Blockchain By Example

A developer's guide to creating decentralized applications
using Bitcoin, Ethereum, and Hyperledger

Bellaj Badr

Richard Horrocks

Xun (Brian) Wu

BIRMINGHAM - MUMBAI

Blockchain By Example

Commissioning Editor: Sunith Shetty
Acquisition Editor: Porous Godhaa
Content Development Editor: Karan Thakkar
Technical Editor: Dinesh Pawar
Copy Editor: Safis Editing
Project Coordinator: Namrata Swetta
Proofreader: Safis Editing
Indexer: Priyanka Dhadke
Graphics: Jisha Chirayil
Production Coordinator: Shantanu Zagade

First published: November 2018

Production reference: 1301118

Published by Packt Publishing Ltd.
Livery Place
35 Livery Street
Birmingham
B3 2PB, UK.

ISBN 978-1-78847-568-6

www.packtpub.com

`mapt.io`

Mapt is an online digital library that gives you full access to over 5,000 books and videos, as well as industry leading tools to help you plan your personal development and advance your career. For more information, please visit our website.

Why subscribe?

- Spend less time learning and more time coding with practical eBooks and Videos from over 4,000 industry professionals

- Improve your learning with Skill Plans built especially for you

- Get a free eBook or video every month

- Mapt is fully searchable

- Copy and paste, print, and bookmark content

Packt.com

Did you know that Packt offers eBook versions of every book published, with PDF and ePub files available? You can upgrade to the eBook version at `www.packt.com` and as a print book customer, you are entitled to a discount on the eBook copy. Get in touch with us at `customercare@packtpub.com` for more details.

At `www.packt.com`, you can also read a collection of free technical articles, sign up for a range of free newsletters, and receive exclusive discounts and offers on Packt books and eBooks.

Foreword

From the time Badr Bellaj first told me about his intention to write a book about blockchain, I was highly supportive of his endeavor. I even managed to suggest topics that I, as a veteran developer, still needed to understand. A year later, after reading this book, my expectations have been surpassed and I could not be happier. Therefore, it's my pleasure to provide this foreword and to recommend Bellaj's book, *Blockchain by Example*.

It is generally agreed that blockchain is a disruptive technology that has shaken the IT scene. Consequently, it has increasingly drawn the interest of a lot of developers. However, according to my experience, it's hard for newcomers to find a helpful guide that explains blockchain in the easiest possible terms, and teaches with concrete examples how to use major blockchain solutions to build projects.

This book is intended to change this situation and acts as an introduction to blockchain technology from a developer viewpoint. It's an undertaking of great potential value, and Bellaj and his coauthors have done it justice.

In fact, this book will help you, step by step, to build realistic projects from scratch using different concepts and technologies, namely Bitcoin, Ethereum, Quorum, and Hyperledger. You'll find, among other topics, how a developer can create a Bitcoin-like coin, run an ICO, and implement privacy-preserving solution in business.

This book isn't just for absolute beginners. It's also a good book for introducing experienced programmers to blockchain technologies or even bringing up to speed developers already familiar with these technologies. It helps if you know a bit about blockchain when you step in, but if you don't, hang on and you should pick up the basic ideas as you go along.

Bellaj is an educator, and a darn good one. He wants us to acquire practical skills instead understanding only the superficial concepts! He knows that if you and I are ready to learn, we have to practice: we have to do the work. In his chapters, he will continually challenge you to propose new features for the presented project. We are well advised to try to implement what he suggests and to create pull requests.

I have enjoyed the book and found it valuable. I think you will, too. Enjoy!

Sam Hauer

Cofounder of NSApps

Contributors

About the authors

Bellaj Badr is an experienced security and software engineer who loves blockchain with a passion. Currently, he is the CTO at Mchain, a blockchain start-up that develops blockchain solutions for companies.

Alongside his role as CTO, he acts as technical consultant, offering strategic and technical consulting to many companies worldwide. Aside from this, he is involved in many blockchain projects involving the establishment of new blockchain business-oriented protocols. Badr is a frequent speaker at developer conferences and is father to two angels.

> *I would like to thank my family for their support and my awesome children, Arwa and Youssef, for letting me finish this book.*

Richard Horrocks is a freelance Ethereum and full-stack developer based in the UK, and holds a BA and MSc in natural sciences from the University of Cambridge. He worked for many years as a technical lead for Cisco Systems, where he worked on the operating systems of carrier-grade routing hardware, before leaving the world of IT to work as an English teacher.

The advent of cryptocurrency piqued his interest sufficiently to lead him back to IT, and, since 2015, he has been working with Ethereum and other cryptocurrencies. His specialist interests are cryptoeconomics and incentive layers, with a particular focus on mechanism design and token engineering.

When not in front of a computer, he enjoys yoga and falling off motorbikes.

Xun (Brian) Wu is the founder and CEO of SmartChart. He has 16+ years of extensive, hands-on, design and development experience with blockchain, big data, cloud, UI, and system infrastructure. He has coauthored a number of books, including *Seven NoSQL Databases in a Week*, *Hyperledger Cookbook*, and *Blockchain Quick Start Guide*. He has been a technical reviewer on more than 50 technical books for Packt. He serves as a board adviser for several blockchain start-ups and owns several patents on blockchain. Brian also holds an NJIT computer science masters degree. He lives in New Jersey with his two beautiful daughters, Bridget and Charlotte.

I would like to thank my parents, wife, and children for their patience and support throughout this endeavor.

About the reviewers

Karthikeyan Sukumaran has been involved in blockchain research and development for the past three years and has over a decade of industry experience in connection with mobile and web platforms. He has been a CEO for his own blockchain start-up, where he architected multiple blockchain projects for various consulting, automobile, supply chain, logistics, and financial companies. He is also a renowned speaker within the Indian blockchain community. Currently, Karthikeyan is an associate director (DLT Labs—Blockchain R&D) for The Depository Trust and Clearing Corporation (DTCC), India.

Aafaf Ouaddah is a veteran security engineer, currently pursuing a PhD involving blockchain. She has wide-ranging experience in distributed systems. Currently, she is a lead researcher investigating security and privacy in distributed systems, blockchain, IoT and fog computing. She has presented more than 10 research papers at various conferences and workshops and has published in reputed international journals with IEEE, Springer, and Elsevier.

Packt is searching for authors like you

If you're interested in becoming an author for Packt, please visit `authors.packtpub.com` and apply today. We have worked with thousands of developers and tech professionals, just like you, to help them share their insight with the global tech community. You can make a general application, apply for a specific hot topic that we are recruiting an author for, or submit your own idea.

About the reviewers

Packt is searching for authors like you

Table of Contents

Preface

Blockchain is a disruptive technology that promises to disrupt many sectors of the global economy. This innovative technology aims to revolutionize those industries that rely on intermediation and trust by shifting the paradigm away from the currently dominant centralized architectures and toward decentralization.

The past couple of years have seen the exponential growth of blockchain, which has evolved into multiple forms and currently comprises many different technologies and tools, some mature, others relatively new, all of which makes understanding and mastering the key ideas and concepts a difficult task.

This is where this book enters the picture. There are many books out there aiming to capitalize on blockchain's current popularity, but, in our opinion, a vast majority of them concentrate on blockchain's theoretical or speculative aspects: in other words, what blockchain could be used for in future, without providing any concrete details on how these things can be achieved in practice. This book is different: it's more pragmatic. From the outset, this book details what can be done with blockchain technology now, and how to do it, by guiding the reader through a series of in-depth, hands-on implementations.

The book is organized into several main parts. It starts by providing an introduction and high-level overview of blockchain's concepts, before moving on to present different use cases and practical implementations based on the Ethereum, Bitcoin, and Hyperledger blockchains.

Who this book is for

This book is aimed at the blockchain novice, and aims to provide an easy way to learn how to conduct a blockchain-based project. It provides comprehensive coverage of the technical details associated with different blockchain solutions, and step-by-step guidance on implementing typical blockchain projects. By the end of the book, the reader will be able to build and maintain reliable and scalable distributed systems based on blockchain.

What this book covers

Chapter 1, *Say Hello to Blockchain*, serves as a general introduction, and explains the general concepts on which blockchain technology is based.

Chapter 2, *Building a Bitcoin Payment System*, introduces the specifics of Bitcoin by first building a customer-friendly payment system, before moving on to looking in more detail at the use of smart contracts on the Bitcoin blockchain.

Chapter 3, *Building Your Own Cryptocurrency*, builds on the general understanding of Bitcoin learned in the previous chapter to then create a new currency based on the Bitcoin code base.

Chapter 4, *Peer-to-Peer Auction in Ethereum*, introduces the basic features, concepts, and tools of Ethereum that are required to build a decentralized application. This chapter introduces the Solidity smart contract language that is used extensively in later chapters.

Chapter 5, *Tontine Game with Truffle and Drizzle*, builds on the previous Ethereum chapter to create a more complex decentralized application, leveraging more advanced features of Solidity, together with the Truffle development environment.

Chapter 6, *Blockchain-Based Futures System*, continues to build on the previous two Ethereum chapters, this time focusing on how smart contracts can interact with the outside world using oracles and third-party APIs.

Chapter 7, *Blockchains in Business*, introduces the idea of private enterprise blockchains and their use cases, before detailing how to implement a private network using an enterprise-focused fork of Ethereum called Quorum.

Chapter 8, *Creating an ICO*, continues the theme of using the Ethereum blockchain for business by describing, in detail, how to create and run an initial coin offering, also known as a token sale.

Chapter 9, *Distributed Storage – IPFS and Swarm*, builds on the previous Ethereum chapters to explore how to incorporate decentralized file storage in a decentralized application.

Chapter 10, *Supply Chain on Hyperledger*, introduces the third blockchain network of the book: Hyperledger. This chapter introduces the main concepts and basic features of Hyperledger, and how it differs from Bitcoin and Ethereum, before describing a practical implementation of how Hyperledger can be used to run a supply chain.

Chapter 11, *Letter of Credit (LC) Hyperledger*, builds on the basics from the previous chapter to implement a letter of credit issued between two banks and two transacting customers.

To get the most out of this book

The book assumes that you are comfortable using a command-line interface, though doesn't require any formal shell scripting skills. Basic language-agnostic programming knowledge is also assumed, and, in some cases, a familiarity with a particular language would be beneficial, though isn't a requirement.

As the book covers many languages and technologies, it is unlikely the reader will be familiar with all of them. As such, a willingness to learn is certainly recommended.

Download the example code files

You can download the example code files for this book from your account at www.packt.com. If you purchased this book elsewhere, you can visit www.packt.com/support and register to have the files emailed directly to you.

You can download the code files by following these steps:

1. Log in or register at www.packt.com.
2. Select the **SUPPORT** tab.
3. Click on **Code Downloads & Errata**.
4. Enter the name of the book in the **Search** box and follow the onscreen instructions.

Once the file is downloaded, please make sure that you unzip or extract the folder using the latest version of:

- WinRAR/7-Zip for Windows
- Zipeg/iZip/UnRarX for Mac
- 7-Zip/PeaZip for Linux

The code bundle for the book is also hosted on GitHub at https://github.com/PacktPublishing/Blockchain-By-Example. In case there's an update to the code, it will be updated on the existing GitHub repository.

We also have other code bundles from our rich catalog of books and videos available at https://github.com/PacktPublishing/. Check them out!

Download the color images

We also provide a PDF file that has color images of the screenshots/diagrams used in this book. You can download it here: `https://www.packtpub.com/sites/default/files/downloads/9781788475686_ColorImages.pdf`.

Conventions used

There are a number of text conventions used throughout this book.

`CodeInText`: Indicates code words in text, database table names, folder names, filenames, file extensions, pathnames, dummy URLs, user input, and Twitter handles. Here is an example: "You can, at any level, use `console.log()` to print the received values in the console."

A block of code is set as follows:

```
var bitcoin = require('bitcoinjs-lib');
var rp = require('request-promise');
```

Any command-line input or output is written as follows:

```
sudo add-apt-repository ppa:bitcoin/bitcoin
sudo apt-get update
```

Bold: Indicates a new term, an important word, or words that you see on screen. For example, words in menus or dialog boxes appear in the text like this. Here is an example: "The customer can check the transaction details before proceeding with the payment by pressing the **Transaction details** button."

 Warnings or important notes appear like this.

 Tips and tricks appear like this.

Get in touch

Feedback from our readers is always welcome.

General feedback: If you have questions about any aspect of this book, mention the book title in the subject of your message and email us at customercare@packtpub.com.

Errata: Although we have taken every care to ensure the accuracy of our content, mistakes do happen. If you have found a mistake in this book, we would be grateful if you would report this to us. Please visit www.packt.com/submit-errata, selecting your book, clicking on the Errata Submission Form link, and entering the details.

Piracy: If you come across any illegal copies of our works in any form on the internet, we would be grateful if you would provide us with the location address or website name. Please contact us at copyright@packt.com with a link to the material.

If you are interested in becoming an author: If there is a topic that you have expertise in, and you are interested in either writing or contributing to a book, please visit authors.packtpub.com.

Reviews

Please leave a review. Once you have read and used this book, why not leave a review on the site that you purchased it from? Potential readers can then see and use your unbiased opinion to make purchase decisions, we at Packt can understand what you think about our products, and our authors can see your feedback on their book. Thank you!

For more information about Packt, please visit packt.com.

Say Hello to Blockchain

1

What is blockchain? Certainly, with the huge hype around it, you must have heard or come across this question—it might be even the reason why you are reading this book. Let's discover, in this first chapter from a developer's standpoint, what's behind the hype.

As you might know, blockchain is an emerging technology that has the potential to dramatically revolutionize many different fields. This potential is primarily based on its ability to offer people a trustworthy channel to transfer value or real assets (tokenization) over the internet.

Blockchain has the capacity to move us from the *internet of information* to the *internet of value*, potentially breaking our existing financial systems.

Blockchain is in many ways a revolution, similar to the internet when it was conceived—certainly not a passing trend. The reason for this is that it presents a solution to a previously unsolved financial dilemma. For the first time in history, we are able to establish trust within trustless environments (such as the internet), without relying on an authority. As a result, some refer to blockchain as a trust machine.

The potential impact of blockchain is huge—it goes far beyond the mere decentralization of the financial sector. In fact, its ability to circumvent intermediaries opens the door to redefine almost every field revolving around technology—even the internet—pushing us toward a peer-to-peer world.

Through this short introduction, I am trying to give you a foretaste of the importance of our topic, and to confirm that your choice to learn about the technology is timely. As the book's name suggests, the approach we will be following throughout this book is to build concrete blockchain projects, instead of laying out abstract concepts.

Nonetheless, in spite of its less technical nature, the prime objective of this introductory chapter is to provide you with the necessary background to build the various projects presented in this book.

In this chapter, we will cover the following topics:

- What cryptocurrency is
- What blockchain is
- How to send and receive bitcoins
- How to store data into a bitcoin blockchain using JavaScript
- An overview of blockchain types

However, this chapter doesn't intend to cover:

- The underlying cryptography
- Cryptocurrency trading

In this chapter, the first part will introduce basic concepts. The second part will be practical, and we will discover how to interact with the blockchain, using the famous Hello World example to get you started.

The emergence of blockchain and cryptocurrency

Many find it hard to understand the logic and the concepts behind blockchain, and why they would need it. This is primarily because we don't have a clear idea what problems it solves, or what advantages it promises.

Therefore, I believe it is necessary to clarify from the start which problems are solved by blockchain. We will start by learning about the concept and history of cryptocurrencies.

From virtual currencies to cryptocurrency

Blockchain didn't appear out of the blue. It was the product of the evolution of fintech and virtual currencies over the last few decades.

At the end of the last century, the widespread use of the internet favored the emergence of digital currencies as an extension of electronic cash systems. Many projects were developed to create new digital currencies: E-cash, E-gold, WebMoney, and Liberty Reserve, to name just a few

Despite huge success in the 1990s, these projects had ceased to exist by the beginning of the new century, either through bankruptcy or being halted by authorities. A currency which is capable of disappearing overnight is a real financial nightmare, but this situation was inevitable due to the centralized nature of such digital currency systems.

There was also always a need for a central authority to be involved, to fight fraud and manage trust within the system.

Because of this fatal weakness, the opposite, decentralized model was presented as a solution. However, it was hard to establish trust in such environments without any central authority. This contrast made creating a reliable digital currency a disentangled Gordian Knot.

Thankfully, the progress of cryptography and the emergence of some clever solutions such as proof of work (for example, the hashcash Project—see `http://hashcash.org`) brought hope of breaking the deadlock.

The invention of bitcoin

In 2008, Satoshi Nakamoto rose to the challenge and unveiled a digital currency called bitcoin. This new currency effectively harnessed cryptography techniques to manage ownership and to secure the system—hence the name cryptocurrency.

Satoshi solved the aforementioned problems by introducing what he called initially a *chain of blocks*. In his published whitepaper (see `https://bitcoin.org/bitcoin.pdf`), he presented his vision for a new peer-to-peer electronic cash system—bitcoin—and described in detail its underlying machinery—blockchain.

Bitcoin was the first reliable and distributed electronic cash system that's fully peer-to-peer, underpinned by the following basic concepts:

- Encryption to ensure ownership and identity
- A proof-of-work consensus mechanism for validating transactions and securing the network against double transactions
- A transparent and shared ledger (a blockchain)
- Pseudonymity

With the assumption that the network majority (>51%) is honest, the bitcoin system operates autonomously following the rules defined by the protocol (consensus rules) to validate a given transaction. By using a shared blockchain, each player has the ability to check the transaction's log history and the sender's solvency, then vote on whether the proceeded transaction is valid or not.

The voting depends on the overall hash-power the player puts into service to secure the network (initially, one CPU is one vote).

To use a cryptocurrency, users need to install a specific client which creates a wallet, generates cryptographic key pairs (private/public keys), and syncs the blockchain with the network. The public key is used by the client (software) to generate valid addresses, and the funds sent to a given address are controlled by the private key from which the address was calculated. In this way, we rely on secure cryptographic principles to manage ownership.

The following diagram depicts how transactions are processed in bitcoin's peer-to-peer network and added into a blockchain:

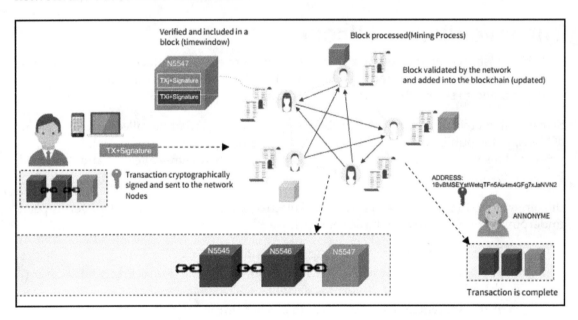

In a bitcoin network where users don't know one another, the blockchain is considered the single source of truth to which they refer to learn about previous consensus outcomes. The blockchain with the consensus protocol allows the network to manage transactions without a single point of failure.

What is blockchain?

Often confused with bitcoin, blockchain is the underlying technology used by bitcoin to operate. Concretely, it's an append-only and chronologically (timestamped) growing database, which harnesses basic cryptographic measures to protect stored transactions from being tampered with (in other words, data can't be deleted or altered).

This database, or ledger, collects and records monetary transactions validated by the network in elementary units called **blocks**. Once validated by the network consensus mechanism, these blocks are added to an existing sequential chain of cryptographic hash-linked blocks, to ensure the integrity of the data—hence the name blockchain.

If a single bit changes in one of the linked blocks, the hash-link collapses, the chain is broken, and it will be rejected by the network.

The following diagram shows how the blockchain is replicated and processed by the members of the network to ensure that everyone has a consistent view of the transaction log. When a new block is validated, all nodes synchronize the same copy:

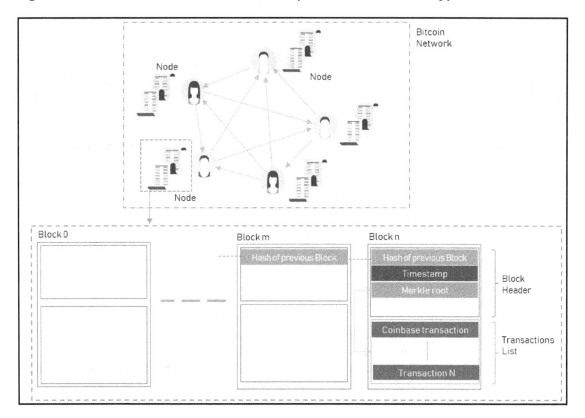

The diagram also shows us that blockchain implements a special data structure, consisting of linked blocks storing transactions and smart contracts. Let us take a closer look at these key elements in detail.

Blocks

If we consider blockchain to be a ledger or a book, a block can be compared to a page or a table in which we record a collection of confirmed transactions. Each block stored in the blockchain is uniquely identified by a hash, and composed of a header and a body.

The header encloses information about its creation (timestamp, Merkle root, Nonce, difficulty target, and version), and a reference to a previous block, whereas the body is a collection of the accepted transactions.

When a block is successfully validated (mined), it becomes part of the official blockchain. New bitcoins are generated in the block (a coinbase transaction) and paid to the validators (or miners).

Transactions

Transactions are the most fundamental building blocks of the blockchain system. They represent the transfer of value (cryptocurrency) within the blockchain network between two addresses.

More tangibly, they are represented by small data structures, defined by the blockchain protocol (such as bitcoin or Ethereum), which specifies their attributes (metadata, inputs, outputs, and so on), and model.

Before broadcasting the transaction, the user sending the funds signs it using their private key (managed by their wallet), and specifies the destination address. Digital signatures and public keys are used to enable network users to validate the transaction, and to check whether the sender has the right to spend the bitcoins held by a specific address.

Smart contracts

Smart contracts are one of the most exciting concepts in blockchain, representing self-executing scripts stored on the blockchain itself. The smart contract takes the blockchain concept to the next stage, enabling it to translate business logic into inviolable contract terms, which will be autonomously executed without relying on a broker, lawyer, or other intermediary.

The earliest form of a smart contract was defined in bitcoin using basic locking and unlocking scripts, but the concept evolved with the emergence of other blockchains.

Smart contracts are one of the more powerful, disruptive forces within blockchain, and are garnering more and more business attention, as described in the Gartner report *Why Blockchain's Smart Contracts Aren't Ready for the Business World* (see `https://www.gartner.com/smarterwithgartner/why-blockchains-smart-contracts-arent-ready-for-the-business-world/`). Gartner estimates that by 2022, smart contracts will be used by more than 25% of global organizations.

Owing to their importance, we will return later in this book to introduce you to smart contracts in leading blockchain platforms—bitcoin, Ethereum, and Hyperledger.

We have now finished describing the concepts—let's practice a little bit to understand what has been presented so far.

Interact with the blockchain

Blockchain as a technology has evolved rapidly, as new techniques deriving from the proliferation of blockchain projects have emerged. Hence the attempts to understand the present day blockchain machinery more closely led to the discovery of bitcoin.

Therefore, in this chapter we will adopt bitcoin as our main example. This choice is due to the fact that bitcoin is the original blockchain implementation, and almost all other projects mimic its design and mechanics.

In the following sections, we will connect to the bitcoin network and store the classic Hello World message into a blockchain. Bitcoin transactions can be used to store small amounts of data in a blockchain—allowing developers to build distributed systems on top of bitcoin, such as Colored Coins, Counterparty, Tierion, and more.

You would be surprised by the number of hidden messages stored in the bitcoin blockchain.

Getting started

In order to store our message into a blockchain, we will set up two bitcoin clients (a receiver and a sender). Then we will build a raw transaction, sending one bitcoin along with our message.

Technically speaking, one of the best-known practices for storing data in the bitcoin blockchain is to create a zero-value OP_RETURN output. As defined in bitcoin's protocol, the OP_RETURN script opcode enables us to store up to 80 bytes. You can check it out in bitcoin's code base—script/standard.h (see https://github.com/bitcoin/bitcoin/blob/0.15/src/script/standard.h):

```
static const unsigned int MAX_OP_RETURN_RELAY = 83;
```

As mentioned in the standard.h header file, the three additional bytes are for the necessary opcodes, and the remainder is for the extra message. More importantly, the OP_RETURN output can be pruned, helping to avoid bloating the blockchain in the future.

Don't worry if you feel lost—we will dive deep into bitcoin concepts such as outputs and scripting in the next chapter.

We will achieve our goal using two different methods:

- By creating a raw transaction with an OP_RETURN output, using RPC commands and a bitcoin client
- By writing a Node.js program to create and send the raw transaction using an online REST API

The second method will require some familiarity with the JavaScript programming language.

Running a bitcoin client for the first time

A bitcoin client is the end-user software that allows us to perform bitcoin operations (sending transactions, receiving payments, and so on). When you run one, you become part of the bitcoin network.

We have chosen two common clients: Bitcoin Core and Electrum. In our example, the sender will use Electrum and the receiver will use Bitcoin Core (the most popular bitcoin client).

For the purposes of this demonstration, I will install them on a single machine using Ubuntu 16.04.

You can install Bitcoin Core (version 15.04) using the following commands:

```
wget
https://bitcoincore.org/bin/bitcoin-core-0.15.2/bitcoin-0.15.2-x86_64-linux
-gnu.tar.gz
sudo install -m 0755 -o root -g root -t /usr/local/bin bitcoin-0.15.2/bin/*
```

Further instructions are available at `https://bitcoin.org/en/full-node#other-linux-distributions`

Electrum is a lightweight wallet, which means it doesn't require you to download the entire blockchain, as we will see in the next section. Download and install the latest version of Electrum as follows:

```
wget https://download.electrum.org/3.2.2/Electrum-3.2.2.tar.gz
sudo apt-get install python3-setuptools python3-pyqt5 python3-pip
sudo pip3 install Electrum-3.2.2.tar.gz
```

Once both clients are installed, we need to synchronize them with the network.

Synchronizing the blockchain

We learned earlier that a blockchain is a transaction database duplicated by all computers on the network. We need to sync a huge amount of data (>200 GB) to enable the sending or receiving of bitcoins.

However, there are two workarounds to this:

- Enabling pruning for a full-node client such as Bitcoin Core
- Using a thin (SPV) client such as Electrum, which fetches blockchain information from Electrum servers instead of having a local copy

We will look at both solutions. Nonetheless, it's always advisable to use a bitcoin full-node client to benefit from the power of blockchain.

Running Bitcoin Core

Depending on your OS, you need to create the `bitcoin.conf` configuration file in the default data directory located under the following paths:

- **Windows**: `%APPDATA%\Bitcoin\`
- **Mac**: `$HOME/Library/Application Support/Bitcoin/`
- **Linux**: `$HOME/.bitcoin/`

In Linux, create a `.bitcoin` directory using `mkdir ~/.bitcoin`, then create the `bitcoin.conf` file using `nano ~/.bitcoin/bitcoin.conf`.

Add the following lines to `bitcoin.conf` to define your client configuration (the comments after each # sign explain the parameters):

```
rpcuser=user_name              #Username for JSON-RPC connections
rpcpassword=your_password      #Password Username for JSON-RPC connections
server=1                       #Tells Bitcoin-Qt and bitcoind to accept JSON-
RPC commands
testnet=1                      #Run on the test network instead of the real
bitcoin network.
prune=550                      #Enables pruning mode
```

Once copied, press *Ctrl + X*, then *Y*, and then *Enter* to save the file.

Now our first client is ready to run on the testnet, which is a bitcoin network created for testing purposes that follows the same rules as a main network. It's a public network using worthless bitcoins. You can use this network to send free transactions and test your applications.

At the time of writing, a blockchain in its entirety exceeds 200 GB. Therefore, we activate pruning mode by setting the `prune=<n>` parameter in `bitcoin.conf`, with n indicating the amount of space you are willing to allocate to the blockchain in MB, with a minimum of 550 MB. Note that the data directory will exceed a few GB (2 GB in my case), because it hosts additional index and log files along with the UTXO database. The prune size only defines how many blocks will be downloaded.

It's now time to run Bitcoin Core. Open a new **command line interface (CLI)** window, and run the following command:

```
bitcoin-qt
```

Bitcoin Core will start running with its standard GUI interface connected to the testnet.

For the first run, it will ask you to set the data directory, which we will set to the default. It will then automatically create a wallet for you, start syncing with the testnet, and download the blockchain:

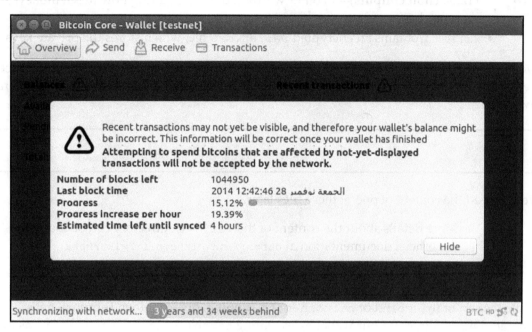

Alternatively, you could run the bitcoin daemon in CLI mode with the following command:

```
bitcoind
```

It's up to you to choose which mode to continue using (bitcoind or bitcoin-qt); the available RPC commands are the same. For my part, I'll continue this guide using btcoin-qt.

As Bitcoin Core starts up, it creates many subdirectories and files in the default data directory (.bitcoin), as shown in the following screenshot:

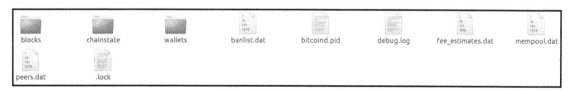

The main subdirectories are:

- `blocks`: Stores actual bitcoin blocks
- `chainstate`: Holds a LevelDB database for available **UTXOs** (short for **Unspent Transaction Outputs**)—in other words, a database storing how much money everyone has
- `wallet`: Contains an encrypted `wallet.dat` file, which stores the private keys

Even if the network sync is not yet finished, you can open the `blocks/` subdirectory to see the blockchain's blocks stored in raw format. Each `blk00*.dat` file is a collection of several raw blocks:

We will read the content of one of these files later.

 More details about the content of the `.bitcoin` directory can be found in the official documentation at `https://en.bitcoin.it/wiki/Data_directory`.

While the server (`bitcoind` or `bitcoin-qt`) is running, open another Terminal. Let's generate a new address for our wallet by executing `bitcoin-cli getnewaddress`, as in the following screenshot:

```
user@ByExample-node:~$ bitcoin-cli getnewaddress
2MsHsi4CHXsaNZSq5krnrpP4WShNqtuRa9U
```

Basically, `bitcoin-cli` is a tool that enables us to issue RPC commands to `bitcoind` or `bitcoin-qt` from the command line (`bitcoin-qt` users can also access the bitcoin RPC interface by using the Debug console, under the Help menu).

Now we have finished with Bitcoin Core, let's leave it to sync with the blockchain and move on to configuring Electrum.

Running Electrum

After you have downloaded and installed Electrum, open Electrum's testnet mode by running electrum --testnet. When you run Electrum for the first time, it will display the new wallet creation wizard. Follow these steps:

1. Select **Auto Connect** in the first dialog box and click **Next**.
2. Select **Standard wallet** and click **Next**.
3. Keep selecting **Next** for each dialog box that appears, until you are asked to save your seed words. Copy them, then reconfirm that you've saved them correctly, as follows:

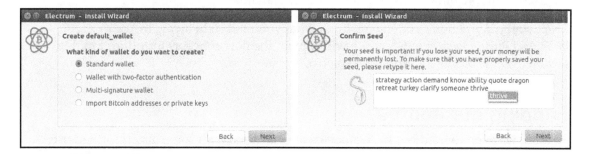

4. In the last step, it will ask you for a password, which you can leave empty.
5. Once finished, Electrum will generate a new wallet with plenty of new addresses. Quit the Electrum GUI, and let's continue in CLI mode. We run Electrum as a daemon process, whereby we execute the JSON/RPC commands as following:

```
electrum --testnet daemon
electrum --testnet daemon load_wallet
```

6. In a new Terminal window, run electrum --testnet listaddresses:

```
user@ByExample-node:~$ electrum --testnet listaddresses
[ecc] warning: libsecp256k1 library not available, falli
[
    "n3CKupfRCJ6Bnmr78mw9eyeszUSkfyHcPy",
    "mhc5YipxN6GhRRXtgakRBjrNUCbz6ypg66",
    "msvrqSHwJFFhS17ReQjMJyd1y4S6n7hirm",
    "mjSiyuBwjS8qeTmK44x97jG7Zmfq3ZB9Ai",
    "mq8izx8q2ydz6P3jhrPjqaPMSurkkwzaTD",
    "myE8qY9MDkRxsuFPUHVZrueMPZxc9TcZBU",
    "mqWMijZC7fdFDWao2KpcGWHgnEviqNN3xu",
    "mwMHzcxBcucgMG1E4CmXK2JjGMwbvEF9Mt",
```

Great, now we have the necessary environment to start transacting with the public bitcoin network. That said, let's discover how a bitcoin transaction is created, exchanged and stored in the blockchain by constructing a bitcoin raw transaction, signing it, and broadcasting it to the network.

Method 1 – Building a raw transaction using Bitcoin Core

For the sake of brevity, we'll focus herein on the instructions needed to create and send raw transactions in Bitcoin Core, without lengthy explanations.

Don't worry if you don't understand all of what you read right away. In `Chapter 2`, *Building a Bitcoin Payment System*, we will explain the new concepts introduced in this section (inputs, outputs, scripts, and so on).

Funding our address

First off, we need to fund our previously created address with some bitcoins in order to make the first transaction. Thankfully, in the testnet we can use a free funding source called a *bitcoin faucet*, which provides worthless bitcoins for testing applications.

For this example, browse to the online faucet website at `http://bitcoinfaucet.uo1.net/` or any other bitcoin's faucet websites, and get a few by providing the first address generated by Electrum and the address created by Bitcoin Core, as shown in the following screenshot:

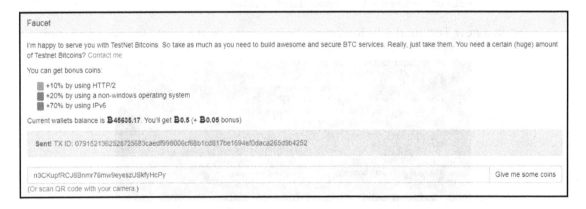

Unspent transaction output

Now that we've sent the bitcoins from the faucet, let's check whether Bitcoin Core can see the transaction. To do that, we'll need to list the available UTXOs in both clients, using the `listunspent` RPC command.

With Bitcoin Core running, run the following command in your Terminal window:

```
bitcoin-cli listunspent
```

This will return the following result:

```
[{ }]
```

Initially, `listunpsnet` returns an empty result, because Bitcoin Core hasn't yet finished syncing the blockchain, which takes time (a few hours). For this reason, we will use Electrum instead of Bitcoin Core for the remainder of this guide, as it avoids us waiting for hours to see the received bitcoins.

However, we will go back using Bitcoin Core from time to time, as it has a powerful command line to deal with raw transactions.

Now run the same command for Electrum, as follows:

```
electrum --testnet listunspent
```

We will get a list of available entries, such as the following:

```
user@ByExample-node:~$ electrum --testnet listunspent
[ecc] warning: libsecp256k1 library not available, falling back to python-ecdsa
[
    {
        "address": "n3CKupfRCJ6Bnmr78mw9eyeszUSkfyHcPy",
        "coinbase": false,
        "height": 1356645,
        "prevout_hash": "0791521362528725683caedf998006cf68b1cd817be1694ef0daca265d9b4252",
        "prevout_n": 1,
        "value": "1.1"
    }
]
```

The previous command's output shows that we have a single available transaction received from the faucet, uniquely identified by its hash (`prevout_hash field`), with 1.1 Bitcoins.

More precisely, we have an available unspent transaction output from a previous transaction, which can be used as an input for the transaction we are willing to build, as follows:

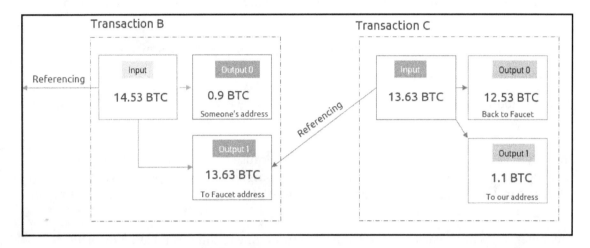

In Bitcoin, transactions spend outputs from prior transactions, and generate new outputs that can be spent by transactions in the future. In fact, users move funds solely by spending UTXOs.

The previous diagram shows that the transaction (Transaction C) we received from the faucet consumes as inputs an existing output(output 1) created earlier by an old transaction. The same transaction creates two outputs: one for us (output 1), and the other returns back the change (output 0). The reason for this is that transaction outputs must be fully spent.

Unlike what you might have expected, in bitcoin, transactions don't update a global user balance (the account/balance model). Instead, they move bitcoins between one or more inputs and outputs (the UTXO model). The total balance is calculated by the bitcoin client as the sum of the values transferred by the received unspent transactions.

Creating the transaction

At this level, it's time to create a transaction that spends the received transaction. From the `listunspent` output, we have the necessary ingredients (`prevout_hash` and `prevout_n`) to construct our raw transaction. Let's see how.

First, you need to convert the `hello world` message into hexadecimal, using an online converter (such as `https://codebeautify.org/string-hex-converter`). The hexadecimal encoded form will be `68656c6c6f20776f726c64`.

Then we have to use the `createrawtransaction` command, which creates a transaction spending the given inputs and creating new outputs. We have to pass as an argument (from the previous output) an object with the following parameters:

- The `txid` of one of the available outputs
- The `vout` index (`prevout_n` for Electrum) of the selected output
- The hexadecimal form of the message
- The destination address (created earlier)
- The total number of satoshis (the smallest unit of the bitcoin currency) to send

Here we are sending one bitcoin, although you can set it to `0`:

```
bitcoin-cli createrawtransaction
"[{\"txid\":\"0791521362528725683caedf998006cf68b1cd817be1694ef0daca265d9b4
252\", \"vout\": 1}]"
"{\"data\":\"68656c6c6f20776f726c64\",\"2MsHsi4CHXsaNZSq5krnrpP4WShNgtuRa9U
\":1.0000000}"
```

You'll get the following serialized long hex-encoded string, representing our raw transaction:

```
020000000152429b5d26cadaf04e69e17b81cdb168cf068099dfae3c6825875262135291070
100000000ffffffff0200000000000000000d6a0b68656c6c6f20776f726c6400e1f5050000
000017a914008051b4d96aa26269dfd36af0eb9c2b2fa894568700000000
```

> To facilitate the usage of the previous CLI commands (and avoid manipulating long hex strings), you can assign the `createrawtransaction` output to a terminal variable, and use this later as an argument for the other commands. For example, we can use `RAW=$(bitcoin-cli createrawtransaction .....)`. The resulting hexadecimal string will be stored in the `RAW` variable, and accessible using `$RAW`.

Transaction structure

At first sight, the previous resultant hexadecimal string seems ambiguous and meaningless. The following table breaks down and examines indepth our transaction, byte by byte:

REPRESENTATION		LENGTH (Bytes)	VALUE
version		4	02000000
input count		1	01
Input 1	previous output ID in little endian (reversed)	32	52429b5d26cadaf04e69e17b81cdb168cf068099dfae3c682587526213529107
	Vout (previous output index	04	100000000
	ScriptSig length	01	00
	ScriptSig		
	sequence	04	ff ff ff ff
Number of generated outputs		1	02
Output 1	amount of Satoshis (1 Satoshi = 0.00000001 Bitcoin)	8	0000000000000000
	script length	1	0d
	ScriptPubKey: OP_RETURN <Push size> <Payload (hello world in hex)>	13	6a 0b 68656c6c6f20776f726c64
Output 2	Value in Satoshis (hex encoded in little endian order)	8	00e1f50500000000
	Script length	1	17
	ScriptPubKey (Actual output script)	23	a914eb949dbde8d3b1755e7f3c20b6a62c1f1403bd9087
Lock time (the earliest time a transaction can be added to the blockchain)		04	00 00 00 00

As you can see, our transaction has one input (the only unspent transaction received from the faucet), with the 0791...252 transaction id, and two outputs:

- An OP_RETURN output with an OP_RETURN script
- An output sending one bitcoin to the specified address

The transaction structure can be visualized by decoding back the raw transaction using the `deserialize` command. If you run `electrum --testnet deserialize <Raw transactions>`, it will output a meaningful JSON representation of our constructed transaction:

```
user@ByExample-node:~$ electrum --testnet deserialize 020000000152429b5d26cadaf04e69e17b81cdb168cf668099dfae3c68258752621352910701000000000ffffffff02
a0b68656c6c6f20776f726c6400e1f5050000000017a914008051b4d96aa26269dfd36af0eb9c2b2fa894568700000000
[ecc] warning: libsecp256k1 library not available, falling back to python-ecdsa
{
    "inputs": [
        {
            "address": null,
            "num_sig": 0,
            "prevout_hash": "0791521362528725683caedf998006cf68b1cd817be1694ef0daca265d9b4252",
            "prevout_n": 1,
            "scriptSig": "",
            "sequence": 4294967295,
            "type": "unknown"
        }
    ],
    "lockTime": 0,
    "outputs": [
        {
            "address": "6a0b68656c6c6f20776f726c64",
            "prevout_n": 0,
            "scriptPubKey": "6a0b68656c6c6f20776f726c64",
            "type": 2,
            "value": 0
        },
        {
            "address": "2MsHsi4CHXsaNZSq5krnrpP4WShNgtuRa9U",
            "prevout_n": 1,
            "scriptPubKey": "a914008051b4d96aa26269dfd36af0eb9c2b2fa8945687",
            "type": 0,
            "value": 100000000
        }
    ],
    "partial": false,
    "segwit_ser": false,
    "version": 2
}
```

To get the same result, you can decode the raw transaction using `bitcoin-cli decoderawtransaction`, or by using an online decoder such as the one at `https://live.blockcypher.com/btc-testnet/decodetx/`.

Signing the transaction

At this point, the transaction is created, but not yet transmitted to the network. To send our transaction, we need to sign it using the `bitcoin-cli signrawtransaction` command. We sign the transaction using our private key (related to the receiving address) to prove to the network our ownership of the output, and therefore our authority to spend the held bitcoins.

The first step will be to extract the private key associated with the first address used to receive the bitcoins from the faucet:

```
electrum --testnet listaddresses | electrum --testnet  getprivatekeys -
```

Notice the presence of a dash at the end of the command. It will be replaced by the values returned from the pipe. As a result, you'll get a list of private keys. Copy the first one without the `p2pkh` prefix, as follows:

```
user@ByExample-node:~$ electrum --testnet listaddresses | electrum --testnet  getprivatekeys -
WARNING: ALL your private keys are secret.
Exposing a single private key can compromise your entire wallet!
In particular, DO NOT use 'redeem private key' services proposed by third parties.
[
    "p2pkh:cOx4Ucd3uXEpa3bNnS1JJ84qWn5diChfChtfHSkRaDNZOYA1FYnr",
    "p2pkh:cVZn69R4DwrPHVPGk5z63VfPebk3HVqbgCPCpDTEd3nw2KRUuSJE",
    "p2pkh:cSKqWnito7E1bNCmA7QW9FehwX8KZ1HwgMaRH8YocJ44ghz1oYNg",
    "p2pkh:cQFuxDStLrqVCzKKLjMhKnSsvsowVEUJwUFoWckhd9RWRrPSuKuu",
    "p2pkh:cQL23Vcj4dXXcn42Vc1LrrvZiFijbBaVx4b5GnnSy6cMtVCYcV15",
    "p2pkh:cRhUCBnUf5fTWGYq1HdeibqcvTdDzhskTtJkjmxeVjrqwrJxAzNW",
    "p2pkh:cRktM73Hvu7EvPNxUQTxZ6733h8wiQ81FcbuCovihKcn3RD5GV3R",
    "p2pkh:cSU4oqXniw3TwsA8kzRh5zjQaUYEriDFpHYmEKKoLSDjbBS1NH4L",
```

Next, we need to get `scriptPubKey` from the output we are willing to spend. For that, firstly, we have to retrieve the transaction from the blockchain, using `electrum gettransaction --testnet "0791521362528725683caedf998006cf68b1cd817be1694ef0daca265d9b4252"`.

Secondly, we use the resultant raw form to get `scriptPubKey`, as follows:

```
electrum deserialize --testnet
0200000001915bf222c2e4e6ff36760168904ae102a0e968d83b3c575077d5475aa94dd9bf0
10000006b483045022100b129bc0fb5631aa668c48bb7a8fef0c81fec131d2f68ba430cd7cd
9de0bd971b02203dabbf054790e31b4fd1b9a333881cd480c19b38a229e70f886dbb88ee467
3f1012103bcf53d63d2fa14ee04d9ebb9170dfa7987298689c7e6ceb765c1d3ccd7f9ad01fe
ffffff02d618b24a000000001976a914b9172e192d2805ea52fa975847eea0657e38fef888a
c80778e06000000001976a914edcce89f510bf95606ec6a79cb28a745c039e22088ac63b314
00
```

Unlike before, here we are loading and deserializing the received transaction from the faucet. We will get the outputs created in this transaction, as follows:

```
"outputs": [
    {
        "address": "mxPd583YeW6iw3cCgfrmrdcXKG6PLM2fBj",
        "prevout_n": 0,
        "scriptPubKey": "76a914b9172e192d2805ea52fa975847eea0657e38fef888ac",
        "type": 0,
        "value": 1253185750
    },
    {
        "address": "n3CKupfRCJ6Bnmr78mw9eyeszUSkfyHcPy",   <=
        "prevout_n": 1,
        "scriptPubKey": "76a914edcce89f510bf95606ec6a79cb28a745c039e22088ac",
        "type": 0,
        "value": 110000000
    }
],
"partial": false,
"segwit_ser": false,
"version": 2
}
```

The part surrounded in red is `scriptPubKey` of the unspent transaction output.

A `scriptPubKey` can be seen in the outputs; it represents the conditions that are set for spending the outputs. The new owner can sign using the private key associated with the address receiving the output to fulfil the conditions of `scriptPubKey`.

The network checks whether the digital signature is valid, and if so makes it an input for the new transaction. The cryptographic parts—`scriptSig` and `scriptPubKey`—are particularly complex, and will be discussed in the next chapter.

Copy `scriptPubKey` from the output, and pass it along the other options to the `signrawtransaction` command, as follows:

```
signrawtransaction "Raw hexstring" (
[{"txid":"id","vout":n,"scriptPubKey":"hex","redeemScript":"hex"},..]
["privatekey",..])
```

The second argument is a JSON array of the previous transaction outputs we are consuming, and the third argument is the private key belonging to the address that received the output. The result will be similar to the following output:

```
user@ByExample-node:~$ bitcoin-cli signrawtransaction "020000000152429b5d26cadaf04e69e17b81cdb168cf068099dfae3c682587526213529107010000000ffffffff02600000000000000000000d
6a0b68656c6c6f20776f726d6f6f400e1f5050000000017a914008051b4d96aa26269dfd36af0eb9c2b2fa894568700000000" '[{"txid":"07915213625287256b3caedf998006cf68b1cd817be1694ef0daca26
5d9b4252","vout":1,"scriptPubKey":"76a914edcce89f510bf95606ec6a79cb28a745c039e22088ac","redeemScript":""}]' '["cQx4Ucd3uXEpa3bNnS1JJ84gWn5djChfChtfHSkRaDNZQYA1FYnr"]'
{
  "hex": "020000000152429b5d26cadaf04e69e17b81cdb168cf068099dfae3c682587526213529107010000006a4730440220537e1923a82b9c910fb552f2facd45ed89a03c5cd7ff66093c7e2d399783c1b
902206edffba148dfaeabeeceace51e06049714169ae5d4c1ce095aafa38723aec2938121024ef6f56dcfe9044cfc6c10b717a503e7f5a910312f25560a99a048a4a21d33c5ffffffff0260000000000000000000d
6a0b68656c6c6f20776f726d6f6f400e1f5050000000017a914008051b4d96aa26269dfd36af0eb9c2b2fa894568700000000",
  "complete": true
}
```

After succeeding in signing the raw transaction, it is time to send the signed transaction to the testnet.

Sending the transaction

To send the transaction into a blockchain, we submit the signed signature using the `broadcast` command provided by Electrum, as shown in the following screenshot:

```
user@ByExample-node:~$ electrum --testnet broadcast 0200000000152429b5d26cadaf04e69e17b81cdb168cf06B899dfae3c6B25875262135291070180000006a4730440220537e1923a82b9c918fb55
2f2facd45ed89a03c5cd7ff66093c7e2d399783c1b902286edffba148dfaeabeeceace51e06049714169ae5d4c1ce095aafa30723aec2930121024ef6f56dcfe9044cfc6c10b717a503e7f5a910312f25560a99
a048a4a21d33c5ffffffff0200000000000000000d6a0b68656c6c6c6f20776f726c6400e1f5050000000017a914008051b4d96aa26269dfd36af0eb9c2b2fa894568700000000
[ecc] warning: libsecp256k1 library not available, falling back to python-ecdsa
[
    true,
    "d3e300c2f2eedf673ab544f4c2b09063353e618ab8a0c9444e931d0145e43ded"
]
```

You'll get back the hex-encoded transaction hash ID:

d3e300c2f2eedf673ab544f4c2b09063353e618ab8a0c9444e931d0145e43ded

Retrieving your message online from the blockchain

If everything goes as planned, you should have successfully stored the `hello world` message into bitcoin's testnet blockchain.

The following screenshot illustrates what we have done so far. We consumed an input (from a previous transaction), then created a transaction with two outputs; the first being an `OP_RETURN` transaction carrying our message along, the other one transferring one bitcoin (BTC):

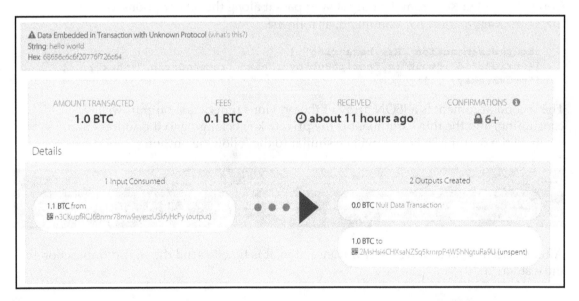

Isn't it just fascinating? You can use a block explorer such as `https://live.blockcypher.com/btc-testnet/tx/<txid>` to inspect the transaction with the printed transaction hash (`txid`), and to retrieve your stored message.

It would be more exciting to retry the same operation using the mainnet (the original and main network for bitcoin), but then you would be dealing with real, expensive bitcoins.

Using the local blockchain

If Bitcoin Core has finished syncing the blockchain, you can locally parse the blocks to locate our transaction and read the stored message.

To open and parse the blockchain blocks, we need to install a graphical hex editor such as `bless`, by running `sudo apt-get install bless`.

Once installed, you can run it and open one of the `.blk` files present in the `blocks` directory:

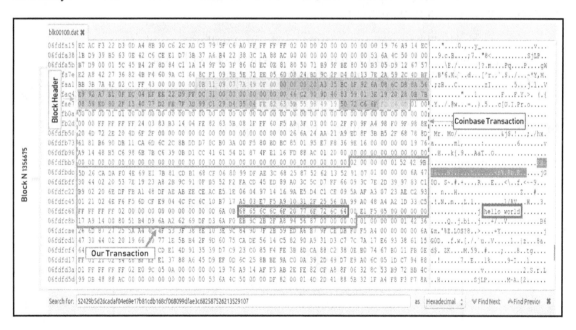

As shown in the screenshot, `bless` will display a pane divided into three parts:

- The left column is the offset column
- The center column displays the blocks' hexadecimal content

- The right column is the same line of data as in the center, with recognized text characters displayed as text and binary values represented by period characters

To locate our transaction, you can search for it by pasting the unsigned raw transaction string into the **Search** field. You may go through a few `blk**.dat` files before you find your transaction. In my case, I found it in the `blk00100.dat` file.

At first glance, it may not be very meaningful, but once you locate your transaction you can easily locate the message you've stored in the blockchain. The `hello world` message will be visible in the ASCII section on the right.

You can also locate the block that encompasses the transaction by searching for the previous block delimiter, called `magic bytes`, represented by `0b110907`. Then you can, by following the structure of the block, determine the meaning of these long hexadecimal strings.

In the previous screenshot, I delimited the block with a yellow border and highlighted the blocks header field with multiple colors. I delimited our transaction and the coinbase transaction in blue and gray, respectively.

As you'll be running in prune mode, you will not be able to see my transaction, as you will have only synced newer blocks. However, you'll be able to see your transaction by following the same process.

To help you visualize the block content, the following table explains the meaning of the

previously highlighted bytes:

Bytes		Size
Magic number		4 bytes
Block size		4 Bytes
Block Header	Version	4 Bytes
	Hash of previous block	32 Bytes
	Hash Merkle root	32 Bytes
	Timestamp	4 Bytes
	Bits	4 Bytes
	Nonce	4 Bytes
Transactions Counter		1-9 Bytes
List of Transactions		-

And that's it! You can now send transactions with extra messages into the blockchain, and retrieve the data online or locally. Although this is not usually required, it may prove useful in the future.

Let's go ahead and send another raw transaction with an OP_RETURN output using a different method.

Method 2 – build a raw bitcoin transaction in JavaScript

At this point, I would guess that you want to write some code. Your wish is my command.

In this section, we will build a simple Node.Js script to perform what we have performed manually before: to send a raw transaction over the testnet. You can stop running Electrum and Bitcoin Core, as we will use an online REST API (chain.so/api) as a middle tier to interact with bitcoin's network.

 By using an online API, we are losing the biggest advantage of blockchain: disintermediation. Instead of trusting our own blockchain copy, we have to trust a third party to read the data for us and send the transaction on our behalf. What would happen if the service provider provided wrong or outdated data?

Preparation

Before you start building your program, make sure you have Node.js and **NPM** (short for **Node Package Manager**) installed.

In order to create an OP_RETURN transaction, we can use one of the many available bitcoin APIs, such as:

- bitcore (https://bitcore.io/)
- php-OP_RETURN (https://github.com/coinspark/php-OP_RETURN)
- python-OP_RETURN (https://github.com/coinspark/python-OP_RETURN)

In our example, we will use a JavaScript library called `bitcoinjs-lib` written for Node.js. We install the corresponding package as follows:

```
npm install bitcoinjs-lib --save
```

In the example code, we will submit requests using Node.js and the `request` package to access the API. Therefore, we install the following modules:

```
npm install request --save
npm install request-promise --save
```

Similar to the first method, we will use the first address and its corresponding private key generated by Electrum to send a raw transaction carrying a `hello world` message programmatically.

Let's code

Start by creating a `hello.js` file and importing the `bitcoinjs-lib` and `request-promise` modules using the `require` directive as follows:

```
var bitcoin = require('bitcoinjs-lib');
var rp = require('request-promise');
```

Then we declare and define the necessary variables:

```
var data = Buffer.from('Hello World', 'utf8');
var testnet = bitcoin.networks.testnet;
var privateKey = 'cQx4Ucd3uXEpa3bNnS1JJ84gWn5djChfChtfHSkRaDNZQYA1FYnr';
var SourceAddress = "n3CKupfRCJ6Bnmr78mw9eyeszUSkfyHcPy";
```

They represent respectively:

- The message to be embedded in the transaction
- The network—testnet
- The private key in **WIF** (short for **Wallet Import Format**)
- The source address from which we spend the UTXO

Then we ask the API to provide us with the available unspent output belonging to a specific address. We read the response from the API to define the available amount and the output `txid`.

We also define the fee (5,000 satoshis) to pay the network (miners) for processing the transaction, as follows:

```
var url = "https://chain.so/api/v2/get_tx_unspent/BTCTEST/"+SourceAddress;
var DestionationAddress = '2MsHsi4CHXsaNZSq5krnrpP4WShNgtuRa9U';
var options = {
    uri: url,
    json: true
};

rp(options).then(function (response) {
    var index = response.data.txs.length - 1;
    console.log(response.data.txs[index]);
    var UtxoId = response.data.txs[index].txid;
    var vout = response.data.txs[index].output_no;
    var amount = Number(response.data.txs[index].value*100000000);
    var fee = 0.0005*100000000;
}).catch(function (err) { console.error(err);});
```

You can use `console.log()` at any point to print the received values in the console.

Now it's time to create our transaction. Inside the previous GET request, add the following lines:

```
const RawTransaction = new bitcoin.TransactionBuilder(testnet);
RawTransaction.addInput(UtxoId, vout);
RawTransaction.addOutput(DestionationAddress, parseInt(amount-fee));
scrypt = bitcoin.script.compile([bitcoin.opcodes.OP_RETURN,data]);
RawTransaction.addOutput(scrypt, 0);
```

Here we are using `TransactionBuilder` from bitcoinjs-lib to create our new raw transaction. Then we add the output we requested earlier from the API as input to our transaction.

We add two outputs: the first is an OP_RETURN output with 0 bitcoins, and the second is the output with 100,000,000 satoshis (one bitcoin), minus the fees.

Great! Everything is set! The only thing we have to do right now is to sign the transaction with our private key, and send it to the bitcoin blockchain:

```
var keyPair = bitcoin.ECPair.fromWIF(privateKeyWIF, testnet);
tx.sign(0, keyPair);
```

The second line—tx.sign(0, keyPair)—is because we are consuming a **Pay-to-Public-Key-Hash** (**P2PKH**) output. However, in bitcoin we have different types of transaction and addresses. The addresses beginning with 2 receive **Pay-to-Script-Hash** (**P2SH**) transactions, instead of the common P2PKH transactions received by addresses starting with m or n.

Of course, this changes the way we spend the output; therefore, we need to know the type of the output prior to signing the new transaction. For P2SH transactions, we need to use the following code instead:

```
const p2wpkh = bitcoin.payments.p2wpkh({ pubkey: keyPair.publicKey,
network: bitcoin.networks.testnet });
const p2sh = bitcoin.payments.p2sh({ redeem: p2wpkh, network:
bitcoin.networks.testnet});
RawTransaction.sign(0, keyPair, p2sh.redeem.output, null,
parseInt(amount));
```

Lastly, we take the signed transaction in and send it to the specified network using a POST request with the API. We provide in our request a JSON object, which contains a hex representation of the signed transaction, as follows:

```
var Transaction=RawTransaction.build().toHex();
var Sendingoptions = { method: 'POST', url:
'https://chain.so/api/v2/send_tx/BTCTEST',
body: {tx_hex: Transaction},  json: true};

rp(Sendingoptions).then(function (response) {
    var Jresponse = JSON.stringify(response);
    console.log("Transaction ID:\n"+Jresponse);
}).catch(function (err) { console.error(err); });
```

Once you have saved the file, run it with the node hello.js command. If the raw transaction is valid and delivered successfully to the network, you will receive a message back that's similar to the following:

```
user@ByExample-node:~/deletme$ node hello.js
{ txid: '0615fe519f4583546ea9d39d3ca7628eeea56cd3037ea64d1bb0e967f48d93e4',
  output_no: 0,
  script_asm: 'OP_DUP OP_HASH160 edcce89f510bf95606ec6a79cb28a745c039e220 OP_EQU
ALVERIFY OP_CHECKSIG',
  script_hex: '76a914edcce89f510bf95606ec6a79cb28a745c039e22088ac',
  value: '1.10000000',
  confirmations: 0,
  time: 1533938378 }
Transaction ID:
{"status":"success","data":{"network":"BTCTEST","txid":"f917abfa314ebd774a4a659c
69c924cab3d8e4e9f4f41ccd7620a985b373a2fb"}}
```

We get the used output details, along with a success message returning the transaction ID.

As before, we can check the transaction processing using a testnet explorer.

Congratulations, you have successfully built your first Node.js application to send bitcoins and to store data into a blockchain. Based on that, you can create advanced applications or develop your own protocol on top of the blockchain.

As a bonus, the full code is available in the following Github repository: `https://github.com/bellaj/HelloWorld`.

Types of blockchains

The blockchain initially started as the technology underpinning bitcoin. However, its early success to prove itself as a trust machine and intermediary killer put pressure on a variety of industries to both adapt to and adopt this new technology.

Consequently, many variations of Satoshi's original blockchain have been developed. In this final section, we will take a look at the major types of blockchain technologies.

Classification of blockchains

Currently, blockchain solutions can be classified into four basic models with different paradigms. The distinction between them is driven by two main criteria: the network type and the implemented access control model; in other words, who is allowed to join the peer-to-peer network (run a node) and access the blockchain records.

The following table gives an overview of the different types, with a basic description of each model:

Model	characteristics	Technologies	Strengths
Public blockchain	The general public can join the network and write (under consensus protocol) and read data. This model is a true representation of the original blockchain used in the cryptocurrencies.	Bitcoin. Zcash. Ethereum, Litecoin. NXT. etc..	Full-Decentralization High Security Censorship-resistant Low-trust Anonymity Transparency
Private or internal blockchain	A network under the governance of one organization. which defines the access rules to join its private network. Therefore. only authorized entities can read the transactions data. The organization defines nodes with high trust levels to accept the transaction.	Monax. Symbiont Assembly. Iroha. Kadena. Chain. Quorum. MultiChain.	Confidentiality Authenticated parties Privacy Faster Less expensive
Consortium or hybrid Blockchain	A partly private and permissioned blockchain network operated by known entities such as stakeholders of a given industry regrouped in a consortium or exploiting a shared platform. The network participants have control over who can join the network. and who can participate in the consensus process of the blockchain.	Hyperledger Fabric. Tendermint. Symbiont Assembly. R3 Corda. Iroha. Kadena. Chain. Quorum. MultiChain	Confidentiality Authenticated parties Privacy Faster Less expensive
Blockchain as a service (Baas)	Cloud platform hosted by a service provider to deploy blockchain applications. The service provider manages the blockchain network while the customer defines the business logic.	Bluemix. Azure. Rubix. Stratis. AWS. SAP. Oracle.	Flexibility Scalability Complexity reduction

You might be wondering—which one of these types of blockchain might be appropriate for your project?

The answers depend on your project's requirements. Generally, in a trustless environment (for remittance systems, proving provenance, and so on), we tend to use a public blockchain, while the other models are fit for actors who share a pre-existing trust and desire to build shared services.

Private blockchains are suitable for building faster local testing environments, or to avoid the cost of transacting, whereas the BaaS model is a suitable solution for easy deployment and high scalability.

Summary

This first chapter is designed to acquaint you with the key concepts behind blockchain, which you'll need to build blockchain projects.

We have seen how to interact with bitcoin's blockchain both manually and programmatically (using JavaScript). Now you can start building innovative solutions harnessing blockchain as a safe and trustworthy vault to help with checking the authenticity of documents, proving the provenance of products, asset digitization, and more.

A deep understanding of bitcoin is key to deciphering blockchain. In the next chapter, we will continue learning about bitcoin, and build an advanced payment application.

Building a Bitcoin Payment System

2

The previous chapter was an excellent starting point for understanding the blockchain and learning about bitcoin. In fact, we covered many basic concepts and elementary operations, such as signing, sending raw transactions, and storing data in the blockchain. In this chapter, we'll continue to explore the blockchain, firstly by building a customer-friendly payment system based on the Bitcoin payment protocol, and secondly, by building our first smart contract in the bitcoin system.

The end goal of this chapter is to help you acquire the necessary technical background to understand bitcoin's mechanics and build your first bitcoin applications using very common languages such as JavaScript and Java. If you're an experienced programmer, most likely you are familiar with one of these technologies; if not, I recommend you spend time reading their official "getting started" documentation.

Throughout this chapter, we will cover the following key points:

- Introducing bitcoin
- Building a BIP 70 payment system using Node.js and `bitcore-lib`
- Building a bitcoin client using `BitcoinJ`
- Writing and deploying a smart contract in bitcoin using `Rootstock`

This is a fully hands-on coding chapter; I will insist that you code each of the snippets presented herein to make sure you get the most out of the chapter. Happy coding!

What is Bitcoin?

As outlined in the previous chapter, Bitcoin is a peer-to-peer electronic cash system based on blockchain technology. Technically speaking, Bitcoin is a protocol maintaining the blockchain data structure and ensuring consensus between different network parties (senders, recipients, miners, and so on). This protocol defines the ruleset for validating transactions, Bitcoin mining, and avoiding counterfeiting or double spending.

Bitcoin is referenced as a cryptocurrency because it uses cryptography to control the creation and transfer of money. Specifically, it uses digital signatures (based on ECDSA public key encryption) to process and verify the transactions, and cryptographic hash functions (SHA-256) to secure the blockchain (integrity, mining process, and so on).

This book's scope isn't about presenting the Bitcoin protocol in fine detail; instead, we will introduce the necessary concepts for building higher-level services. If you are eager to learn about Bitcoin in depth, you can refer to the official documentation at `https://en.bitcoin.it/wiki/Protocol_documentation`.

Why choose Bitcoin as a platform?

Although using Bitcoin directly to build blockchain applications might seem to you somehow obscure, it still can be the best choice to build powerful applications. Apart from the fact that the blockchain and Bitcoin are hot trends, several factors can motivate you to choose Bitcoin as a platform for your next project, including the following:

- Bitcoin is an electronic payment pioneer and the most accessible system for users worldwide.
- Settlement processing is faster than many payment channels.
- Transaction are without chargebacks.
- Bitcoin is the most secure blockchain and more secure than the common payment channels.

I am proposing in the following section that you begin with a simple and easy-to-follow practical introduction before we start developing our first application.

Getting started with Bitcoin

To get started using Bitcoin, there are plenty of Bitcoin clients and different implementations of the Bitcoin protocol. As we saw in Chapter 1, *Say Hello to Blockchain*, the commonly used Bitcoin client is Bitcoin Core, which is maintained by the Bitcoin Core team representing the C++ implementation of the Bitcoin protocol and the continuity of the Satoshi client. I'll assume that you have already installed this client and have become familiar with it.

Setting up a Regtest environment

For learning or testing purposes, it's safer and cheaper to use Bitcoin's test network -- testnet (for more information, refer to https://bitcoin.org/en/glossary/testnet) or regression test mode --regtest (for more information, refer to https://bitcoin.org/en/glossary/regression-test-mode). We learned in the previous chapter how to use the Testnet network but this option stil requires us to download the blockchain and wait for delayed validation. However, there is a solution, and this time we are going to use the Bitcoin client in Regtest mode.

In this mode, we can set up a local testing network and a private blockchain whereby we can instantly validate transactions and create new bitcoins locally. Similar to running a web application in localhost mode, you'll find the Regtest option more suitable for developing and testing new applications.

You have to follow the same procedure as in the previous chapter and add an extra step: change bitcoin.conf to select the Regtest network by defining the parameter regtest=1.

Your bitcoin.conf will look like the following:

```
rpcuser=<user>
rpcpassword=<password>
#testnet=1
#prune=550
regtest=1
server=1
```

We commented out the testnet and prune parameters as they are no longer needed for Regtest mode. In addition, make sure to replace the RPC credentials <user/password> and use them throughout this section when they are needed.

If you want to build a network with multiple Bitcoin instances instead of a single node on your machine, you have to define different data directories with different `bitcoin.conf` files. In each, you'll need to set the new path and different communication ports using the following parameters: `datadir`

`port` (default: 8443)

`rpcport`(default: 18442)

You can find more information about the Bitcoin Regtest mode in the official documentation at `https://bitcoin.org/en/developer-examples#regtest-mode`.

First commands

We will set up a private blockchain with a single node. Start by opening two separate command-line prompts. In the first, run `bitcoind` (Bitcoin node server), while in the other, run one of the available RPC commands using `bitcoin-cli <command>`. To get the full list of RPC calls, you can use the help option `bitcoin-cli --help`, or visit the official documentation at `https://en.bitcoin.it/wiki/Original_Bitcoin_client/API_Calls_list`.

As a first command, we will generate quickly 101 blocks by running the following command:

```
bitcoin-cli generate 101
```

The expected output is a list of created blocks' IDs, similar to the following:

```
user@ByExample-node:~/deletme$ bitcoin-cli --regtest generate 101
[
  "193a6c217cf7918c1f8b040e415691c131721000746d206e37fc347ede25b1f0",
  "44b3f041bef18fc1265268a752834f5456962b0e7ffe7b2584dd87cd194e0fcc",
  "70edb90d0b3dd510998d15d882b340486dd30eac04bc3650c90d31883f771736",
  "76357d14d35adf2f79b562a6cfa2902defe73fb87efdd115deef2179143aa858",
  "1f1e00f9526fda59632943c96838caed9ee338eef86aa2db2a1ed8dc6e7a794a",
  "347250ca8ed505267dde9f305950dc4e8fd69de37c132f8066a66fa6b0d81168",
  "64f4ca37116dbfbabbdd832a81f469bfc7d83e0856952861344ff05ab2ff1df1",
  "69b3db538b64303c42a8eee7d2ac1d433f03c99803d9623eddc6ebdd8958d65c",
  "07fd1a3186d6bbe7d2613b9ca2ff4ba34dc75205c7992e018d947c10d19aa155",
  "09f31ebf056c4d38070b8dfcd243440de58e299d797464c97e8bb488b49d543b",
  "2d3ed1cad6b92de823f2a7d2f9ed2271f6859a54cf610f856a9bb2fb7e6d0e6c",
  "744db4f8983a5f16c88f723754186289c55a5e985f9f4ac4c5dd71cfe27f7d24",
  "1ac745d9a88a4ef11fd8c64c5ba3a263bcc22694923c32d1483834d60e8df319",
  "31c9709fd9a601688f9ed652dc9034512eb19b956052afd564b16e7b8e57b699",
  "0627f6a23c017f073cb58a0e87acc218aec2fc5ef84cde0f69fadcccbe454630",
```

It is worth noting that in Regtest mode, you have to generate 100 blocks (100 confirmations) to get the initial reward (50 bitcoins) generated for the first block. We can check out how many bitcoins we have with the following:

```
bitcoin-cli --regtest getbalance
50.00000000
```

Instead of interacting directly using `bitcoin-cli`, you can run commands via the HTTP JSON-RPC tools. If CURL isn't installed, you can install it with `sudo apt-get install curl`. For example, you can request your balance by using CURL:

```
curl --user user:password --data-binary '{"jsonrpc": "1.0",
"id":"curltest", "method": "getbalance", "params": [] }' -H 'content-type:
text/plain;' http://127.0.0.1:18443
```

Notice the presence of the RPC username and password defined earlier in `bitcoin.conf`, used with the option `--user` in the RPC call.

> You can also use REST calls to communicate with your bitcoin node. However, in this case, you'll need to enable the REST API by adding the option `rest=1` to your `bitcoin.conf` file. The available calls are presented in the official documentation at `https://github.com/bitcoin/bitcoin/blob/master/doc/REST-interface.md`.

After successfully setting up the Regtest environment, what follows is a small introduction to transactions in bitcoin with some basic knowledge required to build the project.

Transactions in bitcoin

Without delving into the working internals of bitcoin in great detail, we need to learn more about the following key concepts:

- Mining
- Scripts

Let's take a look at each one in detail in the following sections.

Mining

When a transaction is sent to the bitcoin network, it is not finalized until it gets included in a "block" of transactions by a "bitcoin miner." Being a miner isn't a reserved role, but an open position for anyone able to provide enough computing power to validate the transactions. All the time, the miners in the network are racing to be the first one to validate a block of transactions by performing a difficult computational operation to solve a function defined by the protocol (Proof of Work). The first miner to succeed is rewarded with a prize of newly generated bitcoins along with "transaction fees" paid for each transaction, as well as his blocks being included in the blockchain.

However, it should be noted that these mechanisms are susceptible to being reversed, hence the need to wait for a few confirmations (more than six blocks) to consider the transaction final.

Bitcoin scripting

One of the amazing features of the bitcoin system is the ability to set a script defining the conditions that a recipient should validate to spend the bitcoins later, making bitcoin a programmable currency. Fundamentally, all bitcoin transactions have scripts, written in the Bitcoin programming language, included in their inputs and outputs. This language is a Forth-like language offering a set of opcodes or instructions, evaluated from left to right using a stack to determine the success or failure of the script execution.

Normally, the transaction embeds into its inputs an unlocking script commonly called
ScriptSig and a locking script called ScriptPubkey into its outputs. When a transaction
is validated, the concatenation of both scripts – ScriptPubkey, which protects the output,
and the ScriptSig provided by the recipient to prove ownership – must execute
successfully (evaluated to true). The following diagram illustrates the location of both
scripts and how they are validated:

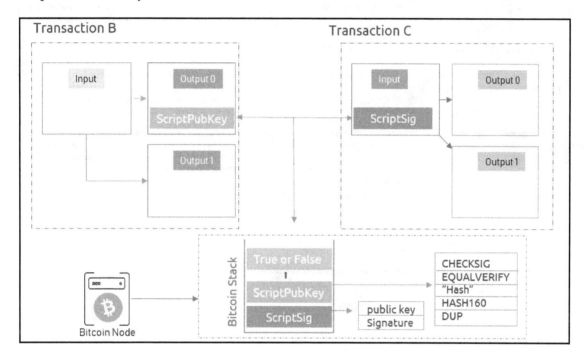

Bitcoin scripting using different combinations of opcodes enables us to create a wide variety of transaction types. The following table summarizes the standard transaction types:

Script Type		Script Format	Description
Pay to PubKey Hash (P2PKH)	ScriptPubKey	OP_DUP OP_HASH160 <PubKeyHash> OP_EQUALVERIFY OP_CHECKSIG	This script is the most popular type in the Bitcoin blockchain. It is used to send Bitcoins to a single address (which is a public key hash encoded in base58check starting with 1).
	ScriptSig	<signature> <PubKey>	
Pay to PubKey (P2PK)	ScriptPubKey	<Public Key> OP_CHECKSIG	This script is usually used by miners to redeem their new mined Bitcoins.
	ScriptSig	<Signature>	
Pay to Script Hash (P2SH)	ScriptPubKey	OP_HASH160 <script Hash> OP_EQUAL	A special script which moves the responsibility for supplying the conditions to redeem a transaction from the creator of the transaction to the receiver(s). This latter must provide a script matching the script hash.
	ScriptSig	<signature> <serialized script>	
Multi-Signature	ScriptPubKey	ScriptPubKey=2 <Public Key A> <Public Key B> <Public Key C> n OP_CHECKMULTISIG	This script locks the output with N public keys, with condition that at least M of those Keys are required. The redeemers should provide M valid signatures corresponding to the N public keys.
	ScriptSig	<Signature1><Signature2>or any permutation of Sig m:n	
P2WSH	ScriptPubKey	zero [32-byte sha256(witness script)]	P2WSH is similar to P2SH but the proof of ownership RedeemScript is moved to the witness instead of ScriptSig (signature + redeem script)
	ScriptSig	Empty (as the signature is located in the witness instead of the ScriptSig)	
Pay-to-Witness-Public-Key-Hash	ScriptPubKey	ScriptPubKey: zero [20-byte hash160(public key)]	P2WPKH is similar to a P2KH but with witness data.
	ScriptSig	Empty	
Null Data:		OP_RETURN OP_DATA_X	This script marks a transaction as provably unspendable and a potential prunable Output. In this case the script is considered as invalid, guaranteeing that there is no corresponding ScriptSig

Lastly, it's worth mentioning that users can define their own locking scripts, but they should ask miners to mine them.

If you're familiar with C++, you can understand how scripts work under the hood by looking at script interpreter code: https://github.com/bitcoin/bitcoin/blob/master/src/script/interpreter.cpp. Moreover, a transaction is considered as standard if it fulfills the requirement defined by Bitcoin Core's IsStandard() and IsStandardTx() functions.

We have now clarified the role of scripts but they will make more sense the more practice you get. Let's take a look at an example of how to build and send bitcoin transactions with custom scripts using JavaScript.

Building a P2PKH script using JavaScript

The first hands-on part of this chapter will be writing a JavaScript snippet using the powerful bitcoin library `bitcore-lib` to build a P2PKH script (used to pay to a bitcoin address). Throughout this chapter, we will run our experiments on Ubuntu LTS 16.04.

Before you proceed with this section, make sure Node.js (`nodejs.org`) is installed with the latest version. Then create a directory in which we install the `bitcore` package:

```
npm install bitcore-lib --save
```

Let's take a look at how to build very simple script:

```
var bitcore = require('bitcore-lib');
var Address = bitcore.Address;
var address = Address.fromString('n3CKupfRCJ6Bnmr78mw9eyeszUSkfyHcPy');
var script = bitcore.Script.buildPublicKeyHashOut(address);
console.log(script);
```

The `bitcore.Script` object provides an interface to construct bitcoin scripts. It also gives simple interfaces to create the most common script types, such as `buildPublicKeyHashOut(address)`, which creates a **Pay-to-Public-Key-Hash** (PPKH) output for the given address.

Save the code in a JavaScript file `script.js` and run it using `node script.js`. The output will show you the following `ScriptPubKey` script (locking script):

```
<Script: OP_DUP OP_HASH160 20 0xedcce89f510bf95606ec6a79cb28a745c039e220
OP_EQUALVERIFY OP_CHECKSIG>
```

The result is a common locking script requiring the receiver to have the private key corresponding to the public key whose `Hash160 ( RIPEMD160(SHA256(publickey)))` is `0xedcce89f510bf95606ec6a79cb28a745c039e220`. This special hash was extracted from the receiver's bitcoin address as follows:

```
Bitcoin address = [Version Byte (1 byte)]+[Hash 160 of public
key]+[Checksum (4 Bytes)]
```

This is then encoded in base 58. If the receiver provides the public key, they have to prove also their ownership of the correct private key by signing the transaction to fulfill the OP_EQUALVERIFY OP_CHECKSIG part.

Building a custom script

As mentioned before, we can define our own scripts instead of using the standards. In the following example, we will define a non-standard bitcoin script based on a simple equation, X+13=15. Therefore, to spend our transaction, the recipient needs to come up with a ScriptSig presenting the correct solution, which is obviously 2, in order to solve the equation and spend the output.

If we translate this equation into bitcoin scripts, we get the following:

Locking Script (ScriptPubKey): "x+13=15"	OP_X OP_13 OP_ADD OP_15 OP_EQUAL
Unlocking Script (ScriptSig): "2"	OP_2

Bitcore enables us to create transactions with custom script. Hence, in the following example, we will create a non-standard transaction with the puzzle (`ScriptPubkey`) described previously.

Firstly, we need to select a UTXO from our bitcoin wallet to construct a new transaction. For that, make sure bitcoin Core is still running in Regtest mode and use the command `bitcoin-cli listunspent` to get an available UTXO with its details: `txid`, ScriptPubkey, and receiving address. Then create a new destination address with `bitcoin-cli getnewaddress`.

On the other hand, the private key can be unveiled using `bitcoin-cli dumpprivkey <utxo address>`. Once you have all these ingredients, edit the following code accordingly (the full code is available at `https://github.com/bellaj/Bitcoin_payment/tree/master/custom%20scripts`):

```
var pkey = 'cPJCt9r5eu9GJz1MxGBGgmZYTymZqpvVCZ6bBdqQYQQ5PeW4h74d'; //UTXO's
private key
var Taddress = 'n1PoDECeUwbXgktfkNkBcmVXtD2CYUco2c'; //Destination address
var lockingscript = bitcore.Script('OP_13 OP_ADD OP_15 OP_EQUAL');
//PubKeyScript
var g_utxos=[{"address":"n1PoDECeUwbXgktfkNkBcmVXtD2CYUco2c",
"txid":"c6758cf22346d3d8b7b6042b7701a5f07d140732bf5b93e1fb92ed250e5b6d20","
vout":0,"scriptPubKey":"210330b8e88054629399e6c90b37503f07fbc1f83aa72444dd2
cfd9050c3d08d75fcac","amount":50.0}]; //UTXO details

var transaction = new bitcore.Transaction();
transaction = transaction.from(g_utxos);
transaction = transaction.to(Taddress, 4000000000); //Add a first output
```

```
with the given amount of satoshis
transaction = transaction.fee(0.0001*100000000);
transaction = transaction.addOutput(new bitcore.Transaction.Output({script:
lockingscript, satoshis: 1000000000,address:Taddress }));
transaction = transaction.sign(pkey); //Sign all inputs
console.log("Raw Transaction\n" + transaction);
```

The preceding code is self-explanatory: we construct a transaction using
the `Transaction()` method, and then we define two outputs – one sending 40 BTC to a
P2PKH address and the other sending 10 with a custom script.

Save this code in a file called `custom_pubkeyscript.js` and run it using `node`
`custom_pubkeyscript.js`. As a result, a raw transaction will be constructed. If you
decode the resulting transaction using `bitcoin-cli decoderawtransaction <your`
`tx>`, you'll be able to see our custom ScriptPubkey:

```
{
    "value": 10.00000000,
    "n": 1,
    "scriptPubKey": {
        "asm": "13 OP_ADD 15 OP_EQUAL",
        "hex": "5d935f87",
        "type": "nonstandard"
    }
}
```

Then send the raw transaction to the local network using `bitcoin-cli`
`sendrawtransaction <your raw transaction>` and you'll get back the transaction ID.
To get it validated, we only have to mine a block using `bitcoin-cli generate 1`.

Now we have a non-standard output carrying 10 bitcoins waiting to be spent. To consume
it, we need to construct a transaction with the correct `ScriptSig op_2` as follows:

```
var unlockingScript = bitcore.Script().add('OP_2');
var transaction = new bitcore.Transaction();
transaction.addInput(new
bitcore.Transaction.Input({prevTxId:'c6758cf22346d3d8b7b6042b7701a5f07d1407
32bf5b93e1fb92ed250e5b6d20', outputIndex: 1, script: unlockingScript }),
unlockingScript, 10000);
transaction = transaction.to(Taddress, 90000000);
transaction = transaction.fee(0.0001*100000000);
console.log(transaction)
```

We define here an input pointing the previously created output with a custom ScriptSig. As
you may notice, the output can be spent without providing a signature. As we did for the
previous transaction, you can send the transaction and mine it.

When `ScriptSig` and `ScriptPubkey` are executed, the opcode `.add('OP_2')` pushes value 2 onto the stack, and then the operands (13 and 2 from ScriptSig) are added using `.add('OP_ADD')`, and the result is compared using `.add('OP_EQUAL')` to 15; therefore the top of the stack will be true, which means the full script (unlocking + locking) is valid and the output is "unlocked" and can be spent.

 To observe the execution of a bitcoin script on the stack., there is an interesting open source IDE for bitcoin transactions called Hashmal, available at `https://github.com/mazaclub/hashmal`.

If everything went correctly, you should be able to successfully spend the previous output with the custom ScriptPubkey. Just a minor warning: in public networks, non-standard transactions may not be validated by the network.

All set. We're done with non-standard transactions and bitcoin scripting. Now you have a basic understanding of bitcoin under your belt, you should be ready to tackle the rest of this chapter and build a real-world application.

Building a payment gateway

If you have never developed bitcoin applications before, this section is the best place to start. We plan here to integrate bitcoin payments into an online e-commerce website. The idea is to create a payment option for the e-commerce customers to pay simply by clicking a direct bitcoin payment URL or scanning a QR code, which opens a payment form with payment details in the wallet, making the payment process very straightforward and easy. Moreover, such a payment option avoids customers filling in any forms or providing personal data.

Project description

This project generally represents how to implement the bitcoin payment protocol proposed in `BIP 70` in order to build an online payment gateway. The BIP 70 protocol enables direct bitcoin payment processing for e-commerce platforms by managing payment transactions between a payment portal and the customer's bitcoin wallet.

 BIPs, or Bitcoin Improvement Proposals, are proposals for introducing features or changes to Bitcoin . You can learn about all the BIPs in the official documentation at `https://github.com/bitcoin/bips`.

The merchant's server application will generate a custom `BIP 72` payment URL (and the corresponding QR code) to help customers check out easily using their bitcoin wallet/client, whether by clicking on the link provided, or by scanning the QR code, as shown in the following diagram:

Basically, we'll perform the following three major steps to set up the project:

1. Build the merchant server using Node.js and the `Bitcore` library
2. Build the JavaScript frontend
3. Build the Java client using BitcoinJ

Bitcoin payment protocol overview

The Bitcoin payment protocol specification is presented in the BIP 70 (`https://github.com/bitcoin/bips/blob/master/bip-0070.mediawiki`), BIP 71(`https://github.com/bitcoin/bips/blob/master/bip-0071.mediawiki`), BIP 72(`https://github.com/bitcoin/bips/blob/master/bip-0072.mediawiki`) and BIP 73(`https://github.com/bitcoin/bips/blob/master/bip-0073.mediawiki`) documents. It was designed to introduce additional features to bitcoin by replacing the use of a bitcoin address with direct payment flow between the sender and recipient of funds using a graphical wallet to offer a seamless checkout process. The main goal of BIP 70 is to provide a bitcoin payment solution, improving the customer experience and securing the online payments.

If you are familiar with C++, you can examine
`paymentserver.cpp` and `paymentrequestplus.cpp` located in the
Bitcoin GitHub repository at `https://github.com/bitcoin/bitcoin/`
`blob/master/src/qt/`.

The user does not have to deal with bitcoin's underlying mechanisms, they only have to simply open their wallet with a payment request and proceed with the payment. The following sequence diagram shows how the customer's and merchant's wallets interact with each other and with the bitcoin network to process the payment operation using BIP 70 protocol:

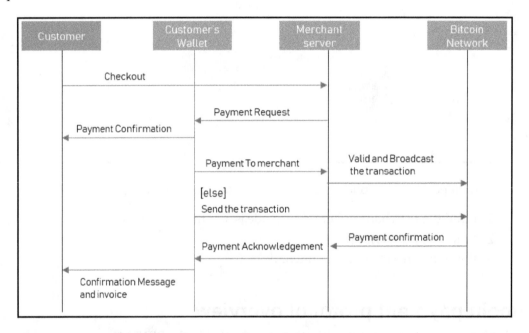

When the customer initiates the checkout process, the merchant launches a payment request to the user's wallet signed with its certificate. Once received, the latter parses and validates the request details, and then authorizes the payment by sending the payment transaction back to the merchant or directly to the network. When the payment is settled, the merchant sends a payment acknowledgment to the user with potential invoice details.

Prerequisites

Before proceeding with this project, a general knowledge of programming concepts and JavaScript is highly recommended. To start coding, we need to have the following elements installed:

- npm (the npm package gets installed along with Node.js)
- bower
- git

For this project, I suggest we switch bitcoin client to operate on the testnet. In your bitcoin.conf file, keep the same user and password and edit the following values:

```
regtest=0
testnet=1
prune=550
```

Afterward, run bitcoin-qt and generate two addresses, one for the merchant and the other for the customer, and then provision some testnet bitcoins to the customer's address from an online bitcoin faucet such as https://testnet.manu.backend.hamburg/faucet.

Project setup

After fulfilling the prerequisite steps, create a new directory dedicated to your project, as follows:

```
mkdir Bitcoin_payment && cd Bitcoin_payment
```

In your workspace, create two new subdirectories: a keys/ directory for storing your keys and certificate, and a views/ directory for storing the web pages and scripts.

To install all the requisite dependencies, create a package.json file from inside the Bitcoin_payment/ directory:

```
{
  "scripts": {
    "start": "node server.js"
  },
  "dependencies": {
    "bitcore-lib": "^0.15.0",
    "bitcore-payment-protocol": "1.2.2",
    "body-parser": "^1.18.3",
    "express": "^4.16.3",
    "request": "^2.88.0",
```

```
        "underscore": "^1.9.1"
    }
}
```

Then run the following command:

```
npm install
```

This will install all the Node packages you need for setting up and running the project.

Certificate management

In order to build a secure payment system, we need to use SSL certificates either for enabling HTTPS or for BIP 70 payment request verification so as to confirm that the payment request was genuinely initiated by the merchant. Basically, the certificate has to be provided by a third-party certificate authority (CA) in order to confirm the merchant's identity.

To obtain SSL certificates, you have the choice between using commercial or private certificate authorities or the Let's Encrypt (https://letsencrypt.org/ project. For demonstration purposes, in this guide, we will use a self-signed certificate to avoid unnecessary details. To obtain such a certificate, you need to use OpenSSL as follows:

```
openssl req -x509 -newkey rsa:4096 -keyout keys/key.pem -out keys/cert.pem
-days 365  -subj
"/C=MA/ST=ByExample/L=Testbip70.com/O=Chapter3/OU=Org/CN=Testbip70.com" -
nodes

openssl x509 -in keys/cert.pem -out keys/cert.der -outform DER
```

You will end up with three files – key.pem, cert.pem, and cert.der – in your keys/ directory.

Merchant side

To start off, we build a basic Node.js server accepting HTTP and HTTPS requests using our generated certificates. As this book is not about either Node.js or JavaScript, I'll put the main emphasis on presenting the code related to bitcoin and the bitcore library. For now, let's start building our web server:

```
'use strict';
var bitcore_lib = require('bitcore-lib');
var PaymentProtocol = require('bitcore-payment-protocol');
var express = require('express');
```

```
var bodyParser = require('body-parser');
var URI = require('bitcore-lib/lib/uri');
var request = require("request");
const https = require('https');
var fs = require("fs");

var dcert = fs.readFileSync('./keys/cert.der');
var mcert = fs.readFileSync('./keys/cert.pem'); // For HTTPS server
var mkey = fs.readFileSync('./keys/key.pem');

var credentials = {key: mkey, cert: mcert};
var app = express();
var os = require('os');
var interfaces = os.networkInterfaces();
var addresses = [];
for (var k in interfaces) {
    for (var k2 in interfaces[k]) {
        var address = interfaces[k][k2];
        if (address.family === 'IPv4' && !address.internal) {
            addresses.push(address.address);
        }
    }
}

var IP = addresses[0];
var port = 8883;
var http_port = 3000;

app.get("/", function(req, res) {
    res.send('Bitcoin Payment protocol');
});

app.listen(http_port, function() {
    console.log("-http Server listening on :"+IP+":"+ http_port);
});

https.createServer(credentials, app).listen(port, function() {
    console.log("-https Server listening on :"+IP+":"+ port);
});
```

This big chunk of code creates a simple Node.js server to serve the HTTP requests. Save this code in a file named `server.js` and run it with `node server.js`. Your server will start and listen on two different ports: 3000 for HTTP and 8883 for HTTPS.

You might get the error **Error: More than one instance of bitcore-lib found**; in this case, refer to `https://github.com/bellaj/Bitcoin_payment`, where I propose a sketchy workaround.

Since the certificate is self-signed, if you open any browser to the server's address with port 8883, it will yield a warning, and not allow the communication to continue without an explicit exception. To solve that, you have to manually install the certificate (`cert.der`) into your browser. Next, try to visit locally `http://localhost:3000`; the browser window should display a **Bitcoin Payment protocol** message.

Before we move on, stop the running server by pressing *Ctrl + C* in the server's Terminal window. Let's expand our code to make use of the bitcore library to create the payment request.

Building a payment request URI

First off, we define the testnet as the default network for our application and a merchant address. Simply put within the server's code the following lines:

```
bitcore_lib.Networks.defaultNetwork = bitcore_lib.Networks.testnet; // the
project runs only on testnet
var Merchant_address = "mhc5YipxN6GhRRXtgakRBjrNUCbz6ypg66";
```

In this example, we used a static bitcoin address but in a real implementation, the merchant has to generate a unique payment address associated with the customer's order. Alternatively, you can generate a random address using the following:

```
var privateKey = bitcore_lib.PrivateKey(merchant_pkey); // we pass a
specific private key as argument
var publicKey = bitcore_lib.PublicKey(privateKey);
bitcore_lib.Address(publicKey, bitcore_lib.Networks.defaultNetwork ));
```

We then define a simple function, `compose_uri()`, to build the bitcoin payment URI:

```
function compose_uri(amount_to_pay) {
    var pay_url = "http://"+IP+":"+http_port+"/request";
    var uriString = new URI({
        address: Merchant_address,
        amount : amount_to_pay, // amount in satoshis
        message: 'payment request'
    });
    var paymentUri = uriString+"&r="+pay_url;
    return paymentUri;
}
```

The `compose_uri()` function generates the request payment URI starting with the prefix `bitcoin:` (defined in BIP 21), and containing the destination and amount. The overall URI is a BIP-72-style with the special query parameter `r`, which specifies from where the payment request will be fetched from. Custom URIs are very helpful as browsers and mobile apps use them to launch the registered protocol handler, in this case a bitcoin client.

So now that we have all that up and running, it's time to actually handle requests.

Routing

The actual application functionality is just a basic user model with a few views and a controller without supporting registration and logging in/out. Unsurprisingly, to handle the HTTP requests, we are using the `expressJs` framework, which provides us with middleware to handle incoming HTTP requests and translate each into an action.

Checkout view

The initial endpoint will be `/checkout`, whereby the customer requests to make a payment. We define the handler associated with a `get` handler to execute `/checkout` as follows:

```
var path = require("path");
app.use(express.static(path.join(__dirname + '/views')));
app.get('/checkout', function(req, res) {
    res.sendFile(path.join(__dirname+'/views/index.html'));
});
```

If you're unfamiliar with Express, we defined here a callback function that behaves like middleware (`https://expressjs.com/en/guide/using-middleware.html`) to handle the `/checkout` route. We are using `sendFile` to make the server send a static `index.html` file from the `views/` directory to the browser, when the user requests the `/checkout` path.

Proceeding with payment

We then define the /ProcessingPayment route, which will be requested when the user clicks the **Pay with BTC** button to generate and render the bitcoin payment URL:

```
app.use(bodyParser.json());
app.post("/ProcessingPayment", function(req, res) {
    var amount_ = req.body.amount;
    var resp = compose_uri(amount_)+"?amount="+amount_;
    res.send(resp);
});
```

Requesting payment details

As defined by the protocol, when the customer clicks on the payment link, its wallet (bitcoin client) will request the /request endpoint to get the merchant's payment request with all the necessary data:

```
var urlencodedParser = bodyParser.urlencoded({ extended: false });
app.get("/request", urlencodedParser, function(req, res) {
    var amount = req.query.amount;
    amount = (amount === undefined) ? 0 : amount; // set amount to 0 if
undefined
    var merchant_outputs = []; // Where payment should be sent
    var outputs = new PaymentProtocol().makeOutput();
    outputs.set('amount', amount);
    var script =
bitcore_lib.Script.buildPublicKeyHashOut(Merchant_address.toString());
    outputs.set('script', script.toBuffer());
    merchant_outputs.push(outputs.message);
});
```

Here, the merchant's server constructs a P2PKH transaction with the amount handed from the client side. Then, within the same route, we wrap inside a PaymentRequest message with relevant details about the payment as follows:

```
var details = new PaymentProtocol().makePaymentDetails();
var now = Date.now() / 1000 | 0;
details.set('network', 'test');
details.set('outputs', merchant_outputs);
details.set('time', now); //Unix timestamp when the PaymentRequest was
created.
details.set('expires', now + 60 * 60 * 24); //timestamp after which the
PaymentRequest should be considered invalid.
details.set('memo', 'A payment request from the merchant.');
details.set('payment_url', "http://"+IP+":"+http_port+"/payment?id=12345");
//location where a Payment message may be sent to obtain a PaymentACK.
```

```
details.set('merchant_data', new Buffer("Transaction N 12345")); //identify
the payment request
```

For more information about these fields, you can visit the official BIP 70 documentation (`https://github.com/bitcoin/bips/blob/master/bip-0070.mediawiki#paymentdetailspaymentrequest`). After defining the payment request details, we form the final request as follows:

```
var request = new PaymentProtocol().makePaymentRequest();
request.set('payment_details_version', 1);
var certificates = new PaymentProtocol().makeX509Certificates();
certificates.set('certificate',dcert);
request.set('pki_type', 'x509+sha256');
request.set('pki_data', certificates.serialize());
request.set('serialized_payment_details', details.serialize());
request.sign(mkey);
var rawbody = request.serialize(); // serialize the request
res.set({
    'Content-Type': PaymentProtocol.PAYMENT_REQUEST_CONTENT_TYPE,
    'Content-Length': request.length,
    'Content-Transfer-Encoding': 'binary'
});
```

A `PaymentRequest` is optionally tied to a merchant's identity using public-key infrastructure (PKI) specified in `pki_type`. We sign it using the private key that corresponds to the public key in `pki_data` before forwarding it to the client side. The response format changes depending on the requester, be it a bitcoin client or a browser:

```
if (req.query.browser==1) {
    var buf = new Buffer(rawbody, 'binary').toString('base64');
    res.contentType(PaymentProtocol.PAYMENT_REQUEST_CONTENT_TYPE);
    res.send(buf);
} else {
    //response for bitcoin core client
    res.status(200).send(rawbody);
}
```

Receiving and acknowledging payment

Once the customer verifies the payment request, they post a payment transaction to the merchant server (toward `payment_url`, which points to the `payment/` route). Therefore, in this route, we extract the payment details (payment message) from the client's transaction as follows:

```
var rawBodyParser = bodyParser.raw({type:
PaymentProtocol.PAYMENT_CONTENT_TYPE});
```

```
app.post("/payment", rawBodyParser, function(req, res) {
    var body = PaymentProtocol.Payment.decode(req.body);
    var payment = new PaymentProtocol().makePayment(body);
    var refund_to = payment.get('refund_to'); //output where a refund
should be sent.
    var memo = payment.get('memo');
    var Rawtransaction = payment.get('transactions')[0].toBuffer();/*One or
more valid, signed Bitcoin transactions that fully pay the PaymentRequest*/
    var TransactionToBrodcast = new
bitcore_lib.Transaction(Rawtransaction).toString('hex');
/* potentially broadcast the transaction as we did in the first chapter
using chain.so/api/ */
});
```

Depending on your design, you can choose which side will broadcast the payment to the bitcoin network, whether the server or the customer's wallet. Still, in the second section (BitcoinJ), we will instead request the customer's approval and then let the merchant forward the transaction to the network using a web API (or by using bitcore-p2p at https:/ /bitcoinj.github.io/payment-protocol).

The final action in the payment process is sending to the client a payment acknowledgment message with a receipt ID. It's possible you can listen on the bitcoin network for whether the transaction took place before sending such a message:

```
var ack = new PaymentProtocol().makePaymentACK();
ack.set('payment', payment.message);
ack.set('memo', 'Payment processed,Thank you ;) \n invoice ID
:'+req.query.id);
//store invoice details in database
var rawack = ack.serialize();
res.set({
    'Content-Type': PaymentProtocol.PAYMENT_ACK_CONTENT_TYPE,
    'Content-Length': rawack.length,
});
res.send(rawack);
```

Invoicing

Finally, the system would be complete if it enabled the merchant to invoice the clients. For this purpose, you can add to your system a database-based invoice system to store the purchase invoices for future access. We can define an /invoice handler to provide the invoice details to the requester:

```
app.get("/invoice", urlencodedParser, function(req, res) {
    var invoice_id = req.query.id;
    var detail="details about the invoice N:"+invoice_id;
```

```
/*....invoice Database access..*/
res.send(detail);
});
```

Now, as the server is ready, we need to proceed to building the frontend part.

Client side

As for the backend, we'll use bitcore in the client side, therefore we need to install the frontend component. For that, create a bower.json file in the views/ folder with the following content:

```
{
  "dependencies": {
    "bitcore-lib": "^0.15.0",
    "bitcore-payment-protocol": "1.2.2"
  }
}
```

Then run the following command (inside the views/ folder):

```
bower install
```

Next, we need to install a QR code library in the views/ directory:

```
git clone https://github.com/davidshimjs/qrcodejs
```

Then create two files – index.html and main.js – in the views/ directory. In the first of these files, paste the following code:

```
<html>
<head>
  <script src="bower_components/bitcore-lib/bitcore-lib.js"></script>
  <script src="bower_components/bitcore-payment-protocol/bitcore-payment-
protocol.min.js"> </script>
  <script src="qrcodejs/qrcode.js"></script>
  <script  src="//ajax.googleapis.com/ajax/libs/jquery/3.2.1/jquery.min.js"
type="text/javascript"></script>
  <link rel="stylesheet" type="text/css" href="style.css" />
</head>
<body>
  <div class="main_div">
    <form id="myForm">
      <img src="watch.jpg" width="200px" class="item">
      <br>
      <h1>MVMT WATCH</h1>
```

```
      <strong>Item Details:</strong> WATER RESISTANT
      <br>
      <strong>Price :</strong> 0.888888 BC.
      <input type="hidden" id="amount" value=888888>
      <br>
      <br>
      <input
        type="submit"
        value="Pay with BTC"
        id="submit"
        onclick="event.preventDefault();ProcessingPayment()" />
    </form>
  </div>
  <script src="./main.js"></script>
</body>
</html>
```

This code builds a demo web page with a single product (a watch) and a payment button. On the other hand, in main.js, we define the frontend functions to interact with the payment server.

First, we define the ProcessingPayment() function, which initiates an Ajax call to request the payment URI:

```
function ProcessingPayment() {
    var amount_ = $('#amount').val();
    $.ajax({
        method: 'POST',
        url: '/ProcessingPayment',
        data: JSON.stringify({'amount' : amount_}),
        contentType: 'application/json',
        processData: false,
        success: function(data) {
            pay(data);
        }
    });
}
```

The server will answer back with a payment link, which will be displayed as a URL and QR code using the method `pay()`:

```
function pay(pay_url) {
    document.write("<body><div class='pay_div'><h1>Quick Checkout</h1><div
class='result' id='result' name='result'> <div class='overview'> Payment
URL : <a href=" +pay_url+ ">"+ pay_url +"</a> </div><br> <div
id='qrcode'></div>  <input type='hidden' id='amount' value='888888'> <br>
<input type='button' value='Transaction Details' onclick='check_details()'
id='check' class='check'><div class='details'></div></div><script
src='./main.js'></script> <link rel='stylesheet' type='text/css'
href='style.css' /></body>");

    var qrcode = new QRCode(document.getElementById("qrcode"), {
        text: pay_url.toString(),
        width: 128,
        height: 128,
        colorDark : "#000000",
        colorLight : "#ffffff",
        correctLevel : QRCode.CorrectLevel.H
    });
}
```

We then define a `check_details()` method to request from the server the payment details when the customer presses the **Transaction Details** button:

```
function check_details() {
    var amount_ = $('#amount').val();
    $.ajax({
        method: 'GET',
        url: '/request?amount='+amount_+'&browser=1',
        datatype:'binary',
        processData: false,
        success: function(data) {
            get_payment_details(data);
        }
    });
}
```

In the last step, once the payment request details are received, they will be unpacked and displayed using the following `get_payment_details` method:

```
function get_payment_details(rawbody) {
    try {
        var body = PaymentProtocol.PaymentRequest.decode(rawbody);
        var request = (new PaymentProtocol()).makePaymentRequest(body);
        var version = request.get('payment_details_version');
        var pki_type = request.get('pki_type');
```

```
        var pki_data = request.get('pki_data');
        var serializedDetails = request.get('serialized_payment_details');
        var signature = request.get('signature');
        var verified = request.verify();
        verified=(verified) ? "Valid" : verified;
        var decodedDetails =
PaymentProtocol.PaymentDetails.decode(serializedDetails);
        var details = new
PaymentProtocol().makePaymentDetails(decodedDetails);
        var network = details.get('network');
        var outputs = details.get('outputs');
        var time = details.get('time');
        var expires = details.get('expires');
        var memo = details.get('memo');
        var payment_url = details.get('payment_url');
        var merchant_data = details.get('merchant_data');
        $('.details').append('<h2>Invoice :</h2><ul><li> Network :
'+network+'</li><li>Transaction Timestamp : '+time+'</li><li>Expiration
Date: '+expires+'</li><li>Merchant data : '+merchant_data+'</li><li>
Merchant Signature verification: '+verified+'</li><li>Memo:
'+memo+'</li><li> Total : 0.0088888</li>');
    } catch (e) {
      console.log(('Could not parse payment protocol: ' + e));
    }
  }
```

The details displayed are very important, especially the validation of the merchant identity status using `request.verify()`, which validates the payment request signature against the merchant's identity.

Instead of building the frontend from scratch, we can use a scaffolding tool such as Yoman generator in order to generate new web project structures in a matter of seconds.

Great! Now the application is ready to be tested. Let's check it out.

Previewing your application

It's time to try out what we have built. First, we need to start the merchant server by running `npm start` from the project root (`bitcoin_payment/`). Then, open your browser to visit the URL, `http://<Machine_IP>:3000/checkout`.

If all went well, the server will serve you a store page with a single item and a **Pay with BTC** button, as shown in the following screenshot:

While I am testing on the same Linux machine, I have changed the domain name for localhost to bip70.com by editing the `/etc/hosts` file and adding `127.0.0.1 bip70.com`.

Once the client chooses to pay with bitcoin, they will be redirected to a new view with a custom payment URL:

Quick Checkout

Payment URL : bitcoin:mhc5YipxN6GhRRXtgakRBjrNUCbz6ypg6 6?amount=0.00888888&message=payment%20request&r=http:// 192.168.1.6:3000/request?amount=888888

Transaction Details

Invoice :

- Network : test
- Transaction Timestamp : 1534338057
- Expiration : 1534424457
- Merchant data : Transaction N 12345
- Merchant Signature verification: Valid
- Memo: A payment request from the merchant.
- Total : 0.0088888

The customer can check the transaction details before proceeding the payment by pressing the **Transaction Details** button. After the customer clicks on the payment link, the browser will open the bitcoin client after asking for authorization:

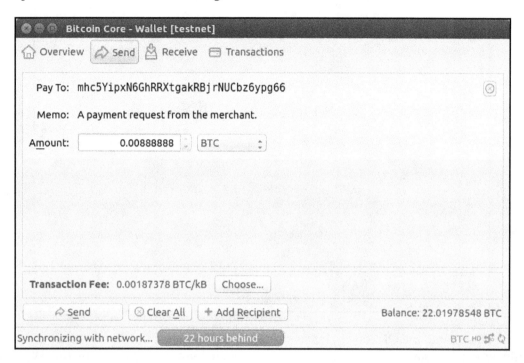

Once loaded, the bitcoin client connects to the payment server and gets the payment details (amount, merchant address, and so on) and prepares a payment transaction. We can see the memo sent from the merchant server displayed in the client interface. After examining the amount (which they can't edit), the client will approve the transaction and send it directly to the bitcoin network.

When the transaction is sent by the client, the bitcoin client will display the payment acknowledgment message sent from the server confirming the payment, as shown in the following screenshot:

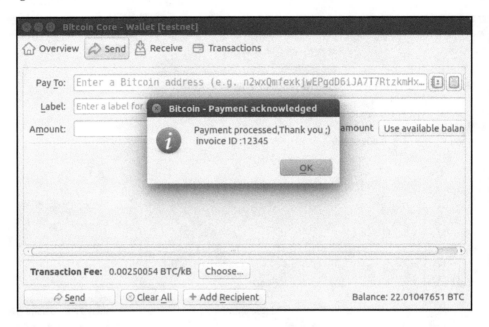

On the other hand, the QR code helps users to pay using their smartphone. To test this ability, you can install a bitcoin wallet from the Google Play store, such as Testnet Wallet or copay, and make sure you're connected to the same network. When you scan the QR code, you'll encounter an unavoidable error indicating that the certificate isn't signed by a trusted authority. Thus, we will need to add the merchant's certificate to the mobile OS. Once done, you can enjoy trying the payment process using the bitcoin mobile wallet as follows:

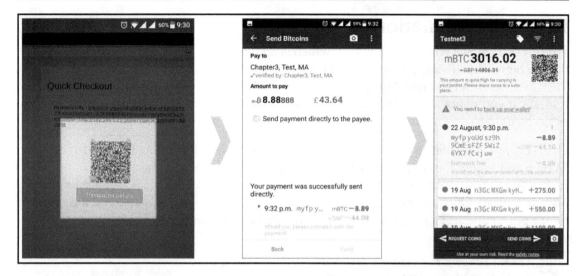

At this point, we have successfully built an online web store that accepts bitcoin payments. To complete the experience, let's build a light Java bitcoin wallet to pay with instead of relying on the installed bitcoin clients.

Payment protocol using BitcoinJ

If you're a Java developer who would like to get started with building bitcoin applications, this part will be your best starting point. We will build a Java client that implements the payment protocol (BIP 70) using BitcoinJ, and interacts with our payment Node.js server.

Prerequisites

The first thing you should do to follow this guide is to set up your own Java development environment. This walkthrough assumes that the latest version of the following elements is installed and running on your platform of choice:

- Java 8
- The Eclipse IDE from https://www.eclipse.org/downloads

You can refer to their official documentation in order to download and install them properly.

BitcoinJ installation

For this section, we will use `BitcoinJ`, which is a Java library designed to interact with the bitcoin network with support for BIP 70 (`https://bitcoinj.github.io/payment-protocol`). In order to make things simpler, we will install Maven's BitcoinJ plugin (version 0.14.17). If you're not a Java developer, Maven is a build automation tool for Java projects, used to download the dependencies required for a project.

Open Eclipse and create a new Maven project via **File** | **New** | **Other...** | **Maven** | **Maven** and follow the wizard instructions to finish the creation process (further instructions about setting up a Maven project are presented in Chapter 6, *Blockchain-Based Futures System*). Once the project is created, browse to the `pom.xml` file and add a reference to `BitcoinJ` and `slf4j-api` dependencies using the following lines inside:

```
<dependency>
  <groupId>org.bitcoinj</groupId>
  <artifactId>bitcoinj-core</artifactId>
  <version>0.14.7</version>
  <scope>compile</scope>
</dependency>
<dependency>
  <groupId>org.slf4j</groupId>
  <artifactId>slf4j-simple</artifactId>
  <version>1.7.21</version>
</dependency>
```

Slf4J is the logging framework used by BitcoinJ. It serves to handle the logs and helps us understand, via valuable logging messages (network connection and transaction information), the behavior of the BitcoinJ application and evaluate its execution. After that, right-click the `pom.xml` file and select **Run As** | **Maven** to build and run the empty project.

Now we can finally start programming using BitcoinJ.

BitcoinJ client

First off, in your Maven project, add a new class to your `src/main/java` folder with the name `Cbip70`. This class should have a main method, which will be used to communicate with the server.

Bitcoin wallet configuration

In the first line of our code, we activate BitcoinJ's logging using a Java logging formatter that writes more compact output than the default:

```
BriefLogFormatter.init();
```

Then we indicate which bitcoin network we want to use. In this scenario, we choose testnet, as our Node.js server is already running on the testnet network by default:

```
final static NetworkParameters params = TestNet3Params.get();
```

The other available options are `MainNetParams` and `RegTestParams`.

Next, we start by initializing (inside the `main` function) a `WalletAppKit` object, to create a lightweight **SPV** (short for **Simplified Payment Verification**) BitcoinJ wallet. As mentioned in the BitcoinJ documentation, the `WalletAppKit` class wraps the boilerplate (`Peers`, `BlockChain`, `BlockStorage`, `Wallet`) needed to set up a new SPV BitcoinJ app:

```
WalletAppKit kit = new WalletAppKit(params, new File("."), "walletappkit");
```

As a result, two files are also created locally – `.wallet` (wallet) and `.spvchain` (blockchain information) – with the specified prefix (the third argument) and stored in the indicated directory (the project root folder). Once created, we download the blockchain and wait until it's done:

```
kit.startAsync();
kit.awaitRunning();
```

In this case, the `kit` will behave as a bitcoin node connecting to other nodes and syncing with them the blockchain (downloading only headers).

 You can use `kit.connectToLocalHost();` if you're using Regtest mode to connect the kit to your local bitcoin client. Have a look at the `WalletAppKit` class to learn about the available functions and understand what's happening behind the scenes.

We then generate a bitcoin address for the client and print it along with its balance:

```
Address CustomerAddress=kit.wallet().currentReceiveAddress();
System.out.println("Customer's address : " + CustomerAddress);
System.out.println("Customer's Balance : "+kit.wallet().getBalance());
```

The wallet is now ready to run but we need to send a few bitcoins from a faucet source to the bitcoin address returned by the `currentReceiveAddress` function. If you run the current code, you'll get output similar to the following about blockchain's synchronization and the account details in Eclipse's log viewer:

```
Problems  Javadoc  Declaration  Console 

<terminated> Cbip70 [Java Application] /usr/lib/jvm/java-8-openjdk-amd64/bin/java (Aug 14, 2018, 2:00:09 PM)
[PeerGroup Thread] INFO org.bitcoinj.core.PeerGroup - Waiting 3375 msec before next connect attempt to [176.9.113.75]:18333
[NioClientManager] INFO org.bitcoinj.net.NioClientManager - Connected to testnet-seed.bitcoin.petertodd.org/82.202.207.182:18333
[NioClientManager] INFO org.bitcoinj.core.Peer - Announcing to testnet-seed.bitcoin.petertodd.org/82.202.207.182:18333 as: /bitcoinj:0
[NioClientManager] INFO org.bitcoinj.net.NioClientManager - Connected to testnet-seed.bitcoin.jonasschnelli.ch/18.222.184.185:18333
[NioClientManager] INFO org.bitcoinj.core.Peer - Announcing to testnet-seed.bitcoin.jonasschnelli.ch/18.222.184.185:18333 as: /bitcoin
[NioClientManager] INFO org.bitcoinj.core.Peer - [195.154.163.75]:18333: Got version=70015, subVer='/Satoshi:0.15.1/', services=0x9, t
[NioClientManager] INFO org.bitcoinj.core.Peer - [195.154.163.75]:18333: New peer     (1 connected, 8 pending, 12 max)
[NioClientManager] INFO org.bitcoinj.core.PeerGroup - Setting download peer: [195.154.163.75]:18333
Customer's address : n3UkyjXiy86dChf5nNwD5tJK2AAJ321odQ
Customer's Balance : 165000000
[NioClientManager] INFO org.bitcoinj.net.NioClientManager - Connected to testnet-seed.bluematt.me/198.251.83.19:18333
[NioClientManager] INFO org.bitcoinj.core.Peer - Announcing to testnet-seed.bluematt.me/198.251.83.19:18333 as: /bitcoinj:0.14.7/
[NioClientManager] INFO org.bitcoin.Secp256k1Context - java.lang.UnsatisfiedLinkError: no secp256k1 in java.library.path
[WalletAppKit STOPPING] INFO org.bitcoinj.core.PeerGroup - Awaiting PeerGroup shutdown ...
```

Requesting payment

Now that our wallet is loaded and synced with the network, we can read the BIP 70 URI provided by the merchant in order to make the payment. You can write a few lines of code to directly parse the bitcoin payment URL and register your app as the bitcoin URI (:bitcoin) handler. But to keep it simple, we will manually copy the payment link provided by Node.js earlier and assign it to a local variable (I've omitted irrelevant parameters):

```
String url
="bitcoin:mhc5YipxN6GhRRXtgakRBjrNUCbz6ypg66?r=http://bip70.com:3000/reques
t?amount=888888";
```

The important part in the URL is the `r` parameter, which represents the merchant server, so edit it to set your server's IP or domain name.

Prior to requesting payment details from merchant's server details, we can add a sanity check to evaluate whether the address has sufficient bitcoins:

```
if (Float.parseFloat(String.valueOf(kit.wallet().getBalance())) == 0.0) {
    System.out.println("Please send some testnet Bitcoins to your address
"+kit.wallet().currentReceiveAddress());
} else {
    sendPaymentRequest(url, kit);
}
```

Then we define `sendPaymentRequest()` as follows:

```
private static void sendPaymentRequest(String location, WalletAppKit k) {
    try {
```

```
            if (location.startsWith("bitcoin")) {
                BitcoinURI paymentRequestURI = new BitcoinURI(location);
                ListenableFuture<PaymentSession> future =
    PaymentSession.createFromBitcoinUri(paymentRequestURI,true);
                PaymentSession session = future.get();
                if (session.isExpired()) {
                    log.warn("request expired!");
                } else { //payment requests persist only for a certain
        duration.
                    send(session, k);
                    System.exit(1);
                }
            } else {
                log.info("Try to open the payment request as a file");
            }
        } catch (Exception e) {
            System.err.println( e.getMessage());
        }
    }
```

This method is comprised of two steps: parsing the bitcoin URI in order to request payment details from the specified URL, and running another function, send(), which proceeds with the payment.

The createFromBitcoinUri method initializes a PaymentSession using the payment URI. If this function is called with a second parameter set to true, the system trust store will be used to verify the signature provided by the payment request and a CertPathValidatorException exception is thrown in the failure case. The future.get() method parses the payment request, which is returned as a protocol buffer.

Once the payment session is established, we call the send() method to proceed with the payment. Note that you'll have to handle a few different exceptions, but I've set here a global try/catch for all expected exceptions to make the code cleaner for the reader.

Sending a payment

The next function is the one to pay the bill. Before sending the bitcoins, this function will check the payment request details, including the merchant's x509 certificate. We print out in the console the payment request details to let the client know whom they are going to pay:

```
private static void send(PaymentSession session,WalletAppKit k) {
    log.info("Payment Request");
    log.info("Amount to Pay: " + session.getValue().toFriendlyString());
    log.info("Date: " + session.getDate());
    // Probably indicates what your are paying for.
```

```
            log.info("Message from merchant : " + session.getMemo());
        PaymentProtocol.PkiVerificationData identity = session.verifyPki();

        if (identity != null) {
            // Merchant identity from the certificate
            log.info("Payment requester: " + identity.displayName);
            // The issuing Certificate Authority
            log.info("Certificate authority: " + identity.rootAuthorityName);
        }
    }
```

The important point in this first part is to validate the merchant's identity and signature using the PKI system. In fact, `session.verifyPki()` checks whether the merchant DER certificate containing the public key corresponding to the private key used to sign the `PaymentRequest` is signed by a trusted root authority. We display to the customer the merchant's identity and the certifying authority.

Then, we call the `getSendRequest` method to get the needed information about precisely how to send money to the merchant. Until now, the transaction in the request is incomplete; we need the client to confirm the payment transaction using `completeTx(req)`, which adds outputs and signed inputs according to the instructions in the request. The client indicates a refund address and a short memo to the intended destination:

```
    final SendRequest request = session.getSendRequest();
    k.wallet().completeTx(request);
    String customerMemo = "Nice Website";
    Address refundAddress = new
    Address(params, "mfcjN5E6vp2NWpMvH7TM2xvTywzRtNvZWR");
    ListenableFuture<PaymentProtocol.Ack> future =
        session.sendPayment(ImmutableList.of(request.tx), refundAddress,
    customerMemo);

    if (future != null) {
        PaymentProtocol.Ack ack = future.get();
        ...
```

The client creates here a transaction that fully pays the `PaymentRequest` using `completeTx`. Then, we call the `sendPayment` method, which does not broadcast the transaction to the bitcoin network, but instead sends a `Payment message` after the customer has authorized payment and indicated a refund address.

More specifically, if `payment_url` is specified in the merchant's payment request, then the payment message is serialized and sent as the body of the POST request to that URL. The server will forward the payment transaction to the network.

Afterward the customer's wallet waits for an acknowledgment of payment from the server:

```
...
System.out.println("Memo from merchant :"+ack.getMemo());
...
```

Then, we put the given transaction into the wallet's pending pool:

```
...
kit.wallet().commitTx(request.tx);
...
```

At this level, we have to edit the server's code (`server.js` file) to make it able to broadcast the received transaction. For that, within the `/payment` route, we have to add a few lines broadcasting the raw transaction using the `chain.so` API as we did in first chapter:

```
...
    var Rawtransaction = payment.get('transactions')[0].toBuffer();
    var TransactionToBrodcast = new
bitcore_lib.Transaction(Rawtransaction).toString('hex');
    var ack = new PaymentProtocol().makePaymentACK();
    ack.set('payment', payment.message);
    console.log("the merchant brodcast")

    var Sendingoptions = {
        method: 'POST',
        url: 'https://chain.so/api/v2/send_tx/BTCTEST',
        body: { tx_hex: TransactionToBrodcast },
        json: true };

    rp(Sendingoptions).then(function (response) {
        var Jresponse= JSON.stringify(response);
        ack.set('memo', 'Payment processed,Thank you ;) \ninvoice ID
:'+req.query.id+"\nTransaction Details : "+Jresponse );
    var rawack = ack.serialize();
    res.set({
    'Content-Type': PaymentProtocol.PAYMENT_ACK_CONTENT_TYPE,
    'Content-Length': rawack.length,
    });
    res.send(rawack);
    });
    ...
```

The server should normally determine whether or not the transaction satisfies the conditions of payment after broadcasting the transaction. It should also wait for confirmations to make sure that the payment is received before returning an acknowledgment message, as a transaction could fail to confirm for many reasons.

However, if the bitcoin URI returned by the payment request doesn't contain a payment URL, we broadcast the signed transaction directly from the client side:

```
...
} else {
    Wallet.SendResult sendResult = new Wallet.SendResult();
    sendResult.tx = request.tx;
    sendResult.broadcast = k.peerGroup().broadcastTransaction(request.tx);
    sendResult.broadcastComplete = sendResult.broadcast.future();
}
```

And with this last function, we are all set to try out our simple BitcoinJ application. Make sure to properly shut down all the running services when you want to stop the kit:

```
log.info("stopping..");
kit.stopAsync();
kit.awaitTerminated();
```

Congratulations! You have finished your first BitcoinJ program and got it to run. The complete source code for this section is available on GitHub at https://github.com/bellaj/BitcoinJ_Bip70.

Testing the code

It's testing time, but before running the project, we need to define a trusted keystore for Java in order to validate the server's certificate, and for that we use the Java keytool (further usage details on keytool can be found in Oracle's documentation):

```
keytool -import -keystore clientkeystore -file /path_to/cert.der -alias
bip70.com -storepass changeit
```

Then import the resulting `clientkeystore` file into the Eclipse project. Afterwards, click **Run as** then **Run Configurations** to define the parameter – `Djavax.net.ssl.trustStore=clientkeystore`—in the **Arguments** tab in the **VM arguments** box:

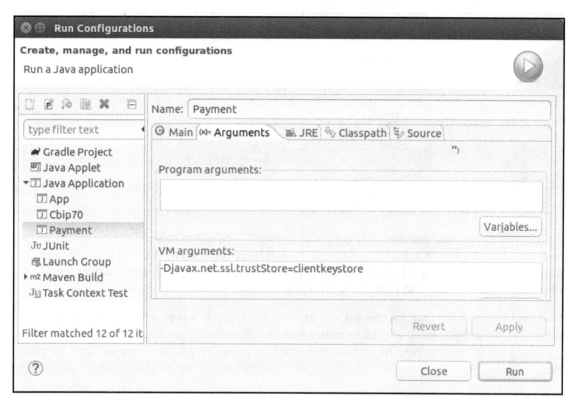

A good alternative way to use a custom trust store is to use `createFromBitcoinUri(BitcoinURI uri, boolean verifyPki, TrustStoreLoader trustStoreLoader)`, where the third argument is a `TrustStoreLoader` that loads the local `KeyStore`. When it's not defined, the system default trust store is used.

When you finish, compile and run your code. If everything runs correctly, you will be able to visualize in the Eclipse log viewer the SVP wallet activity, the merchant's payment request details, and the memo from the merchant when the payment is successfully processed, along with the invoice ID:

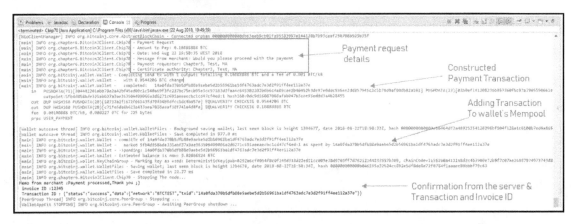

At this point, we have reached our goal of building a Java client to send a payment over the testnet network using the BIP 70 protocol. As you have witnessed, BitcoinJ is an easy-to-use and powerful framework. I would definitely recommend you spend time reading their official documentation and compiling the code samples provided therein.

Finally, I would note that, for the sake of brevity, the overall server and client code is intentionally unoptimized and lacks many features. You could probably go back over the code and try to include new improvements, such as building a GUI. I'll be waiting for your pull requests.

Bitcoin smart contracts

In the previous chapter, we briefly introduced the smart contract concept as self-executing programs that define a set of clauses stored on the blockchain. Although bitcoin was the first blockchain to propose a scripting language (limited for security reasons) to control funds, the smart contract concept is usually associated with the `Ethereum` blockchain, which provides Turing-complete smart contract languages. However, to redress the balance, many projects were initiated, such as Rootstock, Counterparty, and Ivy, to enable building and running advanced smart contracts on bitcoin. Welcome to bitcoin 2.0.

What is Rootstock?

Rootstock is a project to bring smart contracts (Turing-complete smart contracts) to the ecosystem of bitcoin. Rootstock (www.rsk.co) is a separate blockchain attached to the bitcoin blockchain through the use of a two-way peg. When you send a bitcoin over to Rootstock (via a special address where it will be locked and unspendable), it becomes a "smart" bitcoin living in Rootstock, which can be sent back to the bitcoin chain. This concept is known as a sidechain. Technically, Rootstock nodes are using a port of Ethereum (Java source), harnessing the EVM and its Turing-complete language to write and run smart contracts. Moreover, it promises faster payment and scaling up to 100 transactions per second.

Rootstock setup

To get started, we first need to install RskJ (a Java implementation of the RSK protocol). The setup process is quite straightforward, and uses the following commands:

```
sudo add-apt-repository ppa:rsksmart/rskj
sudo apt-get update
sudo apt-get install rskj
```

Once installation finishes, a configuration wizard will prompt you to select your network. Let's choose testnet:

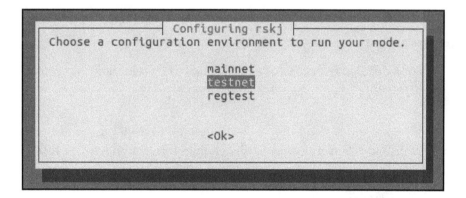

To reconfigure your node once installed, you need to change the configuration files that are located in `/etc/rsk/`. Firstly, in `node.conf`, you have to enable account creation by adding `enabled = true` inside the wallet configuration section:

```
wallet {
  accounts = []
  enabled = true
}
```

Secondly, change the CORS parameter from `cors = "localhost"` to `cors = "*"`.

We also enable the prune service by setting the parameter `enabled = true` in the `prune` section.

Interactions with RSK

After having configured the RSK node, we can then manage it as a service that can be started with the following:

```
sudo service rsk start
```

As a result, RSK will run as a daemon in the background and download the blockchain (a few GBs) in the `/var/lib/rsk/database/testnet` directory. Similarly, you can stop, restart, or check the situation of the service using the following:

```
sudo service rsk restart
sudo service rsk stop
service rsk status
```

For a detailed overview of an RSK node's behavior, you can consult its logs using `tail -f /var/log/rsk/rsk.log`.

The RSK project provides a useful console that enables interaction with an RSK node through RPC calls. We can install this utility using npm:

```
git clone https://github.com/rsksmart/utilities.git
cd utilities/console && npm install
```

After the installation is complete, open a new CLI and run the following command to access the console (by default, the RSK node runs in port 4444):

```
node console.js -server localhost:4444
```

This will open for you an interactive console that allows you to send commands to your RSK smart node. You can find a list of available RPC commands in the official documentation (`https://github.com/rsksmart/rskj/wiki/JSON-RPC-API-compatibility-matrix`).

It is worth mentioning that an RSK node behaves like an Ethereum node by exposing the `Web3` API over RPC, whereas the JavaScript console is a wrapper for the `web3js` API (part of the `Ethereum` project) to execute Web3 available calls in a bitcoin-related environment. We will cover this API in depth in `Chapter 4`, *Peer-to-Peer Auctions in Ethereum*, `Chapter 5`, *Tontine Game with Truffle and Drizzle* and `Chapter 6`, *Blockchain-Based Futures System*.

To check whether the blockchain is synced, we can use the `web3.eth.syncing` command in the RSK console which should return false (which might also mean that the node isn't syncing), and the `web3.eth.blockNumber` command should return the same block number as the latest block in the RSK explorer (`explorer.testnet.rsk.co/blocks`).

Account settings

While waiting for the blockchain to synchronize, let's create a new account from the RSK console:

```
web3.personal.newAccount('YourPassword')
web3.personal.unlockAccount(web3.eth.accounts[0], 'YourPassword', 0)
```

The result should look like the following:

```
user@ByExample-node:~/Chapter2/utilities/console$ node console.js -server localhost:4444
RSK >   web3.personal.newAccount("pwd1234")
0x6dcb977df8fc8b3b82b84bb62d39135b0cb821a9
RSK > web3.eth.getBalance("0xe009f56c37526809bc54089b128c071429938368").toNumber()
0
RSK > web3.eth.blockNumber
17612
```

Obviously, the balance is null because the freshly created account hasn't yet received any free smart bitcoins (SBTCs). To change that, we need to load this account with some SBTCs. For that, we can request them from an online faucet provider such as `http://faucet.testnet.rsk.co`.

You can check your new balance a few moments later using the following command:

```
web3.eth.getBalance(web3.eth.accounts[0]).toNumber()
```

Here, `web3.eth.accounts[index]` is an array of the created accounts.

Note that while the blockchain isn't synced, you'll also get a null balance. You can instead check the balance online using the Testnet RSK explorer: `https://explorer.testnet.rsk.co/address/<your address>`.

Note: If you want to use the sidechain aspect of Rootstock (*two-way peg mechanism*), whereby each bitcoin can be converted into a smart bitcoin, you should first whitelist your address (`https://github.com/rsksmart/rskj/wiki/Whitelisting-in-RSK`) and send the bitcoins to the TestNet Federation address: `2MyqxrSnE3GbPM6KweFnMUqtnrzkGkhT836`. Then, you'll need to convert your private key to an RSK private key using `https://utils.rsk.co` and import it into RSK's `node.conf`.

Writing your first bitcoin smart contract

To write smart contracts in RSK, we should use Solidity, which is an Ethereum smart contract language. In this chapter, we will not go into detail about Solidity, but rather we will limit the explanation to how to deploy and interact with a Solidity smart contract in RSK.

As a first smart contract, we consider the following code snippet:

```
pragma solidity ^0.4.21;

contract store {
    string public Message;

    function set (string NewMessage) public {
        Message = NewMessage;
    }
}
```

If you're unfamiliar with Solidity, know that this smart contract defines a variable called `Message` and a setter method to edit its value. In other words, we read and store a message into the blockchain.

Deploying the contract

If your RSK node is synchronized with the network, we can easily deploy our contract using Remix. Remix is a browser-based IDE that enables developers to compile and deploy Solidity smart contracts into the blockchain. Further instructions and details about Remix will be presented in `Chapter 4`, *Peer-to-Peer Auctions in Ethereum* and `Chapter 5`, *Tontine Game with Truffle and Drizzle*.

We need to connect Remix to our running RSK node by performing the following steps:

1. Open the Remix IDE by visiting `http://remix.ethereum.org`.
2. In the **Run** tab (right menu), select **Environment | Web3 provider**.
3. In the popup, define `http://localhost:4444` as your Web3 provider endpoint.

Once connected, paste the contract code into Remix's code section and, in the right-hand panel, press the **Deploy** button to send a transaction that deploys the selected contract. RSK VM is based on Ethereum VM, therefore the cost of deploying and interacting with the smart contract is calculated in gas. Nevertheless, the gas will be paid in SBTC.

While transferring the contract to the RSK network, Remix will display important information in the console located at the bottom of the main section.

 Due to breaking changes introduced with the newer Solidity compiler +V0.5 (used by default), you have to downgrade the Remix's compiler version to a prior version (for example version 0.4.25+) in order to run without error the presented contract. The process to achieve that is presented in the official documentation (`https://remix.readthedocs.io/en/latest/settings_tab.html`).

Interacting with the contract

After we've deployed the contract, we can interact with the contract instance in the Testnet network, using the same `Remix` tool we used in the deployment. If the deployment succeeded, Remix will provide you with a form in the right-hand pane to execute the contract's methods. In our case, we'll pass a new message as a string (with quotes) `hello` to the method `set()`:

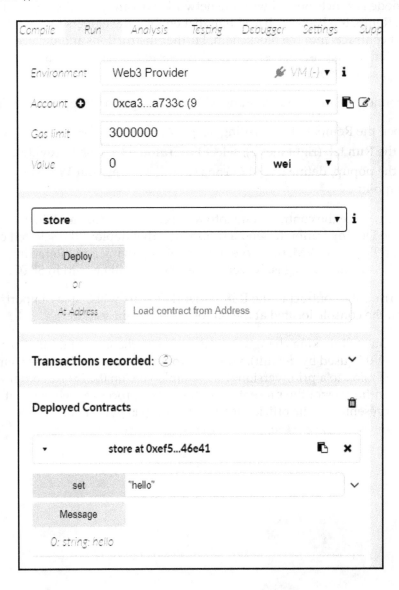

Then press the blue **Message** button to make Remix request the variable value from the contract's storage. It will return the last stored value, `hello`, as expected.

Great! You've successfully built and deployed your first contract in the RSK Testnet network. If you are tempted to deploy your contract in the main network, you have to whitelist your account by making a request to the RSK team, as the network is closed to whitelisted participants.

RSK isn't the only attempt to bring advanced smart contract capabilities to bitcoin. Other projects, such as `Counterparty`, aim to provide a protocol based on bitcoin to enable Ethereum-like smart contracts and building DApps. On the other hand, unlike the former, which is based on Ethereum, Ivy is a new smart contract language that compiles to bitcoin scripts. To play around with Ivy, you can use an online contracting tool: `https://ivy-lang.org/bitcoin`.

Summary

Congratulations! You are now qualified to write production applications using the most popular blockchain – bitcoin – whether as a payment system or as a platform for running advanced smart contracts.

In this walkthrough, we have consolidated our understanding of bitcoin and dissected in depth its underlying scripting mechanism. More importantly, we now know how to integrate bitcoin payments into applications and websites using the bitcore library. Lastly, we discovered how to use an RSK network for deploying and interacting with Solidity smart contracts in a bitcoin environment.

Stay tuned for the next chapter, where we will learn something very exciting: we will discover how to build our own cryptcurrency using bitcoin's code base. For sure, it will be a golden opportunity for you to deepen your understanding of bitcoin's protocol and the blockchain in general.

3
Building Your Own Cryptocurrency

In the previous chapter, you learned about major concepts behind Bitcoin by building a payment system based on the Bitcoin payment protocol. Alongside this, you took earlier advantage of projects such as Rootstock to enable advanced smart contract capabilities. However, there is no better way to cement and deepen your understanding of the blockchain than to build your own cryptocurrency. Although building a currency from scratch is beyond the scope of this book, you will examine instead how to build your own cryptocurrency based on the existing Bitcoin code base.

In this chapter, we'll cover the basic concepts necessary to build an alternative cryptocurrency (known as an **altcoin**) that offers almost all the functionalities of Bitcoin, which we will call Readercoin. I don't expect the reader to have strong programming skills, or any deep knowledge of Bitcoin's details. Consequently I present herein a simplified guide to help anyone to customize Bitcoin and create a new clone—a new cryptocurrency.

This chapter is broken into two main parts:

- Compiling the Bitcoin code
- Designing and building Readercoin

By the end of this two-part guide, you should be able, among other things, to clone Bitcoin and build and mine your new currency.

Compiling Bitcoin from source

The Bitcoin project is open sourced under the MIT license. Therefore, it's possible for you to experiment with its source code and build your own derivative cryptocurrency. As a first step toward creating your own currency, it would be opportune to start by compiling the original Bitcoin source code without modification to get accustomed with the building process.

Preparing your build system

To get the most out of this first section, you'll need the following elements:

- Two or more computers or virtual machines—I will be using my laptop and an Ubuntu 16.04 VM. The guide should work on 14.04 and 17.04 as well.
- Text Editing Software—I'm using nano.
- Time, patience, and lots of coffee.

Preferably, you should have some basic knowledge of C++ programming. At the very least, you should be able to understand basic compiling errors and how to fix them. Furthermore, this chapter covers a number of technical topics regarding the Bitcoin protocol, which you might want to read up on beforehand in the previous chapters along with the official documentation. Go to `https://bitcoin.org/en/developer-documentation`.

Installing dependencies

Before we advance any further, I would like to note that we will be using the Bitcoin core project, as it's the most complete implementation of the Bitcoin protocol. The project is based on many external libraries, including:

- `libssl`: The portion of OpenSSL that supports TLS (`https://www.openssl.org`)
- `Boost C++`: Aset of libraries that provides support for tasks and structures such as multi threading, filesystem operations, and pseudo random number generation, (go to`https://www.boost.org`)
- `libevent`: An event notification library (go to`http://libevent.org`)
- `Miniupnpc`: UPnP IGD client (firewall-jumping support) (`https://github.com/miniupnp/miniupnp`)
- `libdb4.8`: The library for the Berkeley database, which is used for wallet storage (`wallet.dat` file) (`https://github.com/berkeleydb/libdb`)

- `Qt`: Qt SDK (only needed when GUI-enabled) (`www.qt.io`)

- `Protobuf`: A data interchange format used for payment protocol (only needed when GUI-enabled) (`https://github.com/protocolbuffers/protobuf`)

To install these dependencies, make sure you upgrade and update any outdated packages:

```
sudo apt-get update
sudo apt-get upgrade
```

Instead of installing all dependencies in one go, let's install by grouping the packages:

```
sudo apt-get install build-essential libtool autotools-dev automake pkg-
config libssl-dev libevent-dev bsdmainutils python3 git
```

You need to watch the output logs carefully to detect if something goes wrong. The next step will be to install only the necessary part of the boost C++ library:

```
sudo apt-get install
libboost-system-dev libboost-filesystem-dev libboost-chrono-dev libboost-
program-options-dev libboost-test-dev libboost-thread-dev
```

If that doesn't work for any reason, you can install all the boost development packages using the following:

```
sudo apt-get install libboost-all-dev
```

Afterward, you'll need to install the Berkeley database, which is what the Bitcoin software uses for wallet storage, and to store the necessary functions that make the wallet work correctly (BerkeleyDB for wallet files, and LevelDB for blockchain indexes).

To install Berkeley 4.8 libs on Ubuntu 16.04, run the following commands:

```
sudo apt-get install software-properties-common
sudo add-apt-repository ppa:bitcoin/bitcoin
sudo apt-get update
sudo apt-get install libdb4.8-dev libdb4.8++-dev
```

Bitcoin-qt - Qt5 GUI for Bitcoin

If you are interested in running the graphic interface GUI toolkit, all you need to do is install the following QT5 dependencies:

```
sudo apt-get install libqt5gui5 libqt5core5a libqt5dbus5 qttools5-dev
qttools5-dev-tools libprotobuf-dev protobuf-compiler qt5-default
```

Your build system is ready now. With all the packages installed, we can start building the Bitcoin source code.

Cloning the Bitcoin source code

Prior to building the code, start by creating a source directory called `workspace/`, where we can clone the Bitcoin Core source repository:

```
mkdir workspace && cd
```

To download the Bitcoin Core source code, we'll use `git` to clone the latest version of its repository in the current local directory:

```
git clone https://github.com/bitcoin/bitcoin.git && cd bitcoin
```

The download process will take a few minutes. At the end, you'll get a new directory called `bitcoin/` containing all the Bitcoin source code files.

Building Bitcoin Core

As the dependencies are installed, we can build the code using autotools by running these commands in succession as follows:

```
./autogen.sh
./configure --with-gui=qt5 --enable-debug
sudo make
```

Pay attention to the space and double dash in front of both the options: `with-gui` and `enable-debug`.

It's common to supply some options to the `configure` command to change the final location of the executable program. You can explore the different possible options in the official documentation: `https://github.com/bitcoin/bitcoin/blob/master/doc/build-unix.md`.

As you may have noticed, we passed the `configure` file two arguments: `--with-gui=qt5` to build the graphical interface, and `--enable-debug` to produce better debugging builds. If you want to build only a headless Bitcoin client, use `--without-gui`.

In order to accelerate the building process, you can skip running the tests by specifying the --disable-tests argument.

After running the make command, the initial compile will take quite a long time. Think about taking a coffee.

If all the dependencies have been installed correctly, a test compilation should be achieved successfully at the end of the compilation process. If you got an error somewhere, have a look at the compilation output to spot the error.

Alternatively, you can run qmake, which is the qt make tool, before running make, or you can install Qt Creator and open the bitcoin-qt.pro file located under the contrib folder.

Now that the software is built and ready to run, you can optionally install it by running the following command:

```
sudo make install
```

This will add the Bitcoin commands to your PATH so that you can simply run bitcoin-qt or bitcoind to start the Bitcoin client without specifying the binary location. Keep in mind that you have to rerun make install each time you edit and compile your code in order to update your client.

Congratulations! You have compiled Bitcoin successfully from its source code.

Checking your build worked

Here are a couple more commands to make sure that the build worked, and to make sure the executable files it was supposed to generate are actually there. From the bitcoin/ directory, run the following command:

```
ls src/bitcoind
ls src/bitcoin-cli
ls src/qt/bitcoin-qt
```

Running this command will show you the Bitcoin Core **Welcome** screen, similar to the following screenshot:

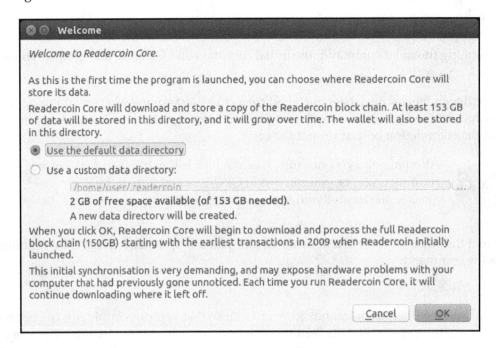

Excellent! If Bitcoin runs without error, that means your build environment has everything you need to create an altcoin. Let's start making your altcoin.

New cryptocurrency – Readercoin

We have finally hit the big time!

Although Readercoin will be a derivative coin from Bitcoin, we will design it differently. We need to define, amongst other characteristics, how the new altcoin is minted, the money supply, and the altcoin brand.

The following table summarizes the important parameters we'll define for **Readercoin**:

Coin's Name	Readercoin
Con's Symbol	RDC
Block Time	2.5 minute
Initial block reward	10
Halving interval	Every 100000 blocks (174 days)
Ports	RPC port: 19333
	P2P port: 9333
Total supply	2000000 units
difficulty readjustment	After 576 blocks
Block size	Up to 8 Mb

Cloning Bitcoin

Bitcoin is a highly active project frequently releasing new releases. The current version at the time of writing is 0.15—you can view a list of project releases at `https://bitcoin.org/en/version-history`. From one version to another, a lot of features get added or removed. Therefore, you must examine the `changelog` to see whether there is any special feature you are interested in. For example, internal mining got removed in version 0.13.

To build Readercoin, I've opted for using the last major version of Bitcoin, that is, version 0.15 (You can also use the newer version 0.16). Create a directory called `readercoin` and clone the Bitcoin 0.15 code as follows:

```
git clone -b 0.15 https://github.com/bitcoin/bitcoin.git readercoin && cd
readercoin
```

`git` gives us access to all past and future versions; hence, you can choose different branches using the `-b` option.

Now, we have to remove Bitcoin's ties to the original Bitcoin repository. This can be done easily with the following command:

```
rm -rf .git
```

To enable `git` versioning, you can initialize a new `git` repository on your newly created folder Readercoin, add the existing files, and commit them:

```
git init
git add -A
git commit -m "initial commit"
```

Besides being a good habit, maintaining a remote repository will help us to compile our Readercoin client on different machines without the need to copy the code each time.

Go to the GitHub website and create a new online repository, and then add your repository's `git` URL as the remote repository. Afterward, push your initial commit:

```
git remote add origin https://github.com/bellaj/Readercoin_.git(use instead
YOUR NEW GITHUB REPO's url)
git push -f origin master
```

Remember, before you start editing the code, that you can compile the code at any level of the following guide using `make` to check whether the addition process has been executed successfully or not. It's advisable to commit and push working changes to your remote repository as it will help you to make rollbacks if there are any compilation issues, or if you want to compile code on other machines.

Readercoin rebranding

We kick off by rebranding the Bitcoin project as Readercoin by renaming the `bitcoin` filenames to `readercoin` using the following commands:

```
find . -exec rename 's/bitcoin/readercoin/' {} ";"
find . -exec rename 's/btc/rdc/' {} ";"
```

These Linux commands will rename every file that has `bitcoin` or `btc` in the name, recursing into subdirectories as needed.

 If rename isn't available on your system you can install it using `sudo apt install rename`

As changing filenames will affect source files and `make` files, breaking paths and `include` statements, we need to replace all the occurrences of the old `Bitcoin` name and its abbreviation as `BTC` recursively in the code with the new name `Readercoin` and the acronym `RDC`. To be sure of replacing all occurrences, we use different capitalizations:

```
find ./ -type f -readable -writable -exec sed -i "s/bitcoin/readercoin/g"
{} ";"
find ./ -type f -readable -writable -exec sed -i "s/Bitcoin/Readercoin/g"
{} ";"
find ./ -type f -readable -writable -exec sed -i "s/BitCoin/ReaderCoin/g"
{} ";"
find ./ -type f -readable -writable -exec sed -i "s/BITCOIN/READERCOIN/g"
{} ";"
find ./ -type f -readable -writable -exec sed -i "s/bitcoind/readercoind/g"
{} ";"
find ./ -type f -readable -writable -exec sed -i "s/BTC/RDC/g" {} ";"
find ./ -type f -readable -writable -exec sed -i "s/btc/rdc/g" {} ";"
```

Instead of running these commands separately, you can put them in a single Bash script. The preceding command will take a few minutes to complete. To check whether there are any remaining occurrences of the Bitcoin string, use `grep -ri "bitcoin"`.

Alternatively, you can use a text editor such as `gedit` to find and replace all `Bitcoin` and `BTC` occurrences in the project source files.

Changing the `Bitcoin` occurrences will also affect the `git` files. Hence, if you want to keep using git, you have to use the following commands to avoid git's bad index file signature error:

```
rm -f .git/index
git reset
git add -A
git commit -m "rename bitcoin into readercoin occurrences"
git push origin master
```

To start code editing, change the working directory to `src`(`cd src`).

Changing the ports

To operate, Bitcoin uses two ports on which the client will listen to establish connections, namely:

- p2p port (by default, 8333 in mainnet and 18333 in testnet)
- RPC port (by default, 8332 in mainnet and 18332 in testnet)

We will define different ports for both mainnet and testnet, in order to be able to run your altcoin alongside a Bitcoin client without port overlap. Remember, mainnet and testnet are abbreviations for the main and test public networks.

Get your favourite text editor and open up `chainparams.cpp` and `chainparamsbase.cpp` located in the `src/` folder. Find the network parameters, including the ports, and then change the following variables:

- For mainnet (`CMainParams` and `CBaseMainParams` classes):

    ```
    chainparams.cpp: nDefaultPort = 9333;
    chainparamsbase.cpp: nRPCPort = 9332;
    ```

- For testnet (`CTestNetParams` and `CBaseTestNetParams` classes):

    ```
    chainparams.cpp: nDefaultPort = 19333;
    chainparamsbase.cpp: nRPCPort = 19332;
    ```

To make modifications consistent with the whole code, change the port occurrences in all files using the following Linux commands:

```
find ./ -type f -readable -writable -exec sed -i "s/8332/9332/g" {} ";"
find ./ -type f -readable -writable -exec sed -i "s/8333/9333/g" {} ";"
```

Feel free to choose any port you like, but avoid the mainstream ones (below 1000, such as 80 for HTTP).

Great! Remember that you can always change either the Bitcoin port or your altcoin's port just by providing the options `-rpcport` and `-port` in the command line or in the `readercoin.conf` file without editing the Bitcoin code base.

Changing pchMessageStart

The Bitcoin node broadcasts, in each P2P frame, 4 bytes known as **magic values** to ensure that only the client/peers belonging to the same network can communicate. The magic bytes are represented in the `pchMessageStart[]` array to identify the used network as described in the following table:

Network	Magic value	Sent over wire as
main	0xD9B4BEF9	F9 BE B4 D9
testnet	0xDAB5BFFA	FA BF B5 DA
testnet3	0x0709110B	0B 11 09 07
namecoin	0xFEB4BEF9	F9 BE B4 FE

To differentiate our Readercoin network, we will change `pchMessageStart` values by incrementing them by 2. Always in `chainparams.cpp`, edit `pchMessageStart` in the `CMainParams` class using the following values:

```
pchMessageStart[0] = 0xfd;
pchMessageStart[1] = 0xc0;
pchMessageStart[2] = 0xb6;
pchMessageStart[3] = 0xdb;
```

For the `CTestNetParams` class:

```
pchMessageStart[0] = 0x0d;
pchMessageStart[1] = 0x13;
pchMessageStart[2] = 0x0b;
pchMessageStart[3] = 0x09;
```

For `CRegTestParams` (which represents the regression test network):

```
pchMessageStart[0] = 0xfc;
pchMessageStart[1] = 0xc1;
pchMessageStart[2] = 0xb7;
pchMessageStart[3] = 0xdc;
```

There is no special reason behind these specific values; you can use any value between the hexadecimal values 0 and 0xFF.

Genesis block

Now we will deal with the crucial part: the genesis block.

A genesis block is the first block in a blockchain. When a node boots, it initializes its copy of the blockchain alongside the genesis block and then begins the synchronization process. To start a new chain for our currency, we need to forge a new genesis block and override the original one hard coded in the Bitcoin code as it was set for an older date (January 2009).

Here's the source code of the function that generates the genesis blocks defined in `chainparams.cpp`:

```
static CBlock CreateGenesisBlock(const char* pszTimestamp, const CScript& genesisOutputScript, uint32_t nTime, uint32_t nNonce, uint32_t nBits, int32_t nVersion, const CAmount& genesisReward)
{
    CMutableTransaction txNew;
    txNew.nVersion = 1;
    txNew.vin.resize(1);
    txNew.vout.resize(1);
    txNew.vin[0].scriptSig = CScript() << 486604799 << CScriptNum(4) << std::vector<unsigned char>((const unsigned char*)pszTimestamp, (const unsigned char*)pszTimestamp + strlen(pszTimestamp));
    txNew.vout[0].nValue = genesisReward;
    txNew.vout[0].scriptPubKey = genesisOutputScript;

    CBlock genesis;
    genesis.nTime    = nTime;
    genesis.nBits    = nBits;
    genesis.nNonce   = nNonce;
    genesis.nVersion = nVersion;
    genesis.vtx.push_back(MakeTransactionRef(std::move(txNew)));
    genesis.hashPrevBlock.SetNull();
    genesis.hashMerkleRoot = BlockMerkleRoot(genesis);
    return genesis;
}
```

We can easily spot some predefined values, such as the key for the genesis coinbase transaction and a timestamp message. Editing the content of this block implies calculating a new genesis hash required for other parameters within the `chainparams.cpp` code.

For creating the new genesis block, we'll use a dedicated Python script called **GenesisH0**.

For that, in a new terminal, clone the genesis generator script (GenesisH0) from its GitHub repository:

```
git clone https://github.com/lhartikk/GenesisH0.git && cd GenesisH0
```

And then install the required package:

```
sudo pip install scrypt construct==2.5.2
```

To reproduce the original genesis block, run GenesisH0 with the following arguments:

```
python genesis.py -z "The Times 03/Jan/2009 Chancellor on brink of second
bailout for banks" -n 2083236893 -t 1231006505 -v 5000000000
```

You need to understand what each argument means to replace it with an appropriate value:

- The `-z` option indicates an optional timestamp represented by an arbitrary paraphrase with a date– usually a headline of a news article can be chosen. The Bitcoin's genesis block famously contains the dated title of an article in the *Financial Times*: *The Financial Times 03/Jan/2009 Chancellor on brink of second bailout for banks*

This is probably intended as proof that no premining has taken place before 2009. You can use a recent news headline or any time-related information. For example, I'll use the book's name with the publication year: *Blockchain By Example 2018*.

- For the nonce (`-n`), you can set any value to be used as a start nonce.
- For the epoch (`-t`), you can use the current time epoch. You can get the current epoch time online from `www.epochconverter.com/`, or you can generate it from the command line of most `*nix` systems with this code: `date +%s`.
- For `-v`, you need to determine the coin reward value and multiply it by * 100000000. For example, if you have a block reward of 50, it would be `-v` 5000000000. We will generate only 10 Readercoins for the genesis block.
- `-b` represents the target in compact representation, associated with a difficulty of 1. To get a block in 2.5 minutes, we will use `0x1e0ffff0`.

We end up with the following command with different arguments to generate the new genesis block:

```
python genesis.py -z "Blockchain by example 2018" -n 1 -t 1529321830 -v
1000000000 -b 0x1e0ffff0
```

After a short while, you should see an output similar to the following:

```
user@ByExample-node: ~/GenesisH0
user@ByExample-node:~/GenesisH0$ python genesis.py -z "Blockchain by example 201
8" -n 1 -t 1529321830 -v 1000000000 -b 0x1e0ffff0
04ffff001d01041a426c6f636b636861696e206279206578616d706c652032303138
algorithm: SHA256
merkle hash: 6bc2585d63185acf3868cc34e0b017b3fb41c00938eb09bc52a3cf73a31ec6a8
pszTimestamp: Blockchain by example 2018
pubkey: 04678afdb0fe5548271967f1a67130b7105cd6a828e03909a67962e0ea1f61deb649f6bc
3f4cef38c4f35504e51ec112de5c384df7ba0b8d578a4c702b6bf11d5f
time: 1529321830
bits: 0x1e0ffff0
Searching for genesis hash..
genesis hash found!
nonce: 490987
genesis hash: 000001a9bbae8bb141c6941838bdacdbcf474b6ed28a0b18b2120b60a68f00ee
user@ByExample-node:~/GenesisH0$
```

Bingo! You now have the genesis block information that you need to use in your code base.

Except the first line, which is the `Scriptsig` of the genesis transaction, the remainder of the output results are identified by an expressive keyword.

Let's edit the `/src/chainparams.cpp` file accordingly to integrate the newly generated genesis block. Specifically, our target will be the function `CreateGenesisBlock`:

```
static CBlock CreateGenesisBlock(uint32_t nTime, uint32_t nNonce, uint32_t nBits, int32_t nVersion, const CAmount& genesisReward)
{
    const char* pszTimestamp = "The Times 03/Jan/2009 Chancellor on brink of second bailout for banks";
    const CScript genesisOutputScript = CScript() << ParseHex("04678afdb0fe5548271967f1a67130b7105cd6a828e03909a67962e0ea1f61deb649f6bc3f4cef38c4f35504e51ec112de5c384df7ba0b8d578a4c702b6bf11d5f") << OP_CHECKSIG;
    return CreateGenesisBlock(pszTimestamp, genesisOutputScript, nTime, nNonce, nBits, nVersion, genesisReward);
}
```

New pszTimestamp

Let's change the original value defined by Satoshi, located inside the `CreateGenesisBlock` function, to the new passphrase we used in the GenesisH0 script:

```
const char* pszTimestamp = "Blockchain by example 2018";
```

New nonce, epoch time, and nbits

We have to locate the following line in `chainparams.cpp` in the three classes `CMainParams`, `CTestNetParams` and `CRegTestParams`:

```
genesis = CreateGenesisBlock(time, nonce, bits, 1, 10 * COIN);
```

In the order, change the arguments of the `CreateGenesisBlock` function using the values computed previously by the `GenesisH0` script as follows:

```
genesis = CreateGenesisBlock(1529321830, 490987, 0x1e0ffff0, 1, 10 * COIN);
```

The argument in the function is the initial reward (10 Readercoins) for generating the genesis block.

New genesis hash

While we have edited some values in the genesis block, the block's hash provided by Satoshi is no longer valid. Therefore, we have to replace it with the new one provided by the `GenesisH0` script.

Under the `chainParams.cpp` file, you will find several occurrences of the following assertion, which refers to the old hash value of the genesis block:

```
assert (hashGenesisBlock == uint256 ("genesis block hash"));
```

These assertions verify whether the genesis block hash is congruous, otherwise code execution fails and halts further code execution. You can either comment out all of these `assert` methods or replace the hash with the new value of your generated genesis block (by adding `0x` as a prefix).

If you get any errors related to these assertions later when you run your client, you can check whether the hashes match by printing out the computed genesis hash:

```
printf ("Readercoin hashGenesisBlock: % s \ n",
consensus.hashGenesisBlock.ToString (). c_str ());
```

Editing the Merkle root

A Merkle tree is an important piece in Bitcoin's puzzle. It's a fingerprint of the entire list of transactions, thereby enabling a user to verify whether or not a transaction has been included in the block.

In `testparams.cpp`, look for the following line:

```
assert( genesis.hashMerkleRoot == uint256s('merkle hash value');
```

Replace the Merkle hash with the hash calculated by `GenesisH0`. To check the genesis block Merkle root, you can print its hash root:

```
printf ("Readercoin hashMerkleRoot:% s \ n",
genesis.hashMerkleRoot.ToString (). c_str ());
```

All set? We have finished defining the new genesis block.

Removing the seed nodes

Next, we'll need to remove the DNS seeds from the code. Bitcoin uses built-in DNS seeds, which are a list of host names for a DNS server to discover other nodes. A Bitcoin client issues DNS requests to learn about the addresses of other peer nodes, and, in response, the DNS seeds return a list of IP addresses of full nodes on the Bitcoin network to assist in peer discovery.

We'll need to remove or comment out the hardcoded seed nodes in the `chainparams.cpp` file. In this file, you'll find a vector of seed (`vSeeds`) to which they append a list of DNS URLs:

```
vSeeds.emplace_back("seed.bitcoin.sipa.be", true);
```

We need to comment out all occurrences of `vSeeds.push_back` and `vSeeds.emplace_back` in both `CMainParams` and `CTestNetParams`.

It's not over yet with seeds, as we'll need to deal with fixed IP seeds, either by commenting out the occurrences on the following line, as follows:

```
vFixedSeeds = std::vector<SeedSpec6>(pnSeed6_main, pnSeed6_main +
ARRAYLEN(pnSeed6_main));
```

Or by replacing this line with the following:

```
vFixedSeeds.clear();
vSeeds.clear();
```

Otherwise, you can include your proper DNS seed servers. In `chainparamseeds.h`, you'll find a list of IPs (wrapped inside IPv6 addresses) of nodes that can be connected to for mainnet and testnet to retrieve more IP addresses of nodes that can be connected to:

```
static SeedSpec6 pnSeed6_main[] = {
    {{0x00,0x00,0x00,0x00,0x00,0x00,0x00,0x00,0x00,0x00,0xff,0xff,0x02,0xe4,0x46,0xc6}, 8333},
    {{0x00,0x00,0x00,0x00,0x00,0x00,0x00,0x00,0x00,0x00,0xff,0xff,0x04,0x0f,0xb4,0x1d}, 8333},
    {{0x00,0x00,0x00,0x00,0x00,0x00,0x00,0x00,0x00,0x00,0xff,0xff,0x04,0x0f,0xb4,0x1e}, 8333},
    {{0x00,0x00,0x00,0x00,0x00,0x00,0x00,0x00,0x00,0x00,0xff,0xff,0x05,0x02,0x43,0x6e}, 8333},
    {{0x00,0x00,0x00,0x00,0x00,0x00,0x00,0x00,0x00,0x00,0xff,0xff,0x05,0x27,0xe0,0x67}, 8333},
    {{0x00,0x00,0x00,0x00,0x00,0x00,0x00,0x00,0x00,0x00,0xff,0xff,0x05,0x2b,0x7c,0x9a}, 8333},
    {{0x00,0x00,0x00,0x00,0x00,0x00,0x00,0x00,0x00,0x00,0xff,0xff,0x05,0xbd,0xa5,0x66}, 8333},
    {{0x00,0x00,0x00,0x00,0x00,0x00,0x00,0x00,0x00,0x00,0xff,0xff,0x05,0xe2,0x95,0x91}, 8333},
    {{0x00,0x00,0x00,0x00,0x00,0x00,0x00,0x00,0x00,0x00,0xff,0xff,0x05,0xe4,0x07,0x92}, 8333},
    {{0x00,0x00,0x00,0x00,0x00,0x00,0x00,0x00,0x00,0x00,0xff,0xff,0x05,0xe4,0x40,0x47}, 8333},
    {{0x00,0x00,0x00,0x00,0x00,0x00,0x00,0x00,0x00,0x00,0xff,0xff,0x05,0xf9,0x98,0x65}, 8333},
    {{0x00,0x00,0x00,0x00,0x00,0x00,0x00,0x00,0x00,0x00,0xff,0xff,0x05,0xfe,0x7c,0x37}, 8333},
    {{0x00,0x00,0x00,0x00,0x00,0x00,0x00,0x00,0x00,0x00,0xff,0xff,0x05,0xff,0x40,0xe7}, 8333},
    {{0x00,0x00,0x00,0x00,0x00,0x00,0x00,0x00,0x00,0x00,0xff,0xff,0x05,0xff,0x5a,0xea}, 8333},
    {{0x00,0x00,0x00,0x00,0x00,0x00,0x00,0x00,0x00,0x00,0xff,0xff,0x0e,0xc0,0x08,0x1b}, 21301},
    {{0x00,0x00,0x00,0x00,0x00,0x00,0x00,0x00,0x00,0x00,0xff,0xff,0x12,0x3e,0x03,0x56}, 8333},
    {{0x00,0x00,0x00,0x00,0x00,0x00,0x00,0x00,0x00,0x00,0xff,0xff,0x12,0x55,0x23,0x50}, 8333},
```

To set up a seed node, you just need to run a normal node for Readercoin and add its IP address to `chainparamseeds.h`, or anticipate a list of IPs that you'll use for your nodes later.

Under `contrib/seeds`, there is a Python script `generate-seeds`, which will help you to generate the `pnSeed6_main` and `pnSeed6_test` arrays that are compiled in the client.

In `nodes_test.txt` and `nodes_main.txt`, remove the existing IPs, set all your node IPs (one IP per line), and then run the following command:

```
~/workspace/readercoin/contrib/seeds$ python3 generate-seeds.py . >
../../src/chainparamseeds.h
```

Checkpoints

The Bitcoin Core client has hardcoded checkpoints verifying that certain specific blocks should be found at certain heights. They are regularly added in new versions of the client to avoid accepting any forks from the network prior to the last checkpoint, thereby making transactions irreversible.

As our blockchain doesn't have previous blocks, you have to disable these checkpoints for Readercoin, otherwise your node will not be able to construct additional blocks nor start mining, as it will be waiting for non-existent blocks.

In the `chainparams.cpp` file, locate the `checkpointData` map:

```
checkpointData = (CCheckpointData) {
    {
        { 11111, uint256S("0x0000000069e244f73d78e8fd29ba2fd2ed618bd6fa2ee92559f542fdb26e7c1d")},
        { 33333, uint256S("0x000000002dd5588a74784eaa7ab0507a18ad16a236e7b1ce69f00d7ddfb5d0a6")},
        { 74000, uint256S("0x0000000000573993a3c9e41ce34471c079dcf5f52a0e824a81e7f953b8661a20")},
        {105000, uint256S("0x00000000000291ce28027faea320c8d2b054b2e0fe44a773f3eefb151d6bdc97")},
        {134444, uint256S("0x00000000000005b12ffd4cd315cd34ffd4a594f430ac814c91184a0d42d2b0fe")},
        {168000, uint256S("0x000000000000099e61ea72015e79632f216fe6cb33d7899acb35b75c8303b763")},
        {193000, uint256S("0x000000000000059f452a5f7340de6682a977387c17010ff6e6c3bd83ca8b1317")},
        {210000, uint256S("0x000000000000048b95347e83192f69cf0366076336c639f9b7228e9ba171342e")},
        {216116, uint256S("0x00000000000001b4f4b433e81ee46494af945cf96014816a4e2370f11b23df4e")},
        {225430, uint256S("0x00000000000001c108384350f74090433e7fcf79a606b8e797f065b130575932")},
        {250000, uint256S("0x000000000000003887df1f29024b06fc2200b55f8af8f35453d7be294df2d214")},
        {279000, uint256S("0x0000000000000001ae8c72a0b0c301f67e3afca10e819efa9041e458e9bd7e40")},
        {295000, uint256S("0x00000000000000004d9b4ef50f0f9d686fd69db2e03af35a100370c64632a983")},
    }
};
```

The map stores a collection of preset checkpoints such that the first element of each pair is the block height, and the second is the hash of that block.

Remove all checkpoint pairs to end up with the following form:

```
checkpointData = (CCheckpointData) { { {}, } };
```

Make the same modification in the mainnet, testnet, and regtest classes. Alternatively, in `validation.h` you can set the following constant to false: `static const bool DEFAULT_CHECKPOINTS_ENABLED = true;` or, in `checkpoints.cpp`, you can hack the `GetLastCheckpoint` function by making it returns a null pointer as follows:

```
CBlockIndex* GetLastCheckpoint(const CCheckpointData& data) {
    const MapCheckpoints &checkpoints = data.mapCheckpoints;
    for (const MapCheckpoints::value_type& i :
reverse_iterate(checkpoints)) {
        const uint256 &hash = i.second;
        BlockMap::const_iterator t = mapBlockIndex.find(hash);
        if (t != mapBlockIndex.end()) {
            // return t->second;
            return null;
        }
    }
    return nullptr;
}
```

Now, the checkpoints are disabled. Nonetheless, if you want to keep them, you can premine 50 blocks, put their weights and hashes in the checkpoints, and then reenable the checkpoints. After all, they are a powerful way for blockchain developers to protect against remining the whole chain.

> The message `readercoin is downloading blocks` will be displayed if the client hasn't yet downloaded all the checkpoint blocks.

ChainTxData

The next maneuver is to change some parameters in the `chaintxdata` structure, which represents the blockchain state at a specific timestamp using the data of a specific block. In the Bitcoin code, you will find recorded the blockchain snapshot's state at January 3, 2017, where the total number had reached 446,482 mined blocks:

```
chainTxData = ChainTxData{
    // Data as of block 59c9b9d3fec105bdc716d84caa7579503d5b05b73618d0bf2d5fa639f780a011 (height 1353397).
    1516406833, // * UNIX timestamp of last known number of transactions
    19831879,   // * total number of transactions between genesis and that timestamp
         //     (the tx=... number in the SetBestChain debug.log lines)
    0.06     // * estimated number of transactions per second after that timestamp
};
}
```

As our chain doesn't yet have any blocks, we can use our genesis block instead and edit the values accordingly. Thus, the first argument, 1,483,472,411, should be changed to the timestamp used in the creation of the genesis block. The second number, 184,495,391, should be set to 1 because there is only the genesis transaction mined at that time. Finally, change the third value to 1.

Rewarding

At this level, we are finally going to change the monetary variables of our new cryptocurrency, such as issuance rate and the total amount of Readercoins circulating. As you might know, the Bitcoin protocol rewards miners by giving them freshly minted coins for doing their jobs. The reward is 50 new coins, which decreases constantly with time.

In `src/validation.cpp`, you'll find a parameter called `nSubsidy` in the `GetBlockSubsidy` function, which defines the initial value of the reward. We will be less generous. We will set this value to `10` as follows:

```
CAmount nSubsidy = 10 * COIN;
```

Remember, we set the same reward value when we generated our genesis block in the `CreateGenesisBlock` function in `chainparams.cpp` to be consistent with the defined reward per block.

Halving

For Bitcoin, the mining reward is cut in half every 210,000 blocks, which will occur approximately every four years. In Bitcoin, the reward, initially set to 50 BTC, fell to 25 BTC in late 2012, to 12.5 BTC in 2016 and so forth, until the reward tends to 0 at the 64th halving.

To change the halving rule, in `chainparams.cpp`, you have to edit the following parameter:

```
consensus.nSubsidyHalvingInterval = 210000;
```

Let's reschedule the halving interval in main and test at 100,000 blocks, equivalent to 174 days.

In `src/validation.cpp`, the halving mechanism formula is defined in the `GetBlockSubsidy` function, which determines the reward amount at a specific height in the blockchain:

```
CAmount GetBlockSubsidy(int nHeight, const Consensus::Params& consensusParams)
{
    int halvings = nHeight / consensusParams.nSubsidyHalvingInterval;
    // Force block reward to zero when right shift is undefined.
    if (halvings >= 64)
        return 0;

    CAmount nSubsidy = 50 * COIN;
    // Subsidy is cut in half every 210,000 blocks which will occur approximately every 4 years.
    nSubsidy >>= halvings;
    return nSubsidy;
}
```

In this instance, we have the following:

- `nHeight` is the number of blocks that have been found.
- `consensusParams.nSubsidyHalvingInterval` specifies the halving's interval block.
- `nSubsidy` finally gives the number of satoshi that the coinbase may create.

After another number of blocks equivalent to `nSubsidyHalvingInterval`, the reward halves again. Thus, the number of bitcoins in circulation asymptotically approaches `nSubsidy*nSubsidyHalvingInterval*2`.

Total supply

Bitcoin is designed in such a manner that it has a total circulation of approximately 21 million bitcoins (20,999,999.9769 bitcoins). In the header file `amount.h`, there is a total supply `MAX_MONEY` sanity check:

```
/** No amount larger than this (in satoshi) is valid.
 *
 * Note that this constant is 'not' the total money supply, which in Bitcoin
 * currently happens to be less than 21,000,000 BTC for various reasons, but
 * rather a sanity check. As this sanity check is used by consensus-critical
 * validation code, the exact value of the MAX_MONEY constant is consensus
 * critical; in unusual circumstances like a(nother) overflow bug that allowed
 * for the creation of coins out of thin air modification could lead to a fork.
 * */
static const CAmount MAX_MONEY = 21000000 * COIN;
inline bool MoneyRange(const CAmount& nValue) { return (nValue >= 0 && nValue <= MAX_MONEY); }
```

Here, `COIN` is equal to 10^8 satoshi (the smallest Bitcoin unit). As per our design, we will set `MAX_MONEY` to 20,000,000 (rounded number).

Contrary to what you might think in the actual Bitcoin code, there is actually no **total supply parameter** that defines how many bitcoins will be generated. Nevertheless, rules are put in place that dictate how many bitcoins will be released depending on the reward and halving rate. The following Python script simulates how the total supply is deduced from the initial reward value and the halving interval. It will print out a total of `1999999.987` units:

```
COIN = 100 * 1000 * 1000
Reward = 10
Halving = 100000
```

```
nSubsidy = Reward * COIN
nHeight = 0
total = 0
while nSubsidy != 0:
nSubsidy = Reward * COIN
nSubsidy >>= nHeight / Halving
nHeight += 1
total += nSubsidy
print "total supply is", total / float(COIN)
```

POW parameters – target

As you know, proof of work is the consensus mechanism used in Bitcoin to validate (mine) the blocks. It's a repetitive brute-force process aiming at finding the hash that meets specific requirements. Each hash basically gives a random number between 0 and the maximum value of a 256-bit number (which is huge). If the miner's hash is below the given target (a special hash value), then he wins. If not, he increments the nonce (completely changing the hash) and tries again.

The target is a 256-bit number that represents a threshold. Actually, it represents a threshold such that the SHA-256 hash of a candidate block's header must be lower than or equal to it in order to be accepted as valid and added to the blockchain:

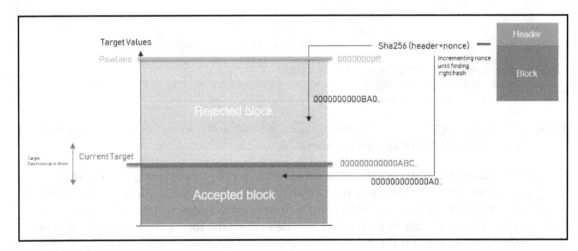

In the `chainparams.cpp` file, there is a `powLimit` parameter that describes the absolute highest target, which, at the same time, is the lowest possible difficulty:

```
consensus.powLimit =
uint256S("00000000ffffffffffffffffffffffffffffffffffffffffffffffffffffffff"
);
```

This limit represents, by definition, a difficulty of 1. In order to produce blocks every 2.5 minutes, we use the following value instead:

```
consensus.powLimit =
uint256S("00000ffffffffffffffffffffffffffffffffffffffffffffffffffffffffffff"
);
```

This target can also be represented in the code by `nBits=0x1e0ffff0`. In fact, the variable `genesis.nBits` defined in `chainparams.cpp` represents the compacted form of the target `powLimit` value.

In the same file, Bitcoin also defines the following parameter:

```
consensus.nMinimumChainWork =
uint256S("0x00000000000000000000000000000000000000000000001b3fcc3e766e365e4
b");
```

This specifies the minimum amount of chain work that a client must have before it will consider itself synchronized. As we are running a new chain, the minimum should be zero for both testnet and mainnet:

```
consensus.nMinimumChainWork = uint256S("0x00");
```

New block time

In Bitcoin, blocks are created and transactions get confirmed every 10 minutes. Therefore, you might assume that Bitcoin is an incredibly slow network and you might want to reduce this delay for Readercoin. On our side, we will produce Readercoin's blocks every 2.5 minutes (as with Litecoin).

Before tinkering, let's understand the mechanics behind the minting rule of 10 minutes.

In Bitcoin, there is no parameter directly defining the block time, but actually it depends on the hashing power of the network and delays. Ten minutes was a choice made by Satoshi for stability and low latency reasons. Initially, he defined an initial hash target (`powLimit`) that needed 10 minutes to be calculated, and then the protocol tried to keep this block time by adjusting the blockhash so it could be found within a specific retargeting period.

Therefore, the first related concept to introduce is the difficulty.

Difficulty adjustment time interval

Difficulty is a concept used to express how difficult it is to reach the current hash target in comparison with the initial hash target used to mine the genesis block. The difficulty value is not used internally in Bitcoin, but it's a metric used to express a target's height change.

In Bitcoin, after each 2,016 blocks, each node looks at the time stamps of the past 2,015 blocks and adjusts the difficulty using the following function defined in `src/consensus/params.h`:

```
int64_t DifficultyAdjustmentInterval() const {
    return nPowTargetTimespan / nPowTargetSpacing;
}
```

Both parameters,`nPowTargetTimespan` and `nPowTargetSpacing`, are defined in `chainparams.cpp`, where we will set the following new values to keep block generation at 2.5 minutes:

```
consensus.nPowTargetTimespan = 24 * 60 * 60;
consensus.nPowTargetSpacing = 2.5 * 60;
```

The `nPowTargetSpacing` parameter indicates the average time (2.5 minutes) in which it should be possible to solve the computational problem of a new transaction block, whereas the `nPowTargetTimespan` parameter adjusts the time interval (a day) during which the difficulty of the proof-of-work problem should be recalculated and adjusted. Therefore, difficulty is adjusted every 576 blocks (24 * 60 * 60 / 2.5 * 60).

If the coins were generated too quickly since the last adjustment on average, the difficulty would be increased. If they were generated too slowly, it would be decreased. We therefore have to change the value of the `consensus.nMinerConfirmationWindow` parameter from 2016 to 576 in the `chainparams.cpp` file.

Difficulty adjustment rate

The `GetNextWorkRequired` function defined in `src/pow.cpp` is responsible for redefining difficulty by defining the next hash target to keep block production on the desired interval time:

```
unsigned int CalculateNextWorkRequired(const CBlockIndex* pindexLast, int64_t nFirstBlockTime, const Consensus::Params& params)
{
    if (params.fPowNoRetargeting)
        return pindexLast->nBits;

    // Limit adjustment step
    int64_t nActualTimespan = pindexLast->GetBlockTime() - nFirstBlockTime;
    if (nActualTimespan < params.nPowTargetTimespan/4)
        nActualTimespan = params.nPowTargetTimespan/4;
    if (nActualTimespan > params.nPowTargetTimespan*4)
        nActualTimespan = params.nPowTargetTimespan*4;

    // Retarget
    const arith_uint256 bnPowLimit = UintToArith256(params.powLimit);
    arith_uint256 bnNew;
    bnNew.SetCompact(pindexLast->nBits);
    bnNew *= nActualTimespan;
    bnNew /= params.nPowTargetTimespan;

    if (bnNew > bnPowLimit)
        bnNew = bnPowLimit;

    return bnNew.GetCompact();
}
```

Let's break this function down and jump directly to the important part, recalculating the new difficulty after the difficulty adjustment time interval:

```
int64_t nActualTimespan = pindexLast->GetBlockTime() - nFirstBlockTime;
```

This calculates the time between the current time and the time 2,016 blocks ago(576 for Readercoin):

```
const arith_uint256 bnPowLimit = UintToArith256(params.powLimit);
```

bnPowLimit is the absolute maximum target corresponding to the lowest difficulty.

bnNew is the new target represented in compact form (current target) using the following:

```
bnNew.SetCompact(pindexPrev->nBits);
```

When we retarget, we move the target value up or down by the ratio (nActualTimespan/params.nPowTargetTimespan).

```
bnNew *= nActualTimespan;
bnNew /= params.nPowTargetTimespan;
```

We cap the difficulty at the powlimit value to avoid using a target above the minimal target hash:

```
if (bnNew > bnPowLimit) bnNew = bnPowLimit;
```

Then, the function returns the result as a 32-bit compact representation of the difficulty, like the nbits we used in chainparams.cpp previously: return bnNew.GetCompact();

Thus, if, for some reason, 576 blocks is taking more or less than 24 hours by 20%, each node will lower or increase the difficulty (hash target value) by 20% to bring block production back to the 2.5-minute block target for a few iterations.

Time maturity

The coinbase maturity indicator indicates a time window of 100 blocks between the creating block and the spending block. For Readercoin, we decrease this limit from 100 to 50. In the `src/consensus/consensus.h` file, we edit the following line of code:

```
static const int COINBASE_MATURITY = 50;
```

The reason behind this measure is to make coinbase transactions with less confirmations than the value of the variable `COINBASE_MATURITY`, unspendable to avoid spending coins generated for orphaned blocks.

Block size

Welcome to the most controversial issue in Bitcoin!

Block size is simply the size, in bytes, of the serialized block. Initially, Bitcoin's block had a maximum size set to 1 MB. This limit was introduced initially by Satoshi to protect the network against DOS attacks, until it was recently raised after the introduction of Segwit. Segwit, or Segregated Witness, is a technique enabling the production of blocks with a size of up to 4 MB by putting their signatures (which use roughly 60 percent of the transaction space) in an extra space, enabling block capacity to be scaled while maintaining backward compatibility. Segwit introduced the concept of weight instead of size, enabling old nodes (which recognize only 1 MB blocks) to see only placeholders, while nodes upgraded to Segwit are still able to see the entire block and validate the signatures (4 MB).

The calculation of the weight is a bit more complicated than the simple `block size = 1` MB. The miners now need to build blocks, which do not violate the conditions determined by the `CheckBlock()` function defined in `validation.cpp`:

```
// Size limits
if (block.vtx.empty() || block.vtx.size() * WITNESS_SCALE_FACTOR > MAX_BLOCK_WEIGHT || ::GetSerializeSize(block, SER_NETWORK, PROTOCOL_VERSION |
SERIALIZE_TRANSACTION_NO_WITNESS) * WITNESS_SCALE_FACTOR > MAX_BLOCK_WEIGHT)
    return state.DoS(100, false, REJECT_INVALID, "bad-blk-length", false, "size limits failed");
```

The `GetSerializeSize` function just computes the size in bytes of a serialized block for the network-ignoring witnesses. Therefore we can deduce that the weight is proportional to size by a factor of `WITNESS_SCALE_FACTOR` as follows: `maximum size = Weight/WITNESS_SCALE_FACTOR`.

Any block, such that `block.vtx.size()` is larger than 1 MB, will be rejected as invalid.

You might find this weight concept a useless fancy hack, but it isn't as it solves the dilemma of scaling Bitcoin without breaking the Bitcoin network consensus (backward compatibility). As we are starting a new network, we can directly increase block size or keep the Segwit solution with a higher block weight. In this guide, we'll opt for the second approach.

Prior to Bitcoin 0.15, the limit was defined in the `src\consensus\consensus.h` as follows:

```
static const unsigned int MAX_BLOCK_BASE_SIZE = 1000000;
```

This set the maximum limit of a Bitcoin block to 1 MB, excluding witness data.

Since Segwit activation, the weight parameters have been defined in `consensus.h`:

```
/** The maximum allowed size for a serialized block, in bytes (only for buffer size limits) */
static const unsigned int MAX_BLOCK_SERIALIZED_SIZE = 4000000;
/** The maximum allowed weight for a block, see BIP 141 (network rule) */
static const unsigned int MAX_BLOCK_WEIGHT = 4000000;
/** The maximum allowed number of signature check operations in a block (network rule) */
static const int64_t MAX_BLOCK_SIGOPS_COST = 80000;
static const int WITNESS_SCALE_FACTOR = 4;
```

To double the weight, we have to double the values of these four parameters.
This theoretically allows us to mine blocks of up to 8 MB, but a more realistic maximum block size will be an occasionally rare 7.7 MB (assuming near 100% Segwit transactions). By processing big blocks, we have to make a trade-off between scalability and the growth in the blockchain's size. As the blockchain is an unalterable database, reaching a big size implies higher centralization as few storage points will be able to store data.

Congratulations! You just replicated the schism of the Bitcoin community, which was proposal BIP141 (Segwit). But what are BIPs?

BIPs: Bitcoin Improvement Proposals

In the previous chapter, we introduced BIPs as a way to bring new features to the Bitcoin protocol. Each new improvement (BIP) is activated at a future block height to give Bitcoin users time to update their software. In `chainparams.cpp`, you'll find some old important BIPs (BIP34/65/66) defined as the following checkpoints:

```
consensus.BIP34Height = 227931;
consensus.BIP34Hash = uint256S("0x000000000000024b89b42a942fe0d9fea3bb44ab7bd1b19115dd6a759c0808b8");
consensus.BIP65Height = 388381; // 000000000000000004c2b624ed5d7756c508d90fd0da2c7c679febfa6c4735f0
consensus.BIP66Height = 363725; // 00000000000000000379eaa19dce8c9b722d46ae6a57c2f1a988119488b50931
```

For checkpoints, we can use either a block height or hash.

As you are creating a new chain from scratch, you can just use the genesis block height or hash to have these BIPs activated from the start:

```
consensus.BIP34Height = 0;
consensus.BIP34Hash =
uint256S("000001a9bbae8bb141c6941838bdacdbcf474b6ed28a0b18b2120b60a68f00ee"
);
consensus.BIP65Height = 0;
consensus.BIP66Height = 0;
```

Alongside the BIP activation time, the next 11 lines describe the activation rules (retargeting period, requisite activation threshold, version bit, fork start, and ending time) for deploying soft forks:

```
consensus.nRuleChangeActivationThreshold = 1916; // 95% of 2016
consensus.nMinerConfirmationWindow = 2016; // nPowTargetTimespan / nPowTargetSpacing
consensus.vDeployments[Consensus::DEPLOYMENT_TESTDUMMY].bit = 28;
consensus.vDeployments[Consensus::DEPLOYMENT_TESTDUMMY].nStartTime = 1199145601; // January 1, 2008
consensus.vDeployments[Consensus::DEPLOYMENT_TESTDUMMY].nTimeout = 1230767999; // December 31, 2008

// Deployment of BIP68, BIP112, and BIP113.
consensus.vDeployments[Consensus::DEPLOYMENT_CSV].bit = 0;
consensus.vDeployments[Consensus::DEPLOYMENT_CSV].nStartTime = 1462060800; // May 1st, 2016
consensus.vDeployments[Consensus::DEPLOYMENT_CSV].nTimeout = 1493596800; // May 1st, 2017

// Deployment of SegWit (BIP141, BIP143, and BIP147)
consensus.vDeployments[Consensus::DEPLOYMENT_SEGWIT].bit = 1;
consensus.vDeployments[Consensus::DEPLOYMENT_SEGWIT].nStartTime = 1479168000; // November 15th, 2016.
consensus.vDeployments[Consensus::DEPLOYMENT_SEGWIT].nTimeout = 1510704000; // November 15th, 2017.
```

As we have edited the `consensus.nMinerConfirmationWindow = 576;` earlier, we can therefore deduce the `nRuleChangeActivationThreshold` value by multiplying the confirmation window by 95% to get the following:

```
nRuleChangeActivationThreshold=574;
```

For the rest of the rules, you can keep the bit element as it is and set the `nStartTime` and `ntimeout` as follows:

```
consensus.vDeployments[Consensus::DEPLOYMENT_CSV].nStartTime = 0;
consensus.vDeployments[Consensus::DEPLOYMENT_CSV].nTimeout = "your genesis
time stamp";
```

Or you can just keep the original values. Just afterwards, you'll find the following assumption:

```
consensus.defaultAssumeValid =
uint256S("0x0000000000000000003b9ce759c2a087d52abc4266f8f4ebd6d768b89defa50
a");
```

This assumes that the signatures in the ancestors of this block are valid. We'll need to set this hash to zero:

```
consensus.defaultAssumeValid = uint256S("0x00");
```

The preceding modifications should be performed for mainnet and testnet as well.

All right. Now our Readercoin is ready to be compiled and tested.

Compiling and testing

Ta-da! The moment we have been waiting for has finally arrived.

As we have done at the beginning of this chapter to build Bitcoin, we will reproduce the same steps. Thus, let's run the following commands:

```
./autogen.sh
./configure --with-gui=qt5 --enable-debug --disable-tests
make && sudo make install
```

Successful compilation and installation should output as follows:

```
user@ByExample-node:~/workspace/readercoin/src$ ./readercoin-cli addnode 192.168.1.4 onetry
user@ByExample-node:~/workspace/readercoin/src$ ./readercoin-cli getblockchaininfo
{
  "chain": "main",
  "blocks": 187,
  "headers": 187,
  "bestblockhash": "00000b6242a3f38d6635be95badbda19263e1cc657de6ad62f67e113b22d186d",
  "difficulty": 0.000244140625,
  "mediantime": 1528732541,
  "verificationprogress": 0.9894736842105263,
  "chainwork": "00000000000000000000000000000000000000000000000000000000bc00bc0",
  "pruned": false,
  "softforks": [
    {
      "id": "bip34",
      "version": 2,
      "reject": {
        "status": false
      }
    },
    {
      "id": "bip66",
      "version": 3,
      "reject": {
        "status": false
      }
    },
    {
      "id": "bip65",
      "version": 4,
      "reject": {
        "status": false
      }
    }
  ],
  "bip9_softforks": {
    "csv": {
      "status": "defined",
      "startTime": 1528707955,
      "timeout": 1528707955,
      "since": 0
    },
    "segwit": {
      "status": "defined",
      "startTime": 1528707955,
```

The expected end result would be to build the executable programs `readercoind` and `readercoin-qt`. You can check this by running the following:

```
ls ./src/readercoind ./src/qt/readercoin-qt
```

Awesome! Start your client using `readercoin-qt`.

A graphical interface will show up asking to set the default directory, but it will show you the Bitcoin logo and icon. Admittedly, it's inconvenient to keep these graphical fingerprints, so let's get rid of them. Before going further, shut down the running Readercoin client.

Design and graphics (Qt wallet)

The cherry on the cake will be defining a unique icon and image for your newborn currency, differentiating it from Bitcoin and other cryptocurrencies.

Under the /src/qt/res directory, you'll find all the other graphical resource files that you'll need to edit, including the logo and icon (the file with an .ico extension) to personalize your graphical interface. Let's start by changing the background image that shows up when the graphical wallet is loaded. You can create a new image with a size of 1024*1024 pixels– let's say a big **R** in a circle with a transparent background—using Photoshop or Gimp—and save it as readercoin.png under the/src/qt/res directory. You also have to convert this readercoin.png to the svg format (readercoin.svg) using an online converter and save the result in the/src/qt/res/src directory:

When Bitcoin is run in testnet mode, the GUI uses a green image. For ReaderCoin's testnet, let's choose a different color for the background—let's say red.

The splash picture can be also converted to an .ico file to serve as an icon. You can use an online converter to get your icon file. For macOS X, you'll need to edit the Bitcoin file with the ICNS file extension.

Once you finish editing the graphical elements, you have to build the code again (by running `make`) to apply the graphical changes. Next time you run your ReaderCoin client's GUI, you'll see your new splash screen and icon as follows:

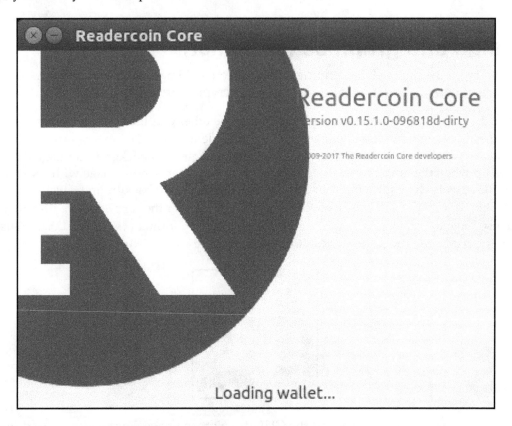

Redesign of the Bitcoin-Qt wallet

Alongside editing graphical resources, you can customize the wallet interfaces to define your own. Most of the dialogs in Bitcoin-Qt are created based on the Qt framework using Qt designer. The resource files corresponding to different dialog forms are editable files with `.ui` extensions and are located under `src/qt/forms`.

If you're not keen to use Qt, you can alternatively design and write your own graphical wallet in other languages and tools such as C#/WPF, and communicate over RPC with Readercoin's RPC API.

Graphical interface addition

To start modifying the UI part, download and install the Qt dedicated IDE, Qt Creator, which includes neat tools for UI design as follows: `sudo apt-get install qtcreator`.

Let's proceed with the import of the project as follows:

1. Run Qt Creator using: `qtcreator`.
2. When the IDE shows up, in Qt Creator start a **New Project**. A new dialog form will show up as shown in the following screenshot. Then choose **Import Project** as the template, followed by **Import Existing Project**:

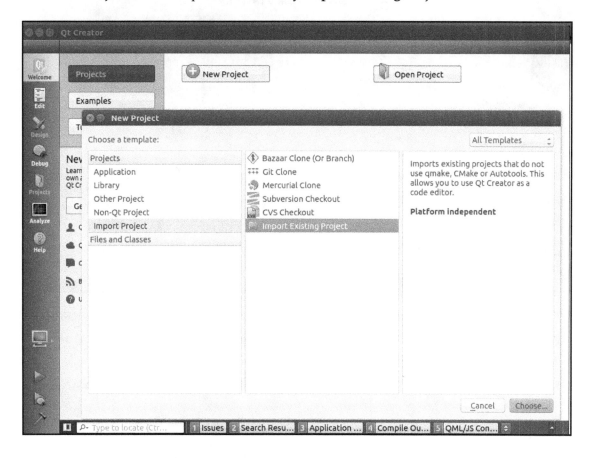

3. Enter `readercoin-qt` as the project name, and then select the location of `src/qt` in your Readercoin project (`workspace/readercoin/src/qt`):

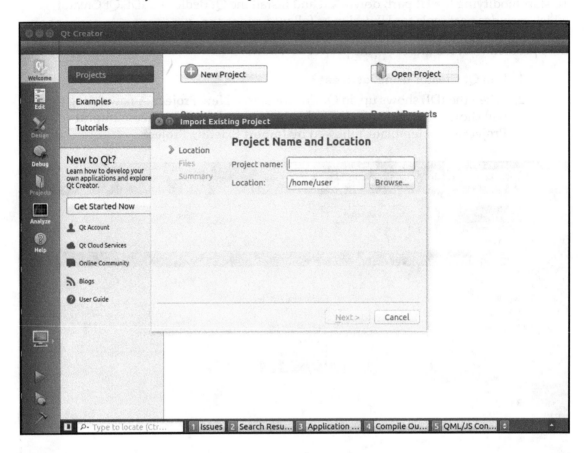

4. A new interface will show up suggesting you choose files to import. Leave the proposed file selection as it is. We then import all the files located under the `src/` folder:

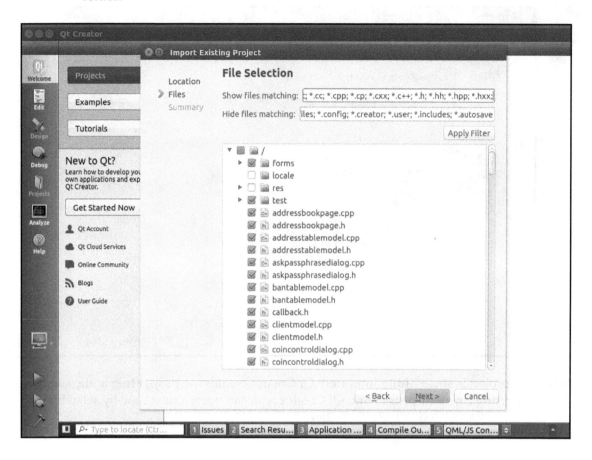

5. A `summary page` dialog will show up where you can optionally indicate your git repository, before finally confirming the project import:

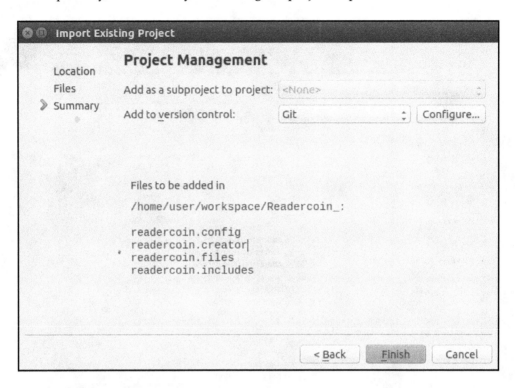

When the project is successfully imported, Qt Creator creates the project tree in the sidebar. After importing a generic project into Qt Creator, you can open it next time by selecting the `.creator` file created in the `src/`folder.

In the **Project** section in the left-hand column, select **Manage Kits...**, and then, in the **Build & Run** section,select the build configuration, and set your compiler and debugger if it is not auto-detected:

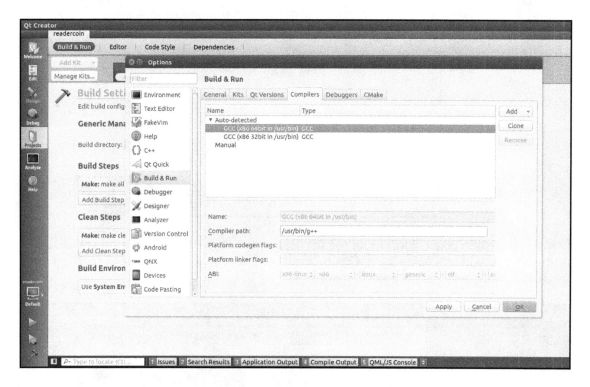

All set? You can start building the project with Qt Creator by pressing the green triangle button. It will ask you to specify the executable name and path, along with the arguments to use when running your executable. Thus, we specify `src/qt/readercoin-qt` or `readercoind` as an executable, and `-printtoconsole` as an argument:

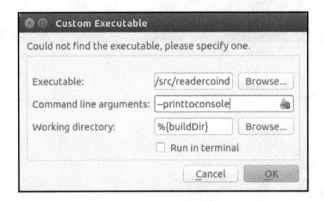

During the project build, you should see the log printed in the Qt Creator application output. If you edit any value using Qt Creator, you'll have to recompile the code to get your modification included in your Readercoin client:

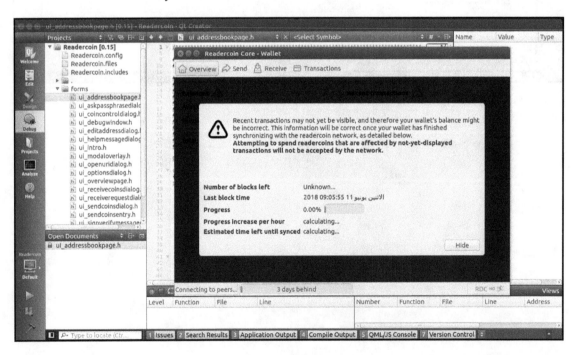

As you'll notice, Qt Creator only gives you access to the client code. In order to edit graphical forms, start `qt-designer` by double-clicking on the file with a `.ui` extension located under `qt/forms/`:

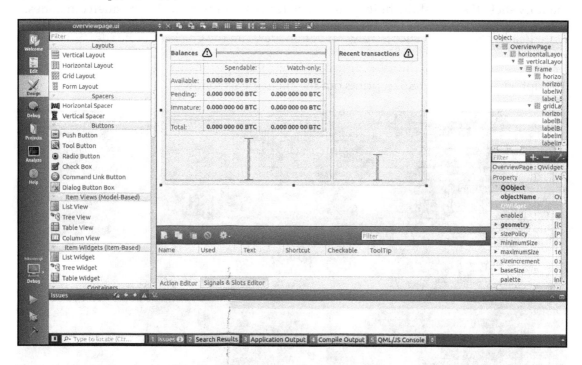

Using both Qt Creator and Qt Designer, play around by removing or adding graphical elements. If you want to add new Qt features, you should have a basic knowledge of Qt/C++. After each modification, compile the code by pressing the green triangle located in the bottom left of `qt-creator`.

Building a Readercoin network

As most of the work is done, let's put the results into practice.

At this level, everything is ready to launch our Readercoin network. We'll need to build a network of two connected machines, called **Node A** and **Node B**. Before advancing further, check that both machines can ping each other. Let's say Node A has the IP address `192.168.1.3`, and Node B `192.168.1.8`.

At this point, we have built Readercoin on a single machine (Node A), so we will need to build it on Node B in the same manner we did in Node A. For that, you can clone the code source from our remote repository, or just transfer the Readercoin folder using a USB memory stick. If successfully built, you will be ready to connect the P2P Readercoin nodes.

Once Readercoin is built successfully on both nodes, run the Qt client or `readercoin-qt -printtoconsole`.

The option `-printtoconsole` prints out the client log as follows:

Running the Readercoin client for the first time will create a `.readercoin` directory in your home directory, along with some other necessary files. Stop the client to create a configuration file named `readercoin.conf` in `~/.readercoin` and insert the following lines:

```
server=1
rpcuser=set a username
rpcpassword=set a password
addnode=the other node's IP
rpcallowip=192.168.0.0/16
```

Instead of using the `addnode` option in the configuration file, you can run the clients on both nodes and execute the `addnode` RPC call:

```
readercoin-cli addnode 192.168.1.3:9333 onetry (in nodeA)

readercoin-cli addnode 192.168.1.8:9333 onetry (in nodeB)
```

A log entry in both peers should appear, confirming a pairing similar to the following. If not, try it again or wait for a bit:

```
user@ByExample-node: ~
2018-06-18 14:06:11 Bound to [::]:7333
2018-06-18 14:06:11 Bound to 0.0.0.0:7333
2018-06-18 14:06:11 init message: Loading P2P addresses...
2018-06-18 14:06:11 Loaded 0 addresses from peers.dat  0ms
2018-06-18 14:06:11 init message: Loading banlist...
2018-06-18 14:06:11 init message: Starting network threads...
2018-06-18 14:06:11 init message: Done loading
2018-06-18 14:06:11 torcontrol thread start
2018-06-18 14:06:11 net thread start
2018-06-18 14:06:11 dnsseed thread start
2018-06-18 14:06:11 Loading addresses from DNS seeds (could take a while)
2018-06-18 14:06:11 msghand thread start
2018-06-18 14:06:11 0 addresses found from DNS seeds
2018-06-18 14:06:11 dnsseed thread exit
2018-06-18 14:06:11 Imported mempool transactions from disk: 0 successes, 0 fail
ed, 0 expired
2018-06-18 14:06:11 opencon thread start
2018-06-18 14:06:11 addcon thread start
2018-06-18 14:06:14 connect() to 192.168.1.7:9333 failed after select(): No rout
e to host (113)
2018-06-18 14:06:14 Leaving InitialBlockDownload (latching to false)
2018-06-18 14:06:14 receive version message: /Satoshi:0.15.1/: version 70015, bl
ocks=0, us=[::]:0, peer=0
```

You can check whether both nodes are connected using `readercoin-cli getpeerinfo`.

You'll need to see all the connected peer information, as shown in following screenshot:

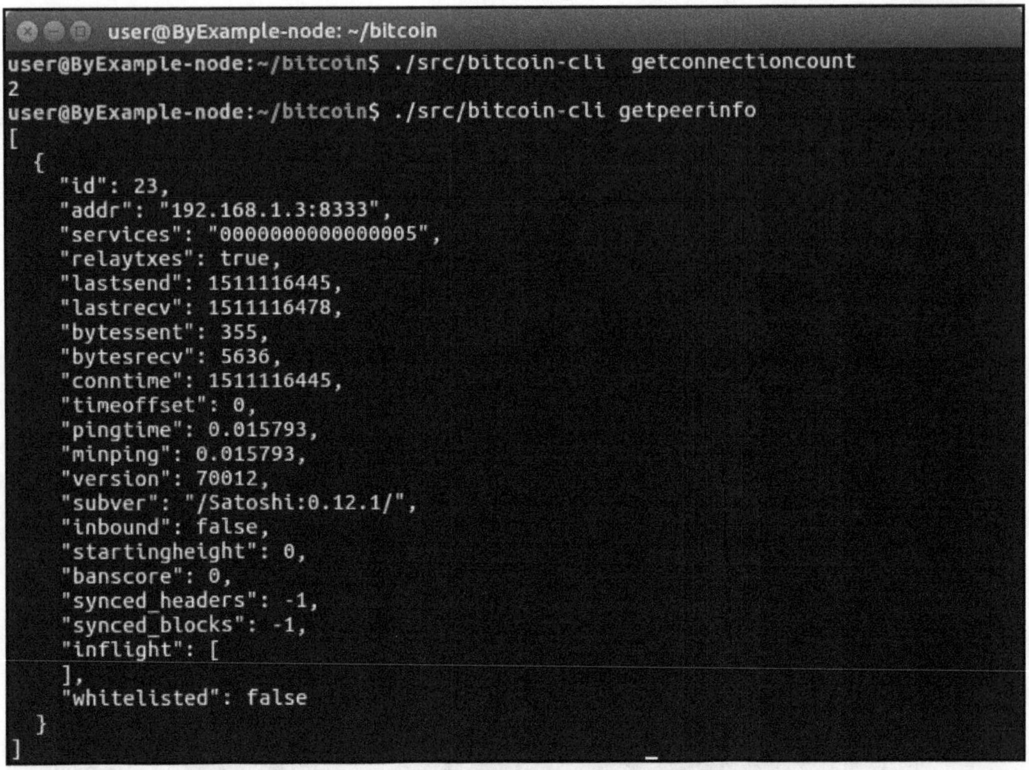

```
user@ByExample-node: ~/bitcoin

user@ByExample-node:~/bitcoin$ ./src/bitcoin-cli  getconnectioncount
2
user@ByExample-node:~/bitcoin$ ./src/bitcoin-cli getpeerinfo
[
  {
    "id": 23,
    "addr": "192.168.1.3:8333",
    "services": "0000000000000005",
    "relaytxes": true,
    "lastsend": 1511116445,
    "lastrecv": 1511116478,
    "bytessent": 355,
    "bytesrecv": 5636,
    "conntime": 1511116445,
    "timeoffset": 0,
    "pingtime": 0.015793,
    "minping": 0.015793,
    "version": 70012,
    "subver": "/Satoshi:0.12.1/",
    "inbound": false,
    "startingheight": 0,
    "banscore": 0,
    "synced_headers": -1,
    "synced_blocks": -1,
    "inflight": [
    ],
    "whitelisted": false
  }
]
```

It's worth noting that you can run RPC commands from the GUI without using a terminal as follows:

1. Open the Readercoin wallet
2. Choose **Help**
3. Select **Debug window**
4. Select **Console**

5. Execute your command line without using `readercoin-cli`:

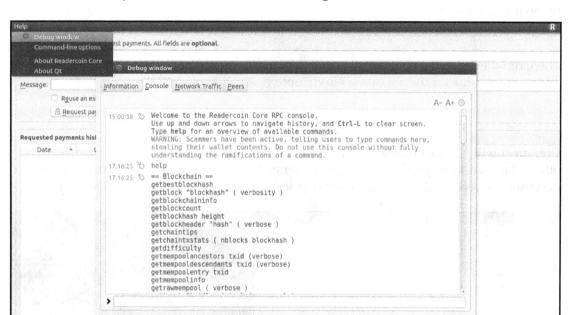

Our nodes are ready to start sending and receiving Readercoins but, as you have noticed, we don't have any yet. Therefore, we need to start mining, either on one of the nodes or on both of them.

Readercoin mining

Bitcoin 0.15, which Readercoin is based on, doesn't have an internal miner, so we will need to use a dedicated mining tool to mine our blocks. Among many, we will use Cpuminer (minerd), which is pretty simple to use and supports CPU mining for `sha256` hashing.

To install it, you can get the binary file from GitHub: `https://github.com/pooler/cpuminer/releases`. Download the last release and extract the binary, you'll get a file called `minerd`.

Prior to running `cpuminer`, we need to generate new addresses in both instances using the following command:

```
readercoin-cli getnewaddress
```

Then, run the following command on one or both clients and provide the generated address as a value for the `coinbase-addr` option:

```
./minerd -o http://127.0.0.1:9332 -u user -p password -a sha256d --no-
longpoll --no-getwork --no-stratum --coinbase-addr=your_address
```

Cpuminer will not start unless both nodes are connected and communicating with each other. Once working, you'll be able to see a series of log entries along with notifications declaring the receipt of new transactions (genesis transactions), each with 10 Readercoins:

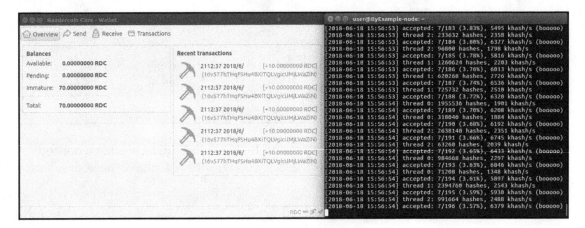

If you're facing any mining problems while using `cpuminer`, you can use a more updated tool, such as `cgminer` or `ccminer`. In parallel, in another terminal, you can get detailed information about the progress of your blockchain using `readercoin-cli Getinfo,`which returns an object containing various state information. A more specific RPC method is `getblockchaininfo`, which provides you with various state information regarding blockchain processing, including the number of mined blocks, the last block hash, the chainwork, and the soft fork situation:

```
user@ByExample-node:~/workspace/readercoin/src$ ./readercoin-cli addnode 192.168.1.4 onetry
user@ByExample-node:~/workspace/readercoin/src$ ./readercoin-cli getblockchaininfo
{
  "chain": "main",
  "blocks": 187,
  "headers": 187,
  "bestblockhash": "00000b6242a3f38d6635be95badbda19263e1cc657de6ad62f67e113b22d186d",
  "difficulty": 0.000244140625,
  "mediantime": 1528732541,
  "verificationprogress": 0.9894736842105263,
  "chainwork": "000000000000000000000000000000000000000000000000000000000000bc00bc0",
  "pruned": false,
  "softforks": [
    {
      "id": "bip34",
      "version": 2,
      "reject": {
        "status": false
      }
    },
    {
      "id": "bip66",
      "version": 3,
      "reject": {
        "status": false
      }
    },
    {
      "id": "bip65",
      "version": 4,
      "reject": {
        "status": false
      }
    }
  ],
  "bip9_softforks": {
    "csv": {
      "status": "defined",
      "startTime": 1528707955,
      "timeout": 1528707955,
      "since": 0
    },
    "segwit": {
      "status": "defined",
      "startTime": 1528707955,
```

To get all the details about a specific block, you need to run `readercoin-cli getblock <block hash>`:

```
Terminal File Edit View Search Terminal Help
user@ByExample-node:~$ readercoin-cli getblockhash 0
000003758b8aa3b5066e2d5b2aa4f5c7516868f50d37bfdb55d52ff581425adc
user@ByExample-node:~$ readercoin-cli getblock 000003758b8aa3b5066e2d5b2aa4f5c7516868f50d37bfdb55d52ff581425adc
{
  "hash": "000003758b8aa3b5066e2d5b2aa4f5c7516868f50d37bfdb55d52ff581425adc",
  "confirmations": 1,
  "strippedsize": 242,
  "size": 242,
  "weight": 968,
  "height": 0,
  "version": 1,
  "versionHex": "00000001",
  "merkleroot": "6bc2585d63185acf3868cc34e0b017b3fb41c00938eb09bc52a3cf73a31ec6a8",
  "tx": [
    "6bc2585d63185acf3868cc34e0b017b3fb41c00938eb09bc52a3cf73a31ec6a8"
  ],
  "time": 1528707955,
  "mediantime": 1528707955,
  "nonce": 690552,
  "bits": "1e0ffff0",
  "difficulty": 0.000244140625,
  "chainwork": "0000000000000000000000000000000000000000000000000000000000100010"
}
user@ByExample-node:~$
```

In the preceding screenshot, the genesis block has a 1 difficulty and `1e00ffff0` bits. We explained earlier that Bitcoin bits represent the `target` hash value in a special format.

Mining using a single node is called **solo mining**, which will be impossible to perform if the difficulty reaches a high level. In that situation, it's appropriate instead to build mining pools formed by multiple mining nodes, which share the work and rewards.

Sending transactions

As we have set the coinbase maturity to 50, we will need to mine 50 blocks to be able to spend our mined Readercoins (reward set in the genesis transaction).

On `node A`, we can use the address generated on `node B` to send 1 Readercoin using the following command:

```
readercoin-cli sendtoaddress <node B readercoin's address> 1
```

Or, alternatively, this can be effected via Qt wallet, as demonstrated in the following screenshot:

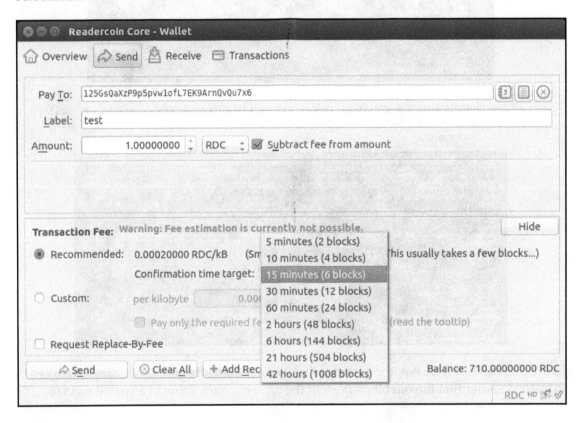

As for Bitcoin,you can define the transaction fee to accelerate your transaction's processing or not.You may notice the confirmation time is expressed according to our block time.

You can now enjoy extending your network and mining new coins. It's a great feeling to use your own, handcrafted cryptocurrency to boost your understanding of blockchain, isn't it?

As a bonus, we will set up an explorer to give users more visibility into the operation processing.

Building a transaction and block explorer

Block explorers are helpful tools, providing all the information about transaction processing and block details. In general, they are web applications communicating with blockchain nodes to display the network situation, avoiding the burden of repeatedly executing RPC calls (`readercoin-cli`) for you. There are multiple open source Bitcoin block explorers and, by searching around GitHub, you'll find projects such as Php-Bitcoin-explorer, and BitcoinJS explorer, Bitcoin-ABE. In the following guide, we will opt for Iquidus explorer.

Iquidus will read the Readercoin blocks, transform and load the data into its database, and present the information via a web interface.

Iquidus setup requirements

To set up Iquidus, we need to install the following tools:

- NodeJs V6:
    - If you have a newer version, you can use `nvm` to manage multiple node versions: `nvm install V6`.
- MonogoDB:
    - To install MongoDB, run the following command line:

```
sudo apt-get install -y mongodb-org=3.6.5 mongodb-org-server=3.6.5 mongodb-org-shell=3.6.5 mongodb-org-mongos=3.6.5 mongodb-org-tools=3.6.5
```

Then, start MongoDB using `sudo service mongod start`. Afterward, follow these steps to set up the explorer's database.

Creating Iquidus's database

Enter the MongoDB cli using the command `mongo`:

```
> use explorerdb
```

Create a user with read/write access:

```
> db.createUser( { user: "iquidus", pwd: "3xp!0reR", roles: [ "readWrite" ]
} )
```

Note: If you're using mongo shell 2.4.x, use the following to create your user:

```
> db.addUser( { user: "username", pwd: "password", roles: [ "readWrite"] })
```

Installing Iquidus

Open a new terminal and clone the project's repository:

```
git clone https://github.com/iquidus/explorer.git readercoin_explorer && cd
readercoin_explorer
```

Then, install all dependencies using the following code:

```
npm install --production
```

Iquidus configuration

To use the Iquidus explorer, you have to edit `settings.json` with the same setting parameters set in your `readercoin.conf` file. First, we rename the settings file to `cp settings.json.template settings.json`.

Then, in your text editor, update the values of the following parameters:

```
"coin": "readercoin",
"symbol": "RDC",
"wallet": {
    "host": "localhost",
    "port": 9332,
    "user": "user", //Readercoin's RPC user defined in readercoin.conf
    "pass": "password"
},
```

For the `genesis_block` parameter, you can set your genesis block's hash.

For `genesis_tx`, you can define the hash of the genesis transaction. This value can be extracted from the `tx` field in the output provided by `readercoin-cli getblock your_genesis_block_hash`.

Pick any block you have in your blockchain and put its details in the following API section:

```
"api": {
    "blockindex": 0,
    "blockhash":
"000003758b8aa3b5066e2d5b2aa4f5c7516868f50d37bfdb55d52ff581425adc",
    "txhash":
"6bc2585d63185acf3868cc34e0b017b3fb41c00938eb09bc52a3cf73a31ec6a8",
    "address": "1Cccex1tMVTABi9gS2VzRvPA88H4p32Vvn"
},
```

Save and close your setting file.

Syncing databases with the blockchain

To sync the explorer's local database with the blockchain information, a dedicated script, `sync.js` (located in `scripts/`), is available. This script must be called from the explorer's root directory as follows:

```
node scripts/sync.js index [mode]
```

For the `mode` option, you can choose one of the following modes:

- `update`: Updates the index from the last sync to the current block
- `check`: Checks the index for (and adds) any missing transactions/addresses
- `reindex`: Clears the index and then resyncs from genesis to the current block

As indicated in the official documentation, it's recommended to have this script launched via a cronjob at 2+ minute intervals. For example, to update the index every minute and market data every two minutes, use the following:

```
*/1 * * * * cd /path/to/explorer && /usr/bin/nodejs scripts/sync.js index
update > /dev/null 2>&1
*/5 * * * * cd /path/to/explorer && /usr/bin/nodejs scripts/peers.js >
/dev/null 2>&1
```

Wallet preparation

Iquidus Explorer is now ready to connect to your node, but first we will need to run the Readercoin node with the option `-txindex` or set `-txindex=1` in your `readercoin.conf`. This will facilitate the obtaining of transaction data for any transaction in the blockchain and your client will maintain an index of all transactions that have ever happened. If you have been running your client for a while, but haven't had `txindex=1` set, then it might take a few hours to rebuild the index.

Starting the explorer

At this level, everything is ready to start the block explorer. Open a terminal window and run it within the `Iquidus` root directory `npm start` and make sure that mongodb is already running.

If we have no errors, you can open your block explorer from `http://ip.address.of.server:3331` to access the explorer web interface:

Congratulations!!

Henceforth, you can get all the blockchain information from your explorer and fetch data for a specific block, transaction, or address. I hope that the steps in setting up your own altcoin explorer were easy and straightforward.

Building an exchange market

You now have your Readercoin wallet, network, and blockchain explorer ready to be deployed widely, so all you need now is to find crypto-lovers to join your project. At this level, you might be thinking about trading your new altcoin to make it more attractive. To achieve that goal, you can ask well-known trading platforms to list your coin, or, more excitingly, you can build your own exchange market.

To avoid you reading a long chapter, I'll just introduce you to the platform to adopt for the second option. Actually, to build your cryptocurrency exchange, there is an amazing open source project called **Peatio**. This great platform is used in well-known trading platforms such as Yunbi Exchange, Binance, and Cex.io. Peatio's code, as well as the installation procedure, are available in the official GitHub repos: `https://github.com/peatio/peatio/blob/master/doc/setup-local-ubuntu.md`.

Peatio is a complete solution, is easy to set up, and provides all the basic exchange platform operations, such as cryptocurrency or fiat deposit and withdrawal, trading, and KYC:

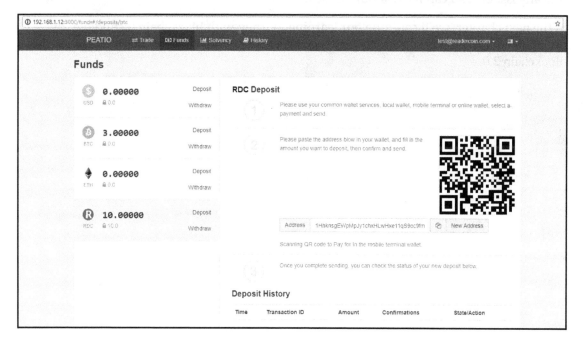

The starting point before creating a new coin would be answering the following question: What's the purpose of your new coin? Do you have an original idea? Do you solve any of Bitcoin's problems? Don't be lured into financial temptation. You should instead focus on improving performance or implementing extended functionalities.

Summary

The main purpose of this chapter was to present the basic steps for creating a cryptocurrency by shamelessly cloning Bitcoin. Although it only scratches the surface of building cryptocurrencies,this chapter was an opportunity to enrich your knowledge of the Bitcoin protocol and also provided a short initiation to understanding Bitcoin's source code.

This chapter concludes our short excursion into the land of Bitcoin; I hope you enjoyed it. Again, here's the GitHub repository: `https://github.com/bellaj/Readercoin_.git`.You can catch up on any things you may have missed, or just get a better look at the code. If you face any issues, you can make a pull request.

In the next chapter, we'll continue our learning journey with blockchain technology by diving deep into the very promising project, Ethereum, which is often referred to as Blockchain 2.0.

4
Peer-to-Peer Auctions in Ethereum

In the first part of this book, we introduced bitcoin as the first embodiment of blockchain technology and the world's most popular cryptocurrency. Throughout the previous chapters, we tried to illuminate from a developmental angle, what a blockchain is, by building applications using bitcoin. In this second part of the book, we'll introduce the most well-established and mature smart-contract-driven blockchain: Ethereum.

As we discussed in `Chapter 1`, *Say Hello to Blockchain*, the primary aim of bitcoin is to establish itself as a payment alternative to regular money, whereas Ethereum focuses more on enabling developers to build and run distributed applications, **decentralized apps (DApps)**, by providing them with built-in tools and currency vehicles.

Faithful to our approach of learning by example, we will start our exploration by building a decentralized auction DApp to sell vehicles on top of the Ethereum blockchain.

The purpose of this chapter is to introduce you, from a developmental standpoint, to the tools, concepts, and fundamental basics required to build decentralized applications. Nonetheless, if you are interested in a detailed overview of the Ethereum protocol, you can refer to its white paper (`https://github.com/ethereum/wiki/wiki/White-Paper`), and for a full technical presentation, you can read its yellow paper (`https://ethereum.github.io/yellowpaper/paper.pdf`).

This chapter is organized around four major topics, as follows:

- A general overview of Ethereum
- Introducing Solidity (auction smart contract)
- Introducing web3.js (auction frontend)
- The smart contract deployment environment

I am quite sure that you'll find Ethereum a developer-friendly blockchain that can help enthusiasts and eager developers like you easily unlock the power of the blockchain. Let's start.

Introduction to Ethereum

In its first years, the bitcoin system has proven impressive, but it has narrow capabilities. It seemed that we would keep whittling away at its constraints, but the situation changed after the introduction of the Ethereum blockchain, which, unlike bitcoin, can be extended to much more than just managing a digital currency. In fact, Ethereum is a general-purpose blockchain that is more suited to describing business logic, through advanced scripts, also known as smart contracts. As you saw in previous chapters, bitcoin scripts are primarily about expressing ownership conditions and payment rules. For instance, the standard pay to pubkey hash script describes a small program that allows a sender to send coins to a receiver identified by a public key; no wonder, as bitcoin was designed as a cash system. In contrast, Ethereum was designed with a broader vision, as a decentralized or world computer that attempts to marry the power of the blockchain, as a trust machine, with a Turing-complete contract engine.

Although Ethereum borrows many ideas that were initially introduced by bitcoin, there are many divergences between the two. The following table summarizes the main areas of difference between Ethereum and bitcoin:

	Ethereum	Bitcoin
Smart Contracting	Universal and Turing-complete scripting language.	Forth-like language Locking unlocking scripts.
Mining algorithm	Ethash PoW, specialized hardware resistant.	PoW based on SHA-256, non-specialized hardware resistant
Cryptocurrency Generation	3 Ethers per block after Byzantium Fork (It will be reduced in near future to 2 Ethers)	Initially 50 Bitcoin, which halves every 210,000 blocks (currently 12,5 Bitcoin)
Average confirmation time	GHOST (fast block confirmation time, 3 ~ 30 sec)	Slow block confirmation (an average of 10 minutes)
stale blocks	Uncles and nephews blocs are accepted	Orphaned blocks are rejected
Blockchain Model	Account model with two types: • External accounts • Contract accounts	UTXO model.

Ethereum virtual machine and smart contracts

The Ethereum virtual machine and smart contracts are key elements of Ethereum, and constitute its main attraction. The smart contract is a concept that was introduced in the 1990s by Nick Szabo, as a set of commitments specified in digital form. In Ethereum, smart contracts represent a piece of code written in a high-level language (Solidity, LLL, Viper) and stored as bytecode in the blockchain, in order to run reliably in a stack-based virtual machine (Ethereum Virtual Machine), in each node, once invoked. The interactions with smart contract functions happen through transactions on the blockchain network, with their payloads being executed in the Ethereum virtual machine, and the shared blockchain state being updated accordingly. The following diagram provides a
general overview of the smart contract execution environment and the interaction between the virtual machine and the blockchain ledger:

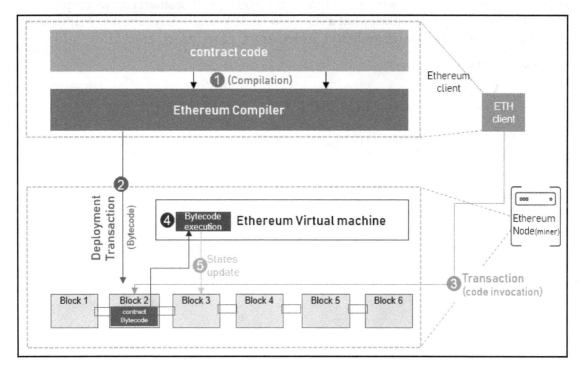

Ether and gas

Like bitcoin, the Ethereum network has a built-in cryptocurrency, called **ether**. In addition to operating as a digital currency for payment, ether is used in Ethereum's pricing mechanism for running DApps on the system. Ethereum isn't a free network; you have to pay in ether, whether for transaction fees, or for smart contract deployment or execution. The protocol defines the cost for each computation in a dedicated unit called gas, and the total cost is paid, in order to incentivize miners and avoid denial of service attacks. We will look at the relationship between ether and gas in the next sections.

Your first smart contract

Before we go any further, let's be concrete and jump into our first smart contract right away. The following code shows what a standard Hello World smart contract, written in a higher programming language (Solidity), looks like:

```solidity
pragma solidity ^0.4.24;

contract HelloWorld {
    string message = "hello world";

    function setMessage(string msg_)  public {
        message = msg_;
    }

    function getMessage() public view returns (string) {
        return message;
    }
}
```

If you're a developer, this code should be understandable; there is nothing complex. We define a variable, message, with two functions, a setter and a getter. What differs is the fact that we are dealing with a contract that easily stores a given message in Ethereum's blockchain, without using an I/O stream or database connection. We will take a closer look at the meaning of each element later in this chapter. You can copy , paste, and compile this code by using an online IDE, such as Remix (remix.ethereum.org). You will find further details on handling Remix in the next section.

Voila! You have created your first Hello World smart contract.

What's a DApp?

Have you heard about Web 3.0?

This buzzword is all about a decentralized web, enabled by blockchain networks running DApps, instead of classic client-server web applications. DApp is an abbreviation for decentralized application, and it refers to an unstoppable application running on top of a peer-to-peer blockchain network. The DApp's unstoppability comes from the fact that it eliminates the need for any middlemen to operate, and its execution is replicated across a distributed network.

DApp architecture

Generally, a DApp is a two-tier application, comprised of two main components:

- A frontend layer on the user side
- A backend (smart contract) hosted in the blockchain network

In the frontend, if you are familiar with Bootstrap or any other framework, you can continue using it. You won't need to manage user accounts, create accounts, or log in to access your DApps, as the network is anonymous, and we only deal with anonymous accounts (addresses), without identification. On Ethereum, the backend operations are ensured by the smart contract, which is validated by the peer-to-peer network. The following diagram shows the layers of a typical DApp and the interactions between the frontend and backend:

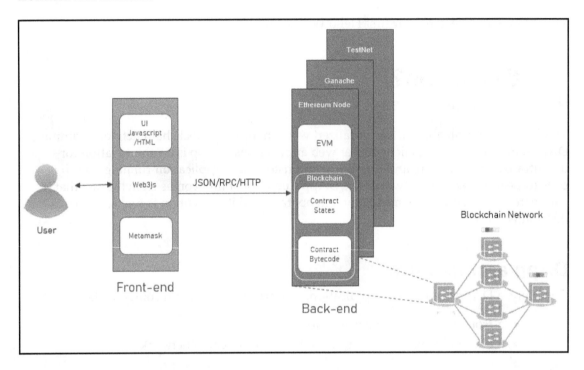

Building an auction DApp

Now that you have a basic idea of what Ethereum and DApps are, we can start to build our auction DApp. An auction is a typical example, but it is complex enough to provide a perfect first DApp. It demonstrates the trustless nature of the blockchain, in which we can manage funds automatically and securely, without requiring legal recourse or relying on a trusted third party. Moreover, auctions are generally needed for building smart contracts for token sales in ICOs, which is a hot topic that we will cover in `Chapter 8`, *Creating an ICO*.

To summarize, our auction DApp will be a web application that enables users to start in auctions using ether. Let's see what we can throw together:

- First, we will write (in Solidity) and compile the auction contract
- We will interact with our contract through a web page
- We will deploy our smart contract on different environments and set up a local blockchain

Auction description

Let's start with the backend layer, represented by the smart contract that manages the auction. We'll consider the following auction design.

A vehicle's owner deploys the contract to the blockchain and becomes the auction owner. The auction is open immediately after the contract deployment, and, once the bidding period is over, the highest bidder wins the auction, and the other participants withdraw their bids. In this example, the bid will be cumulative, which means that if, for example, you bid 100 ETH, and then someone else bids 110 ETH, you can only send an additional 10.000000000000000001 ETH the next time to outbid them; your new bid is the sum of your two bids.

Furthermore, the auction owner can cancel the auction in exceptional cases, and must also be allowed, at the end of the auction, to withdraw the winning bid. The auction interaction flow is illustrated in the following diagram:

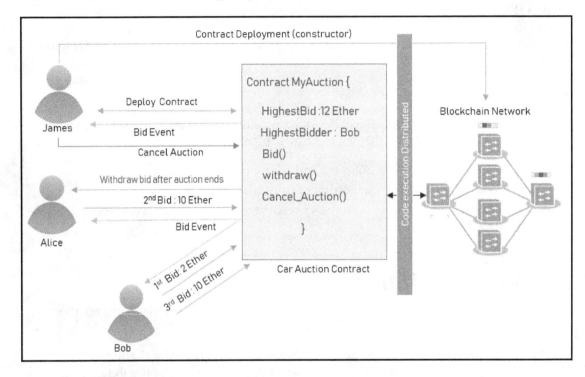

Auction contract in Solidity

To write our auction contract, we will use Solidity, which is the most popular language used to write smart contracts for the Ethereum blockchain. It's a JavaScript-like language, compiled into bytecode running in the Ethereum virtual machine. If you are familiar with object-oriented programming, learning to write Solidity contracts should be fairly straightforward. Through this auction example, I'll try to lay out the basic and important features of Solidity.

Ready, set, go.

Our contract design will be simple. In the first step, we will create an abstract contract, in which we will declare our elementary functions and events. Then, we will use inheritance to create a compliant implementation—a contract with the exact same functions implemented. Abstract contracts help us to decouple the definition of a contract from its implementation, providing better extensibility and code readability.

Start by creating a file called `Auction.sol` (the `.sol` extension refers to Solidity files), and paste in the code of our abstract contract, `Auction`:

```solidity
pragma solidity ^0.4.24;

contract Auction {
    address internal auction_owner;
    uint256 public auction_start;
    uint256 public auction_end;
    uint256 public highestBid;
    address public highestBidder;
    enum auction_state {
        CANCELLED, STARTED
    }

    struct car {
        string  Brand;
        string  Rnumber;
    }

    car public Mycar;
    address[] bidders;
    mapping(address => uint) public bids;
    auction_state public STATE;

    modifier an_ongoing_auction() {
        require(now <= auction_end);
        _;
    }

    modifier only_owner() {
        require(msg.sender == auction_owner);
        _;
    }

    function bid() public payable returns (bool) {}
    function withdraw() public returns (bool) {}
    function cancel_auction() external returns (bool) {}

    event BidEvent(address indexed highestBidder, uint256 highestBid);
    event WithdrawalEvent(address withdrawer, uint256 amount);
```

```
    event CanceledEvent(string message, uint256 time);
}
```

I know this first contract is perhaps enigmatic for you, and maybe it's the first time you have seen a contract of such size (even if it's small). But, don't worry; we will use this first abstract contract as a playground for learning Solidity. In fact, my approach will be to dissect this code line by line and section by section, in order to introduce you to the different major Solidity features.

Contract code analysis

In Solidity, a contract resembles a class in object-oriented languages, and it defines almost all conventional elements: variables, functions, structures, interfaces, libraries, inheritance, and so on.

The first line—`version pragma ^0.4.24;`—is a declaration of Solidity's compiler version that your particular code should use. The caret operator (`^`) indicates that the preceding code will not compile with an earlier compiler, but will compile with both 0.4.24 and any newer version that doesn't introduce any breaking changes.

The second line—`contract Auction {...}`—declares a contract with the name `Auction`.

State variables

In Solidity, we introduce the concept of states, to express variables (used to store information) declared inside of the contract scope and outside of the function scope, similar to the global variable concept in other programming languages. They represent values that are permanently stored in contract storage (on the blockchain); hence, the contract knows their updated values. In general, a state variable in Solidity is declared as follows:

```
<Variable type>  <visibility specifier>  <variable name>
```

In this contract, we'll need to define a set of variables, as follows:

- `auction_owner`: This is an address variable that is used to store the vehicle vendor, who is also the auction's owner. This address is where the winning bid goes after the auction ends.
- `auction_end` and `auction_start`: These represent the auction's start and end epoch times, respectively.

- `highestBid`: This represents the highest amount bid in ether.
- `highestBidder`: This represents the Ethereum address of the highest bidder.
- `bidders`: This is an array of all bidder addresses.
- `Bids`: This is a mapping, matching the address of each bidder with their total bid.
- `STATE`: This represents the auction state, whether it is open or closed (cancelled).

Variable state types

In our code, we used only two basic variable types:

- `uint256`
- `address`

The first represents an unsigned integer of 256 bits. Solidity deals with signed and unsigned integers of various sizes, and to declare an integer, we use one of the keywords, `int` or `uint`, for signed and unsigned integers of 8 to 256 bits (`uint8` to `uint256`, in steps of 8). The type `address` is a dedicated type that holds a 20-byte value (the size of an address), to represent an Ethereum account's address.

Visibility and access modifiers

As you will notice, each variable is preceded by a visibility specifier (`public` or `internal`) that defines the accessibility scope. A `public` state (storage variable) is visible internally and externally (in this case, Solidity creates an implicit public getter for you). An `internal` variable, however, is only accessible within the current contract or contracts deriving from it, not by external calls, making it similar to the `protected` keyword in object-oriented programming languages. By default, variables are `internal`; therefore, the `internal` keyword can be omitted. In order to access an `internal` state, we need to define an explicit public getter function. The following is a getter that we define to read the `auction_owner` as an internal state (we can define this state as public, and avoid such manipulation):

```
address internal auction_owner;

function get_owner() view returns(address) {
    return auction_owner;
}
```

Another access modifier, which is unused in our code, is `private`. This makes the only variable visible within the contract where it is defined, and not in derived contracts.

Enumerations

As in other programming languages, enumerations help us to define our own data type that consists of a list of named constants, to ease reading the code. Here, we define an enumeration representing the auction status, with two possible states: CANCELLED or STARTED.

First, we define our enumeration `auction_state` by using the `enum` keyword, as follows: `enum auction_state { CANCELLED, STARTED }`.

Then, we declare a variable of the `auction_state` type: `auction_state public STATE;`.

The `enum` values are converted into integers and numbered in the order that they are defined, starting at zero. If you want to get the value of your declared `enum` constants, use an explicit conversion `uint(STATE)`. Instead of using the corresponding integer value, you can directly use the `enum` constants, as follows: `auction_state.STARTED` (equals 0) or `auction_state.CANCELLED` (equals 1).

Arrays

Solidity provides three types of data structures: `struct`, `mapping`, and `arrays`.

In our contract, we define a dynamic array to contain all of the bidder addresses. Solidity supports fixed and dynamic sized arrays; therefore, as we don't know the exact number of the bidders a priori, we declare a dynamic array (without fixed length), as follows:

```
address[] bidders;
```

An array of a fixed size n and an element type T is declared as T[n], and an array of dynamic size is declared as T[].

Mappings

A mapping is a special dynamic data structure, similar to a hash table, that maps keys to values. A map cannot contain duplicate keys, because a key is hashed and used as a unique index; thus, each key can map to, at most, one value. You can get the value directly by providing a key, without the need to use indices, like in an array:

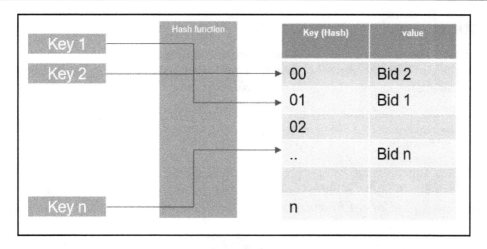

In Solidity, a mapping is declared as a variable by using the mapping keyword, `mapping(KeyType => ValueType)`, where `KeyType` can be almost any type (except for a mapping) and `ValueType` can actually be any type, including further mappings. In our contract, we're creating a mapping that accepts the bidder's address as the key, and with the value type being the corresponding bid:

```
mapping(address => uint) public bids;
```

As with other variables, the mapping can be declared as public, to avoid the need to define a getter for reading its values. Mappings are very useful, as we don't have to manage the indices of the stored elements. For example, to store the bid made by a participant, we use `bids["participant address"] = bid value;`.

Structures

A structure is a collection of variables of different data types, under a single name. As with most programming languages, we define a structure type by using the `struct` keyword. In the following example, we declare a structure with two members:

```
struct car {
    string  Brand;
    string  Rnumber;
}
```

Here, the `struct` represents a car by defining its brand and registration number. We then declare a `car` object by using `car public Mycar;`.

Functions

After defining the auction states, it's time to define the functions that handle the auction's functionalities. In Solidity, a function has the same meaning as in any other language, and is declared using the keyword `function`, as follows:

```
function function_name(<parameter types>)
{internal|external|private|public} [pure|constant|view|payable] [returns
(<return types>)]
```

Like variables, functions can be specified as being `external`, `internal`, `private`, or `public`, while the default visibility is `public`. As our first contract, `auction`, is an abstract contract, we only declare the functions without implementation. They will be implemented later, in a child contract.

Along with the visibility specifier, we can define additional specifiers, such as the following:

- **Constant and view**: These play the same role, and both indicate that the function should not modify the state. The constant keyword, however, is deprecated, and doesn't mean that the function returns a constant result.
- **Pure**: This is more restrictive, and indicates that the function won't even read the storage state.
- **Payable**: This is a keyword that specifies the ability of the function to receive ether.

In this contract, we define the following methods, in order to guarantee the basic auction operations:

- `bid()`: Enables the participant to send their bids in ether, and accordingly, determines the highest bidder. The bidding in our contract is cumulative, which means that if the bidder is no longer the highest bidder, he can only add an additional amount in the next bid.
- `withdraw()`: Enables participants to withdraw their bids once the auction is over.
- `cancel_auction()`: Enables the auction owner to cancel the auction he started.
- `destruct_auction()`: Destroys the auction contract in the blockchain.

Modifiers

One of the most interesting features in Solidity is the function modifiers. They are special control methods that are designated by a special keyword, `modifier`. Their role is to modify the behavior of defined functions, according to specific conditions. For example, they can automatically check a condition prior to executing the function. Consider the two following modifiers:

```
modifier an_ongoing_auction() {
    require(now <= auction_end);
    _;
}

modifier only_owner() {
    require(msg.sender == auction_owner);
    _;
}
```

The first checks whether the auction is still open, whereas the second restricts the authorization to executing a function to the contract's owner (`auction_owner`). The usage of the `only_owner()` modifier makes the contract `ownable`, which is a common smart contract pattern, thereby giving the contract owner specific privileges, similar to an admin in other systems. Generally, in modifiers, we check conditions by using the `require`, `revert`, or `assert` functions. The underscore in the modifier's body will be substituted by the code of the function being modified.

Condition and error verification

Solidity initially used the special keyword `throw` to stop and exit the contract execution when called. Since then, the functions `assert()`, `require()`, and `revert()` have been introduced (in Solidity 0.4.10), in order to enhance the error handling. Although the `throw` function is now being deprecated, you are still able to use it.

With all of these functions in place, we can use them equivalently, as follows:

	if(msg.sender != owner) { throw; }
require(msg.sender == owner);	if(msg.sender != owner) { revert(); }
	assert(msg.sender == owner);

You might have noticed that we have reversed the required conditional statement between, on the one hand, `require()` and `assert()`, and on the other hand, `throw` and `revert()`. In `assert()` and `require()`, we provide the statement that we want to be true, whereas `throw` and `revert()` behave like exit functions that you call when your condition isn't met.

The differences between these functions can be described as follows:

- `assert(bool condition)`: Throws if the condition is not met; this is to be used for internal errors. It uses up all remaining gas and reverts all changes.
- `require(bool condition)`: Throws if the condition is not met; this is to be used for errors in input or external components. Generously, it will refund the remaining gas to the caller.
- `revert()`: Aborts execution and reverts state changes with a gas refund.
- `throw`: Throws and consumes any remaining gas.

As `revert()` and `require()` both refund the unconsumed gas, they should be used to ensure valid conditions, whereas `assert()` should be used to check a harmful statement and to protect your contract, meaning that you can use assert to avoid overflow or underflow. Think of `assert()` as a handbrake that you use when something very wrong has happened, and the other functions as normal brakes.

An important feature that has been introduced in a newer Solidity version (0.4.22) is that you can return an argument to specify the error reason in your `assert` or `require` function:

```
require(msg.sender == owner, "the execution is reserved to the contract's
owner");

if (msg.sender != owner) {
    revert("the execution is reserved to the contract's owner");
}
```

Events

Events allow for the convenient use of the EVM logging facilities. They are an important concept in smart contracts, as any off-chain environment connected to Ethereum's JSON-RPC API can listen to these events and act accordingly.

In general, there are three main use cases for events and logs in DApps:

- To return values from a smart contract to a user interface
- To provide asynchronous triggers with indicative data that we can listen for in the frontend
- As a cheaper form of storage in the blockchain

When they are called, they cause their arguments to be stored in the transaction's log. An event is declared as using the `event` keyword, as follows: `event CanceledEvent(string message, uint256 time);`.

In the declaration, we determine the parameter types that we expect to include in the log. In our case, the previously created event `CanceledEvent` will be emitted once the auction is cancelled and will broadcast a message, **Auction has been cancelled**, with the time of cancellation. We also defined two other events:

- `BidEvent()`: Informs us of a newly registered bid and provides us with the bidder's address and the bid
- `WithdrawalEvent()`: Logs the withdrawal operations, giving the withdrawer's address and the withdrawal amount

As you'll see later when developing the web interface, it is possible to filter for specific values of indexed arguments (using the `indexed` keyword) in the user interface using the filtering functionality of Web 3.0.

So far, we have covered the basic programming constructs (such as variables, data types, and data structure) and introduced the important concept of a contract by defining an abstract contract representing auctions in general. Now, let's move forward and define our main derived contract.

Inheritance

Solidity supports advanced features, such as multiple inheritance, including polymorphism. After writing our abstract class, let's extend our code by writing our second contract (child contract), called `MyAuction`, in the same contract file. It will inherit from the first contract and implement the defined auction functions.

The following is how you declare a derived contract inheriting from our first contract: `contract MyAuction is Auction {..}`.

The keyword is indicates to the compiler that MyAuction is derived from the Auction contract. Hence, the MyAuction contract can access all members, including private functions and storage variables in the Auction contract.

> Instead of defining both contracts in the same Solidity file, you can define the parent in a separate file and import it by using the directive import "filename";.

Constructors

As with object-oriented programming (**OOP**), you can define a constructor for your contract. It's a special function using the same name as the contract it belongs to. Unlike in OOP, a contract's constructor is invoked once and only once during the first deployment to the blockchain, and usually defines the initial contract behavior.

In the MyAuction contract, our constructor is extremely simple:

```
function MyAuction (uint _biddingTime, address _owner, string _brand, string
_Rnumber) public {
    auction_owner = _owner;
    auction_start = now;
    auction_end = auction_start + _biddingTime* 1 hours;
    STATE = auction_state.STARTED;
    Mycar.Brand = _brand;
    Mycar.Rnumber = _Rnumber;
}
```

This constructor, upon creation, sets the relevant states by defining the auction owner, the auction opening and ending date, and the car's details. Consequently, our auction starts immediately, once the contract is deployed. In newer Solidity versions (from the compiler version 0.4.22), you can declare a constructor by using the constructor keyword:

```
constructor(uint _biddingTime, address _owner, string _brand, string
_Rnumber) public {/*code*/}
```

Time in Solidity

As you will notice, in the constructor, we used the keyword now to set the auction start time, whereas the auction's end is calculated by adding to the auction start time a number of hours defined by the _biddingTime argument.

The now keyword is an integer variable that returns the block's timestamp (it's an alias for the special global variable block.timestamp), in which the contract was embedded. Solidity also provides us with some helpful time units (seconds, minutes, hours, days, weeks, and years) that can be applied to a variable as a suffix, to automatically convert a unit to the equivalent time, in seconds. In your constructor, the elapsed number of hours (_biddingTime * 1 hours) is automatically converted to seconds and added to the Linux epoch time provided by the now variable.

We could, alternatively, manage the auction duration by using block numbers instead of the time epoch. In that case, the auction will start once a specific block is mined and stop at a specific future block. For that, you'll use the special variable block.number provided by Solidity, which gives you the current block's number.

Special variables and functions

Earlier, we introduced two special system variables: block.timestamp and block.number. Solidity provides us with a set of global variables and special functions that exist in the global namespace and that are mainly used to provide information about blocks and transactions.

The following is a list from the official documentation:

- block.blockhash(uint blockNumber): Returns a hash of the given block (bytes32)—only works for the 256 most recent blocks, excluding the current block
- block.coinbase (address): Provides the current block miner's address
- block.difficulty (uint): Represents the current block difficulty
- block.gaslimit (uint): Represents the current block gas limit
- block.number (uint): Represents the current block number
- block.timestamp (uint): Represents the current block timestamp, as seconds since Unix epoch
- gasleft() (uint256): Returns the remaining gas
- msg.data (bytes): Represents a copy of calldata
- msg.sender (address): Represents the address of the sender of the message (current call)
- msg.sig (bytes4): Represents the first four bytes of calldata (that is, function identifier)
- msg.value (uint): Represents the number of wei sent with the message

- `tx.gasprice (uint)`: Represents the gas price of the transaction
- `tx.origin (address)`: Represents the sender of the transaction

The values of all attributes of the `msg` object, including `msg.sender` and `msg.value`, vary for every external function call according to the sender and the amount carried by the transaction. In our constructor, we can provide the auction owner as an argument, using `msg.sender` to directly set the sender of the deployment transaction as the owner:
`auction_owner = msg.sender;`.

The fallback function

In Solidity, there is another special method, which is the fallback function. It's an unnamed function that cannot have arguments, nor return anything, and it is declared as follows:
`function () public payable { }.`

The fallback function is executed if the contract is called and no function in the contract matches the specified function's signature. This is not a mandatory function to declare, but you can include it, in order to define your contract's behavior when it receives transactions without data. To accepts funds, you have to declare it as `payable`.

> If your contract will be called by another contract, you can't put much code into your fallback function. At most, you can define an event log, as for security reasons, it only has access to a 2,300 gas stipend.

Function overloading

At this level, we need to overload the functions in the child contract, `MyAuction`, that we defined earlier in the abstract contract, `Auction`. In order to achieve that goal, we need to keep the same name and declaration (the same visibility and return type) as in the `Auction` contract and then define the function's body. You'll overload the function in the sequence in which they were defined in the abstract contract, as follows.

The bidding function

Let's start by defining the bidding function, which will allow participants to place bids in ether (wei):

```
function bid() public payable an_ongoing_auction returns (bool){
    require(bids[msg.sender] + msg.value > highestBid, "can't bid, Make a
higher Bid");
```

```
        highestBidder = msg.sender;
        highestBid = msg.value;
        bidders.push(msg.sender);
        bids[msg.sender] = bids[msg.sender] + msg.value;
        emit BidEvent(highestBidder, highestBid);
        return true;
    }
```

Nothing is different from the original declaration; we only add a modifier at the end of the function declaration, to enable its execution only during the auction period; otherwise, an exception will be raised. As I have stated repeatedly, the `payable` keyword enables the function to receive ether carried by the bidding transactions.

In the body of the `bid()` function, we initially check whether the total of the bids sent by a participant is higher than the highest bid, using `require(bids[msg.sender] + msg.value > highestBid);`.

Depending on how much ether the bidder sends, either they will be the new highest bidder or their bid will be refused. If the bid was successful, the contract will fire the `BidEvent` event, to announce the new highest bid and bidder. In the newer Solidity versions, you can use the `emit` keyword to fire an event.

Before emitting the event, we add the bidder's address to the array of participants, using the `push` function. Afterwards, we update the participant's bid in our mapping bids: `bids[msg.sender] = bids[msg.sender] + msg.value;`.

At the end, this function returns `true` to indicate a successful execution (bidding). We will use this return pattern in all other functions.

Canceling an auction

Wouldn't it be logical to enable the auction owner to cancel the auction?

Such a function should be executed exclusively by the auction owner, while the auction is still open; thus, we use the modifiers `only_owner` and `an_ongoing_auction`:

```
    function cancel_auction() only_owner an_ongoing_auction returns (bool) {
        STATE = auction_state.CANCELLED;
        CanceledEvent("Auction Cancelled", now);
        return true;
    }
```

This function will change the state of the auction status to `Cancelled`, using the enum value `auction_state.CANCELLED` we defined earlier, and the event `CanceledEvent` will be fired announcing the auction cancellation.

Withdrawing bids

After the auction ends, you'll need to enable bidders to get their ether back. For security reasons, it's better to adopt a withdrawal pattern—this helps us to avoid security issues that could cause funds to be lost:

```
function withdraw() public returns (bool){
    require(now > auction_end , "can't withdraw, Auction is still open");
    uint amount = bids[msg.sender];
    bids[msg.sender] = 0;
    msg.sender.transfer(amount);
    WithdrawalEvent(msg.sender, amount);
    return true;
}
```

There is nothing new here except, as you might have noticed, the use of a new function, `transfer()`. Along with another function, `send()`, both methods enable the contract to send funds to a designated address (`msg.sender`). In this case, the contract sends the corresponding bid amount back to the withdrawal requester's address.

Notice that we're following the recommended pattern for functions that send ETH:

- Check preconditions
- Send ether and throw if the send fails (roll back method execution)
- Emit a log event and return `true`

You might be wondering why we don't just define a function that automatically refunds all participants once the auction is over, a function similar to the following:

```
function payback_participants() internal returns (bool){
    uint256 payback = 0;
    for (uint256 i = 0; i < bidders.length; i++)
    {
        if (bids[bidders[i]] > 0) {
            payback = bids[bidders[i]];
            bids[bidders[i]] = 0;
            bidders[i].transfer(payback);
        }
    }
    return true;
}
```

Well, it's a risky anti-pattern. You should know that `send` or `transfer` methods can actually fail (for different reasons) and therefore, the payment loop won't end by successfully paying back all of the participants. For example, a malicious user that bid only 1 wei from a contract with a non-payable fallback can block the refund process by making the transfer method fail (and therefore throw) forever, meaning that the loop will never get executed completely.

Contract destruction

At this final step, let's have some fun.

What about introducing a nuclear launch button in our contract that, once pushed by the auction owner, will make the contract disappear from the blockchain? The contract destruction will be ensured by the `destruct_auction()` method, which can be invoked if all participants have withdrawn their bids, as follows:

```
function destruct_auction() external only_owner returns (bool) {
    require(now > auction_end, "You can't destruct the contract,The auction
is still open");
    for (uint i = 0; i < bidders.length; i++)
    {
        assert(bids[bidders[i]] == 0);
    }
    selfdestruct(auction_owner);
    return true;
}
```

The first thing that we can see here is that Solidity defines for-loops like standard languages, and you can access the length of a dynamic size array by using the `.length` member.

More importantly, Solidity defines a special function, `selfdestruct(address)`, to destroy the current contract (it will no longer be accessible) and send all its funds to the address given as the argument. This is a space- and cost-saving feature as, when you are finished with a contract, it will cost you far less gas using `selfdestruct` than just sending the contract funds using `address.transfer(this.balance)`.

But wait! Isn't the blockchain immutable?

The answer needs a little dive into the Ethereum block structure, which is out of the scope of this book. However, it's worth noting that the `selfdestruct` method clears all the contract's data, and frees up space from the current and future state tree (the mapping between the contract's account and its states), but not from the previous blocks. The contract bytecode will remain in an old block but its account will no longer be accessible in the state tree; therefore, the data is still immutable. In other words, after calling `selfdestruct`, the state tree will be updated without the destroyed contract states.

> In old Solidity code, you will notice the use of the `suicide(address recipient)` method, which is used as an alias to `selfdestruct`.

All set! We have finished our auction smart contract. Now let's enjoy compiling and running our first achievement.

Remix IDE

As we'll see later in this chapter, different tools and options are available to compile and deploy smart contracts. But at this level, we don't want to waste time in setting up complicated tools, or our environment. Thankfully, the Ethereum project provides us with the Remix web browser IDE (also known as Browser-Solidity), which is an online IDE that can be used to compile, deploy, and invoke smart contracts.

Let's make our way over to Remix by visiting `https://remix.ethereum.org/`, then paste the complete contract code into a new contract file. To make it easier for you, I have published the code on GitHub, under the link `https://github.com/bellaj/Car_Auction`:

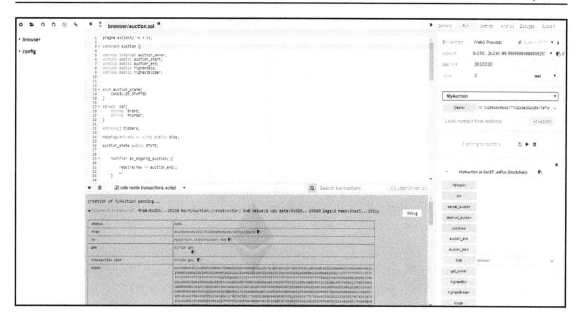

After pasting the code into Remix, you can compile it by pressing the **Start to compile** button:

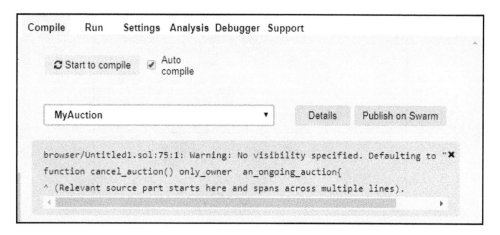

You might get some warnings (sometimes irrelevant), but if it compiles without any errors, you can visualize the result of the compilation process by pressing the **Details** button. Among other things, you'll get a list of contract details, ranging from metadata and bytecode to ABI, and even our contract's web3.js deployment code. There is an auto-compile option, which if checked will make Remix recompile the contract each time you edit the code.

Due to breaking changes introduced with the newer Solidity compiler +V0.5 (used by default), you have to downgrade the compiler version used by Remix to a prior version (for example 0.4.25+) in order to run the presented code without error . The process to achieve that is presented in the official documentation (`https://remix.readthedocs.io/en/latest/settings_tab.html`).

On the upper-right side of our screen, we have several tabs. The **Settings**, **Debugger**, **Analysis**, and **Support** tabs all have their use cases and are worth exploring. We're going to be using the **Run** tab. When you select it, you'll see a few different contract settings that we need to define, as shown here:

Under the **Run** tab, you'll have a panel of two forms. The first helps you to define the following settings:

- **Environment**: Represents the deployment environment to which you want to connect Remix. At this level, you'll choose the JavaScript VM option to simulate an EVM in your browser.
- **Account**: A set of virtual accounts that generated and funded with 100 virtual ether each.
- **Gas limit**: Specifies the maximum gas you are willing to pay for the transaction (leave it unchanged).
- **Value**: Represents the amount of ether that you are willing to send in your transaction (leave it at zero for the deployment).

The second form is dedicated to deploying the contract. The first element is a drop-down list to select which contract you want to deploy, in case you have multiple declared contracts in your file code. In our case, we have to select the child contract (`MyAuction`) not the main contract (`Auction`). Just below ,you have the **Deploy** button to deploy your contract and a text input to provide the constructor's arguments (comma-separated). In our case, we will need to provide the auction duration time in hours, the address of the auction's owner, and the car's brand and registration number, for example:

```
1,"0xca35b7d915458ef540ade6068dfe2f44e8fa733c","ferrari","IS2012"
```

 If you need to provide an address (to set the owner, for example), you can copy the address of one of the virtual accounts from the first section using the small copy button located to the right of the account drop-down list.

The last thing to mention is that if you want to interact with an already deployed contract, you can use the **At Address** button by providing the contract's address.

Once the deployment is successful, you'll get a form representing your contract methods and states' as shown here:

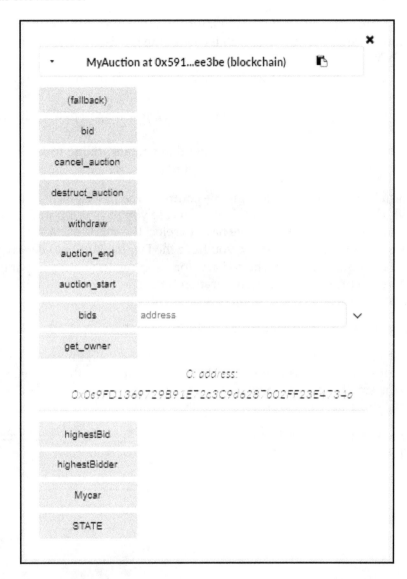

In contrast to the red button, the blue one means that you can read a variable or execute a function without initiating a transaction as it represents `public` variables, and `pure` or `view` functions. Therefore, the constructor is executed and the auction is opened and lives at a virtual address in the memory.

Finally, let's bid. To execute the `bid()` function, enter in the **value** field in the **transaction** section the amount of your bid in a specific ether unit, then press the red bid button. To simulate multiple bidders, you can bid using a different virtual account each time. Once the function is executed, you'll get information about the status and result of your bid action, displayed in Remix's log panel. If you click on the **Details** button, it will provide you with further details, as follows:

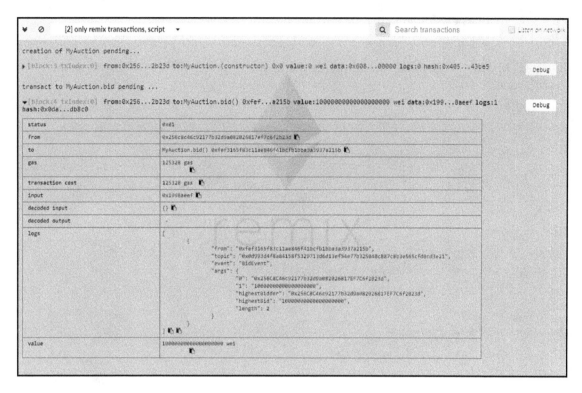

Notice there are the transaction cost and execution cost, which represent an estimation of the execution fee that senders of transactions (in our case, the bidder) will pay for bidding; they can be defined as follows:

- **Transaction cost:** This is the cost (in units of gas) of sending the transaction, which depends on the data size that it's carrying (function call and parameters)
- **Execution cost:** This is the cost (in units of gas) of the computational operations which are executed as a result of the transaction instructions

If everything is fine (no out-of-gas or any other kind of error), you can start creating the frontend side—a bidding form.

Bidding form in web3.js

After a first validation of the auction contract using Remix, it's time to move to the frontend and build a simple web interface that allows participants to interact with the auction. Ethereum is JavaScript-friendly, so you can build your DApp's interfaces using whatever JavaScript framework you prefer: JQuery, ReactJS, or AngularJS.

First off, create a new folder called DAPP/, inside of which you create two files: index.html and auction.js.

In the HTML file, we'll create a bidding form and a display board. The following is the HTML code:

```
<html>
<script src="https://code.jquery.com/jquery-3.2.1.min.js"></script>
<link rel="stylesheet"
href="https://maxcdn.bootstrapcdn.com/bootstrap/3.3.5/css/bootstrap.min.css
">
<script
src="https://maxcdn.bootstrapcdn.com/bootstrap/3.3.5/js/bootstrap.min.js"><
/script>
<script
src="https://cdn.rawgit.com/ethereum/web3.js/develop/dist/web3.js"></script
>
<script src="./auction.js"></script>
</head>

<body onload="init()">
  <div class="col-lg-12">
    <div class="page-header">
      <h3>Car Auction Dapp</h3>
    </div>
    <div class="col-lg-6">
      <div class="well">
        <div>
          <legend class="lead">Car Details</legend>
          <label class="lead"> Brand: </label>
          <text id='car_brand'></text>
          <br>
          <label class="lead">Registration Number: </label>
          <text id='registration_number'></text>
        </div>
        <legend class="lead">Bid value</legend>
        <small>eg. 100</small>
        <div class="form-group">
          <input class="form-control" type="text" id="value" value="10"
></input>
```

```
            <text id="valueValidation"></text>
          </div>
          <div>
            <button class="btn btn-default" id="transfer" type="button"
onClick="bid()">Bid!</button>
            <br>
            <text id="biding_status"></text>
          </div>
        </div>
      </div>
      <div class="col-lg-6">
        <div class="well">
          <div>
            <legend class="lead">Auction Details</legend>
          </div>
          <div>
            <ul id='transfers'>
              <li>
                <label class="lead">Auction End: </label>
                <text id="auction_end"></text>
              </li>
              <li>
                <label class="lead">Auction Highest Bid: </label>
                <text id="HighestBid"></text>
              </li>
              <li>
                <label class="lead">My Bid: </label>
                <text id="MyBid"></text>
              </li>
              <li>
                <label class="lead">Auction Highest Bider: </label>
                <text id="HighestBidder"></text>
              </li>
              <li>
                <label class="lead">Auction Status: </label>
                <text id="STATE"></text>
              </li>
            </ul>
          </div>
          <br>
          <div>
            <legend class="lead">Events Logs </legend>
            <text id="eventslog"></text>
          </div>
        </div>
      </div>
    </div>
```

```html
        <div class="col-lg-6" id="auction_owner_operations">
          <div class="well">
            <div>
              <legend class="lead">Auction Operations</legend>
              <button class="btn btn-default" id="transfer" type="button"
    onClick="cancel_auction()">Cancel auction!</button>
              <button class="btn btn-default" id="transfer" type="button"
    onClick="Destruct_auction()">Destruct auction!</button>
            </div>
          </div>
        </div>
    </body>

</html>
```

I assume you are familiar with HTML; therefore I'll avoid explaining what all these tags mean. In the preceding code, we have introduced four JavaScript functions, namely `bid()`, `init()`, `destruct_auction()`, and `cancel_auction ()`, which need to be defined in the separate `auction.js` file, in order to represent the basic auction operations.

The other important part is the line importing the `Web3Js` library:

```html
<script
src="https://cdn.rawgit.com/ethereum/web3.js/develop/dist/web3.js"></script
>
```

Introduction to the web3.js API

Ethereum provides us with web3.js, which is a useful API to make the web developer's life easier. This JavaScript API enables us to communicate with an Ethereum node using JSON RPC endpoints exposed on top of HTTP, WebSocket, and/or IPC transports from a web page.

In `auction.js`, copy and paste the following code, so we can walk through it step by step while introducing the main web3.js features:

```javascript
var web3 = new Web3();
web3.setProvider(new web3.providers.HttpProvider("http://localhost:8545"));
var bidder = web3.eth.accounts[0];
web3.eth.defaultAccount = bidder;
var auctionContract = web3.eth.contract("Here the contract's ABI"); // ABI
omitted to make the code concise

function bid() {
    var mybid = document.getElementById('value').value;
```

```
        auction.bid({
            value: web3.toWei(mybid, "ether"),
            gas: 200000
        }, function(error, result) {
            if (error) {
                console.log("error is " + error);
                document.getElementById("biding_status").innerHTML = "Think to
bidding higher";
            } else {
                document.getElementById("biding_status").innerHTML =
"Successfull bid, transaction ID" + result;
            }
        });
    }

    function init() {
        auction.auction_end(function(error, result) {
            document.getElementById("auction_end").innerHTML = result;
        });
        auction.highestBidder(function(error, result) {
            document.getElementById("HighestBidder").innerHTML = result;
        });
        auction.highestBid(function(error, result) {
            var bidEther = web3.fromWei(result, 'ether');
            document.getElementById("HighestBid").innerHTML = bidEther;
        });
        auction.STATE(function(error, result) {
            document.getElementById("STATE").innerHTML = result;
        });
        auction.Mycar(function(error, result) {
            document.getElementById("car_brand").innerHTML = result[0];
            document.getElementById("registration_number").innerHTML =
result[1];
        });
        auction.bids(bidder, function(error, result) {
            var bidEther = web3.fromWei(result, 'ether');
            document.getElementById("MyBid").innerHTML = bidEther;
            console.log(bidder);
        });
    }

    var auction_owner = null;
    auction.get_owner(function(error, result) {
        if (!error) {
            auction_owner = result;
            if (bidder != auction_owner) {
                $("#auction_owner_operations").hide();
            }
```

```javascript
    }
});

function cancel_auction() {
    auction.cancel_auction(function(error, result) {
        console.log(result);
    });
}

function Destruct_auction() {
    auction.destruct_auction(function(error, result) {
        console.log(result);
    });
}

var BidEvent = auction.BidEvent();
BidEvent.watch(function(error, result) {
    if (!error) {
        $("#eventslog").html(result.args.highestBidder + ' has bidden(' +
result.args.highestBid + ' wei)');
    } else {
        console.log(error);
    }
});

var CanceledEvent = auction.CanceledEvent();
CanceledEvent.watch(function(error, result) {
    if (!error) {
        $("#eventslog").html(result.args.message + ' at ' +
result.args.time);
    }
});

const filter = web3.eth.filter({
    fromBlock: 0,
    toBlock: 'latest',
    address: contractAddress,
    topics: [web3.sha3('BidEvent(address,uint256)')]
});

filter.get((error, result) => {
    if (!error) console.log(result);
});
```

Step 1 – talking to the blockchain

Web3Js provides the web3 object that enables us to exploit the Web3 API functions in JavaScript. Therefore, the first action to take is to instantiate a web3 object as follows: var web3 = new Web3();

This object needs to be connected to an RPC provider to communicate with the blockchain. We set a local or remote web3 provider using web3.setProvider(new web3.providers.HttpProvider("http://RPC_IP:RPC_Port"));, where RPC_IP is the RPC provider's IP and RPC_Port is its RPC port.

Step 2 – interaction with the smart contract

Web3 also provides a JavaScript object, web3.eth.Contract, which represents your deployed contract. To find and interact with your newly deployed contract on the blockchain, this object needs to know the contract's address and its **application binary interface (ABI)**:

```
var auctionContract = web3.eth.contract("your contract's ABI");
var auction = auctionContract.at("contract address");
```

The ABI

For many, the ABI is a slightly confusing concept. The ABI is essentially a JSON object containing a detailed description (using a special data-encoding scheme) of the functions and their arguments, which describes how to call them in the bytecode.

Based on the ABI, the web3.js will convert all calls into low-level calls over RPC that the EVM can understand. In other words, web3.js needs to know some information (in a predefined format) about the functions and variables, in order to generate instructions that can be interpreted by an Ethereum node (EVM), and to get you the result back in a human-readable way. The EVM doesn't know about function names or variables, it processes only the data as a sequence of bytes accordingly to predefined rules. For example, the first four bytes in a transaction payload specify the signature of the called function, hence the need for an ABI that helps any API or tool to generate a transaction with correct low-level payloads and to read returned values by the contract.

Call versus send transactions

In our JavaScript script, we define the following functions previously called in the HTML file:

- `init()`: Serves to read contract states and display auction details such as the current highest bid and bidder, the auction status and more
- `bid()`: Enables participants to make a bid
- `cancel_auction()`: Enables the owner to cancel the auction
- `destruct_auction()`: Destroys the contract

Each of these functions invokes methods defined in your contract. In Ethereum, there are two ways to invoke a method present in a smart contract, whether by addressing a function call or by sending a transaction.

Invoking contract methods via a call

A call is a contract instance invocation that doesn't change the contract state, and includes calling `view` or `pure` functions or reading public states. The call only runs on the EVM of your local node and saves you the expensive gas as there is no need for broadcasting the transaction. In your `init()` function, we need exactly that, as we only have to read the contract states. We can call a method `foo()` on the local blockchain without having to send out a transaction using `myContractInstance.foo.call(arg1,arg2...)`.

Invoking contract methods via a transaction

To change the state of the contract instance, instead of making a call, you need to send a transaction that costs you real money (gas) to validate your action.

For instance, to invoke the `bid()` method, you have to send a transaction to the blockchain network with the necessary arguments and fees. Just like with the call, to invoke the `foo()` method, you need to explicitly make the invocation using `sendTransaction()` as follows:

```
myContractInstance.foo.sendTransaction(param1 [, param2, ...] [,
transactionObject] [, callback]);
```

Why not let Web3 decide for you!

Web3.js is smart enough to automatically determine the use of call or `sendTransaction` based on the method type indicated in the ABI, therefore you can directly use the following:

```
auction.bid({value: web3.toWei(mybid, "ether"), gas: 200000},
function(error, result){...});
```

In general, to execute a function `foo(argument1, argument2)`, we use the following:

```
auction.foo(argument1, argument2,{Transaction object},
fallback_function{...});
```

Here, `auction` is a web3.js contract object. In the invocation, we provide the following arguments in the following order:

- The contract's function arguments.
- A transaction object that represents details of the transaction that will execute the function (source, destination, amount of ether, gas, gas price, data). As the address for the sending account, we use the coinbase that is the default account that the Ethereum client will use. You can have as many accounts as you want and set one of them as a coinbase.
- At the end, we define a callback function which will be executed once the transaction is validated.

In your `bid()` function, the bid amount is specified in the transaction object, while in the UI form, the bidder will specify the amount in ether, therefore we will need to convert the bid into wei by using `web3.toWei(mybid, "ether")`.

Callbacks

Web3.js is designed to work with a local RPC node, and all of its functions use synchronous HTTP requests by default. If you want to make an asynchronous request, you can pass an optional callback as the last parameter to most functions. All callbacks us an error-first callback pattern, as follows:

```
web3.eth.foo(argument1,..,argumentn, function(error, result) {
    if (!error) {
        console.log(result);
    }
});
```

Reading state variables

As reading the public state doesn't change any information in the blockchain, it can be performed locally using a call. For example, to read the auction's `highestbid` variable, you can use `auction.highestBid.call();`.

Watching events

One more important thing to take care of in your frontend is handling events. Your DApp should be able to listen for fired events by applying the function `watch()` to the expected event to detect changes, or `get()` to read a specific log. The following code shows an example of event watching:

```
var CanceledEvent = auction.CanceledEvent();
CanceledEvent.watch(function(error, result) {
    if (!error) {
        $("#eventslog").html(result.args.message + ' at ' +
result.args.time);
    }
});
```

Each time a new bid is received by the contract, the callback function will display the log.

Indexing events and filtering

In our auction smart contract, we used the indexed argument in `BidEvent()` declaration for a clever reason:

```
event BidEvent(address indexed highestBidder, uint256 highestBid);
```

When you use the `indexed` keyword in your event, your Ethereum node will internally index arguments to build on indexable search log, making it searchable, meaning you can easily perform a lookup by value later on.

Suppose that the event was emitted by the `MyAuction` contract with the arguments `BidEvent(26, "bidder's address");`. In this case, a low-level EVM log with multiple entries will be generated with two topics and a data field as shown in the following browser console screenshot:

The topics and data fields are as follows:

- Topics:
    - **The event signature**: The large hex number
      0d993d4f8a84158f5329713d6d13ef54e77b325040c887c8b3e5
      65cfd0cd3e21 is equal to the Keccak-256 hash of `BidEvent (address, uint256)`
    - **HighestBidder**: The bidder's address, ABI-encoded
- Data:
    - Highest bid value, ABI-encoded

> **TIP**
> The `indexed` attribute can be granted to up to three arguments and will cause the respective arguments to be treated as log topics instead of data.

As you know, logs tend to be much larger and sometimes longer. In web3.js, you can filter data in your contract's log by simply applying a `filter` as follows:

```
var contractAddress="0x00..."
const filter = web3.eth.filter({fromBlock: 1000000,toBlock:
'latest',address: contractAddress,topics: [web3.sha3('BidEvent(address,
uint256)')]})
filter.get((error, result) => {
    if (!error) {
        console.log(result);
    }
});
```

The preceding filter will give you all the log entries for the `BidEvent` event corresponding to your filtering object, in which we define the blocks (`fromBlock`, `toBlock`) to read the log from, along with the account address and the event we are interested in. To listen for state changes that fit the previous filter and call a callback, you can use the `watch` method instead, as follows:

```
filter.watch(function(error, result) {
    if (!error) {
        console.log(result);
    }
});
```

To stop and uninstall the filter, you can use the `stopWatching` method: `filter.stopWatching();`

As shown in the preceding screenshot, the log outputs are ABI-encoded, and to decode a log receipt, you can use `decodeParameter` available in `web3Js 1.0` as follows:

```
web3.eth.abi.decodeParameter('uint256',
'0000000000000000000000001829d79cce6aa43d13e67216b355e81a7fffb220')
```

Alternatively, you can use an external library such as `https://github.com/ConsenSys/abi-decoder`.

Numbers in Ethereum and floating point

You might be surprised to learn that the Ethereum VM doesn't support floating point numbers. Discussing the reasons behind that choice is out of the scope of this book, so let's focus on how to deal with this limitation, in order to enable bidding in floating point numbers.

In Ethereum, we can overcome this issue by using the system used to represent different units of ether. In this system, the smallest denomination or base unit of ether is called wei (Ether=10^{18} wei) along with other units:

- 10^9 wei = 1 Shannon
- 10^{12} wei = 1 Szabo
- 10^{15} wei = 1 Finney

Although we didn't set the units of any bids in the contract, the received bids will be counted in wei. This will help us to accept floating point numbers, as they will become integers after being multiplied by 10^{18}. For instance, 1234.56789 ether will be represented as 123456789E+14 wei. While the bid is done through the auction form in ether and stored in the contract in wei, to display back the bid's value in ether, we convert from wei to ether using `var value = web3.fromWei('21000000000000', 'ether');`.

Transaction status receipt

Since the Byzantium Fork, it's been possible to find out whether a transaction was successful. Indeed, you can check the transaction status using the following:

```
var receipt =
web3.eth.getTransactionReceipt(transaction_hash_from_60_minutes_ago);
```

It returns a set of information including a status field, which has a value of zero when a transaction has failed and 1(0x1) when the transaction has succeeded (it has been mined).

Great!

So far, we have tested our contract and our user interface is ready to interact with it. We now have to assemble the puzzle pieces. To get our DApp working, we need to deploy our contract in a test environment other than Remix's VM JavaScript that we used earlier.

Deployment environment – multiple ways to enjoy!

In Ethereum, we have multiple ways to deploy a smart contract without spending real ether. In this section, we will present how to set up and deploy your contract in the following testing environments:

- Ganache and Remix
- Testnet
- Private network

Option 1 – Ganache

If you're looking for a testing blockchain with a graphical
interface, Ganache (previously TestRpc) is for you. It's an in-memory blockchain (think of it
as a blockchain simulator) that runs locally.

Download and install it from the official Ganache repository (`https://github.com/trufflesuite/ganache/releases`) for the appropriate version for your OS.

When you run Ganache, you will get a graphical screen showing some details about the
server, the blocks created, transactions, and a list of created accounts, each loaded with 100
ether:

To interact with Ganache, you can use Remix, but this time, you have to specify a new
web3 provider with Ganache's IP and RPC port; for example, `http://localhost:7545` (if
you have connection troubles, try to use Remix over HTTP, not HTTPS):

Once Remix is connected to Ganache, deploy your smart contract as you did earlier and start bidding through Remix. In Ganache's interface, you'll be able to visualize the transactions and the created blocks:

If you think Ganache is enough for you, you can stop here and jump directly to the Running the auction DApp section, in order to run the auction DApp using Ganache. However, if you're interested in learning about other possible deployment environments so you can choose the suitable one for you, continue reading.

Option 2 – Testnet

Similar to bitcoin, Ethereum's Testnet is a public network dedicated to testing developers' contracts online without using real ether. You can join this network without the need to run a full node, by using a plugin called MetaMask on your browser. Let's see how it's possible.

Connecting MetaMask to Testnet

MetaMask is a browser plugin that allows your normal browser to behave as a web3 browser, to interact with DApps, and to send transactions without running an Ethereum node. MetaMask achieves this by injecting the web3js API into every web page's JavaScript context.

The necessary instructions for installing and setting up MetaMask are well documented on their official website, at: https://metamask.io. After the process of wallet creation, switch to the Ropsten test network in MetaMask's settings by clicking on the network selector located on the upper left corner. Once you're connected to Ropsten, you'll need to get some free worthless ether by choosing to buy some coins as shown in the following screenshot:

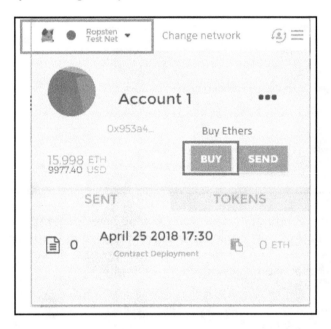

MetaMask can be connected to any RPC provider locally (Ganache, Geth) or online (testnet, Mainnet). For a detailed step-by-step guide to using MetaMask, I point you to the official documentation available at https://github.com/MetaMask/faq/blob/master/USERS.md.

All set; now, go back to your Remix browser (you may need to refresh it) and select (in Remix) injected web3 as the environment option, in order to deploy your contract directly online. MetaMask will initiate the deployment transaction and give you back the contract address:

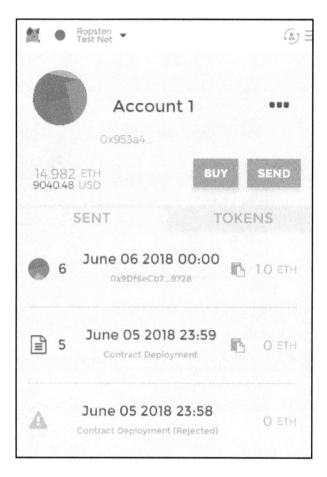

MetaMask provides an Ethereum Etherscan link for each transaction, in order to visualize, among other details, the transaction status and gas cost:

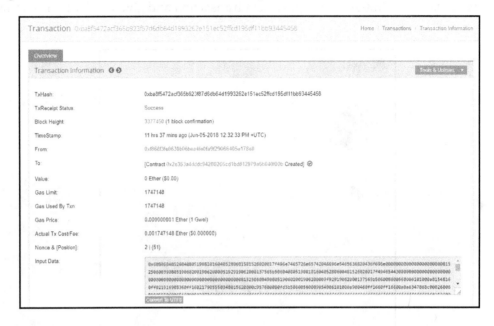

Voila! The contract is easily deployed in the testnet.

Alternatively, you can connect Remix to the testnet by setting up a light node connected to the testnet network as explained in the next section. To test your auction web page using MetaMask, you have to add the following code snippet to the beginning of your `auction.js` file to detect MetaMask's injected web3 instance:

```
if (typeof web3 !== 'undefined') {
    App.web3Provider = web3.currentProvider;
    web3 = new Web3(web3.currentProvider);
} else {
    // change to your RPC provider IP and Port
    App.web3Provider = new
web3.providers.HttpProvider('http://127.0.0.1:7545');
    web3 = new Web3(App.web3Provider);
}
```

Instead using only `web3.setProvider(new web3.providers.HttpProvider("http://127.0.0.1:8545"));` as we did earlier in section *talking to the blockchain*.

The testnet network is very helpful as it gives you an accurate idea of the delay processing and cost of your transactions. However, the implied delay time and limited ether won't be helpful for developers who regularly change their DApp's code, hence the following third option or Ganache is more suitable as a starting environment. You can then you move to this testnet option before going into production on the Mainnet.

Option 3 – private network

Despite the ease of using the previous environment, which abstracts away all the details, it is still good to know how things work at a granular level. Besides, you might face the need to deploy private Ethereum blockchains for private entities to use in production, or during the software development process.

Let's set up our private Ethereum network (a kind of localhost), composed of two running nodes on the same machine.

Geth installation

To start, you'll need to install an Ethereum client, for example Geth (Golang Ethereum client). You'll find the instructions to install Geth for your operating system on the Ethereum repository on GitHub (`https://github.com/ethereum/go-ethereum/wiki/Installing-Geth`). For Ubuntu, you can install the Geth client using the following command:

```
sudo add-apt-repository -y ppa:ethereum/ethereum
sudo apt-get update
sudo apt-get install ethereum
```

For this local network, we will be running two nodes (on the same machine), therefore we need to create two different folders to host their blockchain copies and wallets. Create a directory called `Mytestnet` with the following two subdirectories:

```
~/Mytestnet
 |-- nodeA
 |-- nodeB
```

Creating new accounts

We will create new accounts for our new network. Note that an account is not tied to any specific chain, it's just a private/public key pair.

Change directory to the newly created folder `Mytestnet` and run the following commands:

```
geth account new --datadir nodeA
geth account new --datadir nodeB
```

Repeat the same command to get different accounts on both nodes that we will use to interact with the contract as bidders. Geth will print out the address for each user, so think of saving these addresses in a file, in order to use them later.

You can list the created account for node A or B by using `geth account list --datadir nodeA/nodeB`:

```
user@ByExample-node: ~/Mytestnet
user@ByExample-node:~$ mkdir Mytestnet
user@ByExample-node:~$ cd Mytestnet/
user@ByExample-node:~/Mytestnet$ mkdir nodeA
user@ByExample-node:~/Mytestnet$ mkdir nodeB
user@ByExample-node:~/Mytestnet$ geth account new --datadir nodeA
WARN [06-04|13:40:08] No etherbase set and no accounts found as default
Your new account is locked with a password. Please give a password. Do not forge
t this password.
Passphrase:
Repeat passphrase:
Address: {0e9fd1369729b91e72c3c9d6287b02ff23e4734a}
user@ByExample-node:~/Mytestnet$ geth account new --datadir nodeB
WARN [06-04|13:40:19] No etherbase set and no accounts found as default
Your new account is locked with a password. Please give a password. Do not forge
t this password.
Passphrase:
Repeat passphrase:
Address: {1f00d3ff65d0709be473f8798f81498d0ee761f7}
user@ByExample-node:~/Mytestnet$ geth account list  --datadir nodeA
Account #0: {0e9fd1369729b91e72c3c9d6287b02ff23e4734a} keystore:///home/user/Myt
estnet/nodeA/keystore/UTC--2018-06-04T13-40-12.571747847Z--0e9fd1369729b91e72c3c
9d6287b02ff23e4734a
user@ByExample-node:~/Mytestnet$
```

Genesis file

As you know, each blockchain starts with a genesis block and keeps building on top of it. Therefore, before running your private network, you first have to prepare your own genesis block by defining a genesis file.

You can easily create new genesis files with a command-line tool called `puppeth`, which is a private blockchain manager that comes as a utility with Ggeth. Run `puppeth` and follow the configuration wizard. You'll need to answer a few questions as shown in the following screenshot:

```
⊗ ⊙ ⊙    user@ByExample-node: ~/Mytestnet
user@ByExample-node:~/Mytestnet$ puppeth
+---------------------------------------------------------+
| Welcome to puppeth, your Ethereum private network manager |
|                                                         |
| This tool lets you create a new Ethereum network down to |
| the genesis block, bootnodes, miners and ethstats servers |
| without the hassle that it would normally entail.       |
|                                                         |
| Puppeth uses SSH to dial in to remote servers, and builds |
| its network components out of Docker containers using the |
| docker-compose toolset.                                 |
+---------------------------------------------------------+

Please specify a network name to administer (no spaces, please)
> Mytestnet
Sweet, you can set this via --network=Mytestnet next time!

INFO [06-04|13:50:39] Administering Ethereum network          name=Mytestnet
WARN [06-04|13:50:39] No previous configurations found        path=/home/user
peth/Mytestnet

What would you like to do? (default = stats)
 1. Show network stats
 2. Configure new genesis
 3. Track new remote server
 4. Deploy network components
> 2

Which consensus engine to use? (default = clique)
 1. Ethash - proof-of-work
 2. Clique - proof-of-authority
> 1

Which accounts should be pre-funded? (advisable at least one)
> 0x1f00d3ff65d0709be473f8798f81498d0ee761f7
> 0x0e9fd1369729b91e72c3c9d6287b02ff23e4734a
> 0x


Specify your chain/network ID if you want an explicit one (default = random)
> 1234

Anything fun to embed into the genesis block? (max 32 bytes)
>

What would you like to do? (default = stats)
 1. Show network stats
 2. Manage existing genesis
 3. Track new remote server
 4. Deploy network components
> 2


 1. Modify existing fork rules
 2. Export genesis configuration
> 2

Which file to save the genesis into? (default = Mytestnet.json)
> genesis.json
INFO [06-04|13:51:36] Exported existing genesis block

What would you like to do? (default = stats)
 1. Show network stats
 2. Manage existing genesis
 3. Track new remote server
 4. Deploy network components
> ▊
```

When it asks you about accounts to pre-fund, give it the addresses that were created earlier. At the end of the process, save the genesis file as a JSON file, `genesis.json`:

```
user@ByExample-node: ~/Mytestnet
user@ByExample-node:~/Mytestnet$ cat genesis.json
[
 "config": {
   "chainId": 1234,
   "homesteadBlock": 1,
   "eip150Block": 2,
   "eip150Hash": "0x0000000000000000000000000000000000000000000000000000000000000000",
   "eip155Block": 3,
   "eip158Block": 3,
   "byzantiumBlock": 4,
   "ethash": {}
 },
 "nonce": "0x0",
 "timestamp": "0x5b1543b2",
 "extraData": "0x0000000000000000000000000000000000000000000000000000000000000000",
 "gasLimit": "0x47b760",
 "difficulty": "0x100000",
 "mixHash": "0x0000000000000000000000000000000000000000000000000000000000000000",
 "coinbase": "0x0000000000000000000000000000000000000000",
 "alloc": {
   "0000000000000000000000000000000000000000": {
```

Node initialization

Now that we have the `genesis.json` file, let's forge the genesis block. Both nodes should initialize their chain using the same genesis file by running the following commands:

```
geth --datadir nodeA init genesis.json
geth --datadir nodeB init genesis.json
```

All set. Now you can start your new chain on both nodes using two Terminals.

Starting node A as follows:

```
geth --datadir nodeA --networkid 1234 --rpc  --rpcport 8545 --port 8888  --rpcapi "db,eth,net,web3,personal,miner,admin"  --cache=128 --rpcaddr 0.0.0.0 --rpccorsdomain "*" console
```

And it's the same for node B (update parameters specific to the node):

```
geth --datadir nodeB  --networkid 1234 --rpc  --rpcport 9545  --port 9999 --rpcapi "db,eth,net,web3,personal,miner,admin"  --cache=128 --rpcaddr 0.0.0.0 --rpccorsdomain "*" console
```

Running Geth with the `--rpc` argument makes it operate as an HTTP JSON-RPC server. We have chosen different ports because, in this example, both nodes are running on the same physical machine. The following lists the meaning of some specified arguments, and you can refer to the official documentation for the others:

- `id`: Network identifier. You can pick any value you want but avoid an ID of 0 to 3 as they are reserved.
- `rpcaddr`: Specifies the HTTP-RPC server listening address (default: "localhost").
- `rpcport`: Specifies the HTTP-RPC server listening port (default: 8545).
- `rpcapi`: Specifies the APIs offered over the HTTP-RPC interface (default: eth, net, web3).
- `rpccorsdomain`: Domains from which Geth accepts cross origin requests (browser enforced).

To connect both nodes, you can use any distinct, unused ports but you should set the same network ID. Be aware that the JSON RPC server is not recommended to be used over public internet, but only as a local interface:

```
user@ByExample-node:~/Mytestnet$ geth --datadir node8 --networkid 1234 --rpc  --rpcport 9545 --port "9999" --rpcapi db,eth,net,web3,personal,miner,admin  --cache=128
--rpcaddr 0.0.0.0 --rpccorsdomain "*" console
INFO [06-04|14:20:12] Starting peer-to-peer node               instance=Geth/v1.7.2-stable-1db4ecdc/linux-amd64/go1.9
INFO [06-04|14:20:12] Allocated cache and file handles         database=/home/user/Mytestnet/node8/geth/chaindata cache=128 handles=1024
INFO [06-04|14:20:12] Initialised chain configuration          config="{ChainID: 1234 Homestead: 1 DAO: <nil> DAOSupport: false EIP150: 2 EIP155: 3 EIP158: 3 Byzantium
: 4 Engine: ethash}"
INFO [06-04|14:20:12] Disk storage enabled for ethash caches   dir=/home/user/Mytestnet/node8/geth/ethash count=3
INFO [06-04|14:20:12] Disk storage enabled for ethash DAGs     dir=/home/user/.ethash count=2
INFO [06-04|14:20:12] Initialising Ethereum protocol           versions="[63 62]" network=1234
INFO [06-04|14:20:12] Loaded most recent local header          number=0 hash=347cc2…0973a8 td=1048576
INFO [06-04|14:20:12] Loaded most recent local full block      number=0 hash=347cc2…0973a8 td=1048576
INFO [06-04|14:20:12] Loaded most recent local fast block      number=0 hash=347cc2…0973a8 td=1048576
INFO [06-04|14:20:12] Loaded local transaction journal         transactions=0 dropped=0
INFO [06-04|14:20:12] Regenerated local transaction journal    transactions=0 accounts=0
INFO [06-04|14:20:12] Starting P2P networking
INFO [06-04|14:20:14] UDP listener up                          self=enode://7649de56ad54a0e6c712bb31db22ad9475bc59d89ecba96a82548c226ef17f10c315bee7e0e8442b11b12069524
223306e6a5ab894bf1c91679fcdf32a789b9e@[::]:9999
INFO [06-04|14:20:14] RLPx listener up                         self=enode://7649de56ad54a0e6c712bb31db22ad9475bc59d89ecba96a82548c226ef17f10c315bee7e0e8442b11b12069524
223306e6a5ab894bf1c91679fcdf32a789b9e@[::]:9999
INFO [06-04|14:20:14] IPC endpoint opened: /home/user/Mytestnet/node8/geth.ipc
INFO [06-04|14:20:14] HTTP endpoint opened: http://0.0.0.0:9545
Welcome to the Geth JavaScript console!

instance: Geth/v1.7.2-stable-1db4ecdc/linux-amd64/go1.9
coinbase: 0x1f00d3ff65d0709be473f8798f81498d0ee761f7
at block: 0 (Mon, 04 Jun 2018 13:50:42 WET)
 datadir: /home/user/Mytestnet/node8
 modules: admin:1.0 debug:1.0 eth:1.0 miner:1.0 net:1.0 personal:1.0 rpc:1.0 txpool:1.0 web3:1.0

> admin.nodeInfo
{
  enode: "enode://7649de56ad54a0e6c712bb31db22ad9475bc59d89ecba96a82548c226ef17f10c315bee7e0e8442b11b12069524223306e6a5ab894bf1c91679fcdf32a789b9e@[::]:9999",
  id: "7649de56ad54a0e6c712bb31db22ad9475bc59d89ecba96a82548c226ef17f10c315bee7e0e8442b11b12069524223306e6a5ab894bf1c91679fcdf32a789b9e",
  ip: "::",
  listenAddr: "[::]:9999",
  name: "Geth/v1.7.2-stable-1db4ecdc/linux-amd64/go1.9",
  ports: {
    discovery: 9999,
    listener: 9999
  },
  protocols: {
    eth: {
      difficulty: 1048576,
      genesis: "0x347cc2de7186f480cdee259f224ad464b3368575b22a2e9966f12ce7410973a8",
      head: "0x347cc2de7186f480cdee259f224ad464b3368575b22a2e9966f12ce7410973a8",
```

Connecting Ethereum nodes

As we have enabled the console mode in each node, we can execute commands provided by Geth. Therefore, to connect both nodes, we need to first get the node URL using `admin.nodeInfo.enode`.

As a result, you'll get a value uniquely identifying your node, which can be used by another node to connect both nodes:

```
admin.addPeer({"enode://7649de56ad54a0e6c712bb31db....32a789b9e@[::]:9999"})
```

Replace `[::]` with the node's IP address if you are using nodes in a network.

If everything went well, the `net.peerCount` command should return 1 in both consoles and `admin.peers` should return the list of currently connected peers.

It's worth noting that, for security reasons, Geth unlocks the accounts to prevent anyone other than the owner from performing any action or moving its funds. Therefore, you have to unlock an account before you start sending a transaction using the following:

```
web3.personal.unlockAccount("account address", "password", 0);
```

As account address, you can provide an address from those you got earlier, or just use `eth.coinbase`, which refers to the first account (in Ethereum, a single wallet can have many accounts, each having its own address). The second parameter is the password you provided when you created your account, and the last argument is the duration of unlocking. Having zero as a value means that the account will be unlocked until Geth stops running.

RPC tests

You can communicate with your nodes over RPC (outside of the Geth Terminal) to execute methods defined in web3 API. For instance, we can use CURL or some other command-line HTTP-fetching utility to request Geth's version over RPC as follows:

```
curl -X POST --data
'{"jsonrpc":"2.0","method":"web3_clientVersion","params":[],"id":67}' -H
'content-type: text/plain;' http://127.0.0.1:8545/
  {"jsonrpc":"2.0","id":67,"result":"Geth/v1.7.2-stable-1db4ecdc/linux-
amd64/go1.9"}}
```

Mining process

As in other blockchains, to validate a transaction, whether it is intended to deploy or to interact with the contract, we need to have it mined and included in a block. To start mining with Geth, you'll need to run the following command in the `geth` console:

```
miner.start(x)
```

Here, `x` is an optional parameter representing the number of miner threads. This command will start the mining process, which will keep running even if there are no transactions to validate, creating empty blocks until you stop it manually using `miner.stop()`. The good news is that the mining process will generate new ether for you (valueless, of course).

A more convenient way would be to automatize the process of starting and stopping the mining process only when it's needed (when there are pending transactions). For this purpose, we need to first create a JavaScript file named `mining.js`, in which we define the following script:

```
var mining_threads = 1;
function check() {
    if (eth.getBlock("pending").transactions.length > 0) {
        if (eth.mining) {
            return;
        }
        console.log("Mining in progress...");
        miner.start(mining_threads);
    } else {
        miner.stop(0);
        console.log("Mining stopped.");
    }
}

eth.filter("latest", function(err, block) {
    check();
});

eth.filter("pending", function(err, block) {
    check();
});
check();
```

Then load this script in the `geth` Terminal using `loadScript("/file_path/mining.js")`.

Contract deployment

Now your local Ethereum network is ready to process your transactions and to host your smart contract. Don't forget to make sure you unlocked your account and to mine a few blocks to get some ether.

In the Remix environment, you have to specify one of your node's IP address and RPC port will as the web3 provider. Thereafter, deploy your contract and edit your `auction.js` file with your new contract's address.

Congratulations! You have finished deploying the contract and you can start auctioning from the web page.

Compiling and deploying contracts using solc

If you love compiling and running code using command lines, you can use the Solidity compiler, `solc`. To use the latest stable version of the Solidity compiler, run the following:

```
sudo apt-get update
sudo apt-get install solc
```

Start by copying the contract code into a file named `auction.sol`, and afterwards run the following command to compile the contract and generate the needed ABI and bytecode. The output will be saved in a `details.js` file as follows:

```
echo "var ContractDetails=`solc --optimize --combined-json abi,bin
auction.sol`" > details.js
```

If you see a set of warnings, neglect them and then run in succession the following commands in your Geth CLI, in succession:

```
loadScript("your Path/details.js")
var ContractAbi = ContractDetails.contracts["auction.sol:MyAuction"].abi;
var ContractInstance = eth.contract(JSON.parse(ContractAbi));
var ContractBin = "0x" +
ContractDetails.contracts["auction.sol:MyAuction"].bin;
```

Before you continue, make sue you have unlocked your first account:

```
var deploymentTransationObject = { from: eth.accounts[0], data:
ContractBin, gas: 1000000 };
var auctionInstance = ContractInstance.new(deploymentTransationObject);
var AuctionAddress =
eth.getTransactionReceipt(auctionInstance.transactionHash).contractAddress;
```

From the console, to interact with the contract, you can create an object pointing to your contract's address as follows:

```
var Mycontract = ContractInstance.at(AuctionAddress);
```

This is similar to what we have done so far in Web3Js and, depending on the nature of the function, we can execute a call using `Mycontract.FunctionName.call()` or send a transaction using `Mycontract.FunctionName.sendTransaction(FunctionArguments, {from: eth.accounts[0], gas: 1000000})`.

In order to validate your transaction, you'll need to run the mining process in Geth using `miner.start()` or use the mining script we used earlier when we configured the private chain.

Here, we have seen a winding path for compiling and deploying a contract using `solc`, web3.js, and a local blockchain. Tools such as Truffle (that you'll discover in the next chapter) do all that for you under the hood, and make perfect alternatives for quick development and testing.

Proof of authority (POA) and difficulty adjustment

In the previous procedure of running a local network, we used the Geth client with POW mining to validate the transaction. However, you may find mining a daunting process as its difficulty will rise, causing annoying, heavy computations reducing your system capacity even if we set it as low as possible in the genesis file.

To solve this issue, you have two choices: either configure the network to use an alternative mining mechanism called POA, or fix the mining difficulty in the Geth client source code. Let's have a look at these possibilities.

Option 1 – editing the Ethereum client code

To explore this option, you'll need to do some Golang hacking! Don't worry; there's nothing complex.

In Geth's code (the `consensus.go` file
at; `https://github.com/ethereum/go-ethereum/blob/master/consensus/ethash/consensus.go`), there is a function called `CalcDifficulty` that represents the difficulty adjustment algorithm. It returns the difficulty that a new block should have when created, given the parent block's time and difficulty. To fix the difficulty, we need to fix the returned value as follows:

```
func CalcDifficulty(config *params.ChainConfig, time uint64, parent
*types.Header) *big.Int {
    return big.NewInt(1)
}
```

Afterwards, compile your new Geth client following the instructions presented in the official Geth GitHub repository at `https://github.com/ethereum/go-ethereum/wiki/Installing-Geth`.

Option 2 – POW

An alternative solution to avoid relying on **proof of work (POW)** mining is to use a replacement consensus mechanism known as POA, in which we trust a set of known validators (authorities) to accept transactions. In other words, POA validators are staking their identity and voluntarily disclosing who they are in exchange for the right to validate the blocks. Unlike POW, POA is a centralized mechanism that delivers comparatively fast transactions, thus POA deployment is used by private (enterprise) and some public testing networks (for example, the popular Kovan and Rinkeby test networks).

 Both main Ethereum clients, Parity and Geth, support POA.

To set up a private chain with Geth and POA, you will need to reiterate the same `Puppeth` procedure that was presented earlier, except for choosing the consensus engine. Start `Puppeth`, follow the questionnaire, and choose POA as the consensus engine. In this case, you'll need to determine the validator accounts (accounts that are allowed to seal). For that, copy and paste the Ethereum accounts that were created earlier by Geth. Of course, you can define as many sealers as you like but POA is able to work with a single node and only one sealer:

```
◉ ◉ ◉    user@ByExample-node: ~/Mytestnet
user@ByExample-node:~/Mytestnet$ puppeth
+-----------------------------------------------------------+
| Welcome to puppeth, your Ethereum private network manager |
|                                                           |
| This tool lets you create a new Ethereum network down to  |
| the genesis block, bootnodes, miners and ethstats servers |
| without the hassle that it would normally entail.         |
|                                                           |
| Puppeth uses SSH to dial in to remote servers, and builds |
| its network components out of Docker containers using the |
| docker-compose toolset.                                   |
+-----------------------------------------------------------+

Please specify a network name to administer (no spaces, please)
>
>
> Mytestnet
Sweet, you can set this via --network=Mytestnet next time!

INFO [06-04|14:28:01] Administering Ethereum network           name=Mytestnet
WARN [06-04|14:28:01] No previous configurations found         path=/home/user/.puppeth/Mytestnet

What would you like to do? (default = stats)
 1. Show network stats
 2. Configure new genesis
 3. Track new remote server
 4. Deploy network components
> 2

Which consensus engine to use? (default = clique)
 1. Ethash - proof-of-work
 2. Clique - proof-of-authority
> 2

How many seconds should blocks take? (default = 15)
>

Which accounts are allowed to seal? (mandatory at least one)
> 0x87366ef81db496edd0ea2055ca605e8686eec1e6
> 0x
```

Keep in mind that POA doesn't have mining rewards, and therefore it's highly recommended that you allocate enough ether (defined in the unit of wei) to your accounts first, and then initialize your nodes with the resultant POA genesis file.

Ta-da! No more mining.

After laying out the different available deployment environments, it's time to run our auction DApp.

Running the auction DApp

At this level, you should have already deployed your contract on one of the deployment environments presented beforehand. To try what we have built so far, follow these instructions:

1. In `auction.js`, define your RPC and port provider: `web3.setProvider(new web3.providers.HttpProvider("http://<IP>:<port>"));`.

2. Change the contract's address: `var contractAddress = "your contract address";`.

3. Afterwards, open the `index.html` file directly in your browser or by using a web server. The loaded web page looks as follows:

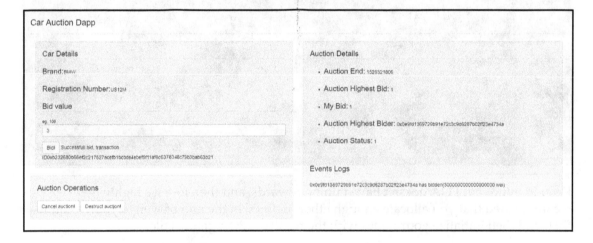

To start interacting with this DApp, the easiest method is to use MetaMask connected to Ganache. In this case, we'll need to import some of the accounts created by Ganache into MetaMask. To do that, we copy the private key from the Ganache interface and in MetaMask, we import the corresponding accounts by following the instructions presented in the official documentation (`https://metamask.zendesk.com/hc/en-us/articles/360015489351-Importing-Accounts`) or if you're using the new UI (`https://metamask.zendesk.com/hc/en-us/articles/360015489331-Importing-an-Account-New-UI-`). Once the accounts have been imported, write your bid amount in the bid input and press the **Bid!** button. MetaMask will prompt you to accept this transaction and let you know the fee you have to pay. To make it competitive, change the bidder account in MetaMask and make a new bid. Each time a new bid is accepted, the auction details board on the right will be updated.

Contract and transaction cost

One of good signs of good Solidity code is the cheap cost of its operations, thus in your contract you should optimize your code cost as much as possible.

As we stated in the introduction, Ethereum is a "paying" network and you're invoiced in gas. We learned earlier that gas has multiple metrics associated with it:

- **Gas cost:** A static value for how much a computation costs in terms of gas.
- **Gas price**: Expresses how much the gas costs in ether. The price of gas itself is meant to stay generally constant.
- **Gas limit**: There are two limits, the block gas limit and transaction gas limit. Each transaction has a gas limit set by the sender, whereas the block gas limit (defined by the network) determines how many transactions can fit in a block.
- **Gas fee**: Effectively, the amount of gas needed to be paid to run a particular transaction or program (called a contract).

The idea behind the gas system is to have a dedicated unit to quantify transaction or computation cost on the Ethereum network. This fueling system is used to incentivize miners and to avoid denial of service attacks through malicious scripts that run forever. If the smart contract cannot complete before running out of ether, it is halted at that point.

In general, gas is consumed by a contract in two situations:

- Contract deployment
- Contract execution through transactions

How cost is calculated

Higher-level languages such as Solidity compile down to EVM bytecode, translating the contract code into a list of smallest units of computation, called opcodes. These include operations such as ADD (addition operation), SLOAD (load word from storage), and CREATE (create a new account with associated code). The gas cost for each opcode can be found in the yellow paper, and is also listed at `https://github.com/bellaj/evm-opcode-gas-costs`. The total cost for a given instruction is the sum of the executed corresponding opcodes.

The Ethereum yellow paper defines approximately 130 opcodes. Each of these opcodes has an associated fixed gas price, with some opcodes costing more gas than others. For example, ADD uses three gas units while MUL (multiply two integers) uses five gas, hence MUL is more complex than ADD. Knowing these costs mean that you can optimize your code by avoiding expensive operations (opcodes).

Deployment cost

To deploy the contract, you have to pay for adding bytecode (the runtime bytecode stripped of initialization data) to the blockchain at a cost of 200 gas/byte, plus a fee of 32,000 gas for creating the contract account (create opcode), as indicated in the Ethereum yellow paper. In our case, the contract deployment costs approximately 1,054,247 gas units, and with a gas price of 2 gwei (1 ether = 1000000000 gwei), it will cost a total of 0.002108494 ether.

To reduce your cost, at this level, you'll need to optimize the code size and get rid of useless code and state variables.

Function execution cost

You can use Remix connected to the testnet to get an estimation cost of each function call. The following table presents the cost of the main methods defined in the auction contract according to Remix:

Functions	Transaction Gas cost estimation
bid()	125350
withdraw()	21008
cancel_auction()	21272
destruct_auction()	14211

A basic transaction (simple transfer of ETH) has a minimum gas requirement of 21,000 gas. Consequently, if you are just transferring funds and not interacting with a contract, your transaction takes 21,000 gas. If you are interacting with a contract, your transaction takes 21,000 gas, plus any gas associated with the executed method.

Contract destruction cost

The `selfdestruct()` function has an interesting feature as it enables us to reduce the cost of the destruction transaction. It's based on the `SUICIDE` opcode, which uses negative gas because the operation frees up space on the blockchain by clearing all of the contract's state data. This negative gas is deducted from the total gas cost of the transaction, therefore reducing your gas cost. In our case, this method costs 14,211 gas, less than a normal transfer (which costs 21,000 gas):

Potential optimization

The opcode gas prices give us an idea about which operations to use with moderation. For instance, reading from storage costs 200 gas per `SLOAD` instruction, and writing to storage `SSTORE` costs 5,000 gas, but reading from the EVM's memory and writing to it costs only 3 gas. Therefore, it's preferable to avoid extensive reading/writing operations from and into storage but instead use the memory.

The cost also depends on data size, with the fee being 20,000 gas to store a 256-bit word. For example, a kilobyte (8,000 bits) costs 640k gas, and with a gas price of 18 Gwei, you'll have to pay 11,520,000 Gwei (0.01152 Ether), or about 6.8659 USD (at 595.997$ per ether), making Ethereum an expensive storage infrastructure. Another bottleneck of storing data is the current block gas limit of approximately 8,000,000 gas/block (`https://ethstats.net`). At this cap of gas per block, it would take over 80 blocks to write 1 MB of data to the blockchain, and that is assuming you can manage to reserve all of the gas per block and that there are no other operations required!

The following is some optimization advice related to data storage:

- Use `bytes1` to `bytes32` instead of `string` for small strings or bytes data that's longer than 32 bytes. They are much cheaper.
- Preferably, use fixed length arrays instead of dynamically sized arrays.
- The `indexed` parameters in events have additional gas cost.
- For `struct` elements, you should use shorter types, as well as sorting them so that short types would be grouped together into single storage slot. By doing this, you can decrease the gas costs by combining multiple `SSTORE` operations into one.
- According to the yellow paper, it costs 375 gas for each topic in a `LOG` operation and 8 gas for each byte of a `LOG` operation's data. Consequently, logs are considered as a cheaper storage solution; however, unlike storage, logs aren't readable by a smart contract.
- By making the state of your contracts `public`, you have your compiler create getters automatically, which reduces contract size and therefore cost.

For a better design in our example, we can use an off-chain environment to store the car or user details, and only keep in the contract a referencing URL. In general, it's wise to find the balance between using on-chain and off-chain environments, while still leveraging the decentralized capabilities of the blockchain.

Solidity tips and tricks

We end this chapter with some recommendations and best practices you can adopt while you write your smart contracts:

- There is no size limit to the data sent along your transaction. You will be only limited by how much ether you have and the block gas limit.
- Constants are not stored in contract storage. A constant state such as `uint256 constant x = block.timestamp;` means that contract will re-evaluate `x` every time it is used.
- Remember that calls to `external` functions can fail, therefore always check the return value.
- For transferring funds, it's preferable to use `transfer()` over `send()` as `transfer()` is equivalent to `require(send())` and will `throw` if it doesn't execute successfully.
- Be aware that the block's timestamp can be influenced a little bit by miners. It's safe to use `block.timestamp` if your contract function can tolerate a 30-second drift in time, since the tolerated NTP drift is 10 seconds, as defined in `https://github.com/ethereum/go-ethereum/blob/master/p2p/discover/udp.go#L57`. Don't be confused if you read in the yellow paper (the old version) that a tolerable drift interval of up to 900 seconds (15 minutes) is allowed. This is outdated information.
- There's a limit in Solidity to how many variables you can define in a function (including parameters and return variables). The limit is 16 variables, otherwise you get the `StackTooDeepException` error.
- Contracts can't trigger themselves but they need an external poke (for example, a contract can't automatically do something at specific time, like a Cron job, unless it receives an external signal).

Summary

Tired? I really hope not, because this was just the beginning of a long adventure. Hopefully, throughout this chapter, you were able to develop an understanding of the fundamentals of DApps and smart contract development. We covered, in a simplified way, the basics of Solidity and web3.js and how to build and deploy a simple full DApp.

While we have created a working DApp, it's by no means the final word in smart contract security and structural optimization. You'll still need to define functions to transfer ownership and open a bid, and add over- and underflow protection measures, just to name a few. I'll be glad to receive your propositions on the project's repository (`https://github.com/bellaj/Car_Auction`).

In the next chapter, we will take the learning process a step further, covering new concepts in Ethereum and digging deeper into Solidity's advanced features, such as optimization, debugging, and security.

5
Tontine Game with Truffle and Drizzle

In the previous chapter, we learned a lot about the Ethereum ecosystem, but we are yet to realize the full potential of its different components. More precisely, we explored how Ethereum works, what a **decentralized application** (**DApp**) is and how to build one, and also covered the key concepts of Solidity and web3.js. We then introduced some of the most common smart contract design patterns (withdrawal from a contract, restricting access, state machines), before ending with a discussion of a contract's cost optimization.

To brush up your knowledge and skills, in this chapter, we are going to build a Tontine DApp game. We will exploit this example to explore new tools that are going to change the way you build DApps, and introduce new Solidity features. I hope you enjoy playing games as much as building them.

In this walkthrough, we will discover how a tool such as Truffle can aid in building, testing, debugging, and deploying our DApp. In a nutshell, we are going to cover four main topics:

- Exploring the Truffle suite
- Learning Solidity's advanced features
- Contract testing and debugging
- Building a user interface using Drizzle

The last point is something seldom covered in a book as it's a relatively new framework. We are going to bridge that gap by building this game from the ground up using Truffle and a Drizzle box.

This chapter will be another step in our continuous learning process, and therefore it's the occasion to clarify any remaining ambiguous points and re-evaluate your understanding of Ethereum's fundamental concepts. The project's source code is available at `https://github.com/bellaj/TontineGame`. It is advised that you download a copy before continuing to read.

One last thing to mention, as in the previous chapter my approach during the process of building the DApp will be to step through details from time to time when it is needed to introduce or explain new related concepts.

Background

Before kicking off the project, let me introduce the concept behind the game.

As this chapter's name suggests, we are going to build a Tontine game. The concept behind the weird word Tontine appeared at the end of 17th century. Initially, it represented a collective investment scheme plan, where each participant paid a sum into a fund and received dividends from the invested capital. But behind this simple idea, a weird rule is hidden: when a subscriber dies, their share is divided among the others and the last lucky survivor recovers the whole capital.

In our game, we will adapt this idea to our smart contract and gaming logic. Players will deposit funds in the game's smart contract to join the game. Afterwards, they should keep pinging it during a specific time interval to avoid being knocked out by other opponents. For instance, if anybody misses pinging the contract within a day for any reason, the other players are able to eliminate them. So, nobody will die in our case but they will be eliminated. Similar to the original Tontine, the last player standing will win the funds controlled by the contract.

Let's start by preparing the environment in which we'll build the Tontine smart contract.

Prerequisites

Before proceeding with this chapter, you should already be familiar with developing in Solidity. If not, I recommend reading the previous chapter, *Peer-to-Peer Auctions in Ethereum*. Moreover, the following prerequisites should be installed:

- Ubuntu 16.04
- MetaMask browser plugin
- Node.js and NPM

Don't forget a cup of good coffee.

Truffle quick start

So far, the only method we have used to compile and interact with our contracts was Remix. Let me now introduce you to a new DApp development toolkit: Truffle.

Truffle is the most popular development environment and testing framework for DApp developers. It is a true Swiss Army knife that helps you easily compile, test, and deploy your contracts to the blockchain. Moreover, Truffle helps you set up and hook your frontend up to your deployed contracts. It also has other features:

- Built-in smart-contract compilation, linking, deployment, and binary management
- Automated contract testing
- Scriptable, extensible deployment and migrations framework
- Network management for deploying to any number of public and private networks
- Interactive console for direct contract communication

Installing Truffle

To start using Truffle, you can install the latest release using **Node Package Manager (NPM)**: `npm install -g truffle`.

You can also choose a specific version to install, such as `npm install -g truffle@4.0.4`.

Once installed, you can check your Truffle version in the Terminal using `truffle version`:

```
user@ByExample-node: ~/tontine
user@ByExample-node:~/tontine$ truffle version
Truffle v4.1.12 (core: 4.1.12)
Solidity v0.4.24 (solc-js)
user@ByExample-node:~/tontine$
```

By typing `truffle` into your Terminal without any arguments, you'll get all of Truffle's available options. If you are unsure about something, or you want to learn about an option, have a look at the documentation: `http://truffleframework.com/docs`.

Saying hello to Truffle

Now, Truffle is ready. Start by creating a folder called `tontine/` for this first project, then initialize it with Truffle as follows:

```
mkdir tontine
cd tontine
truffle init
```

Within a few seconds (equivalent to a sip of coffee), this last command will download a template of a Truffle project for you:

```
⊗ ⊖ ⊙    user@ByExample-node: ~/tontine
user@ByExample-node:~/tontine$ truffle init
Downloading...
Unpacking...
Setting up...
Unbox successful. Sweet!

Commands:

  Compile:         truffle compile
  Migrate:         truffle migrate
  Test contracts:  truffle test
user@ByExample-node:~/tontine$ █
```

Once the initialization is completed, you'll get the following files and directory structure:

- `contracts/`: A directory that houses all Solidity contracts.
- `migrations/`: A directory that hosts JavaScript migration files that helps in deploying our contracts to the network.
- `test/`: A directory holding test scripts for testing your contracts.
- `truffle.js`: Truffle's configuration file, used to define project-related settings.
  - `truffle-config.js` is a copy of `truffle.js` used to ensure compatibility with Windows. Feel free to delete it when you are under Linux.

- `Contracts/Migrations.sol`: A separate Solidity file that manages and updates the status of your deployed smart contracts. This file comes with every Truffle project and is usually not edited.
- `Migrations/1_initial_migration.js`: A migration file for the `Migrations.sol` contract. You can create new migrations with increasing numbered prefixes to deploy other contracts.

Running Truffle for the first time

Now, let's focus on the interesting part. To examine how we can compile and deploy a contract using Truffle, we will use a simple introductory example. Don't worry! We will start building the game soon. We will use the hello world example we built in the previous chapter, *Peer-to-Peer Auctions in Ethereum*. Copy the contract code into a `hello.sol` file and put it into Truffle's `contracts/` folder.

Let's see how can we use Truffle to compile and deploy this first contract.

Preparing the migration

Truffle uses the migration concept to refer to deploying and switching old contracts to new instances. To deploy our hello world contract, we need to indicate to Truffle how to deploy (migrate) it into the blockchain. To achieve that, open the `migrations/` folder and create a new migration file named `2_initial_migration.js`.

Paste the following content into this migration file :

```
const Hello = artifacts.require("HelloWorld");
module.exports = function(deployer) {
  deployer.deploy(Hello);
};
```

At the beginning of the migration, we tell Truffle which contracts we would like to interact with via the `artifacts.require()` method, in the same way we do with `require` in Node.js.

In the case where you have multiple contracts defined, you'll need to define an `artifacts.require()` statement for each contract:

```
var ContractOne = artifacts.require("ContractOne");
var ContractTwo = artifacts.require("ContractTwo");
```

Configuring Truffle

Now, it is time to configure Truffle. First, we need to define the networks to which we want to migrate the contracts. In the `truffle.js` file (`truffle-config.js` for Windows), insert the following code:

```
module.exports = {
  networks: {
    my_ganache: {
      host: "127.0.0.1",
      port: 7545,
      network_id: "*"
    }
  }
};
```

We define a deployment network with the name `my_ganache` along with a few parameters. The network name is used for user-interface purposes, to help you easily choose to run your migrations on a specific network with a name, as we can configure Truffle to use multiple networks.

Basically, this configuration file says to Truffle that when we choose the `my_ganache` network, connect to the host at `127.0.0.1`, using port `7545`. For `network_id`, we used `*` to match any network ID. Beyond that, there are many other configuration options, such as gas limit and gas price, which are detailed in the documentation: `https://truffleframework.com/docs/truffle/reference/configuration`.

Compiling the contract

Now, it's time to compile and deploy the hello world contract. Start by running the `truffle compile` command in your console.

After a short while, you will get the compilation result. You may notice the message indicating that artifacts are saved in the default build folder, `./build/contracts`:

```
user@ByExample-node:~/tontine$ truffle compile
Compiling ./contracts/hello.sol...
Writing artifacts to ./build/contracts
```

If you go there, you will find a JSON file (the artifacts) created by the compilation with details about your contract (ABI, bytecode, and so on).

As Truffle hasn't complained about any errors, you can move forward and deploy your contract. In other cases, you might get warning messages that you can safely ignore, or adjust your code accordingly.

Migrating the contract

We have now compiled our contract and configured Truffle to deploy the bytecode into the local blockchain network called `my_ganache`. To specify the deployment network, we need to run Truffle with the `--network` option, as follows: `truffle migrate --network my_ganache`.

But, wait! It won't connect unless you start the `my_ganache` network, right? This is what we will configure in the next step.

Setting up Ganache

If you remember, in the previous chapter,*Peer-to-Peer Auctions in Ethereum*, we introduced Ganache as a virtual blockchain for local testing. This tool is available under two formats:

- Ganache CLI (previously known as TestRPC)
- GUI version (we used it in the previous chapter)

In this chapter, we will use `ganache-cli`. Hence, install Ganache CLI globally using NPM, as follows:

```
npm install -g ganache-cli
```

Once installed, open a separate command line or tab and type in the following command:

```
ganache-cli -p 7545
```

As you may have guessed, the `-p` option specifies which port to listen on as Ganache CLI runs by default on `8545` (the same as Geth). If you are unsure about an option, refer to Ganache's GitHub page (`https://github.com/trufflesuite/ganache-cli`) where you can find ample information.

When Ganache starts up, it generates 10 accounts (unlocked) preloaded with a balance of 100 ether each, and displays their Ethereum addresses and the corresponding private keys, as shown in the following picture :

These accounts will be very helpful to build raw transactions or import the created accounts later.

After this step, you can deploy the contract by running the `truffle migrate --network my_ganache` migration command.

After the successful execution of the deployment script, Truffle will output the `HelloWorld` contract's address, as depicted here:

```
user@ByExample-node:~/tontine$ truffle migrate --network my_ganache
Using network 'my_ganache'.

Running migration: 2_initial_migration.js
  Deploying HelloWorld...
  ... 0x65440f0f09fd0c917c9e43214e80ffbaf8c4011a23fe7704ebf909d74b2c6e91
  HelloWorld: 0x279841fcc40a59b161e1a1e5076fb8665820d9c7
Saving successful migration to network...
  ... 0x7dcf44eae29483b2651b3c3a462ce9e873a99e84e1b79442ce46301c2d7f973e
Saving artifacts...
```

> Truffle will automatically use the first account generated by Ganache to deploy your contract.

At the same time, in Ganache's output, you should see the deployment transaction details, as shown in the following screenshot:

```
Transaction: 0x65440f0f09fd0c917c9e43214e80ffbaf8c4011a23fe7704ebf909d74b2c6e9
1
  Contract created: 0x279841fcc40a59b161e1a1e5076fb8665820d9c7
  Gas usage: 281139
  Block Number: 30
  Block Time: Wed Jul 25 2018 17:08:56 GMT+0100 (WEST)

eth_newBlockFilter
eth_getFilterChanges
eth_getTransactionReceipt
eth_getCode
eth_uninstallFilter
eth_sendTransaction

  Transaction: 0x7dcf44eae29483b2651b3c3a462ce9e873a99e84e1b79442ce46301c2d7f973
e
  Gas usage: 27008
  Block Number: 31
  Block Time: Wed Jul 25 2018 17:08:56 GMT+0100 (WEST)

eth_getTransactionReceipt
```

You have now set up the necessary development and deployment environment to build a DApp, and learned how to compile and deploy a given contract into Truffle.

Next, we kick off the most exciting part: building the game. Let's start from the smart contract side.

The Tontine contract

As stated in the introduction, Tontine is a competitive multiplayer game. When it starts, players pool their money into the Tontine contract, and once the game is over, all the funds are handed to the last surviving participant. Meanwhile, players take turns trying to stabilize their position and eliminate their opponents. The main rules of our Tontine game are as follows:

- A player can join the game by paying at least 1 ETH to the contract.
- The game starts when the first player enters.
- The player needs to ping the contract every day.
- If the player hasn't pinged the contract during the last 24 hours, other users can eliminate them.
- The last player will get all the money out of the contract and the game ends.

General structure

Technically speaking, unlike a traditional online game, which has all of its business logic defined and executed on a private server owned by a company, our game's business logic is defined and executed in a smart contract on the decentralized Ethereum blockchain.

In our design, we will define two main contracts with a single interface. This wouldn't be the best approach out there, but I designed it as such to make it easier to discover new Solidity features, such as interfaces, contract interactions, and overloading. It's worth mentioning that for the purpose of removing complexities and to help learn advanced Solidity features, optimization and security are intentionally not considered.

Again, as we did in the previous chapter,*Peer-to-Peer Auctions in Ethereum*, we will separate the function declarations from their definitions by using an interface instead of an abstract contract. Obviously, you don't have to create an interface or abstract class for each contract you build, but I am adopting this pattern for learning purposes to show you that such a well-known pattern in object-oriented programming is applicable in Solidity as well.

UML model

For building this game, we will adopt the following straightforward UML diagram:

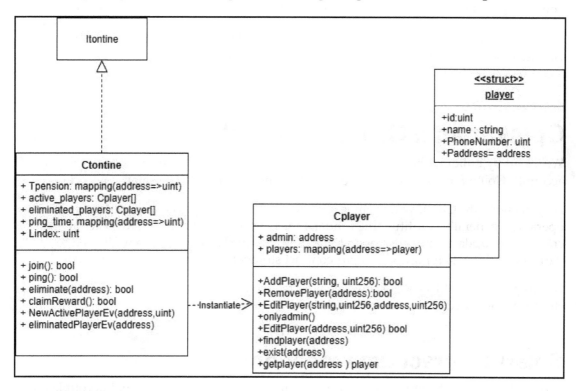

So far, we have three main components:

- Itontine: Interface for Tontine game functions
- Cplayer: A class for managing players (enrollment, modification, and so on)
- Ctontine: A contract for implementing Tontine game functions

As you'll notice, the interface name starts with an I prefix, whereas contracts starts with a C prefix.

Now, let's talk code.

Preparing the contracts

All our code will be hosted in a single Solidity file, so first create an empty file called `tontine.sol` in Truffle's `contracts/` folder using `touch contracts/tontine.sol`.

If you don't like to copy the code from books, no worries, you can grab the code from this GitHub repository: `https://github.com/bellaj/TontineGame/blob/master/tontine/contracts/tontine.sol`.

Cplayer as a CRUD contract

We'll start by building the `Cplayer` contract, which is responsible for managing player accounts. Going forward, we will use Solidity to build it as a CRUD smart contract.

As you know, the CRUD paradigm is common in constructing web applications as its operations generally constitute the fundamental structure. In fact, the CRUD acronym's create, read, update and delete operations represent the basic operation we'll need to perform on the data repository (Smart contract storage) while managing the players.

At this point, to build a CRUD contract, we first need to understand where and how data is stored and accessed in Ethereum's blockchain.

Smart contract data location

Although each smart contract has its own separate storage space, we do not decouple the storage-layer code from the other layers of the application as we do in classical development methods. Therefore, there is no querying language, such as SQL, or separated database component, but the smart contract through its code provides the ability to initiate permanent states, and read or store data.

As we introduced in the previous chapter, *Peer-to-Peer Auctions in Ethereum*, the smart contract is executed in the EVM to update the system state. This virtual machine provides dedicated storage, which is a persistent associative map where the contract stores states (permanent data). It also provides volatile memory to hold transient data while a contract is being executed. On the other hand, the contract's bytecode (encoded sequence of opcodes) is stored separately, in a virtual ROM. The following figure illustrates a simplified architecture of the EVM and its interactions with the blockchain:

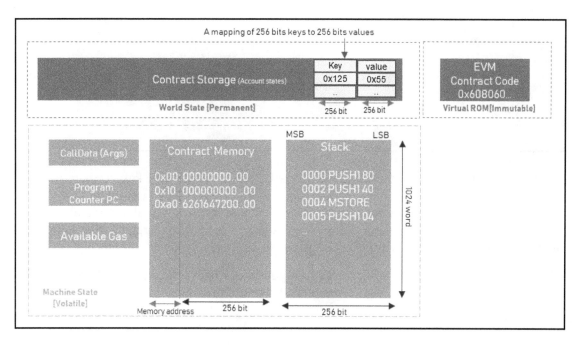

We learned in the previous chapter, `Peer-to-Peer Auctions in Ethereum` that a contract has state variables (we call them the contract's state) similar to global variables (defined in the contract scope) that are located by default in permanent storage.

There are also default locations depending on which type of variable it concerns:

- Function arguments (in `CALLDATA`) and their return values are in memory by default.
- Local variables of the `struct`, `array`, and `mapping` types reference storage by default.
- Local variables of normal types (such as `uint` and `bool`) are stored in memory.

The following picture presents the default locations for different elements in a smart contract (storage in red, memory in green) :

```
contract Cplayer{

    address admin;
    mapping(address=>string) public players;      Storage
    uint[] Array1;                                 (Permanent states)

    constructor() public {
        admin=msg.sender;
    }

    function test(string arg1, uint256 arg2, uint[] argArray1, uint[] storage argArray2) public returns (bool arg3){
    address _address=msg.address;
    uint[4] memory adaArr = [1,2,3,4];     Memory

    return true;
}
```

Depending on the context, you can use dedicated `memory` or `storage` keywords to change the data location. These locations are important to determine how an assignment is performed. In general, assignments between storage and memory variables, and also to a state variable, are passed by value. However, assignments to local storage variables (arrays or structs declared within the function scope) pass the state's value by reference.

 You can read the contract's storage directly using the web3.js API with the `eth.getStorageAt()` method. Have fun reading stored values.

That said, let's jump back to our CRUD `Cplayer` contract.

The CRUD data repository

As our main data repository, we will use a mapping structure to index all enrolled players using their address. If you remember, in the previous chapter, *Peer-to-Peer Auctions in Ethereum* we learned that a mapping is similar to a big key-value database with all possible key values filled with zeros.

In the `tontine.sol` file, add the following code:

```
pragma solidity ^0.4.24;

contract Cplayer{
    struct player{
        string name;
        uint PhoneNumber;
        address Paddress;
        uint id;
    }
    mapping(address => player) players;
}
```

The code is pretty self-explanatory: we declare a new type called `player`, which is a structure (`struct`) that represents a user's details.

We also declare a `players` mapping to store the users' details. In the mapping definition (key ≥ value), the key (which acts like a unique ID) can be almost any type, except for a mapping, a dynamically sized array, a contract, an enum, or a struct. The corresponding value can actually be any type, including a mapping.

It's magic that the data storage is fully managed by a single line of code. In our case, declaring a mapping in the code is enough to store players. We don't have to create a database or table or install a database driver.

To give you an idea, the previous Solidity code is similar to creating a table in SQL:

```
CREATE TABLE players (`address` varchar(32) NOT NULL,  PRIMARY KEY
(`address`) ...);
```

Generally, in a standard RDBMS, you define a unique key as an incremental integer, whereas for a mapping, the uniqueness is ensured by the collision-resistance property of `sha256` used to manage the keys, therefore two different keys can't have the same hash.

CRUD – Create

Great, now that our storage is initiated, let's define the first CRUD operation.

The CREATE operation represents adding new entries to our persistent storage structure (player mapping). To insert a new player, we will define an addPlayer method, as follows:

```
function addPlayer(string _name, uint256 _phonenumber) public returns
(bool) {
    players[msg.sender].name = _name;
    players[msg.sender].Paddress = msg.sender;
    players[msg.sender].PhoneNumber = _phonenumber;
    return true;
}
```

This function enables a new player to enroll themselves in the players, database. Similar to an INSERT statement, the different assignments will create (or, more accurately, fill) a new record in the mapping, indexed using the player address. By analogy, in SQL we can do the same thing using insert into players values (_name, _msg. sender, _phonenumber);.

CRUD – Read

In the CRUD pattern, the READ operation expresses the action of retrieving, searching, or viewing existing entries. Correspondingly, we define the findPlayer method in the Cplayer contract to read the mapping records based on the primary key (player address) specified as an argument:

```
function findPlayer(address _address) public view returns (string, uint,
address) {
    return (players[_address].name, players[_address].PhoneNumber,
players[_address].Paddress);
}
```

This simple, magical function will directly access a player's details, by providing only its address without the need of looping through the mapping. Moreover, as you may have noticed, Solidity enables us to return multiple values for a function.

Similarly, if we suppose that the players mapping is a table with three columns, then the findPlayer method will be similar to performing the following SQL request: Select * from players where Paddress=_address;.

Remember, you can define the mapping as public to retrieve the player information directly without using a find method.

Furthermore, we can check the existence of an element in the mapping by defining the following function:

```
function exist(address _address) public view returns (bool) {
    return (players[_address].Paddress != 0x0);
}
```

The preceding method will read and check whether the player address is not null (not zero), as mappings are initialized to zero for each possible key/value. In Solidity, the `null` statement is not defined.

Furthermore, to retrieve a `player` as a compact structure object, instead of returning a tuple of values, we use the following method:

```
function getplayer(address _adress) public view returns (player) {
    return players[_adress];
}
```

However, Solidity, at the time of writing this chapter, doesn't allow us to return `struct` objects from a function unless you are using a compiler newer than 0.4.16. In this case, you will need to activate the new ABI decoder, which is still an experimental feature, by adding the `pragma experimental ABIEncoderV2;` directive.

Why's that? Because Solidity doesn't recognize `struct`s as real objects, therefore standard ABI doesn't support them.

At the time of writing, passing structs between contracts isn't a good idea. Nevertheless, I have chosen this pattern knowing that in the future, Solidity compilers will provide full support for this feature. You can instead use an `unpacker` method to return the struct elements, such as `findPlayer`. If you plan to deploy your contract to the Mainnet, think of removing the experimental features, such as ABIEncoderV2, to avoid any malfunctioning.

Mapping iterations

While we are talking about search logic, let me open a parenthesis about mappings to answer a recurring question.

Are mappings iterable? The answer is no, they aren't.

Currently Solidity doesn't support iterating a mapping, as they don't have a fixed length (number of non-null key-values entries). However, you can use an auxiliary array and structure in which you store the keys to your mapping to tie each element to its key. Using this pattern, the `IterableMapping` library was built by Solidity developers to iterate over the mapping keys. Its code is available in the following GitHub repository: `https://github.com/ethereum/dapp-bin/blob/master/library/iterable_mapping.sol`.

CRUD – Update

Next up, we're going to perform entry updates. As its name suggests, the update operation in CRUD performs an update or edit to existing entries in our players' mapping storage. Our update method will be `editPlayer()`, which enables the players themselves to edit their own details by sending a transaction to the `Cplayer` contract. Here's the code for `editPlayer()` and the logic for editing individual contacts:

```
function editPlayer(string _name, uint256 _phonenumber, address
_address,uint256 _id) public returns (bool) {
    players[msg.sender].name = _name;
    players[msg.sender].PhoneNumber = _phonenumber;
    players[msg.sender].Paddress = _address;
    players[msg.sender].id = _id;
    return true;
}
```

As every user has their details mapped to their address (ID), we need only to target the ID in the mapping and update the attribute of the corresponding struct.

Again, let's make a point about immutability in Ethereum.

Every time you update a new entry, you don't erase or override the old value. When you update a contract's state, you define a new value that will be included in the current block (on the blockchain), but the old value will still be living in a previous block. This is similar to Lavoisier's law: nothing is lost, everything is transformed.

In SQL, we can do the same thing using an UPDATE statement on the players, table based on the primary key for a record specified in the WHERE clause:

```
UPDATE players
  SET name = name,...
  WHERE ID = msg.sender;
```

However, unlike in SQL, you can't alter an existing mapping as you do for tables. The code is definitively immutable.

Function overloading

As for other languages, Solidity has the ability to define different semantics for a function using different types and numbers of arguments. The following example shows the overloading of the editPlayer function:

```
function editPlayer(address _address,uint256 _id) public returns (bool) {
    players[_address].id = _id;
    return true;
}
```

This is essentially the same as the EditPlayer function we defined before, the difference being it will edit only the player's ID attribute. This overloaded function will be executed if EditPlayer is called with two arguments (string and uint256).

CRUD – Delete

So far, we have implemented three of the main CRUD operations. Now it's time to define the last, the DELETE operation, to deactivate or remove existing entries. To achieve that, we define the following removePlayer() method:

```
modifier onlyadmin(){
    require(msg.sender == admin);
    _;
}

function removePlayer(address _address) public onlyadmin returns (bool) {
    delete players[_address];
    return true;
}
```

removePlayer() will remove an element (player) at a specific index (address). Solidity provides the delete operator to reset deleted elements to the default value. In the mapping, the corresponding value to the specified key (address) will be set to zero, and the mapping structure will remain the same.

Moreover, we can apply `delete` to a given array member as `Delete MyArray[3]`. This implies that the value of `MyArray[3]` will equal zero without reducing the array length. If we want to physically remove the element with reindexing, we need to delete it and manually resize the array. Deleting elements in Solidity behaves like an update with the initial value for the type.

The equivalent SQL statement to the previous function would be `DELETE from players where address=_address;`.

You might be wondering about deleting the mapping as we do in SQL for a table: `DROP TABLE players;`

This is currently impossible for a mapping, but it's possible to delete a dynamic array or a structure.

One last thing to mention: in your CRUD contract, you can manage contract roles and permissions using modifiers. For example, we can define fixed roles and assign permissions based on specific attributes (owner, and player) to control access to specific functions (actions).

At this point, we have accomplished the goal of this first section. We have built our `Cplayer` contract following a CRUD pattern. Now, let's move on to building the `Ctontine` contract while creating an `Itontine` interface.

Tontine interfaces – Itontine

As per our design, now we will define an interface for our Tontine game.

Interfaces are universal concepts in programming languages used to represent collections of abstract methods. They are useful since they implement an agreed set of functions that enable interactions without forcing a contract relationship (they might be considered as a protocol).

Nevertheless, in Solidity, unlike abstract contracts, interfaces present the following limitations:

- Cannot inherit other contracts or interfaces
- Cannot implement their own functions
- Cannot define a constructor
- Cannot define variables
- Cannot define `structs`
- Cannot define `enums`

Here is the definition of our `Itontine` interface:

```
interface Itontine {
    function join() external payable returns (bool);
    function ping() external returns (bool);
    function eliminate(address a) external returns (bool);
    function claimReward() external returns (bool);
    event NewActivePlayerEv(address _address, uint time);
    event EliminatedPlayerEv(address _address);
}
```

As you can see, we define an interface in the same way as we do for an abstract contract, the difference being the use of the `interface` keyword. Let's have a look at what these methods are for:

- `join()` enables players to join the ongoing Tontine game. It's declared as `payable`, which means it can receive ether.
- `ping()` keeps a track record of the player activity (pinging).
- `eliminate()` enables players to knock out inactive players.
- `claimReward()` sends the total amount controlled by the contract to the last surviving player.
- `NewActivePlayerEv` and `EliminatedPlayerEv` are two events emitted when a new player joins the game or a player is eliminated, respectively.

The most important benefit of using interfaces is making the main smart contract upgradeable. Such design can facilitate rolling out future releases of the Tontine game (`Ctontine`) without introducing breaking changes.

At this point, we need to build out the implementation part.

Interface implementation – Ctontine contract

The next step is to define the main contract behind our game: Ctontine. In Solidity, when a contract implements an interface, the class agrees to implement all of its methods. Hence, if you miss implementing a function defined in the inherited interface, you'll get the following error (in Remix):

```
This contract does not implement all functions and thus cannot be created.

                                                                    OK   null
```

As we do for inheritance, we use the `is` keyword to implement the interface, as follows:

```
contract Ctontine is Itontine {..}
```

Now, let's fill this empty contract. Within the preceding bracket, we start by declaring the following contract states:

```
mapping (address => uint256 ) public Tpension;
Cplayer.player[] public active_players;
Cplayer.player[] public eleminated_players;
mapping (address => uint) public ping_time;
uint256 public Lindex;
Cplayer Tplayer:
```

Here are the contract states:

- `Tpension`: This is a mapping object storing the funds deposited by each player.
- `active_players`: This is an array of active players.
- `eliminated_players`: This is an array of eliminated players.
- `ping_time`: This is a mapping storing the last ping time for each player.
- `Lindex`: This is an integer variable tracking the index of the last active user.

We will deal with an instance of the `Cplayer` contract and `Cplayer.player` objects to represent the players managed by the aforementioned contract. Therefore, we should find out how to access the remote states and call methods from a remote contract.

Smart contract interaction

In Ethereum, contracts communicate between each other using message calls. Practically, a smart contract is able to communicate with another one that it deploys or with an instance of an existing contract. In Solidity, for both cases, we can declare a Cplayer instance as follows: Cplayer Tplayer. Let's discuss how contracts interact between Ethereum and Solidity.

Contract instantiation

To instantiate an existing contract, we need to know its address. For example, in our contract, we will instantiate the Cplayer contract in the Ctontine constructor as follows:

```
constructor(address _CplayerAddress) public {
    Tplayer = Cplayer(_CplayerAddress);
}
```

The Cplayer(_CplayerAddress); expression will perform an explicit conversion of the Cplayer type, stating that "we know that the contract at the given address of _CplayerAddress is of the Cplayer type." It's worth noting that instantiating a contract using its address doesn't imply the execution of its constructor.

The interaction with a deployed contract is a very powerful feature as it allows code reusability, since deployed contracts can be used like libraries. Furthermore, if we implement a pattern that enables us to change the used contract, instantiation can help us avoid reusing faulty contracts by changing the contract address.

Contract creation

The second option is to deploy a new instance of a given contract. To achieve that, Solidity provides the new keyword, which can be used as follows:

```
contract ContractA {
    uint256 x;

    function ContractA (uint256 y) payable {
        x = y;
    }
}

contract ContractB {
    ContractA CAinstance = new ContractA(10);
}
```

As you can see, we can pass arguments when we create a contract, since the created contract has a constructor that accepts arguments. The `new ContractA(arg)` line will execute the created contract's constructor and return its address. Note that an instance of each smart contract is implicitly convertible to its address, and in Solidity we are not dealing with real objects as in OOP to represent contracts as we do for classes.

Moreover, you can send ether from your source contract to the newly created contract using the `.value()` option, as follows:

```
ContractA CAinstance = (new ContractA).value(amount)(arg);
```

Once the instance is created, the caller contract can pass messages to call remote methods or to read or edit remote states. Let's see how to perform such calls.

Reading the storage of a remote contract

In our project, we have a `Ctontine` contract that instantiates a `Cplayer` object. As we presented in the game design, the player should sign up using the `Cplayer` contract, and then join the game using the `Ctontine` contract. This implies that the `Cplayer` contract manages the player details and that `Ctontine` needs to access them.

In Ethereum, each contract has its own storage space, which can't be accessed directly or overridden by another contract. Given the `ContractA` and `ContractB` contracts, the former can only access the storage of the latter by invoking a method (getter) that returns data from the storage of `ContractB`.

I'll make an exception for the preceding rule. A contract can access three things from another contract: the contract's balance (`contract_Address.balance`), the contract's code (`EXTCODECOPY`), and the contract's code size (`EXTCODESIZE`).

You might be wondering, "What if we declare states variables as `public`? Wouldn't they be accessible?" It's not important whether the variable is `public` or not, as the `public` specifier provides a free getter function within the contract scope, and not external access.

Back in our contract code, if we try to read the `admin` variable in the `Ctontine` contract from the `Cplayer` contract directly – `Address Cplayer_admin = Tplayer.admin;` – we'll get the following message error, even if `admin` is declared as public:

```
browser/ballot.sol:98:19: TypeError: Member "admin" not found or not visible after argument-dependent lookup in ✖
contract Cplayer
address public ad=Tplayer.admin;
                  ^-----------^
```

So how do we solve this?

In the target contract, we should have a getter that reads for us and returns the intended value.

Editing the storage of a remote contract

As was the case for reading contract storage, you cannot modify states of another contract without defining a setter function.

Let's have a look at the following example:

```
contract ContractA {
    uint256 public state;
    function setstate(uint _value) {
        state = _value;
    }
}

contract ContractB{
    ContractA public OneInstance = new ContractA();
    function getstateA() public {
        OneInstance.state = 12;
        OneInstance.setstate(12);
    }
}
```

The `OneInstance.state = 12;` line in the `getstateA` method will raise an error. We need instead to call the `setstate()` setter to update the state value.

The need for getters (read) and setters (update) in intra-contract interactions demonstrates the importance of the CRUD pattern.

Let's get back to our game code. So far, in our Ctontine contract, we have declared the required states and our constructor is already defined. All we are missing is implementing the Ctontine contract methods.

Joining the game

In order to start the game, a player has to call the join() method while sending more than one ether to the Tontine contract. Therefore, in the Ctontine contract, we need to implement this function as follows:

```
function join() public payable returns(bool) {
    require(Tplayer.exist(msg.sender), "player doesn't exist");
    require(msg.value >= 1 ether && Tpension[msg.sender] == 0, "send higher
pension");
    Tpension[msg.sender] = msg.value;
    Tplayer.EditPlayer(msg.sender, active_players.length);
    active_players.push(Tplayer.getplayer(msg.sender));
    Lindex += (active_players.length - 1);
    ping_time[msg.sender] = now;
    emit NewActivePlayerEv(msg.sender, now);
    return true;
}
```

Let's go over this implementation, line by line.

First of all, the join() function is marked as payable to allow the contract to accept ether via standard transactions. It is also defined as external, specifying that the method has to be called from other contracts or via transactions. We made this choice following the game design and because an external function is cheaper than a normal public function.

The join() method implements the game rules. Thus, a player should be able to join the game if the following requirements are met:

- Player should be registered in the Cplayer contract:
  `require(Tplayer.exist(msg.sender), "player doesn't exist");`
- Player should send enough money (more than one ether): `msg.value >= 1 ether`

- Player hasn't joined the ongoing Tontine game before: `msg.value >= 1 &&`
  `Tpension[msg.sender] == 0`

If they fulfill the conditions, we save the supplied ether in the `Tpension` array.

The `Tplayer.EditPlayer(msg.sender, active_player.length);` line edits the value of the `id` attribute for the given player. We use this element to keep track of the index of each player in the active player array. That will help us to know which case to delete if we want to remove this player.

Then the `active_player.push()` function is used to add a new player into the `active_player` array.

> In Solidity, dynamic arrays support the `push` method to add elements, but there is no `pop` method to retrieve the last added item.

We use a `Lindex` global state, which sums up the index values of the active players. Why? Because it will help us to know the last surviving player's index in the active players array.

The `ping_time[msg.sender] = now;` line initially stores the time when the players join the game as their first ping time.

At the end of the function, we emit an `ewActivePlayerEv(msg.sender,now)` event to announce the signing of a new player.

So far, within this function, we have introduced a lot of new things related to intra-contract interaction. Let's again take a pause in writing the `Ctontine` contract and learn some new concepts. You can skip the next two sections if you want to concentrate on building the game.

Calling remote functions

In Solidity, you can call functions either internally or externally. Only the functions of the same contract can be called internally, whereas external functions are called by other contracts.

If you were to call a function from another contract, the EVM uses the CALL instruction, which switches the context, making its state variables inaccessible. In the following sections, we will discover two ways to call a function from another contract.

Option one – using the ABI

As we did in the Ctontine contract, the regular way to interact with other contracts is to call (invoke) a function on a contract object (we borrow here the OOP terminology). For example, we can call a remote function from a remote contract, ContractA, as follows: ContractA.Remotefunction(arguments).

But to be able to make the invocation this way, we need to define (in the same Solidity file) an abstract form of ContractA. For instance, if we have a contract, ContractA, then the code is as follows:

```
contract ContractA {
    function f(uint256 a, string s) payable returns (bool) {
        //your code here
        return true;
    }
}
```

If this contract is deployed in the blockchain, let's say under the 0x123456 address, and we want to call the f() function within a caller contract, ContractB, then we have to include the abstract form of ContractA in the ContractB file, then instantiate ContractA and execute f(). Here is how the ContractB contract file will look:

```
contract ContractA {
    function f(uint256 a, string s) payable returns (bool);
    function h() payable returns (uint);
}

contract ContractB{
    address ContractAaddress = 0x123456;
    ContractA ContractAInstance = ContractA(ContractAaddress);

    function g() returns (bool){
        return ContractAInstance.f(10, "hello");
    }
}
```

If we invoke a `payable` function, we can specify the number of wei, as well as limit the amount of gas available to the invocation using the `.gas()` and `.value()` special options, respectively: `ContractAInstance.h.value(10).gas(800)();`.

The parentheses at the end serve to receive the arguments needed to perform the call. If the function doesn't accept any arguments, we keep them empty.

> The argument provided for the `.value()` function is considered by default in wei. You can indicate other units, such as `finney` or `ether`. For instance `.value(10 ether)` will send 10 ether instead of 10 wei.

Option two – using low-level calls

When the called contract doesn't adhere to the ABI, we can't just use `ContractAInstance.f();` or `ContractA ContractAInstance = ContractA(0x123456)` to define a new instance.

In this case, we have to use the special low-level `call` function, using the following call structure:

```
contract_address.call(bytes4(sha3("function_name(arguments types)")),
parameters_values)
```

In the previous example, we could call `f()` with two arguments using `ContractAaddress.call(bytes4(keccak256("f(uint256,string)")), 10, "hello");`.

This is a sort of tedious manual construction of the ABI function signature. However, things are getting better with newer Solidity. Since release 0.4.22, the `abi.encode()`, `abi.encodePacked()`, `abi.encodeWithSelector()`, and `abi.encodeWithSignature()` global functions have been defined to encode structured data, therefore helping us to build a valid call, as follows:

```
OneInstance.call(abi.encodeWithSignature("function_name(arguments
types)")),parameters_values)
```

`call` can be used along with the `.gas()` and `value()` methods to adjust the supplied gas and value in the call.

`call` returns `true` if the called function executes without exception. Also, it will fire an exception if the call contract does not exist, or if it throws an exception or runs out of gas. If we apply `call` to a contract without specifying a function name, its `fallback` will be executed (maybe that's why the fallback function doesn't have a name).

 Let's clear up some potential ambiguity about the `call` function. The `call` function used in Solidity to pass messages (the `CALL` opcode) between contracts is different from the `call` method (based on the `eth_call` RPC message) we introduced in the previous chapter, which is part of the web3.js API. The main difference to keep in mind is that the former can change a contract's states while the latter can't.

Using call to send ether

For security reasons, there is a capped stipend of 2,300 gas that applies to internal sends (using the `transfer()` or `send()` methods) from one smart contract to another. Therefore, the triggered fallback has a limited amount of gas to operate. However, the `call` function doesn't have a similar limitation, which represents a risk for your contract. In order to define the same security measure, you have to set `gas` to 0 in your calls: `contract_address.call.gas(0).value(xyz)`.

Mind you, the `call` method or other low-level functions should be used with care as they may cause some security issues if we deal with a malicious contract.

After this long introduction about contract remote calls, let's get back to our `Ctontine` contract.

The ping() method

After implementing the `join()` function, it's time to define the `ping()` function, which will allow the player to update their activity, as follows:

```
function ping() external returns(bool) {
    ping_time[msg.sender] = now;
    return true;
}
```

There's nothing complex about this code. Each time `ping()` is called, we will store the current time returned by `now` as the new ping time. Players will not literally ping the contract as we do in a network, they will only send a transaction invoking the ping method to prove their activity.

The eliminate() method

The game logic enables a player to eliminate another unlucky opponent by triggering the `eliminate()` method, which we define as follows:

```
function eliminate(address PlayerAddress) external  returns(bool) {
    require(now > ping_time[PlayerAddress] + 1 days);
    delete Tpension[PlayerAddress];
    delete active_players[Tplayer.getplayer(PlayerAddress).id];
    Lindex -= Tplayer.getplayer(PlayerAddress).id;
    eliminated_players.push(Tplayer.getplayer(PlayerAddress));
    Tplayer.EditPlayer(msg.sender, 0);
    share_pension(PlayerAddress);
    emit eliminatedPlayerEv(PlayerAddress);
    return true;
}
```

Take a close look, and I'm sure you'll make sense of this code.

The `require(now > ping_time[PlayerAddress] + 1 days);` line ensures that we can eliminate only players who didn't ping the contract within the last 24 hours.

This function will remove the eliminated player from the active player list (`active_players`) and move it to the eliminated player list (`eliminated_players.push`). Then we set the player's ID to zero as it has been removed from the active player list. Afterward, we call `share_pension()`, which will share the balance of the eliminated player between the remaining active players. We end by firing an event, declaring the elimination of the player.

The share_pension() method

As you saw, in the previous function we called `share_pension()` to share the eliminated player's deposit. Here's its implementation:

```
function share_pension(address user) internal returns (bool) {
    uint256 remainingPlayers = remaining_players();
    for(uint256 i = 0; i < active_players.length; i++){
```

```
            if (active_players[i].Paddress != 0x00)
                Tpension[active_players[i].Paddress] = Tpension[user] /
remaining_players;
            }
            return true;
    }

    function remaining_players() public view returns (uint256) {
        return (active_players.length-eliminated_players.length);
    }
}
```

We declare this function `internal` as it's intended to be used only within the contract scope. As we can see, `share_pension()` shares the eliminated players' balances between the remaining active players. This function has to allocate the `Tpension[user]/remaining_players` quotient to each active player. However, we are facing a problem here! Have you spotted it?

Standard integer division

Handling the division in the previous scenario is just the same as working with integer divisions, as Ethereum doesn't adopt floating point numbers. The division would result in a floor of the calculation with the remainder discarded. For example, the division 17/3 equals 5, with the remainder of 2 discarded. To fix this, we create a new method that does the following:

```
function calcul(uint a, uint b, uint precision) public pure returns (uint)
{
    require(b != 0);
    return a * (10 ** (precision)) / b;
}
```

Note that the double asterisk, `**`, is a Solidity operator representing the exponentiation operation. In our example, 10 is the base whereas `precision` is the exponent.

If we divide 17 by 3 using the `calcul()` function, and we call the function with a precision of 5 (the number of digits after the decimal point), it will output 566,666, which can be displayed to the player as 5.66666. In this way, we can produce a float using integer division, though it still requires that in the frontend you divide the result by the equivalent value of `(10 ** (precision))` to display the floating-point number.

Therefore, in the `share_pension()` function, we substitute the quotient by performing the following:

```
Tpension[active_players[i].Paddress] = calcul(Tpension[user],
remainingPlayers, 18);
```

 To avoid security flaws, you can perform a division operation using the `SafeMath` secure library, available at the OpenZepplin repository: `https://github.com/OpenZeppelin/openzeppelin-solidity/blob/master/contracts/math/SafeMath.sol`.

The claimReward method

At the final stage of the game, the last active player can claim their reward by calling `claimReward()`, which we define as the following:

```
function claimReward() external returns (bool) {
    require(remaining_players() == 1);
    active_players[Lindex].Paddress.transfer(address(this).balance);
    return true;
}
```

I'm sure the `this` keyword has caught your attention more than the rest of the code. So what is it?

The this keyword

The `this` keyword in Solidity is pretty similar to `this` in OOP, and represents a pointer to the current contract, which is explicitly convertible to an address. Moreover, all contracts inherit the members of `address`, thus it is possible to query the balance of the current contract using `address(this).balance` (you'll find `this.balance` in old code).

As `this` returns the address of the current contract, we can use it as follows: `address ContractAddress = this;`.

`this` is also used to access internally a method declared as `external`, otherwise the compiler won't recognize it. In that case, the function will be called through a `call` message instead of being called directly via `jumps`.

Great, at this level, we're nearly done with the game contracts. However, the code should be tested before we start working on the user interface side. I hope you didn't forget how to use Truffle. To make it easy for you, I've consolidated the contract's full source code into a single source file on github.

Truffle unit tests

I believe software developers are artists, and they love testing their *chefd'oeuvres* before deploying them. If you're one of them then that's good news for you, as Truffle allows you to easily test your Solidity smart contract.

Under the hood, Truffle leverages an adapted version of the famous Mochajs (https:// mochajs.org/) unit-testing framework to test Solidity contracts. Consequently, you can write your tests in JavaScript and take advantage of all the patterns Mocha provides. In addition, Truffle enables you to write tests using Solidity directly. In this section, I will opt for starting with JavaScript to implement all of the Tontine test cases, then we will explore how to use Solidity as a testing framework.

Let's start by writing our test files.

Preparing the testing environment

To test our contracts, we need first to check whether they compile properly without any errors. As we did at beginning of this chapter, open your Terminal and place yourself in the tontine/ folder we created earlier, then compile the contracts using either truffle compile or truffle compile-all.

The second of these will compile all contracts instead of intelligently choosing which contracts need to be compiled. Now, have a look at the console output:

```
user@ByExample-node: ~/tontine
user@ByExample-node:~/tontine$ truffle compile-all
Compiling ./contracts/Migrations.sol...
Compiling ./contracts/tontine.sol...

Compilation warnings encountered:

/home/user/tontine/contracts/tontine.sol:2:1: Warning: Experimental features are
  turned on. Do not use experimental features on live deployments.
pragma experimental ABIEncoderV2;
^------------------------------^

Writing artifacts to ./build/contracts

user@ByExample-node:~/tontine$ ▊
```

We will get a single, irrelevant warning that we can ignore and advance toward migrating
the contract.

Migrating the contracts

In this second step, we need to write a migration file to let Truffle know how to deploy
your contract to the blockchain. Go to the `migrations/` folder and create a new file called
`3_initial_migration.js`. Notice the incremented numerical suffix:

```
var Ctontine = artifacts.require("Ctontine");
var Cplayer = artifacts.require("Cplayer");

module.exports = function(deployer) {
    deployer.deploy(Cplayer).then(function() {
        return deployer.deploy(Ctontine, Cplayer.address);
    }).then(function() { })
};
```

In the migration file, the first thing we need to do is get the reference to our contract in
JavaScript. This migration script will first deploy the `Cplayer` contract, then it will pass its
address to the constructor of `Ctontine` to deploy it.

> Changing the smart contract or deployment script after the migration has
> run has no effect, but the `--reset` option is specified as `truffle`
> `migrate --reset`.

Running Ganache

Before migrating your contract, don't forget to make sure that Ganache is running. If not, keep the same configuration file, `truffle.js`, as in the earlier example, and run Ganache as we did before: `ganache-cli -p 7545`.

 Ganache will mine blocks instantly, but you can pass in a blocktime to delay block creation to be able to track what's happening. The block time is set using the `-b` option followed by a number (delay in seconds).

Preparing the tests

Everything is ready to build our Truffle test.

First off, create a `test.js` file within Truffle's `test/` folder, then paste in the following code:

```
var Cplayer = artifacts.require("Cplayer");
var Ctontine = artifacts.require("Ctontine");
contract('Cplayer', function(accounts) {
});
contract('Ctontine', function(accounts) {
});
```

As you guessed, `artifacts.require` references the contract to use in the test script. Then, for each contract we need to test, we define a `contract()` function to create a test suite, as follows:

```
contract(Cplayer, function(accounts) { });
```

Here, the `contract()` function is similar to the `describe()` function in Mocha, which holds a collection of tests. Its first parameter is an array with the accounts coming from Ganache.

Note that every call or transaction you execute from `web3.js` or Truffle is asynchronous, with the difference being that the first uses promises and `web3.js` uses callbacks. Either way, while testing, you're going to be writing plenty of asynchronous code.

Testing addPlayer()

Moving on, it's time to define our first test. We will check whether the `addPlayer()` function operates properly. Put the following code inside the first contract function in your test file:

```
it("..should ADD players", async () => {
  let Cp = await Cplayer.new();
  for (let i = 0; i < 3; i++) {
    await Cp.addPlayer("player" + i, 123, { from: accounts[i] });
    const P = await Cp.players.call(accounts[i]);
    assert.equal(P[2], accounts[i], "player not added");
  }
});
```

As you can see, the test adopts Mocha's `it` syntax. If you're not familiar with the Mocha framework, know that `it` is a function that is actually a test itself, which takes two arguments. The first is a message using natural language to describe our expectation for the test, and the second is a function that holds the body of the test.

In the preceding test, we create a new `Cplayer` contract and then add three players using the `addPlayer()` method. As you can see, we use `await` as we are dealing with an asynchronous call.

The test ends with an assertion test using `assert.equal(<current>, <expected>, <message>);`.

Obviously, as its name indicates, this function tests whether two values are equal. If this wasn't the case, it would cause an assertion failure and communicate the message you defined (optionally) as the third argument.

Now, run this first test using `truffle test --network my_ganache`.

Alternatively, you can specify a path to a specific file you want to run, for example, `truffle test ./path/fileName.js --network my_ganache`.

Each time you run the test, Truffle will automatically compile and migrate your contract for you. The test script should compile without any errors. Henceforth, you can continue using Truffle for testing each `it` block we define, or leave it until the end.

Great! Let's move on and add the next test.

Testing findPlayer()

In a single-testing contract function, it is common to have multiple `it` blocks instead of combining multiple tests in a single `it` block. This time, we would like to test the `findPlayer()` function:

```
it("..should FIND a player", async () => {
  let Cp = await Cplayer.new();
  for (let i = 0; i < 3; i++) {
    await Cp.addPlayer("player" + i, 123, { from: accounts[i] });
    const P = await Cp.findplayer(accounts[i]);
    assert.equal(P[0], "player" + i, "player not found");
  }
});
```

This is pretty similar to what we did in the previous test. We only changed the test message and the function we tested.

You may have noticed the redundancy (contract creation) between the two previous `it` blocks. To remove this inconvenience, we can put this redundant code function into the special `beforeEach()` function in the contract function:

```
const [firstAccount, secondAccount, thirdAccount] = accounts;

let Cp;
beforeEach(async function() {
  Cp = await Cplayer.new();
});
```

Consequently, before each test, we instantiate the `Cplayer` contract, so each test is executed with a clean contract state. We also named three first accounts to avoid using `accounts[index]`. That way, the test looks cleaner and more elegant.

Testing removePlayer()

Here, we will experiment with something interesting. As you know, in the `Cplayer` contract, the ability to remove players is restricted to an administrator, which is the deployer's account. The following test will check whether an exception will be raised if a different account tries to call `removePlayer()`:

```
it("..Only admin can REMOVE players", async function() {
  let error;
  await Cp.addPlayer("player1", 123, { from: secondAccount });
  try {
```

```
        await Cp.removePlayer(secondAccount, { from: thirdAccount });
        assert.fail();
    } catch (error) {
        const msgexist = error.message.search('revert') >= 0;
        assert.ok(msgexist);
    }
}
```

As we are expecting an error, we can just use `try {...} catch{}` blocks to handle the exception.

The test will be successful if the contract returns an error with the `'VM Exception while processing transaction: revert'` message. This is because the contract will be deployed with the default account (`accounts[0]` is the admin), and we then try to remove the player using a different account, `accounts[2]` (who is not admin).

Within the `try` block, we use `assert.fail()` to throw a failure with the error message, and in the `catch` block, we use `assert.ok()` to test whether the specific `revert` keyword exists in the error message.

At this level, we've tested almost all the main functions and behaviors in the `Cplayer` contract. Now, it's time to test `Ctontine`.

Testing Ctontine

We start by removing the redundancy in the test block as we did previously for the `Cplayer` tests. We will create a `beforeEach` hook, which takes care of the contract's creation and adds three players to the `Cplayer` instance. All these elements will help us to perform unit tests for the `Ctontine` contract. Keep in mind that all the `Ctontine` tests should be defined within the second contract function in the test file. As a result, we add the following code to the `Ctontine` test suite:

```
contract('Ctontine', function(accounts) {
    const [firstAccount, secondAccount, thirdAccount] = accounts;
    let Cp;
    let Ct;
    beforeEach(async function() {
        Cp = await Cplayer.new();
        Ct = await Ctontine.new(Cp.address);
        for (let i = 0; i < 3; i++) {
            await Cp.AddPlayer("player" + i, 123, { from: accounts[i] });
        }
    });
});
```

Testing a payable function

The first function to test in `Ctontine` will be `join()`, which is `payable`. We therefore need to check whether a player registered in `Cplayer` is able to deposit ether and join the active players list:

```
it(".. should enable players to join the game", async () => {
    await Ct.join({ from: firstAccount, value: 1 * Ether });
    let P1 = await Ct.active_players(0);
    assert.equal(P1[0], "player0", "Player hasn't joined the game");
    let CtBalance = await getBalance(Ct.address);
    assert.equal(CtBalance, 1 * Ether, "Contract hasn't received the
deposit");
});
```

As you know, by default, the amount sent in a transaction is specified in wei, so if you only put 1 in the `value` field, it will be considered as 1 wei, which doesn't fulfill the requirement. In addition to this, Truffle doesn't recognise ether as a unit, therefore as a solution, we need to define a global constant at the top of our test file: `const Ether = 10 * 18`. By using this constant, we will be able to express values directly in ether.

After calling the `join()` method, we assert whether the player has been added to the active player list by comparing the player's name stored in the active player list with the name used in the test: `assert.equal(P1[0], "player0", "Player hasn't joined the game");`.

We also assert that funds have been successfully deposited by comparing the deposited amount to the contract balance. If the player has successfully joined the game, the contract balance should be 1 ether.

In Truffle's tests, to get the contract's balance, we had to use the web3.js method, getBalance(address). In this example, I have encapsulated the getBalance() method in a separate module, defined in a new getBalance.js file:

```
module.exports.getBalance = function getBalance(address) {
    return web3.eth.getBalance(address);
};
```

This is then imported into the test file using const { getBalance } = require("./getBalance");.

Testing events

As you know, events are very useful for the functioning of DApps. Thus, we need to test whether our contract emits them properly. Here's an example of testing the NewActivePlayerEv event:

```
it(".. should emit 'NewActivePlayerEv' event  when a player joins the
game", async function() {
    let NewActivePlayerEvtListener = Ct.NewActivePlayerEv();
    await Ct.join({ from: firstAccount, value:1 * Ether });
    let proposalAddedLog = await new Promise((resolve, reject) =>
      NewActivePlayerEvtListener.get((error, log) => error ? reject(error) :
resolve(log)));
    assert.equal(proposalAddedLog.length, 1, " event not emitted");
    let eventArgs = proposalAddedLog[0].args;
    assert.equal(eventArgs._address, firstAccount);
    let time = await Ct.ping_time.call(firstAccount);
    assert.equal(eventArgs.time, time.toNumber(), "ping time");
});
```

The important part in the preceding code snippet is the following line:

```
let proposalAddedLog = await new Promise( (resolve, reject) =>
    NewActivePlayerEvtListener.get((error, log) => error ? reject(error) :
resolve(log)));
```

Here, we create a new Promise to check whether the event was stored in the contract log. The proposalAddedLog object is expected to be an array containing one entry per event, representing the result of get(), which reads all the log entries .

Then we use `assert.equal(proposalAddedLog.length, 1);` to check whether a new event was stored (log array isn't empty).

Once we have ensured that an event has been emitted, we assert that the `address` and `timestamp` returned by the event match the player's address and pinging time.

If you're wondering why we use a `toNumber()` method, it ensures the result, which is a `BigNumber`, is converted into an integer.

Testing claimReward()

Good news! This will be the last test we perform, but also the longest one. Here, we would like to test the procedure for claiming a reward. As we did before, it's easy to simulate players joining the game, but to eliminate the opponents, we need to wait a day (the game's rule) without a ping!

It's silly to wait a day to perform a test, isn't it?

Don't worry, there's a workaround for this issue. Let's look at the test:

```
it(".. should send the reward to the last active player", async () => {
   await Ct.join({ from: firstAccount, value: 1 * Ether });
   await Ct.join({ from: secondAccount, value: 1 * Ether });
   await Ct.join({ from: thirdAccount, value: 1 * Ether });
   await increaseTime(DAY + 1);
   await Ct.eliminate(secondAccount, { from: firstAccount });
   await Ct.eliminate(thirdAccount, { from: firstAccount });
   let initialBalance = getBalance(firstAccount).toNumber();
   let Nactive = await Ct.remaining_players.call();
   assert.equal(Nactive, 1, "players not eliminated");
   let finalBalance=getBalance(firstAccount).toNumber();
   await Ct.claimReward({ from: firstAccount });
   assert.equal(finalBalance, initialBalance + 3);
});
```

I think you're now able to decipher the preceding test code, except the following line of code: `await increaseTime(DAY + 1);`.

As its name indicates, this function is used to move Ganache's clock forward. If you run this test, you'll get an error as `increaseTime()` is not yet defined.

Time manipulation

In a separate file, called `increaseTime.js`, within the `test/` directory, define the following module to move time forward for a given duration:

```
module.exports.increaseTime = function increaseTime(duration) {
  const id = Date.now();
  return new Promise((resolve, reject) => {
    web3.currentProvider.sendAsync({
      jsonrpc: "2.0",
      method: "evm_increaseTime",
      params: [duration],
      id: id
    }, err1 => {
      if (err1) {
        return reject(err1);
      }
      web3.currentProvider.sendAsync({
        jsonrpc: "2.0",
        method: "evm_mine",
        id: id + 1
      }, (err2, res) => {
        return err2 ? reject(err2) : resolve(res);
      });
    });
  });
};
```

Don't let this strange chunk of code fool you. It is actually very easy to read and understand, so have a second look.

To understand what's going on, you should know that Ganache provides two nonstandard RPC calls: `evm_mine` and `evm_increaseTime`. The former simply forces a block to be mined instantly, whereas the latter jumps forward in time. As you can see, in the earlier code, `evm_increaseTime` takes one parameter, which is the amount of time to increase in seconds. It will use this literally to instruct Ganache to push the clock forward and help us to perform the `claimReward` test instantaneously instead of waiting for a whole day.

Once the module is defined, you have to import it into your test file using `const { increaseTime } = require("./increaseTime");`.

Finally, we also define `constant DAY = 3600 * 24;` to increase the duration in days easily instead of dealing with seconds.

Running the tests

After writing the game contracts and the tests, let's run our test suite to ensure that we have the expected behavior. For that, we run `truffle test --network my_ganache`.

The outcome will be a detailed output similar to the following:

```
user@ByExample-node:~/tontine$ truffle test --network my_ganache
Using network 'my_ganache'.


  Contract: Cplayer
    ✓ .. should ADD three Players (496ms)
    ✓ .. should find a player (114ms)
    ✓ .. should authorize Only admin can remove players (221ms)

  Contract: Ctontine
    ✓ .. sould enable players to join the game (395ms)
    ✓ .. should emit 'NewActivePlayerEv' event  when a player join the game (373
ms)
    ✓ .. should send the reward to the last active player (1437ms)


  6 passing (5s)

user@ByExample-node:~/tontine$ █
```

If the tests were successful, you'll see green checkmarks along with a short description (the `it` block's description) for each unit test. Otherwise, you'll get a red failure message indicating the faulty test.

Under the hood, in one shot, Truffle compiles your contracts and runs migrations to deploy the contracts to the network, then runs the tests against the deployed instances. Isn't it a lifesaver?

Testing with Solidity

As we mentioned before, Truffle enables us to run unit tests using Solidity as well as JavaScript. In order to start testing with Solidity, create a file called `TontineTest.sol` (`.sol` extension not `.js`) in Truffle's `test/` folder with the following code:

```
import "truffle/Assert.sol";
import "../contracts/tontine.sol";
import "truffle/DeployedAddresses.sol";
contract TontineTest { }
```

This is an empty test contract, so we start by importing the needed testing libraries, `DeployedAddresses.sol` and `Assert.sol` (created dynamically at the time of deployment), along with the contract being tested (`tontine.sol`).

> When we import external contracts, filenames are always treated as a path with "/" as the directory separator. All path names are treated as absolute paths unless they start with . or . . . .

Let's go over how to write a Solidity unit test. In the `TontineTest` contract, define the following testing methods:

```
contract TontineTest {
    uint public initialBalance = 10 ether;
    Cplayer cplayer_;
    Ctontine tontine;

    function beforeEach() public {
        cplayer_ = Cplayer(DeployedAddresses.Cplayer());
        tontine = Ctontine(DeployedAddresses.Ctontine());
    }

    function testplayer() public {
        cplayer_.AddPlayer("Player1", 1234);
        bool expected = cplayer_.exist(this);
        Assert.isTrue(expected, "Player doesn't exist");
    }

    function testjoingame() public {
        cplayer_.AddPlayer("Player1", 1234);
        uint expectedBalance = 2 ether;
        tontine.join.value(2 ether)();
        Assert.equal(expectedBalance, address(tontine).balance, "Contract
balance should be 2 ether");
    }
}
```

It's a bit of a long test, but let's look at it after disassembling.

First off, the `initialBalance` variable indicates to Truffle how much ether to allocate to this test contract on deployment (10 ethers, in our case).

In just the same way as we did in the JavaScript tests, we can define a `beforeEach` hook as well as `beforeAll`, `afterAll`, and `afterEach` to perform setup and teardown actions before and after each test is run. We also use `DeployedAddresses` objects to manage the address of the contracts deployed at test time.

In this example, we are performing two unit tests:

- `testplayer()`: Checks whether a player added using `addPlayer()` has been successfully added
- `testjoingame()`: Checks whether the `Ctontine` contract has accepted funds deposited through the `join()` method

Similarly to the JavaScript tests, we rely on assertions (`ChaiJS`) to perform our unit tests. Various testing functions, such as `equals()`, `greaterThan()`, `isFalse()`, and `isEqual()`, are defined in Truffle's Assert library.

In the first test, we use the `this` variable, which represents the address of the current contract. Why? Because when we call the `addPlayer()` method, the `Cplayer` contract will see the test contract as the sender. Thus, we add the contract as a player, and then we check whether a player has been created with the same address.

In the second test, we add a player and then call the `join()` method while also depositing two ethers into the game. Afterward, we check whether the contract balance is equal to the deposited amount.

Run the tests again in the same way we did before: `truffle test test/TontineTest.sol --network my_ganache`.

In the test output, you should see the tests successfully passed, as follows:

```
user@ByExample-node:~/tontine$ truffle test test/TontineTest.sol --network my_ganache
Using network 'my_ganache'.

Compiling ./contracts/tontine.sol...
Compiling ./test/TontineTest.sol...
Compiling truffle/Assert.sol...
Compiling truffle/DeployedAddresses.sol...


TontineTest
  ✓ testplayer (107ms)
  ✓ testjoingame (189ms)


2 passing (2s)
```

Building a test suite while developing new smart contracts is an absolute necessity. I would suggest looking at the tests provided by the `OpenZeppelin` framework. You will find their cleanly written and reusable test patterns.

Compared to JavaScript, Solidity presents limited testing features. For example, unlike JavaScript tests, Solidity tests provide us with a single account (contract account), which can be used as the transaction sender.

Hopefully, this section helps you get started with your tests. Alright, after validating execution correctness with our tests, let's walk through how to spot potential bugs with debugging.

Debugging with Truffle and Remix

Developers familiar with debugging will find this a welcome relief.

Thankfully, Truffle and Remix provide built-in debugging features to help us understand where the code fails. This section provides a general overview of debugging in Truffle and Remix. If you are familiar with debugging using other IDEs, such as Eclipse or NetBeans, you will find Truffle and Remix similarly useful, even though they're less powerful.

Debugging with Truffle

Truffle includes a built-in debugger to debug transactions made against your contracts. It supports elementary debugging operations, such as code-stepping (over, into, out, next, and instruction), breakpoints, and watching expressions.

To try the debugging features, let's intentionally introduce a bug into the Ctontine contract and redeploy it into Ganache. Afterward, we will run the tests and use Truffle's debugger to detect the source of the error.

First, in the Ctontine contract code, change the first require() statement in the join() method as follows:

```
require(!Tplayer.exist(msg.sender));
```

As you can see, we reversed the required condition by adding an exclamation mark, "!", indicating that the player shouldn't be registered in the Cplayer contract. This goes against our previous test's logic as we add the testing player before calling each unit test, including a test for the join() method.

Now, if you run the truffle test test/test.js --network my_ganache tests, you will see the following error:

```
user@ByExample-node: ~/tontine

Contract: Cplayer
  ✓ .. should ADD three Players (455ms)
  ✓ .. should find a player (160ms)
  ✓ .. should authorize Only admin can remove players (181ms)

Contract: Ctontine
  1) .. sould enable players to join the game
  > No events were emitted
  2) .. should emit 'NewActivePlayerEv' event  when a player join the game
  > No events were emitted
  3) .. should send the reward to the last active player
  > No events were emitted


3 passing (4s)
3 failing

1) Contract: Ctontine
   .. sould enable players to join the game:
    Error: VM Exception while processing transaction: revert
      at Object.InvalidResponse (/home/user/.nvm/versions/node/v8.11.2/lib/node_
modules/truffle/build/webpack:/~/web3/lib/web3/errors.js:38:1)
        at /home/user/.nvm/versions/node/v8.11.2/lib/node_modules/truffle/build/we
```

The output shows that we have a serious problem with the Ctontine tests and the VM exception while processing transaction error message isn't much help in detecting the cause behind it. Let's chase the bug.

Spotting the error

To debug the previous error, copy the transaction ID from ganache-cli:

```
 ☒☻☻  user@ByExample-node: ~
eth_sendTransaction

  Transaction: 0x101b45064173614becb9d30322f58f651dc97dbea379ab07339c7d4faa71b1c

  Gas usage: 84574
  Block Number: 643
  Block Time: Thu Aug 02 2018 10:04:30 GMT+0100 (WEST)

th_getTransactionReceipt
th_sendTransaction

  Transaction: 0x90e02cc211733cade22bd5ff3b1ea1600781b48a1c792d867cda83190f77331

  Gas usage: 24944
  Block Number: 644
  Block Time: Thu Aug 02 2018 10:04:31 GMT+0100 (WEST)
  Runtime Error: revert
```

Then feed it as an argument to the truffle debug <tx id> --network my_ganache debug command.

In this case, we run:

```
truffle debug
0x90e02cc211733cade22bd5ff3b1ea1600781b48a1c792d867cda83190f773319 --
network my_ganache
```

Once executed, you'll enter Truffle's debugging mode, as shown the following screenshot:

```
^ (Relevant source part starts here and spans across multiple lines).

Gathering transaction data...

Addresses affected:
 0xcc69cf6888720e2a33bc89bf81f647cac4f14404 - Cplayer
 0x791200dd814f6966e55500882c7acf709f52edcb - Ctontine

Commands:
(enter) last command entered (step next)
(o) step over, (i) step into, (u) step out, (n) step next
(;) step instruction, (p) print instruction, (h) print this help, (q) quit
(b) toggle breakpoint, (c) continue until breakpoint
(+) add watch expression (`+:<expr>`), (-) remove watch expression (-:<expr>)
(?) list existing watch expressions
(v) print variables and values, (:) evaluate expression - see `v`


tontine.sol:

77:
78:
79: contract Ctontine is Itontine {
    ^^^^^^^^^^^^^^^^^^^^^^^^^^^^^^^^^^

debug(my_ganache:0x90e02cc2...)>

tontine.sol:

131:   }
132:
133:   function join() public payable returns(bool){
       ^^^^^^^^^^^^^^^^^^^^^^^^^^^^^^^^^^^^^^^^^^^^^^^

debug(my_ganache:0x90e02cc2...)>
```

Keep pressing the *Enter* button to step through the code and trace the execution steps. Finally, the debugger will stop with an error message:

```
133:   function join() public payable returns(bool){
134:       require(!Tplayer.exist(msg.sender),"player doesn't exist");
           ^^^^^^^^^^^^^^^^^^^^^^^^^^^^^^^^^^^^^^^^^^^^^^^^^^^^^^^^^^^^^^^^

debug(my_ganache:0x90e02cc2...)>

Transaction halted with a RUNTIME ERROR.

This is likely due to an intentional halting expression, like assert(), require(
) or revert(). It can also be due to out-of-gas exceptions. Please inspect your
transaction parameters and contract code to determine the meaning of this error.
user@ByExample-node:~/tontine$
```

As a result, Truffle's debugger indicates that the exception (error) is raised due to a failed `require()` statement, as the evaluated expression (`!Tplayer.exist(msg.sender)`) will definitely always be false. This is because, if you remember, in the `join()` test we added the player first, therefore the `exist()` function will be always true, and hence our faulty `require()` will fail. The important point is that Truffle indicates to us where the code fails with an interesting message, instead of the previous error message generated by the VM.

Breakpoints and watching values

More importantly, Truffle's debugger console enables you to toggle a breakpoint by pressing b and then pressing c to debug until reaching the breakpoint. Additionally, you can choose a variable (state or local) to watch using `+:variable_name` or by pressing v at any debugging step.

For example, if we debug the transaction initiated by the first (successful) `Cplayer` test (the `addPlayer()` test), we can visualize the values of each variable using the v option, as follows:

```
32: function AddPlayer(string _name, uint256 _phonenumber) public returns (bool){
33:   players[msg.sender].name=_name;
34:   players[msg.sender].Paddress=msg.sender;
                         ^^^^^^^^^^^

debug(my_ganache:0x81860524...)> v

         _name: 'player1'
  _phonenumber: 123
             : true
         admin: '0x00'
       players: null

debug(my_ganache:0x81860524...)> +:_name
'player1'
```

Make sure to experiment with all the debugger features introduced earlier. A good start point would be to read Truffle's documentation.

Now, roll back the changes, and save the contract to try debugging with Remix.

Debugging with Remix

If you're not a fan of CLI tools, Remix is a good debugging alternative for you. In fact, Remix provides a graphical interface with many more options.

Start and connect Remix to Ganache as we did in the previous chapter. Once connected, you will be able to debug the previous transaction we debugged using Truffle. First of all, we need to activate the debugging mode. There are several ways to achieve that, the easiest way being to browse to the debugger tab in the right-hand panel, and then provide either a transaction hash (transaction index) or a block number in the debugging input:

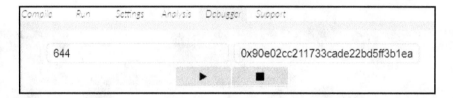

In Remix's right-hand pane, on the debugging form with several controls, press the play button to start debugging. You'll get a debugging menu with the views depicted here:

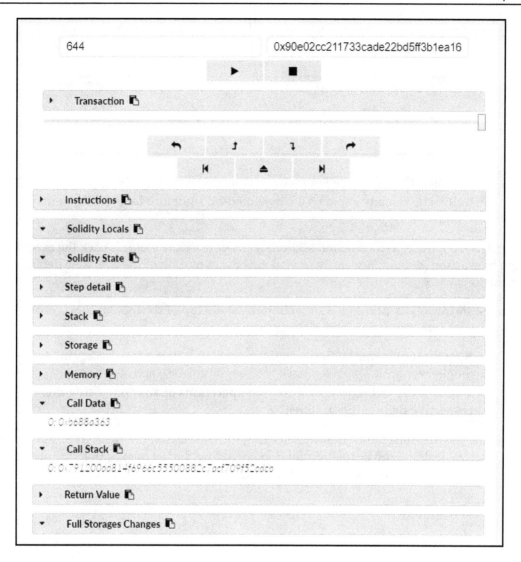

The views are listed as follows:

- **Instructions**: Lists the executed opcodes
- **Solidity Locals**: Shows the content of local variables in the current scope
- **Solidity State**: Displays state variables of the current executing contract
- **Step detail**: Displays the current step's execution details (remaining gas and VM trace step)

- **Stack**: Displays the local variables values stored in the stack
- **Storage**: Displays the contract storage entries(key, value) as shown here:

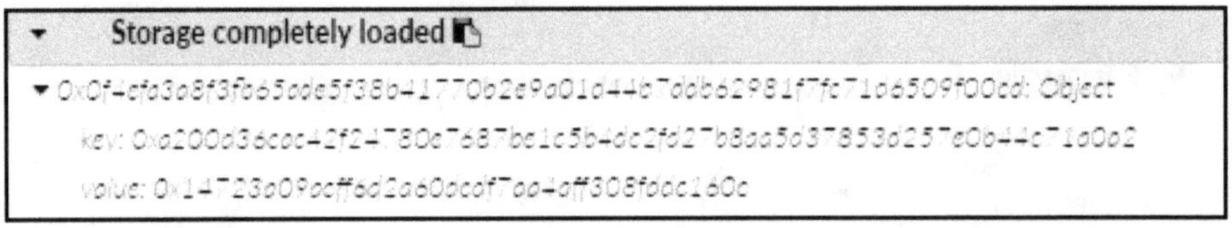

- **Memory**: Provides a view into the memory space that is used by the contract
- **Call Data**: Usually contains a 4-byte method signature followed by serialized arguments

The slider bar at the top (transaction section) helps you advance or roll back the execution of the transaction (debugging) easily to visualize the evolution of the available debugging information.

Below the slider, Remix provides a set of buttons at the top of the toolbar for controlling the execution of the transaction you are debugging:

- **Step through a transaction's payload execution using the debugging buttons**: Single over back ⌃ , step back ↓ , step into ↓ , and step over ⌃
- **You can stop debugging and resume operations at any time using the respective debugging buttons**: ▪ and ▸

Debugging the previous faulty transaction using the transaction's ID with Remix debugger boils down to dealing with crude information, including the list of executed opcodes. In this first case, the debugger shows us that the execution ends with a REVERT instruction:

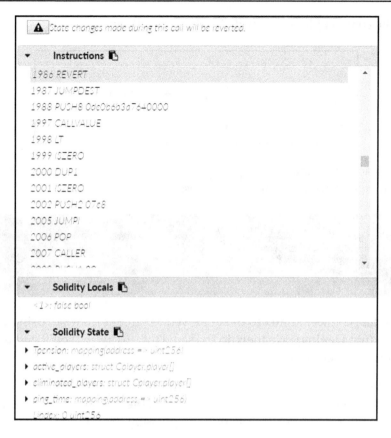

If you follow the JUMP instructions and the values being loaded into the stack, you'll be able to trace the source of the exception. However, I highly suspect you can't (or don't want to) deal with this hard task, which is why I am proposing an easier alternative in the remainder of this section.

Attaching the debugger to the code

Using Remix's debugger with only the transaction ID can be a little troublesome for beginners trying to spot where the code breaks, without having the debugger attached to the code. To make the attachment, we need to load the contract code and connect Remix to the new instance you've migrated in Ganache.

First, import the contract file from Truffle's folder, as follows:

Deploy the contract into Ganache using `truffle migrate -reset -network my_ganache`, then retrieve the contract's address:

```
Running migration: 2_initial_migration.js
  Deploying Cplayer...
  ... 0xce5b12c84a4f0fb96f917afc5964be1622eeefcb01bceb6534f255b8cfcdccac
  Cplayer: 0x7bd9dc68a0d268d9e07e6811d042d2b1bb63608d
  Deploying Ctontine...
  ... 0x5fc630529fd815c5c892f5f8590f3ca086cdc261a97ba7c3092d39f94c7acd61
  Ctontine: 0x081cad5cf649e07e8351b4e45a30db3997e0688a
```

Under the **Run** tab, connect Remix to the deployed `Ctontine` contract using the **At Address** button (not **Deploy**). We then do the same for `Cplayer`. You'll end up with two contracts loaded into Remix.

Then, we add three fictional players using `addPlayer()`. To add different players, change the account indicated in the transaction parameters in the top of the right-hand panel each time and execute the `addPlayer()` function (by pressing the `addPlayer()` button):

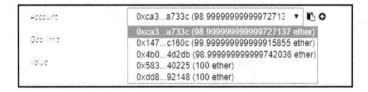

Now that we have three registered players, we can start interacting with the `Ctontine` contract.

Watching values

Remix provides us with a watch window to observe and inspect contract variables. To use this feature, in the right panel, second tab from the left, fill in the **Value** input with 1 and **ether**:

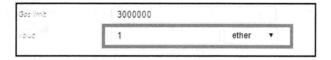

Then make the first player join the Tontine game by pressing the join button. When it completes successfully, change the account and call the join method with zero ether, and you'll get the following error in the messages output:

```
[vm] from:0xdd8...92148 to:Ctontine.join() 0x1df...bda71 value:0 wei data:0xb68...8a363
logs:0 hash:0x369...ba838                                                          Debug

transact to Ctontine.join errored: VM error: revert.
revert  The transaction has been reverted to the initial state.
Reason provided by the contract: "send higher pension". Debug the transaction to get more information.
```

Have you noticed the **send higher pension** message in the output console? If you remember, this message was defined in the require function to show us the reason behind the exception: `require(msg.value >= 1 ether && Tpension[msg.sender] == 0, "send higher pension");`.

Press the **Debug** button in the console or go to the **Debugger configuration** tab to go through the steps!

The **Solidity State** section will show us that, unlike the first player, the second player wasn't added successfully, as depicted in the following diagram:

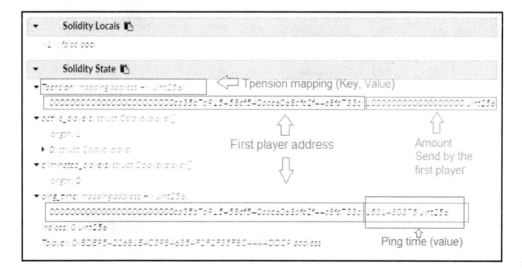

In addition, when the debugging panel loads up, you will see a blue highlight that marks the part of the code being executed as the debugging progresses, which provides precious assistance.

Notice the existence of a warning button under the debugging buttons. Once pressed, it will rethrow the exception and jump directly to the last opcode before the exception happened:

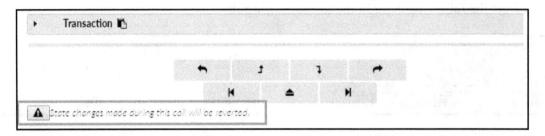

Setting breakpoints

As you know, breakpoints are the most basic and essential feature of reliable debugging. They represent a handy tool to help you examine in detail the execution of a specific section of code. As in other popular IDEs, in Remix breakpoints can be added and removed by clicking on the left margin of a line of code:

```
261 ▾  function join() public payable returns(bool){
262
263        require(Tplayer.exist(msg.sender),"player doesn't exist");
264
265        require(msg.value>=1 && Tpension[msg.sender]==0,"send higher pension");
266
267        Tpension[msg.sender]=msg.value;
268
269        Tplayer.EditPlayer(msg.sender,active_players.length);
270
271        active_players.push(Tplayer.getplayer(msg.sender));
272
273        indices +=(active_players.length-1);
274
275        ping_time[msg.sender]=now;
276
277        emit NewActivePlayerEv(msg.sender,now);
278
279        return true;
280
281    }
```

For example, let's define two debugging breakpoints. Set the first at the line where the player is added to the active players array, and the second at the line where the current timestamp is recorded.

Now, make the second player join the game properly with one ether, then debug the transaction. Once the debugger starts, you can jump directly to your fixed breakpoints using the **Jump to previous breakpoint**, **Jump to next breakpoint**, or **Jump out debugger** buttons:

At the breakpoint, Remix's debugger suspends your running code so you can take a look at the values of contract's states and explore the memory or storage at the current execution level.

For the sake of brevity, breakpoints will be the last debugging feature we cover. You can refer to Remix's documentation (`https://remix.readthedocs.io/en/latest/tutorial_debug.html`) for more information about the debugger's advanced features.

This has been a long discourse on writing, testing, and debugging our contracts. With that in place, we can safely shift to the frontend and start building the UI components.

Frontend with Drizzle

Thankfully, Truffle makes it possible to kick off a DApp project easily using a collection of delicious Truffle boxes. A box is basically a boilerplate template for giving developers the ability to build robust and adaptable DApps quickly. One of these boxes is the Drizzle box.

In this section, we will build a web interface for our game with Drizzle instead of using bare-metal JavaScript and web3.js, as we did in the previous chapter.

Prerequisites

To get started with Drizzle, it's preferable to have basic knowledge of ReactJS, and will require the installation of the following ingredients:

- MetaMask
- Ganache CLI (a version that supports Websockets)
- Truffle

What is the Drizzle box?

Yes, another tool with a delicious name: Truffle, Ganache, Drizzle, these names make me hungry.

Drizzle is a collection of frontend libraries that make writing DApp frontends easier and more predictable. Drizzle is based on the popular React framework, Redux, which is a predictable state container for JavaScript applications most commonly used with ReactJS for building user interfaces. Thus, it helps you write applications that behave consistently, solving the problems related to state mutation in highly asynchronous and non deterministic environments.

The Drizzle box comes with everything you need to start using smart contracts from a React app. As you'll see in a moment, Drizzle is easy to use. We just unpack its box and then we can build a DApp in a few steps. You can write a React app from scratch using Drizzle packages, but to save you time and effort, I opt for using the box template and editing its code.

Getting started with the Drizzle box

Let's start by setting up your first Drizzle template.

First, you have to create a new empty folder for the Drizzle box, otherwise Truffle will refuse to download the Drizzle box files. Start by creating a new dedicated folder: `mkdir DrizzleTontine`.

Then, install the Drizzle box: `truffle unbox drizzle`.

After a few seconds (two sips of coffee), it should output the following:

```
user@ByExample-node: ~/deleteme
File Edit View Search Terminal Help
user@ByExample-node:~/deleteme$ truffle unbox drizzle
Downloading...
Unpacking...
Setting up...
Unbox successful. Sweet!
```

Once the installation is done, you'll get a full DApp demo including sample contracts.

Running the demo

To run the example packed within the Drizzle box, you should already have the local Ganache network running. If not, start Ganache on port 7545: Ganache-cli -p 7545.

As we have a new Truffle project, we need to edit truffle.js, as we have done many times before, to add the my_ganache network. Otherwise, you can edit the development network (port 7545) defined already in truffle.js. If you use the latter option, you won't need to specify the network using --network.

The next step is to compile and publish the smart contracts that come with the truffle compile box. Then, publish the compiled smart contracts to the truffle migrate Ganache blockchain.

Starting the web UI

You can run the example that comes with the Drizzle box by running npm run start from within the DrizzleTontine/ directory.

As a result, you'll see the Webpack server launching, and inside the browser, a nice DApp web interface. As well as showing the Drizzle logo, the page will show a few forms to interact with the sample contracts provided by the box, as illustrated in the following screenshot:

If you don't have MetaMask already installed, or your account is locked, you'll see the following message:

We can't find any Ethereum accounts! Please check and make sure Metamask or you browser are pointed at the correct network and your account is unlocked.

If MetaMask is not already connected to Ganache, you can skip to the *Connecting ganache to MetaMask* section to fix this issue.

Awesome, isn't it? In a few steps, you have deployed a full DApp with a clean interface, interacting with three different contracts, without writing a single line of code.

Now, stop the Webpack server using *Ctrl + C* and let's customize the box to build our Tontine game user interface.

Hacking the Drizzle box

The previous Drizzle unboxing initiated a Truffle workspace along with a ReactJs project located under the `src/` folder. Here are the steps to follow in order to adapt this example to our needs.

First, copy the `tontine.sol` file into the `contracts/` folder and remove the other existing contracts, except for `Migration.sol` and `tontine.sol`.

Then edit the `2_deploy_contract` file (as we did in the "truffle quick start" and "Truffle unit tests" section), and substitute the existing deployment script with the following:

```
var Ctontine = artifacts.require("Ctontine");
var Cplayer = artifacts.require("Cplayer");

deployer.deploy(Cplayer).then(function() {
    return deployer.deploy(Ctontine, Cplayer.address);
}).then(function() { })
```

Next, edit `drizzleOptions.js`, which is located under the `src/` folder, as follows:

```
import Cplayer from './../build/contracts/Cplayer.json'
import Ctontine from './../build/contracts/Ctontine.json'

const drizzleOptions = {
    web3: {
        block: false,
        fallback: {
            type: 'ws',
            url: 'ws://127.0.0.1:7545'
        }
    },
    contracts: [ Cplayer, Ctontine ],
    events: {
        Ctontine: [
            'NewActivePlayerEv',
            'EliminatedPlayerEv'
        ],
    },
    polls: { accounts: 1500 }
}

export default drizzleOptions;
```

Here, we define a `drizzleOptions` object with the following parameters:

- The `fallback` attribute indicates the URL to use for the web3 connection if no web3 provider, such as MetaMask, is available.
- `contracts` represents an array of the contract artifacts to interact with.
- In the `events` option, we set an object consisting of contract names, along an array of the event names we would like to listen for. Furthermore, event names may be replaced with an object containing both `eventName` and `eventOptions`, where the `eventOptions` field defines an event filter. For example, to listen for the `eliminatedPlayerEv` event from block 0 to the latest we use `{ eventName: 'eliminatedPlayerEv', eventOptions: { fromBlock: 0 } }`
- Finally, `polls` indicates how often Drizzle will ping the blockchain to synchronize changes in state. `polls` is set in milliseconds (by default, `3000`). In our case, Drizzle will poll every 1.5 seconds.

Once you are done with the `drizzleoptions.js` editing, move to the `src/layout/home` directory.

The game's homepage

Using the default homepage shipped with the Drizzle box, we will set up a web page for our game. Open the `src/layouts/home/Home.js` file and make the following changes:

```
import React, { Component } from 'react';
import { AccountData, ContractData, ContractForm } from 'drizzle-react-
components';
import PropTypes from 'prop-types';
import logo from '../../logo.png';

class Home extends Component {
    constructor(props, context) {
        super(props);
        this.contracts = context.drizzle.contracts;
    }

    render() {
        return (
            <main className="container">
                <div className="pure-g">
                    <div className="pure-u-1-1 header">
                        <img src={logo} alt="drizzle-logo" />
                        <h1>Tontine Game</h1>
                        <p>Examples of how to get started with Drizzle in
various situations.</p>
                    </div>
                    <div className="pure-u-1-1">
                        <h2>Active Account</h2>
                        <strong>My details:  </strong>
                        <AccountData accountIndex="0" units="ether"
precision="3" />
                    </div>
                    <div className="pure-u-1-1">
                        <h2>Cplayer Contract</h2>
                        <ContractData
                            contract="Cplayer"
                            method="findplayer"
                            methodArgs={[this.props.accounts[0]]} />
                        <h3>Register</h3>
                        <p>Before you start playing, players should
register themselves using AddPlayer from.</p>
                        <ContractForm contract="Cplayer" method="AddPlayer"
```

```
        />
                                </div>
                                <div className="pure-u-1-1">
                                    <h2>Ctontine</h2>
                                    <strong>Last Ping:  </strong>
                                    <ContractData
                                        contract="Ctontine"
                                        method="ping_time"
                                        methodArgs={[this.props.accounts[0]]} />
                                    <strong>Your Game pension:  </strong>
                                    <ContractData
                                        contract="Ctontine"
                                        method="Tpension"
                                        methodArgs={[this.props.accounts[0]]} />

                                    <h3>join game</h3>
                                    <p>Press the button below to join the game (only
        the first time)</p>
                                    <ContractForm
                                        contract="Ctontine"
                                        method="join"
                                        methodArgs={[{value:
        this.context.drizzle.web3.utils.toWei('2','ether'), from:
        this.props.accounts[0]}]} />
                                    <strong>Ping game:  </strong>
                                    <p>Keep pinging the contract to avoid being
        eliminated (ping interval is 1 day)</p>
                                    <ContractForm
                                        contract="Ctontine"
                                        method="ping"
                                        methodArgs={[{from:
        this.props.accounts[0],data:1}]} />
                                    <h3>Eliminate an opponent</h3>
                                    <p>use this form to eliminate your opponent</p>
                                    <ContractForm
                                        contract="Ctontine"
                                        method="eliminate"
                                        labels={['Opponent Address']} />
                                    <h3>Claim your reward</h3>
                                    <ContractForm contract="Ctontine"
        method="claimReward" />
                                </div>
                        </div>

                        <h2>First Active players</h2>
                        <ContractData contract="Ctontine" method="active_players"
        methodArgs={"0"} />
                        <h2>First Eliminated players</h2>
```

```
                <ContractData contract="Ctontine"
method="eliminated_players" methodArgs={"0"} />
                </main>
            )
        }
}

Home.contextTypes = { drizzle: PropTypes.object };
export default Home;
```

Since this is not a CSS nor a ReactJs book, I'm skipping some of the ReactJs explanations and focusing on Drizzle.

Drizzle comes with its own React components, through the `drizzle-react-components` library, which makes it easier for you to display contract-related information and call the contract methods. In the preceding code, we started by importing three components from Drizzle: `AccountData`, `ContractData`, and `ContractForm`. These components are very powerful, so let's discover what they are used for:

- `AccountData`: Displays the account address and balance for a given index. To use this component, we specify these attributes:
  - **accountIndex (int)**: Index of the account to use (zero is the first account)
  - **units (string)**: Denomination of the balance (expressed in wei)
  - **precision (int)**: Number of digits after the decimal point

For example, the `<AccountData accountIndex="0" units="ether" precision="3" />` element will render the first active account's balance and address:

Active Account

My details:

0xd0B60088575D7dcC2FBcb633813aadFae8677c8A

74.378 Ether

- `ContractData`: Displays the contract call's output and accepts the following parameters:
  - **contract(string, required)**: Name of the contract to call
  - **method(string, required)**: Method to call from the contract
  - **methodArgs(array)**: Arguments for the contract method call

For example, in the previous code we had the following:

```
<ContractData contract="Ctontine" method="ping_time"
methodArgs={[this.props.accounts[0]]} />
```

This element will display the ping time value (`ping_time`) for the specified player (`this.props.accounts[0]`) from the `Ctontine` contract. As you can see, there's no such method as `ping_time` in our contract, but while it's a public state, `ContractData` element accepts it as a method argument:

- `ContractForm`: Contrary to `ContractData`, the `ContractForm` Drizzle component can automatically generate a form to read input and interact with the smart contract.

For example, when we use `<ContractForm contract="Ctontine" method="eliminate" labels={['Opponent Address']} />`, we will generate the following form with one input (as `eliminate` accepts a single argument). Once submitted, it will call the specified `eliminate()` method and pass the input value as an argument:

The Drizzle `ContractForm` element accepts the following parameters:

- **contract(string, required)**: Name of the called contract
- **method(string, required)**: Method whose input will be used to create corresponding form fields
- **labels(array)**: Optional custom labels for the generated form input (following ABI input ordering)

At the time of writing, the `ContractForm` component doesn't support a value field (maybe soon) to send ether, but there is a workaround for that listed in this GitHub discussion: `https://github.com/trufflesuite/drizzle-react-components/issues/17`.

One more thing: you may have noticed the use of `web3.utils.toWei`. Interestingly, Drizzle maintains access to the underlying functionality of web3 1.0, thus you can use all `web3.js` methods in your React code without needing to initiate a web3 object.

Save all the changes you've made so far and now let's try our Drizzle DApp.

Trying the DApp

Good work, you have built your first Drizzle app using the Drizzle box. More importantly, you have set up a great development and deployment environment that will make DApp development and testing even easier.

We're getting close to our final goal of running our drizzle DApp, but there's one more important step before we try the game: preparing MetaMask. To summarize, Truffle will compile and deploy the contract into Ganache and ensure connectivity with Drizzle, whereas MetaMask will connect the end user to Ganache (blockchain) in order to let a user play and manage their funds.

Connecting Ganache to MetaMask

In the previous chapter, we introduced the MetaMask plugin, which allows users to send transactions through the browser without having to install a full node.

To interact with Ganache from the browser, we need to configure MetaMask. For that, in the top-left of MetaMask, you can select **Custom RPC**. A new dialogue box, titled **New RPC URL** will show up; here, you should enter `http://127.0.0.1:7545` (Ganache's IP and port) and click **Save**.

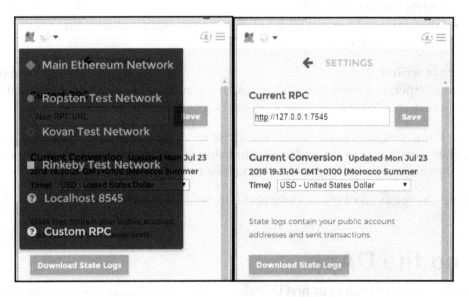

Now that we've connected MetaMask to Ganache, your previous MetaMask accounts will be loaded with 0 ether, which won't help us to try our DApp. Thankfully, `ganache-cli` generated a collection of virtual accounts, each with 100 ether. We need to import some of these accounts to be able to interact with the contract. To do that, copy a few private keys from the `ganache-cli` output and use them in MetaMask to import the corresponding accounts:

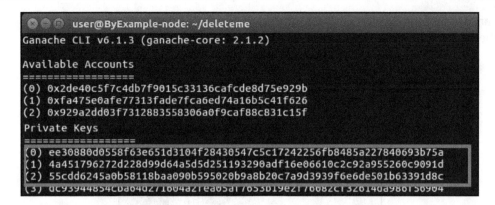

In order to import an existing wallet into a MetaMask account, click on the account-switcher icon in the upper-right corner (see the following screenshot) and select **Import Account**, as shown here:

You can, at any time, switch between imported accounts by using the same account-switcher icon:

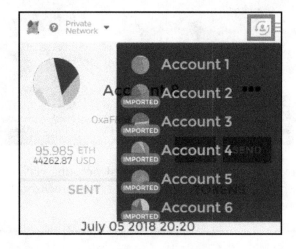

The imported account should appear in the list of accounts and should be marked **Imported** with a red background. That's it! You have successfully imported the necessary wallets into MetaMask.

Now let's run our Tontine DApp.

Running the Tontine DApp

The compilation and migration processes are the same as we've done multiple times already using the following:

```
truffle compile-all
truffle migrate -reset
```

Once the contracts are migrated, let's taste the fruit of our labor in action. In the Drizzle box folder, run the following:

```
npm run start
```

The tontine DApp web page comes up immediately in your web browser, as shown here:

Tontine Game

Examples of how to get started with Drizzle in various situations.

Active Account

My details:

0x6D03B4073651C08d1e4145356beb8Ab3b08B7A2F

9.991 Ether

Cplayer Contract

Register

Before start playing, players should register themselves using AddPlayer from.

> name

> phonenumber

Submit

Ctontine

Last Ping: 1532560156
Your Game pension: 200000000000000000

join game

Press the button below to join the game (only the first time)

Submit

Ping game:

Keep pinging the contract to avoid being eliminated (ping interval is 1 day)

Submit

Eliminate an opponent

use this form to eliminate your opponent

> Opponent Address

Submit

Claim your reward

Submit

Isn't it amazing! We have got a clean web page with plenty of forms and game details. Eager to play? Let's have some fun!

Showtime – ready to play?

Let's imagine a scenario where we have two players who are willing to play. We will use a different account for each player from those previously imported into MetaMask. Afterward, register the first player with details (name, phone number) by filling in the **Add Player** form in the game interface, and clicking **Submit**. A popup will open up in MetaMask, allowing you to submit the transaction. At any time, you can check the transaction status in MetaMask. Wait until it's marked as **Successful**:

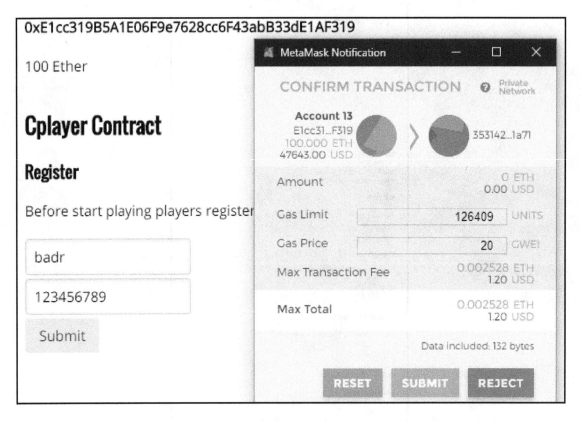

Then, switch between MetaMask accounts and repeat the same operation to add the second player. Note that each player is identified by their wallet address.

Great! Now, as you have two registered players, you can make them join the Tontine game. Successively, for each account, press the **Submit** button under **join game** label:

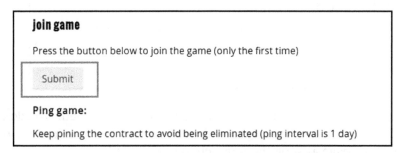

This time, you'll get a MetaMask popup showing that you are sending 2 ether to the game (as we fixed that amount in our Drizzle code). Confirm the deposit for both players:

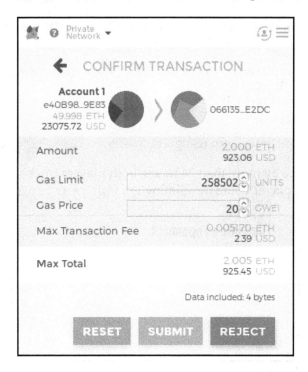

In the same way, you can ping the contract for each player.

Ping game:

Keep pining the contract to avoid being eliminated (ping interval is 1 day)

Submit

I'm sure you've noticed that once the join or ping action is dispatched, Drizzle will update the `ContractData` components (player and Tontine details) automatically without refreshing the whole page as soon the transaction is validated.

As we did in testing, you can increase the time in the trial process to try the elimination feature. From a new Terminal, launch Truffle's console: `truffle console`.

This will spawn an interactive console connected to Ganache. We use it to run the following RPC calls:

```
web3.currentProvider.send({ jsonrpc: "2.0", method: "evm_increaseTime",
params: [90000], id: 1 })
web3.currentProvider.send({ jsonrpc: '2.0', method: 'evm_mine', params: [],
id:1 })
```

You can check the block's timestamp using `web3.eth.getBlock("latest").timestamp`.

After increasing the time by more than 24 hours, both players can be eliminated. Consider eliminating the second player using the elimination form here:

Eliminate an oponnent

use this form to eliminate your opponent

Opponent Address

Submit

Once the player is eliminated, Drizzle will automatically display the details at the bottom of the web page:

First Eliminated players

name
bellaj

PhoneNumber
2126130384875

Paddress
0x953a435b43b605079b42b5e26922d425fDC31c89

id
0

The remaining player should be able to claim and get the due reward (4 ether).

During this tryout, we ensured that the Tontine game is working as expected!

As you can see, we have built a minimalist DApp frontend for the game. This choice was intended to give you the chance to elaborate on the design and create a complete frontend for the game. Count it as an exercise for you. You can even build a small Whisper-based chatroom module for the players. For your information, Whisper (not supported by Ganache) is a direct-messaging protocol in the Ethereum network, and it's fun to work with. I'll be waiting for your pull requests.

Getting help

Even though we have spent ample time exploring Ethereum and Solidity principles in such a way that you should be able to build DApps, this book has its limits and you'll probably need help at some point.

There is good online documentation covering all aspects of Solidity, which is maybe not up to date but is good to start with. For instance, an excellent in-depth introduction to Solidity can be found in the official documentation at `http://solidity.readthedocs.io/en/v0.4.24/solidity-in-depth.html`.

Subscribing to and asking questions on Gitter (`https://gitter.im/ethereum/solidity/`) allows you to communicate with some of the leading figures in the Ethereum community as well as many other talented developers. I should also mention that there is a dedicated Stack Exchange community for Ethereum (`https://ethereum.stackexchange.com/`), which can provide further help.

Summary

This has been an awesome experience. I hope building the Tontine game was a lot of fun for you.

An important takeaway from this chapter is to think twice before deciding to deploy your final contract and release your DApp. It's good practice to always plan your contract-development process before jumping into the code, along with conducting thorough testing either using JavaScript or Solidity to ensure quality and security. Keep in mind that writing smart contracts is a critical task as you'll be dealing with real money. You don't want your project to end up in the blockchain graveyard (`https://magoo.github.io/Blockchain-Graveyard/`), do you? The rule of thumb is begin with testing locally on Ganache, and then on a Testnet before going onto the real Mainnet. Besides this, asking other developers to review your code is always a good habit.

To summarize, in this long chapter, we built a Tontine game from scratch in about 30 minutes. That's a remarkable feat on its own. We also learned new things about Solidity and explored how to use plenty of tools, including Truffle, Remix, and Drizzle, to build a full DApp.

However, the journey doesn't end here. In the next chapter, we are going to learn how to build a Java application to interact with an Oracle-based smart contract using web3.js. If you are a big fan of Java, the next chapter is for you.

Catch you later!

6
Blockchain-Based Futures System

Reaching this chapter is a notable accomplishment in your Ethereum learning trip, during which you've thoroughly learned how to write smart contracts with Solidity, and how to build a complete DApp using web3.js and Drizzle. We focused, in the last two chapters, on building a decentralized web application on Ethereum using a set of tools, such as Remix or Truffle. In this walkthrough, we will learn how to harness a powerful language, such as Java, to build an Ethereum desktop or mobile application. Along the way, we will discover new concepts in Solidity, such as calling third-party APIs in your smart contracts or libraries.

As we learn by example in this book, we will break into finance and build a financial project that manages a futures smart contract using Java (SE). Throughout this interesting use case, we will go over the following points:

- Building futures solidity contract
- Introducing oracles
- Introducing the web3j API

Another benefit of this chapter is that building a futures smart contract will help you to understand the disruptive force of the blockchain and how smart contracts can alter the financial industry (for example, futures trading market) by automating payments and facilitating business processes.

Project presentation

I know you're a developer and not a financial nerd. Hence, I will try to introduce the futures concept in the easiest terms. Futures contracts (more colloquially, futures) are legal agreements to buy or sell a given quantity of commodity or asset (barrel of oil, gold, and silver) at a predetermined price at a specified time in the future, hence the name futures.

For the sake of ease and clarity, let's consider an oversimplified version of a real futures contract from the financial industry. Let's suppose that an airline company wants to lock in the fuel price to manage their exposure to risk and to avoid any unpleasant surprises. Instead of buying the oil and storing it until they need it, they buy a futures contract for oil with a specific date of delivery and price per gallon. For example, an airline company can agree on a futures contract to buy 1,000,000 gallons of fuel, taking delivery 60 days in the future, at a price of $3 per gallon.

In this example, the airline company is considered as hedger while the seller might be considered as a speculator. As the futures contracts may become more valuable if the price goes up, the owner of that contract could sell that contract for more to someone else. That said, we will build a smart contract that implements the logic described here and defines the futures contract's details (asset, quantity, unitary price, and delivery date) along with holding the funds. We will also build a Java application enabling a third party (exchange market authority) to define a futures contract between the other two parties.

The smart contract will also enable the speculator to sell the futures contract to another speculator and calculate its investment offset by comparing the market price to the futures contract price.

This will be a straightforward contract with only a few main abilities and minimalist design. Before going any further, I recommend you grab the project's code from GitHub (`https://github.com/bellaj/web3j`) if you want to follow along without copying code from the book.

Futures smart contract

As usual, we kick off the chapter by writing the smart contract code. First, create a directory called `FuturesWeb3j` (in your home folder) and initiate an empty Truffle project using `truffle init`.

Afterward, in the `contracts/` folder, create a `Futures.sol` file with the following code:

```
contract CFutures {
    address user;
    address hedger;
    address speculator;
    struct asset{
        uint id;
        uint Quantity;
        uint price;
        address seller;
        address buyer;
        uint date;
    }
    asset TradedAsset;

    event DepositEv(uint amount, address sender);

    function CFutures(
        uint assetID,
        uint Quantity,
        uint price,
        address buyer,
        address seller,
        uint date) public {
        TradedAsset.id = assetID;
        TradedAsset.Quantity = Quantity;
        TradedAsset.price = price;
        TradedAsset.seller = seller;
        speculator = seller;
        hedger = buyer;
        TradedAsset.buyer = buyer;
        TradedAsset.date = date;
    }

    function deposit() public payable returns(bool) {
        require(msg.value == TradedAsset.Quantity * TradedAsset.price);
        DepositEv(msg.value,msg.sender);
        return true;
    }

    modifier onlyhedger() {
        require(msg.sender == hedger);
        _;
    }

    function sellcontract(address newhedger) public onlyhedger
returns(bool){
```

```
            hedger = newhedger;
            return true;
    }

    function getpaid() public returns(bool){
        require(now >= TradedAsset.date && address(this).balance > 0);
        speculator.transfer(address(this).balance);
        return true;
    }

}
```

This is the shortened version of a futures smart contract code. I assume you're now familiar with the Solidity language and you can develop the code for adding advanced features.

As you can see, the starting point is to define a constructor that will determine the contract's details, namely: asset ID, agreed quantity to buy, unit price, buyer's address, seller's address, and delivery date.

We'll also define a few functions:

- `deposit()`: The hedger (airlines) will call this function to deposit the agreed funds.
- `sellcontract()`: The speculator can sell the contract to another investor.
- `getpaid()`: The contract will release the funds to the oil vendor at the delivery date.
- `onlyhedger()`: This is a modifier that restricts actions to the initial buyer (the hedger).

Blockchain oracles

At this level, the previous contract enables basic operations to lock and unlock funds against commodities delivery. Nevertheless, once the contract expires, we want the contract to calculate the offset benefit (savings) or loss made by the futures deal – in other words, how much the hedger has economized or lost.

In this case, at settlement time, the smart contract needs a solid and reliable source of information to determine the underlying commodity (oil) price to calculate the offset. But a question arises here: is the contract able to know by itself what the oil market price is?

As we introduced in a previous chapter, the smart contract is deterministic code executed in an isolated VM without direct connection to an outside source of information!

However, there is a workaround for that situation: oracles.

Oracles are trusted agents or data suppliers that read and send requested information to the smart contract from reliable external data sources. We have a few providers of this type of service in the blockchain space, such as Chainlink, Link, Blocksense, and Oraclize. In our example, we will use Oraclize (http://www.oraclize.it/) as it is an industry leader in oracle servicing.

Let's see how we can connect our contract to an oracle contract. In our previous code, we have to bring in the following changes:

```solidity
pragma solidity ^0.4.24;

import "./oraclizeAPI_0.5.sol";

contract CFutures is usingOraclize {
    uint public fuelPriceUSD;

    event NewOraclizeQuery(string description);
    event NewDieselPrice(string price);

    function CFutures(
        uint assetID,
        uint Quantity,
        uint price,
        address buyer,
        address seller,
        uint date) public {
... // keep it as defined previously
}
function __callback(bytes32 myid, string result) public {
    require(msg.sender == oraclize_cbAddress());
    NewDieselPrice(result);
    fuelPriceUSD = parseInt(result, 2);
    }

function updateprice() public payable {
NewOraclizeQuery("Oraclize query was sent, standing by for the answer..");
oraclize_query("URL", "xml(https://www.fueleconomy.gov/ws/rest/fuelprices).f
uelPrices.diesel");
    }
}
```

In result we end up with a simple contract using the Oraclize service to request `Fuelprice` (let's consider fuel as equivalent to oil).

As you can see, we start by importing the Oraclize API: `import "./oraclizeAPI_0.5.sol";`.

Then, we inherit the `usingOraclize` contract to access the library methods.

Next, to help the compiler resolve the import, we need to download the Oraclize API contract and libraries into Truffle's `contracts/` folder by running `wget https://raw.githubusercontent.com/oraclize/ethereum-api/master/oraclize API_0.5.sol`.

In the Oracle code part, we defined, along with `fuelPriceUSD`, two new functions: `updateprice()` and `__callback`.

The first one uses `oraclize_query` to send a query to the Oraclize's smart contract with two arguments: the type of request (URL, WolframAlpha, IPFS multihash) and the requested information (a specific property in the XML response). The `updateprice` function is declared as `payable` because the Oraclize service isn't free, and this function should accept ether to be able to pay for the Oraclize service. However, the first query made by a contract is free, so we include a call for the `updateprice()` function without sending ether in our constructor.

On the other hand, the second function, `__callback` is defined by the API and, as its name indicates, it's a callback function executed once Oracle sends back the response. Its first parameter is the `id` of the request, while the second parameter is the result of your request. In this example, we use the `parseInt` function, which is defined by the Oraclize API file, to set the number precision. In the preceding example, $3.20 will be returned as 320 cents.

The following diagram represents the interaction between the initial contract and the data source using Oraclize:

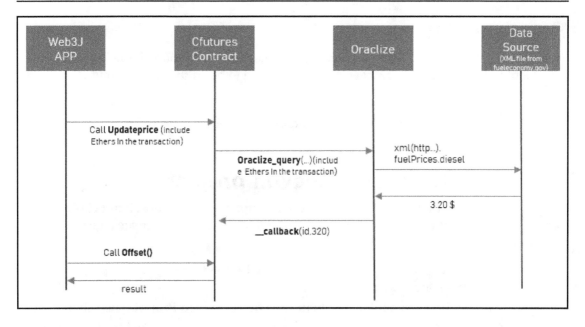

Lastly, let's implement the `offset()` method that will calculate the offset profit the hedger made by taking this futures contract based on the price variation:

```
function offset() public view returns (uint) {
    return TradedAsset.Quantity * (fuelPriceUSD - TradedAsset.price);
}
```

Now that the contract is complete, compile the contract using `truffle compile` and check whether there are any errors.

Web3j

Web3j is a real treat for Java lovers who want to make their first steps in the new blockchain environment. It represents a lightweight Java and Android API for integration with Ethereum clients. It enables you to build a decentralized Java application easily based on Ethereum. You can find all the details about the project at their official website: `https://web3j.io/`.

Prerequisites

To get the most out of the following sections, you need to have a basic knowledge of Java. You should also have the following elements installed to build the application:

- Java 8 JDK
- Eclipse and Maven – for coding and development

Setting up the Web3J Maven project

If you have already downloaded the code from GitHub, you can import it in Eclipse. Otherwise, if you want to build the project from scratch, you have to create a new Maven project, as follows:

1. In the Eclipse IDE, navigate to **File | New | Other** to bring up the project-creation wizard.
2. Scroll to the Maven folder, open it, and choose **Maven Project**. Then choose **Next**.
3. Keep passing the dialogue forms by pressing next until you get the following form:

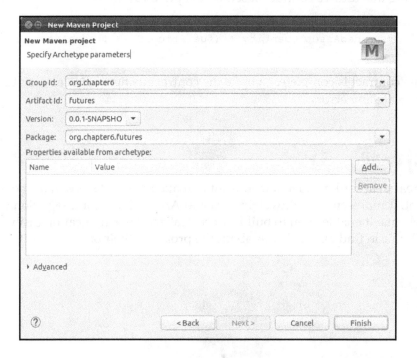

Here, you will need to enter information regarding the Maven project you are creating. Choose the names you want and press **Finish**. The following is what your sample project structure will look like at the end of the Maven project-creation process:

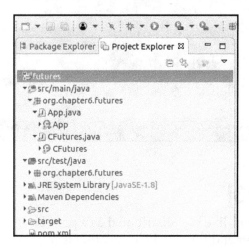

Then, in the Maven POM file (`pom.xml`), we'll need to add the following lines in the corresponding POM tags:

```
<properties>
  <project.build.sourceEncoding>UTF-8</project.build.sourceEncoding>
  <maven.compiler.source>1.8</maven.compiler.source>
  <maven.compiler.target>1.8</maven.compiler.target>
</properties>
<plugins>
  <plugin>
    <groupId>org.apache.maven.plugins</groupId>
    <artifactId>maven-compiler-plugin</artifactId>
    <version>3.7.0</version>
    <configuration>
      <source>1.8</source>
      <target>1.8</target>
    </configuration>
  </plugin>
</plugins>
<dependency>
  <groupId>org.slf4j</groupId>
  <artifactId>slf4j-simple</artifactId>
  <version>1.7.21</version>
</dependency>
```

After editing the Maven POM file, we have to update the project to download the necessary dependencies. Right-click on **Project**, click on **Maven**, then choose **Update Project...**:

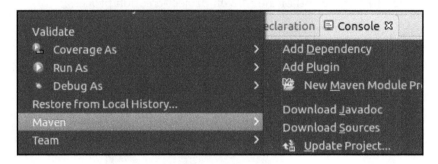

Installing web3j

Web3j provides a command-line tool distributed as a portable `.jar`. In a few steps, you can start using the web3j command line, so no installation is required. In your home folder. run wget
`https://github.com/web3j/web3j/releases/download/v3.4.0/web3j-3.4.0.tar`
.

Unzip the downloaded TAR file:

```
tar  xvf web3j-3.4.0
```

Then add the resultant folder to the system's path:

```
export PATH=$PATH:~/web3j-3.4.0/bin
```

You're all set. Now, you can create Ethereum accounts or generate wrapper classes for your smart contracts.

Wallet creation

The web3j command-line tools allow us, among other features, to create wallets or send transactions.

To create a new Ethereum account, run `web3j wallet create`. You'll be asked to provide a password (don't forget it) and then a location where you want to back up your account (wallet JSON file). At the end, you'll get a JSON file with a long name (you can change this) that carries lots of information, including the account address and private key:

```
user@ByExample-node:~/eclipse-workspace/futures/src$ web3j wallet create



         __  _____ ___  ___
 \    / /_   |  _ \  | |  \/ | | |   / \
  \  /\  /  '_ \  | |_) | | | | | |  / _ \
   \/  \/   |___/  |_.__/  _| |_|  \___/
                          |_/

Please enter a wallet file password:
Please re-enter the password:
Please enter a destination directory location [/home/user/.ethereum/testnet/keystore]: .
Wallet file UTC--2018-07-15T16-44-45.169000000Z--8f9539c3f78cc24597d74978318d1e6ce7f18a1a.json successfully created in:
user@ByExample-node:~/eclipse-workspace/futures/src$ ls
main  test  UTC--2018-07-15T16-44-45.169000000Z--8f9539c3f78cc24597d74978318d1e6ce7f18a1a.json
```

Alternatively, instead of using web3j, you can export one of your Testnet accounts created in MetaMask or Geth.

In this project, we will be running our contract in the Testnet, therefore we need to supply test ethers to our freshly created account. To do that, we can use MetaMask to get free ethers and send them to our new account's address. Be careful, you should add `0x` and wait until the transaction is confirmed, as shown here:

The account's address is saved inside the wallet's JSON file created earlier, with the address being the last part of the file's name.

Java client

As introduced earlier in this chapter, we are building a simple Java application using web3j. Let's understand briefly the mechanics behind this API.

Web3j is the Java port of Ethereum's web3 API, which manages communication (JSON-RPC) between Ethereum clients and the network. For each smart contract, web3j generates a wrapper class, simplifying the access and smart contract interaction with Ethereum. Thus, all complexities will be hidden and you will not be forced to initiate RPC calls on your own. The following diagram (from the official documentation) depicts the interaction flow between web3j and Ethereum:

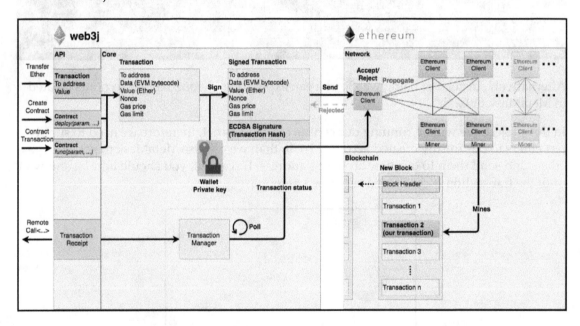

The wrapper generator

Before using web3j, we need to build the Java wrapper class for our smart contract. The web3j command-line tool supports the autogeneration of Java smart contract function wrappers directly from Truffle's contract schema, as follows:

```
web3j truffle generate ~/FuturesWeb3j/build/contracts/CFutures.json -o
~/eclipse-workspace/futures/src/main/java/ -p org.chapter6.futures
```

The first argument is the build file compiled by Truffle for the CFutures contract, and the second is the path of your Java project destination where the class wrapper will be generated. In addition, the -p parameter should be the Java packaging structure for the generated class:

This will result in creating a CFutures.java file with a new class with the same name as the smart contract:

```
public class CFutures extends Contract {
    private static final String BINARY = "0x60606040523415600e576...";
}
```

As you can see, the BINARY string represents your compiled contract (bytecode). Remove the \ and \n, if there are any. You'll find in this class a Java implementation for all of your smart contract methods.

Remember that if you make any changes, you'll have to compile the smart contract and then generate the new ABI, bytecode, and web3j wrapper as we did previously.

Now that we have our smart contract class wrapper, let's move on and write our Futures main class. We have to write a Java class that deploys and interacts with the Cfutures smart contract using the Futures class wrapper.

Initializing web3j

Let's now focus on the `App.java` file created in the Maven project.

The first step is to initialize a web3j object. We do that by passing in a provider (for example, the endpoint of a third-party or local Ethereum node) to the web3j `build` function:

```
Web3j web3j = Web3j.build(new HttpService("https://ropsten.infura.io"));
```

In this example, we will use the Infura gateway (`https://infura.io/`) to access the Testnet network. If you remember, in Ethereum, we always need an entry point, which is an RPC/HTTP provider (node) that carries the orders or actions dispatched by the user to the network. Normally, the end user should have a local RPC client connected to the network. However, we directly use an online provider (used also by MetaMask) to avoid needless instructions and to keep communication with the oracle straightforward.

Remember that if you want to use a private network instead, you'll need to use the Ethereum-Bridge API (`https://github.com/oraclize/ethereum-bridge`) to keep using the Oraclize service.

Setting up Ethereum accounts

To interact with the blockchain network, we need to build transactions, thus we need to have a wallet. We can use an existing one, as follows:

```
Credentials credentials = WalletUtils.loadCredentials("PASSWORD",
"/path/to/walletfile.json");
```

Or, we can create a new wallet: `WalletUtils.generateNewWalletFile("PASSWORD", new File("/path/to/destination"), true);`.

Once loaded or created, you can check the current balance of your wallet using the following:

```
EthGetBalance AccountBalance =
web3j.ethGetBalance(credentials.getAddress(),
    DefaultBlockParameterName.LATEST).sendAsync().get();
log.info("The accounts balance " + AccountBalance);
```

Deploying the contract

As the wallet credentials are defined and the web3 is initialized, we can construct and deploy our `Cfutures` contract using the deploy method:

```
CFutures CFuture_ = CFutures.deploy(web3j, credentials, CUSTOM_GAS_PRICE,
GAS_LIMIT, assetID,
    Quantity, price, buyer, seller, date).send();
```

The first four arguments are needed to construct the deployment transaction, while the rest are the arguments needed by the contract's constructor.

Among these four parameters, we need to define the gas limit and the gas price. In this example, I have defined them as global variables, as follows:

```
private static final BigInteger GAS_LIMIT = BigInteger.valueOf(4_700_000);
private static final BigInteger CUSTOM_GAS_PRICE = Convert.toWei("140",
    Convert.Unit.GWEI).toBigInteger();
```

Here, we define a gas limit of 47,00,000 units of gas and a gas price of 140 GWei. Web3j uses a default price of 22 GWei – feel free to define your own values. To choose the right value, you can check the current gas price for Ropsten at `https://ropsten.etherscan.io/chart/gasprice`.

Once the `deploy()` function is executed, it will result in creating a new instance of the `CFutures` smart contract on the Ethereum blockchain using the supplied credentials and constructor parameter values. If, for any reason, the deployment transaction isn't validated within 600 seconds, an exception will be raised.

At any time, you can visit the Ropsten explorer to examine whether the contract has been deployed using the link printed by the log here:

```
String CFuturesAddress=CFuture_.getContractAddress();
log.info("View contract at https://ropsten.etherscan.io/address/" +
CFuturesAddress);
```

Interacting with smart contracts

If you wish to construct an instance of a smart contract wrapper with an existing smart contract, simply pass in its address to the predefined load function:

```
CFutures CFutureInstance = CFutures.load("contract_address", web3j,
credentials,
    CUSTOM_GAS_PRICE, GAS_LIMIT);
```

Once you instantiate a new CFuture object (using deploy or load), Eclipse will help you with the autocompletion feature to choose the functions to call or to access contract proprieties:

```
CFutures CFuture2 = CFutures.load(CFuturesAddress, web3j, credentials, CUSTOM_GAS_PRICE, GAS_LIMIT);
CFuture.|
    // if yo ⊙ deposit(BigInteger weiValue) : RemoteCall<Trans  gInteger weiValue)
            ⊙ equals(Object obj) : boolean - Object
    /* BigInt ⊙ getClass() : Class<?> - Object                    ials.getAddress()).send();
            ⊙ getContractAddress() : String - Contract
blems  @ Javadoc ⊙ getContractBinary() : String - Contract                                    ▪ ✖ ▸
ated> App (1) [Jav ⊙ getDeployedAddress(String networkId) : String - ' /java (Jul 16, 2018, 10:20:19 AM)
  INFO org.chapte ⊙ getfuelPriceUSD() : RemoteCall<BigInteger> - CFu
1.8.3-stable/lin ⊙ getGasPrice() : BigInteger - Contract          70
  INFO org.chapte
  INFO org.chapte ⊙ getpaid() : RemoteCall<TransactionReceipt> - CFu
1.8.3-stable/lin ⊙ getSyncThreshold() : long - ManagedTransaction ddress 0x7cd884e217c638b04990af8adb5efec6e4aac015
  INFO org.chapte ⊙ gotTransactionReceipt() : Optional<TransactionR sten.etherscan.io/address/0xf1848cf419ce5a68b7dce743105384d
  INFO org.chapte            Press 'Ctrl+Space' to show Template Proposals  sten.etherscan.io/address/0x7cd884e217c638b04990af8adb5efec
```

Calling a contract function

In our example, once the contract is loaded for the first time, we need to deposit the amount both parties agreed on. Hence, we need to execute the deposit function along with sending the contract value in ethers.

In web3j, all methods are defined identically to their equivalent Solidity methods and take the same parameters. To transact with a Cfutures function, we invoke the equivalent object's method using dot notation, as follows:

```
BigInteger Quantity = BigInteger.valueOf(120000);
BigInteger Price = BigInteger.valueOf(300);

TransactionReceipt DepositReceipt =
CFutureInstance.deposit(Price.multiply(Quantity)).send();
```

As you can see, the argument passed to the deposit function is a BigInteger (price * quantity), not an integer or int, and so all variables should be declared as BigInteger in web3j.

For the sake of preserving our testing ethers, we will make a deposit in wei and we will assume that a wei is worth a cent (I know it's unrealistic). We suppose here that at the agreement time, an oil gallon costs 300 cents (300 wei). The quantity and price are declared as separated variables.

If you look at the wrapper class in CFutures.java, you'll find a defined Java function for each function defined in the smart contract. For instance, you'll find the following:

```
public RemoteCall<TransactionReceipt> deposit(BigInteger weiValue) {
    ...
    return executeRemoteCallTransaction(function, weiValue);
}
```

You can see that the function definition has changed, as the original doesn't accept any parameters:

```
deposit() payable returns(bool) {}
```

Web3j defines this new argument for payable functions to make it possible to pass in the amount of Wei to send.

It's worth noting that, **as stated in the official documentation** (https://web3j.readthedocs.io/en/latest/smart_contracts.html), transactional calls do not return any values, regardless of the return type specified on the method. Hence, for all transactional methods, the transaction receipt (https://github.com/ethereum/wiki/wiki/JSON-RPC#eth_gettransactionreceipt) associated with the transaction is returned.

The transaction receipt is useful for two reasons:

- It provides details of the mined block that the transaction resides in
- Solidity events that are called will be logged as part of the transaction, which can then be extracted

For example, we can get from the transaction receipt the transaction hash and examine the corresponding transaction on Etherscan as shown in the picture below:

[This is a Ropsten **Testnet** Transaction Only]	
TxHash:	0x4ef437fce1a877c3b155a03b0ba11309695ac4d84d351f6f3aefee1c60202278
TxReceipt Status:	Success
Block Height:	3648112 (1 block confirmation)
TimeStamp:	25 secs ago (Jul-16-2018 09:56:11 AM +UTC)
From:	0x8f9539c3f78cc24597d74978318d1e6ce7f18a1a
To:	Contract 0x7cd884e217c638b04990af8adb5efec6e4aac015 ⊘
Value:	360 wei ($0.00)
Gas Limit:	4700000
Gas Used By Txn:	21998
Gas Price:	0.00000014 Ether (140 Gwei)
Actual Tx Cost/Fee:	0.00307972 Ether ($0.000000)
Nonce & {Position}:	30	{0}
Input Data:	

```
Function: deposit() ***

MethodID: 0xd0e30db0
```

View Input As ▾

Calling view methods

For view methods (which only read a value in a smart contract), they are invoked using an ordinary method call, except they will not return a `TransactionReceipt` as no transaction will be initiated (no cost associated). In our smart contract, we have a `view` method, `offset()`, that can be invoked as follows:

```
BigInteger  Offset=CFutureInstance.offset().send();
log.info("your offset is "+Offset.intValue());
```

In the same manner, it is possible to query the public states of a smart contract, for instance to read the last `fuelPriceUSD` state's value:

```
BigInteger LastfuelPrice = CFutureInstance.fuelPriceUSD().send();
Integer fuelPriceUSD = LastfuelPrice.intValue();
log.info("Last fuel Price Fuel price According to the Oracle is: " +
fuelPriceUSD);
```

But, to update the `fuelPriceUSD` to the current price, we need to go through two steps.

The first is to update the price, which we request from the oracle. The second is to wait for the event informing us of the oracle's response to read the new value:

```
BigInteger txcost = Convert.toWei("0.01",
Convert.Unit.ETHER).toBigInteger();
TransactionReceipt UpdateReceipt =
CFutureInstance.updateprice(txcost).send();
for (CFutures.NewDieselPriceEventResponse event :
    CFutureInstance.getNewDieselPriceEvents(UpdateReceipt)) {
    log.info("The oil price has been updated:" + event.price);
}
```

Keep in mind, when you call the oracle, you are initiating an asynchronous exchange, which means there will be a delay between the query and the response (request and a callback transaction). Thus, in our Java code, we will need to update the price by listening for the `NewDieselPrice` event before calling the `offset()` method to give us an accurate value.

Notice that we used `Convert.toWei("0.01", Convert.Unit.ETHER)` to convert from ethers to wei while calling `updateprice()`, to cover the call charges.

Web3j events

In the smart contract, we have defined a few events. Each one will be represented in the smart contract wrapper with a method named identically, which takes the transaction receipt and returns a decoded result (event parameters) in an instance of the `EventValues` object. Given that, here's how to get the event data and display its content in our console:

```
for (CFutures.DepositEvEventResponse event :
CFutureInstance.getDepositEvEvents(DepositReceipt)) {
    log.info("Depoist event detected:" + event.amount+"wei has been
deposited");
```

```
        log.info("The funds has been sent by: " + event.sender);
    }
```

Alternatively, you can use `Observables` (RxJava's observables), which will listen for events associated with the smart contract. Then use an `EthFilter` object to filter your observable, as follows:

```
EthFilter filter = new EthFilter(DefaultBlockParameterName.EARLIEST,
    DefaultBlockParameterName.LATEST,
CFutureInstance.getContractAddress());
web3j.ethLogObservable(filter).subscribe(Clog -> {
    log.info("contract log"+ Clog.toString());
});
```

For `EthFilter`, we specify the topics that we wish to apply to the filter, including the contract address. We can also provide specific topics (only for indexed Solidity event parameters) to filter using: `filter.addSingleTopic(EventEncoder.encode(event));`

At the time of writing, listening for events (filters/subscriptions) is supported by `Infura` only using websocket endpoints on `mainnet`, `Ropsten`, and `Rinkeby`. However, web3j doesn't yet support websockets, so we can't use filters in web3j while using `Infura`.

This was the last web3J feature we needed to cover in this chapter – it's time to test the code. Grab the full code from `https://github.com/bellaj/web3j.git` and then import and run the project in Eclipse.

Enhancement

The last thing to consider is adding a textual or a graphical menu to this application to help the user make their choices. To avoid bloating the project with irrelevant code to our purpose, I have opted for a simple text-based menu:

```
input = new Scanner(System.in);
CFutures CFutureInstance = null;
System.out.println("Please make your choice:");
System.out.println("1 - Deploy New Cfutures contract.");
System.out.println("2 - Load contract");
System.out.println("3 - Make deposit");
System.out.println("4 - current Fuel price");
System.out.println("5 - Update Fuel price");
System.out.println("6 - Investment offset");
System.out.println("0 - exit");
int selection;
choice: while(input.hasNextInt()) {
```

```
            selection = input.nextInt();
            switch (selection) {
                case 0:
                    break choice;
                    ...
            }
        }
    }
```

Great, now run your APP.java file to check whether everything is working as expected. You should see message logs detailing the execution steps, similar to the following:

You might get the event results in arbitrary order, as they are executed asynchronously in parallel and their results are later captured. Therefore, it would be preferable to use a CompletableFuture class to wrap your web3j methods and handle these asynchronous calls.

Summary

In this chapter, we have scratched the surface of working with the Ethereum blockchain using your beloved language, Java. Indeed, it was a gentle introduction to web3j by building an Oracle-based application, opening the door to build complex Ethereum applications in Java. From now on, all you need is to dive deep into the web3j documentation. You will find a number of smart contract examples in their main project repository (https://github.com/web3j/web3j/tree/master/codegen/src/test/resources/solidity).

To enrich your knowledge, you can also explore `EthereumJ`, which is a Java implementation of the Ethereum protocol, or Ethereum Harmony. To step outside of the Java world, you can explore Web3py (`https://github.com/ethereum/web3.py`), which is a complete Python implementation of `web3js`.

In the next chapter, our Ethereum journey will continue as we examine how to use Ethereum as an infrastructure for business. We will, among other things, discover the interesting concept of blockchain as a service.

Stay tuned!

7
Blockchains in Business

The Ethereum main network, and its corresponding test networks, are all open for public use. All transactions made on the networks are 100% transparent, and anybody with access to the network—which is potentially everybody—can see and access all data.

The users of these networks don't necessarily know each other: they are mutually distrustful parties who must assume that the other participants in the network are dishonest. For this reason, public blockchain networks require a way for such parties to reach an agreement without needing to trust each other, and this is where decentralized consensus algorithms, such as **proof of work** (**PoW**), come into the picture.

There are cases, however, where transacting parties in a network are more trusting of each other, and where the use of a blockchain isn't solely centered on allowing mutually distrustful parties to interact.

In this chapter, we will explore the main types of blockchain networks available – public and private—before looking in more detail at how blockchains can be used in business settings, and what options are currently available for keeping data private. We will then implement a very basic private network that makes use of certain privacy features.

Public versus private and permissioned versus permissionless blockchains

The Ethereum main network is public, meaning anyone is free to join and utilize the network. There are no permissions involved: not only can users send and receive transactions, they can also take part in a consensus, as long as they have the appropriate hardware to mine blocks. All parties in the network are mutually distrustful, but are incentivized to remain honest by the mechanisms involved in the PoW consensus. This is an example of a public, permissionless network. These networks offer high resistance to censorship and good data persistence, but are less performant due to the decentralized nature of consensus.

The idea of permission, when applied to blockchains, could take one of several forms: it could be explicit, as in the case of an access control list, or implicit, as in a requirement placed on users to enable them to join a network. An example of a public, permissioned blockchain, could take the form of a public proof of stake network, in which permission to participate in the network as a validator is granted in exchange for a deposit or stake.

Of more concern for this chapter is the idea of networks run by companies, either for their own internal use, or as a shared resource used by a group of companies wanting to transact. Such networks are private: they are not open to the general public, but only to those companies authorized to join. These are sometimes also referred to as consortium blockchains, and as such, networks often also impose different types of permissions for different participants. For example, different members of the network may have read, write, or access permissions, while another subset of members may take on the job of validation.

Such private networks can take advantage of permissioning to be more performant than their public and permissionless counterparts. If a set of nodes can be trusted as validators, then consensus can be reached more quickly. There is, however, a tradeoff: a set of permissioned validators must be trusted to correctly and honestly validate blocks. In the world of business, where time is money, such a tradeoff can often be worth making.

Privacy and anonymity in Ethereum

We have so far discussed the differences between public and private networks, where it is the network itself, and access to it, which is either public or private. We now turn our attention to the data—both transaction and contract data—inside a given network.
The Ethereum main network can be joined by anyone. Furthermore, all transaction and smart contract data is public, meaning all transactions between a *to* and *from* address can be seen by everybody using the network. There is no way to hide these transactions, or the addresses transacting, and as such, there's no way for a user on Ethereum to be truly anonymous. If a way were found to link an address with a real-world identity—either at the present time, or at a point in the future—then the identity of the transacting party would be known. This might seem obvious: on public networks, all data is public. What is less obvious is that even in a private Ethereum network, data within the network is visible to all participating nodes.

Other cryptocurrencies, such as Zcash, Monero, and Dash, provide differing degrees of anonymity, and we will briefly discuss two of the techniques for doing so in this chapter, and look at how these could be applied to Ethereum.

Monero uses a type of digital signature called a ring signature, which helps anonymize the transacting addresses as well as the amount being sent. It's possible to use a similar technique in Ethereum by using mixing services based on ring signatures, but these generally aren't accepted as being robust and scalable methods that could be used in an enterprise.

Zcash uses a different technique, leveraging **Zero-Knowledge Succinct Non-Interactive Argument of Knowledge (zk-SNARK)** proofs. In this scheme, a user is able to prove possession of some data without needing to reveal what the data is, and without needing to interact with the user verifying the data. Some work has been done to incorporate zk-SNARKs with Ethereum, though at the time of writing this work is still experimental.

So, there is currently no reliable method to make addresses and transactions anonymous in a guaranteed way – what about the contents of those transactions?

The contents of a transaction, as well as the code and data associated with a smart contract, are publicly viewable and cannot be obscured. Though a smart contract's code is compiled to bytecode, it should not be assumed that an adversary wouldn't be able to decompile and read the code. As such, sensitive information should neither be hardcoded into a contract nor sent to it as part of a transaction.

What can be done, however, is to encrypt any sensitive data off-chain before sending it to the network. Using public-key cryptography, one method would be as follows:

1. The sensitive data is encrypted with the recipient's public key, which could have been published either on- or off-chain
2. The encrypted data is sent either to a smart contract written for the purpose of receiving it, or in the data field of a normal transaction
3. The received data is decrypted using the recipient's private key

Why are privacy and anonymity important?

If we consider the case of a private or consortium blockchain run by a group of companies, then certain aspects of privacy are clearly important.

For example, companies A, B, and C create a consortium blockchain. Although the network is closed to the outside world, any transactions between A and B are visible to company C, which could be undesirable for a number of reasons, especially if the three companies are in competition with each other. In addition to any **business-to-business** (**B2B**) interactions between the companies themselves, it's possible the network would involve some form of **business-to-customer** (**B2C**) interaction , meaning further types of confidentiality and privacy would be required.

Before we look in detail at this chapter's project, let's take a look at the currently available Ethereum-based business platforms.

The Ethereum Enterprise Alliance

The **Enterprise Ethereum Alliance** (**EEA**) is a nonprofit working group whose aim is to define an open, standards-based architecture for business and enterprise use of Ethereum. Group members include many large companies from the world of software and finance, such as Microsoft, Accenture, and J.P.Morgan. The group is currently working toward defining the Ethereum Enterprise Architecture Stack, which itself will help guide the development of the EEA's overall standards-based specification.

EEA's specification will help define a standard way in which Ethereum's blockchain can be used for business purposes. However, given the opensource nature of Ethereum's codebase, adhering to EEA's specification won't necessarily be required: Ethereum's codebase can be used in any way desired.

More information can be found online at `https://entethalliance.org`.

Ethereum's licensing

The Ethereum Foundation has stated that Ethereum:

> *"is both open-source software and Free software after the definition of the Free Software Foundation (so-called FLOSS)."*

In reality, different parts of the Ethereum technology stack are licensed – or will be licensed—in different ways.

The core parts of the stack, including the consensus engine, networking code, and supporting libraries, haven't yet been licensed, but are expected to be covered by either the MIT, MPL, or LGPL license. It's important to understand that the first of these is a permissive license, while the latter two are more restrictive, and restrict a user's ability to distribute any modifications under commercial terms, therefore potentially restricting how businesses can use the code.

Regardless of the potential future restrictions that may appear once licensing is confirmed, several enterprise-centric implementations of Ethereum have already been created, with two such implementations being Quorum, created by J.P.Morgan, and Monax. Later in the chapter we will be discussing and implementing a project based on Quorum.

Blockchain-as-a-Service

Blockchain-as-a-Service (**BaaS**), is a service that allows customers to create and run their own client nodes on popular public blockchain networks, or to create their own private networks for their own use and testing. The provisioned services are based in the cloud, and are analogous to the **Software-as-a-Service** (**SaaS**) model. Several of the large cloud computing providers are now offering BaaS, such as the following:

- Microsoft Azure enables users to quickly deploy and manage applications in the cloud, and has templates available for Ethereum, Hyperledger (see later chapters), and R3's Corda (see `https://azure.microsoft.com/en-gb/solutions/blockchain/`).
- AWS Blockchain Templates is a very similar offering, and again provides templates for Ethereum and Hyperledger (see `https://aws.amazon.com/blockchain/templates/`). Further services are offered by IBM, HP, and Oracle, all along the same lines.

Quorum

Quorum (`https://www.jpmorgan.com/global/Quorum`) is an enterprise-focused fork of the Ethereum codebase, and offers a private blockchain infrastructure aimed specifically at financial use cases. It was created by J.P.Morgan, and claims to address three of the topics that would make a public blockchain network unsuitable for business use:

- Privacy, of both transaction and contract data
- Higher performance and throughput
- Permission and governance

Privacy

To achieve its headline feature of making transactions and contract data private, Quorum builds on Ethereum's existing transaction model, rather than completely redefining it.

Public transactions and public contracts are visible to everyone on the network, and make use of Ethereum's existing infrastructure—Quorum doesn't implement anything different in this respect. As well as these public transactions, Quorum offers the ability to mark transactions as private, making them visible only to the intended recipients.

This privacy is achieved using public-key cryptography, specifically by setting the recipient's public key in a new, Quorum-specific transaction parameter, `privateFor`. This allows the transaction to be encrypted, and therefore read-only by the owner of the private key.

Higher performance and throughput

Private and consortium blockchains are only open to certain authorized parties, rather than completely open to the public. As a consequence, there is little need for the consensus algorithms that are usually used between distrustful parties, namely PoW in the case of the Ethereum main network.

Quorum ultimately aims to offer pluggable and changeable consensus algorithms, and currently there are two to choose from:

- **Raft-based consensus**: This provides a much faster block time—in the order of milliseconds as opposed to seconds—as well as transaction finality, meaning once a transaction is placed into a block, there comes a point where it is impossible to remove it. A further difference from PoW is that this mechanism only creates blocks when there are transactions ready to go into them. It doesn't create empty blocks in the way that the Ethereum main network does.

- **Istanbul Byzantine fault-tolerance**: This is a PBFT-inspired algorithm that again includes short block times and transaction finality. For those wanting to learn more about it, the details can be found in EIP-650 (see: `https://github.com/ethereum/EIPs/issues/650`.)

Permission and governance

The third of Quorum's headline features is its ability to permission only chosen nodes to join a given network. This is achieved by each node in the network that has a whitelist specifying the remote nodes that are permitted for both inbound and outbound connections. We will later look in detail at a practical implementation of this.

The Quorum client

At a high level, a Quorum client consists of the following components:

- **Quorum Node**: This is based on the Ethereum Geth client
- **Constellation**: This is a general-purpose system for submitting information in a secure way, and is itself composed of **Transaction Manager** and **Enclave** subcomponents, as shown in the following diagram:

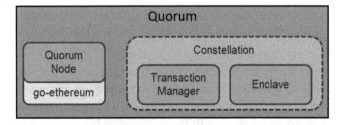

Souce: https://github.com/jpmorganchase/quorum/wiki/Quorum-Overview

Quorum Node

Quorum Node is based on Ethereum's Geth client, but with a series of changes:

- Ethereum's PoW consensus algorithm has been replaced. There is currently a choice of two alternatives, which were briefly discussed previously.
- The P2P protocol has been modified to allow only authorized nodes to connect, preventing connections from the wider public.
- The way Ethereum maintains and records its state has been changed to allow public and private states to be handled separately in two different Patricia Merkle trees.
- Block validation has been altered to handle private transactions as well as public transactions.
- The gas-pricing mechanism has been removed, though the concept of gas is still used.

So far, Geth has been altered in such a way to allow both public and private transactions to occur.

Constellation

Constellation could be considered a P2P system in which each node in the system can act as a distributed key server and **mail transfer agent** (**MTA**), using PGP encryption to encrypt messages. It is this part of Quorum that allows for transactions to be made private, and is composed of two parts: the Transaction Manager and Enclave.

The Transaction Manager handles transaction privacy by storing and making transaction data available, as well as exchanging transaction payloads with Transaction Manager instances on other nodes. It does not have access to any of the private keys required for encryption, which is the job of the Enclave. The Enclave's job is to handle both key-generation and the encryption of transaction data. As its name suggests, handling these jobs separately allows sensitive operations to be isolated.

Our project

To demonstrate Quorum's privacy characteristics, we will set up a small private network using an online example as a basis. Through this, we will explore how the nodes communicate, and show how private transactions—in this case, in the scope of interacting with a smart contract—can be broadcast to the network while being accessible only by the intended recipients.

Prerequisites

While it would be possible to set up our network manually, it will be cleaner to do so in a separate environment that we can bring up and take down easily.

As a first step we'll need to install the following applications:

- **VirtualBox**: https://www.virtualbox.org/wiki/Downloads
- **Vagrant**: https://github.com/hashicorp/vagrant

VirtualBox is a virtualization application that will let us run our network inside a virtual machine, while Vagrant is a tool that will allow us to configure the environment easily so that our network can be initialized and run on command. Once the two applications are installed, we can move onto installing our Quorum-related code.

We first want to download the appropriate code from Quorum's GitHub repository. If Git isn't already installed on your system, now would be the time to do so (see https://git-scm.com/downloads):

```
git clone https://github.com/jpmorganchase/quorum-examples
cd quorum-examples
```

The quorum-examples/ directory contains a file called Vagrantfile, which will be read by Vagrant when it starts. This file defines the parameters of our VirtualBox VM, and includes the ports that will be associated with each node in our network. It also calls a script, called vagrant/bootstrap.sh, which is run to create the node software from scratch.

Running the following will create a virtual machine in VirtualBox and configure it from the Vagrantfile file:

```
vagrant up
```

The first time this is run, it will take somewhere in the order of 5-10 minutes. Vagrantfile defines the image that should be run on our VM—in this case, an Ubuntu Xenial image—which has to be downloaded. On subsequent runs, the startup time will be much quicker. When it has finished, we will have our configured virtual machine. To interact with our new environment, we have to connect to our virtual machine using SSH on the command line:

```
vagrant ssh
```

Our instantiated VM comes with a predefined network that we'll use for our examples, which can be found inside our virtual environment under the `quorum-examples/7nodes/` directory. As the name suggests, our test network will consist of seven nodes in total.

Bringing up the network

Inside the `quorum-examples/7nodes/` directory are the scripts we will use to bring up our network, detailed as follows.

The first script is `raft-init.sh`, which is run only once and performs the following actions:

- Initializes the Quorum Node part of each node by running `geth init --datadir qdata/dd<x> genesis.json`, where `<x>` is the number of the node. This uses the same genesis file for each node, meaning they all share the same network.
- Creates the key pair for each node and places it in each node's `qdata/dd<x>/keystore` directory.

From inside `quorum-examples/7nodes/`, run the following:

```
./raft-init.sh
```

The second script is `raft-start.sh`, which is used to start the network properly. This script instantiates each node by doing the following:

- Runs the Geth client with appropriate parameters, thereby starting the Quorum Node component of the node.
- Runs the `constellation-start.sh` script, which starts the Constellation component of each node, creating the appropriate `qdata/c<x>` directory, and copying the Transaction Manager keys created by the initialization script to the proper place.

From the same directory, run:

```
./raft-start.sh
```

When this completes, you will see the following message:

```
All nodes configured. See 'qdata/logs' for logs, and run e.g. 'geth attach
qdata/dd1/geth.ipc' to attach to the first Geth node.
```

Having brought up the network, it will now look like the following diagram, which shows three of the seven nodes in the network. The **Quorum Node** portions of the nodes are connected via Geth's P2P protocol, while the **Transaction Managers** are connected via **Constellation**:

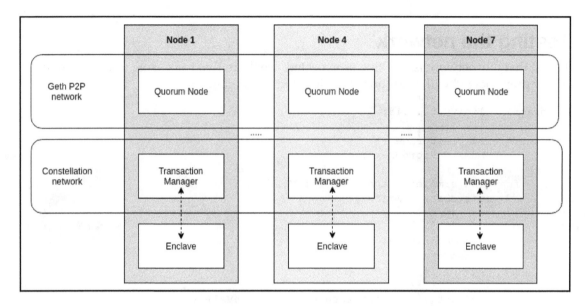

When we need to tear down the network, we can use a third script from the same directory, stop.sh.

Interacting with the network

When we started the Geth clients during the second step, we also created IPC endpoints under each node's data directory. Using these endpoints, we can attach to each of our nodes. First, open three new terminals, navigate to your host machine's quorum-examples/ directory in each window, and run vagrant ssh to connect each of them to the VM.

From within the environment, using the familiar Geth commands, we can attach to three of the running nodes in our network. For example, to attach to node 1, perform the following:

```
geth attach qdata/dd1/geth.ipc
```

This provides us with a familiar JavaScript console through which to interact with the node. For this tutorial, we recommend attaching to nodes 1, 4, and 7, each in their own Terminal window. Repeat the preceding step for each of these nodes, substituting the appropriate number in the command.

Testing the network

To test that our network is working as expected, we'll run two tests using a contract that comes prepackaged with the Quorum code, `simplestorage.sol`:

```solidity
pragma solidity ^0.4.15;

contract simplestorage {
    uint public storedData;

    function simplestorage(uint initVal) {
        storedData = initVal;
    }

    function set(uint x) {
        storedData = x;
    }

    function get() constant returns (uint retVal) {
        return storedData;
    }
}
```

This is a very simple contract that will allow members of the network to read and write a variable on the condition that they have authorization to do so. We'll first deploy the contract publicly, check that all nodes are able to interact with it, and then redeploy the contract in such a way that only two of the nodes are able to interact with it.

 It should be noted that the contract is compiled with an older version of the compiler, in this case 0.4.15. This is because there have been issues with using later releases of the Solidity compiler with Quorum (see `https://github.com/jpmorganchase/quorum/issues/371`.)

To deploy the contract, we can make use of the `runscript.sh` script, together with the following:

- `public-contract.js`
- `private-contract.js`

These preprepared files contain references to both the ABI and bytecode required to deploy the contracts using Web3. If we look at the two files, we can see that the ABI and bytecode are identical – we're deploying exactly the same contract. The only difference is how the contract is deployed.

For `public-contract.js`, we use the following:

```
var simple = simpleContract.new(42, {from:web3.eth.accounts[0], data:
bytecode, gas: 0x47b760}, function(e, contract) { ... }
```

And for `private-contract.js`, we use this code:

```
var simple = simpleContract.new(42, {from:web3.eth.accounts[0], data:
bytecode, gas: 0x47b760, privateFor:
["ROAZBWtSacxXQrOe3FGAqJDyJjFePR5ce4TSIzmJ0Bc="]}, function(e, contract) {
... }
```

In each case, the `simple` variable is the reference to the newly deployed contract. The initial value passed to the constructor is 42, and the contract is deployed by the first account on node 1. The specific difference is that the private contract is deployed with the `privateFor` parameter, with a public key being passed as the value. The transaction being used to deploy the contract is therefore private, and intended only for the owner of the specified public key.

We can check which node this public key equates to by checking the keys held by the Constellation Transaction Manager on each node. Upon inspection, we see that this equates to node 7, meaning once the contract is deployed, only nodes 1 (the deployer) and 7 will be able to access and view the data belonging to the contract as shown here:

```
$ cat examples/7nodes/keys/tm7.pub
ROAZBWtSacxXQrOe3FGAqJDyJjFePR5ce4TSIzmJ0Bc=
```

Deploying the public contract

Let's first deploy the public contract by running the relevant scripts from the console of our main session. It's not necessary to attach to any of the nodes as `runscript.sh` performs the attach for us:

```
$ ./runscript.sh public-contract.sh
```

Having deployed our public contract, we want our nodes to be able to interact with it, and to do so requires each of our three nodes to know the contract ABI and address to which it's deployed.

Using the transaction hash returned during the preceding deployment, we can get the contract address by running the following from one of the nodes directly, from within one of the `geth attach` consoles:

```
> eth.get.transactionReceipt("<transaction_hash>");
```

From here, we can read the `contractAddress` value, which we can set to a variable for ease of use. Make sure you use the address output by your particular instance:

```
> var address = "<your_contract_address>";
```

The ABI can be copied directly from the `public-contract.sh` script, and again assigned to a variable for convenience:

```
> var abi =
[{"constant":true,"inputs":[],"name":"storedData","outputs":[{"name":"","ty
pe":"uint256"}],"payable":false,"type":"function"},{"constant":false,"input
s":[{"name":"x","type":"uint256"}],"name":"set","outputs":[],"payable":fals
e,"type":"function"},{"constant":true,"inputs":[],"name":"get","outputs":[{
"name":"retVal","type":"uint256"}],"payable":false,"type":"function"},{"inp
uts":[{"name":"initVal","type":"uint256"}],"type":"constructor"}];
```

We can then use these values in our node consoles to generate a reference to the deployed public contract:

```
> var public_contract = eth.contract(abi).at(address);
```

These steps should be followed for each of the nodes we have attached to. Now that we have a reference to the deployed contract, we can read the value of the `storedData` variable that we set in the constructor by calling the contract's `get()` function.

From our Terminal attached to node 1, use the following:

```
> public_contract.get()
42
```

Repeating the same command on each of the other attached nodes will yield the same result. All the nodes can read the contract because it was marked as public – or, rather, it was not marked as private—during deployment.

Deploying the private contract

Now, let's test that by deploying a private contract if we make data visible only to those nodes or not that are authorized.

Using the same methodology as before, let's first deploy our private contract:

```
> ./runscript.sh private-contract.js
```

Then, follow the same steps to allow each node to understand the contract:

1. Get the contract address from the returned transaction hash.
2. Set the address to a variable.
3. Get the ABI from the .js file and set it to a variable. (Note: This is the same for both private and public contracts, so there's no strict need to update this.)
4. Get a reference to the contract using the address and ABI:

```
> var private_contract = eth.contract(abi).at(address);
```

We can now show Quorum's privacy in action. On nodes 1 and 7, we are able to read the variable and be returned the expected value:

```
> public_contract.get()
42
```

On node 4—or any other node, if we attach to them—we are unable to read the value as shown here:

```
> public_contract.get()
0
```

Great! We have demonstrated how Quorum is able to keep data private within a network by using its `privateFor` option when deploying a contract.

Permissioning the network

Unlike public networks, which are open for anyone to join, Quorum includes an explicit permissioning system. This can be used to specify both the nodes that can make inbound connections to a network, as well as which nodes can be connected to from inside a network.

In our network, the whitelist is contained in the `permissioned-nodes.json` file, the contents of which are shown as follows (the full node identifiers have been truncated):

```
[
    "enode://ac6b1096...@127.0.0.1:21000?discport=0&raftport=50401",
    "enode://0ba6b9f6...@127.0.0.1:21001?discport=0&raftport=50402",
    "enode://579f786d...@127.0.0.1:21002?discport=0&raftport=50403",
    "enode://3d9ca595...@127.0.0.1:21003?discport=0&raftport=50404",
    "enode://3701f007...@127.0.0.1:21004?discport=0&raftport=50405",
```

```
"enode://eacaa74c...@127.0.0.1:21005?discport=0&raftport=50406",
"enode://239c1f04...@127.0.0.1:21006?discport=0&raftport=50407"
]
```

When the network was brought up, the `raft-init.sh` script copied the same whitelist to the data directory of each node (`qdata/dd<x>/`). When we then called `raft-start.sh`, each node was started with a `--permissioned` flag, meaning the `permissioned-nodes.json` file was parsed, and the permissioning came into effect. Every node on our network could connect to every other node.

To test the permissioning system, we will remove one of the nodes from the whitelist and check whether it can see other nodes in the network. Start by taking down the network from the original console you ran `vagrant ssh` on:

```
./stop
```

Next, we want to remove the original JSON file from the data directory of each node:

```
rm qdata/dd*/static-nodes.json
rm qdata/dd*/permissioned-nodes.json
```

Then edit the master copy of `permissioned-nodes.json` to remove node 6 using your favorite editor. Having done that, we can reinitialize the network using `./raft-init.sh`, before restarting it with `./raft-start.sh`.

To check that our changes have worked, attach to node 1 (`geth attach qdata/dd1/geth.ipc`) and check the active connections using the following:

```
> admin.peers
```

The output should show that node 6 is now excluded, meaning that it's unable to connect to any nodes, nor be connected to. Our network permissions are now in force.

Summary

In this relatively short chapter, we learned how to create a private Quorum network inside a virtual environment. We then explored how transactions can be made private by using the public keys of those nodes that we want to have access to the transaction data, or in our specific case, the data associated with a smart contract. We then briefly looked how our network could be permissioned using Quorum's whitelisting and the `--permissioned` flag.

8
Creating an ICO

An **Initial Coin Offering** (**ICO**) is a fundraising tool that allows a project to raise equity by trading a cryptocurrency that has immediate, liquid value, for a new currency or tokens that might have value in the future. It is a quick and easy way to run a kickstarter campaign in a decentralized manner.

As the name suggests, ICOs are akin to IPOs, but in which participants receive cryptocoins or tokens instead of stocks or shares. For the sake of simplicity, our tutorial will assume that an ICO is the same as a token sale, though it is often argued that there are differences in what these terms mean.

In this chapter, we will discuss a practical implementation of an ICO on Ethereum in detail. We won't be discussing anything related to the wider financial aspects of ICOs, and to this end, this chapter won't do any of the following:

- Give advice on whether your project requires an ICO
- Give advice on which ICOs to invest in
- Discuss whether ICOs should be regulated, or what type of financial instrument they should be classed as

What is an ICO?

During an ICO on Ethereum, participants send ether to a special smart contract, and, in return, receive tokens of equal value, depending on the price of the token set at the start of the sale.

In Ethereum, a token is just a balance – itself just a number – stored in a smart contract and associated with an owner's wallet address. A minimal implementation of a token would therefore only require a way to store how many tokens a given address owns. In Solidity, this can be achieved simply by using a mapping:

```
mapping (address => uint256) balances;
```

It's important to note that a token isn't something that resides in a user's wallet, nor is it something that can be moved around. When a user sees a token in their wallet, the wallet software is really making a call into the token contract and reading the balance associated with its address. Likewise, when a wallet sends a token to another address, the wallet is really calling into the contract to change the balances associated with the to and from addresses.

In addition to the contract that defines the new token, an ICO also requires a contract to define the terms of the sale itself. This contract only needs to exist while the sale is ongoing, and is used to receive ether in exchange for the tokens and to define variables such as the length of the sale and the price of the new tokens.

Finally, while it should be possible to interact with the ICO contracts directly, projects running an ICO almost always create a more user-friendly interface in the form of a web page.

In light of this, in this chapter, we will cover the following topics:

- Project setup.
- Token contracts (together with our implementation).
- Token sale contracts.
- Implementing our token sale contract.
- Contract security.
- Testing the code.
- Deploying to a test network.
- Verifying our contract on Etherscan.
- Creating a frontend website.

At the end of the chapter we will summarize what we have done, and look briefly at suggestions for future work.

Project setup

Before we start to look in detail at the ICO implementation, it's a good idea to set up our working environment so we can incrementally add to the code as we walk through the explanation. For this project, we'll be using the Truffle framework and the Solidity language, which were introduced in `Chapter 4`, *Peer to Peer Auction in Ethereum*, and `Chapter 5`, *Tontine Game with Truffle and Drizzle*. The tutorial assumes you are working from a Linux-style terminal.

If you haven't already installed Truffle, do so by running the following command on the command line:

```
npm install -g truffle
```

 For complete details on dependencies, and to troubleshoot any Truffle-specific issues, please refer to the official documentation at https://truffleframework.com/docs/truffle/getting-started/installation.

Next, create a project directory:

```
mkdir PacktCoin
cd PacktCoin
```

And finally, initialize the Truffle project, which will generate an empty Truffle project with the directory structure that was introduced in Chapter 5, *Tontine Game with Truffle and Drizzle*:

```
truffle init
```

Our project environment is now ready for use. Before we jump into our implementation, let's first explore the types of tokens that are currently available.

Token contracts

As mentioned in the introduction, a token contract can take any form, as long as there is a way to map between an address and a token balance. However, standard token implementations are available that contract creators can use. These standard implementations provide a simple and uniform interface through which interactions with contracts can occur, and allow wallets and exchanges to easily list a multitude of tokens while only implementing the integration logic once.

These standards are defined as **Ethereum Request for Comments** (ERC) token standards, and are submitted through the **Ethereum Improvement Proposal** (EIP) process. The open source nature of Ethereum means that anybody can submit such a proposal to the community for discussion and consideration.

Various token standards exist, the most important of which we'll discuss here. It's important to note that the standards define an interface, which defines what a token contract can do, but not how it does it. The implementations are not defined by the standards.

ERC-20 token standard

(For reference during this section, the standard can be found at the following link: `https://github.com/ethereum/EIPs/blob/master/EIPS/eip-20.md`)

This is the most common type of token in use today, and the one we will use in our implementation. We'll go through each part of the standard and discuss its purpose. Note that there are certain parts of the interface that must be included to adhere to the standard, and certain parts that are optional.

Using your editor of choice, create a new file in the `contracts/` directory of your project, named `PacktToken.sol`. This file will become our ERC-20 token contract.

At the top of the file, we must first declare our Solidity compiler version, which, at the time of writing, is 0.4.24:

```
pragma solidity ^0.4.24;
```

Under this we can declare our contract, as follows:

```
contract PacktToken {

}
```

Let's begin by taking a look at the initial parts of the ERC-20 standard.

Name and symbol (optional)

The name of our token and the associated symbol are not mandatory parts of the implementation, but both are commonly included. We will define them as public state variables at the top of our contract, meaning the associated getter functions will be generated automatically:

```
string public name = "Packt ERC20 Token";
string public symbol = "PET";
```

totalSupply (required)

This public state variable defines the total number of tokens across all address balances. Again, the associated getter function will be automatically generated at compile time. In the case of our token, we will pass in a value for `totalSupply` to our constructor, so we only want to declare it here:

```
uint256 public totalSupply;
```

decimals (optional)

Fixed-point numbers aren't supported in Solidity or inside the EVM, so a different method of representing them has to be used. If we want our contract to be able to represent fractional tokens, then we need a way to represent them as fixed-point numbers. To do this, we use a scaling factor, given by decimals, which describes the number of places after the decimal point that our fractional tokens can be represented to.

For example, if we want to be able to represent 4.5001 tokens, then we require a decimal value of at least 4. In general, the use of 18 is the de facto standard:

```
uint8 public decimals;
```

For the sake of simplicity, our implementation will only deal with whole tokens, so we won't implement the decimals variable in our contract.

Transfer event (required)

The standard dictates that upon the successful transfer of tokens from one address to another, an event must be emitted. Both the to and from address should be included in the event, as well as the number of tokens:

```
event Transfer(address indexed _from,
               address indexed _to,
               uint256 _value);
```

balanceOf (required)

As described earlier in the *What is an ICO?* section, a minimal implementation of a token would only really need a way to store the balance of a given address (in reality, a way to transfer balances between different addresses would also be required for such a minimal implementation). In Solidity, we can represent balances by using a mapping, as follows:

```
mapping (address => uint256) public balanceOf;
```

Again, by declaring this state variable as public, we generate the associated getter function.

transfer() (required)

This is the other essential part of any minimal token implementation, and allows a balance to be transferred from one account to another:

```
function transfer(address _to, uint256 _value)
    public
    returns (bool success)
{
    require(balanceOf[msg.sender] >= _value);

    balanceOf[msg.sender] -= _value;
    balanceOf[_to] += _value;

    emit Transfer(msg.sender, _to, _value);
    return true;
}
```

Let's break down what's happening:

- The contract requires that the user making the transfer has a sufficient number of tokens to do so.
- The balance of the sender is reduced and the balance of the receiver is increased.
- The transfer event described earlier must be emitted.
- The function returns true to show a successful transfer. If the transfer isn't successfulthat is, if the sender has insufficient funds—then the function can either return false, or revert. In our implementation, the `require()` call will cause a revert.

The constructor

Every contract must contain a constructor function that is run only once when the contract is first deployed. In our implementation, the constructor takes the initial supply of tokens as a parameter, which is assigned to the owner of the contract. We also emit a `Transfer` event, indicating a transfer from address 0 to the contract owner's account. This is considered best practice, but is not required by the standard:

```
constructor(uint256 _initialSupply) public {
    balanceOf[msg.sender] = _initialSupply;
    totalSupply = _initialSupply;
    emit Transfer(address(0), msg.sender, totalSupply);
}
```

We've now written sufficient code to have a functional token, though there are still things we must add before it adheres completely to the ERC-20 standard. The following code represents our implementation thus far, with our variables defined:

```
pragma solidity ^0.4.24;

contract PacktToken {
    string public name = "Packt ERC20 Token";
    string public symbol = "PET";

    uint256 public totalSupply;
    mapping (address => uint256) public balanceOf;

    event Transfer(address indexed _from,
                   address indexed _to,
                   uint256 _value);

    constructor(uint256 _initialSupply) public {
        balanceOf[msg.sender] = _initialSupply;
        totalSupply = _initialSupply;
        emit Transfer(address(0), msg.sender, totalSupply);
    }

    function transfer(address _to, uint256 _value)
        public
        returns (bool success)
    {
        require(balanceOf[msg.sender] >= _value);

        balanceOf[msg.sender] -= _value;
        balanceOf[_to] += _value;

        emit Transfer(msg.sender, _to, _value);
```

```
        return true;
    }
}
```

Delegated transfer

In addition to the functionality we've described so far, the standard also defines a way for a token owner to delegate responsibility for transferring all or some of their balance. The owner isn't transferring the tokens themselves, but giving permission for another account to transfer on their behalf. This allows exchange-brokered token transfers, and, more generally, for smart contracts to accept tokens in exchange for a service.

We will describe the parts of the standard that provide the functionality, and then discuss the flow of operations.

allowance (required)

A token owner can approve not only one, but multiple different accounts as delegates. So, for example, Alice can grant both Bob and Carol permission to make transfers from her account on her behalf. Extending this example, Alice can approve any number of any other accounts as delegates. These delegate accounts must be kept track of, and to do so again utilizes Solidity's mapping type, this time in a nested way:

```
mapping(address => mapping(address => uint256)) public allowance;
```

Here, the outer mapping maps Alice's address to an inner mapping. The inner mapping maps the delegate accounts (that is, the accounts granted permission to transfer on Alice's behalf) to the values they have been granted control over.

As in previous cases, this public state variable can be accessed using its getter function.

approve() (required)

This function is called by the token owner to delegate control of a certain balance to a particular account. This can be called multiple times for different delegate accounts:

```
function approve(address _spender, uint256 _value)
    public
    returns (bool success)
{
    allowance[msg.sender][_spender] = _value;
    emit Approval(msg.sender, _spender, _value);
```

```
        return true;
}
```

Note that there is no check to confirm that the approving account, associated with `msg.sender`, has a large enough balance to cover the amount being delegated. This is only the approval step of the delegation—the actual transfer step occurs later. It is assumed that the token owner's balance could change before the eventual transfer event, so any checks are deferred until then.

The standard requires that the function returns true, even though there are no parts of the function that can fail. An `Approval` event, explained next, must also be emitted.

Approval event (required)

As mentioned, the standard dictates that an event be emitted when the `approve()` function is called:

```
event Approval(address indexed _owner,
               address indexed _spender,
               uint256 _value);
```

transferFrom() (required)

This is the final piece of the delegated transfer jigsaw. This function allows the delegate account, set in the original call to `approve()`, to transfer tokens from the token owner's account to another account:

```
function transferFrom(address _from, address _to, uint256 _value)
    public
    returns (bool success)
{
    require(_value <= balanceOf[_from]);
    require(_value <= allowance[_from][msg.sender]);

    balanceOf[_from] -= _value;
    balanceOf[_to] += _value;
    allowance[_from][msg.sender] -= _value;
    emit Transfer(_from, _to, _value);
    return true;
}
```

Let's look at what is happening here:

- The token owner's balance is checked for sufficient funds. This check was deferred from the original call to `approve()`.
- The allowance mapping is checked to ensure that the caller of the function isn't trying to transfer more than they've been allocated.
- The balances of the two accounts are changed.
- The delegated account's allowance is decreased.
- A `Transfer` event is emitted.

Now that we have the required parts, let's look at the flow of the delegation's functionality:

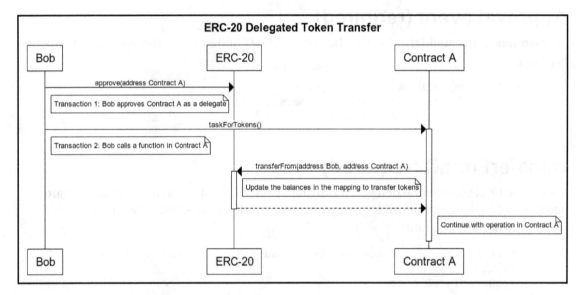

The flow is explained as follows:

1. The token owner calls the `approve()` function, passing in the address of the account that will be the delegate, and the amount of funds being delegated to them. Let's suppose that Bob wants to pay a contract – **Contract A** – to carry out some function, and he wants to pay for that function in tokens that Contract A accepts. He therefore calls `approve()` with Contract A's address, and the allowance value for that address is updated.

2. He calls a function in Contract A that performs some task that he wants to pay for in tokens. The function in Contract A first calls the ERC-20 contract's `transferFrom()` function with Bob's address and Contract A's address.

3. If Bob has approved a sufficiently large balance, `transferFrom()` will succeed and the rest of the function in Contract A can be executed.

4. If Bob hasn't approved a sufficiently large balance, `transferFrom()` will fail, either reverting or returning false, depending upon the implementation.

The complete token contract

Having added the code to support delegated transfers, we now have a complete implementation of our ERC-20 token:

```solidity
pragma solidity ^0.4.24;

contract PacktToken {
    string public name = 'Packt ERC20 Token';
    string public symbol = 'PET';

    uint256 public totalSupply;
    mapping (address => uint256) public balanceOf;
    mapping(address => mapping(address => uint256)) public allowance;

    event Transfer(address indexed _from,
                   address indexed _to,
                   uint256 _value);

    event Approval(address indexed _owner,
                   address indexed _spender,
                   uint256 _value);

    constructor(uint256 _initialSupply) public {
        balanceOf[msg.sender] = _initialSupply;
        totalSupply = _initialSupply;
        emit Transfer(address(0), msg.sender, totalSupply);
    }

    function transfer(address _to, uint256 _value)
        public
        returns (bool success)
    {
        require(balanceOf[msg.sender] >= _value);

        balanceOf[msg.sender] -= _value;
        balanceOf[_to] += _value;
```

```
            emit Transfer(msg.sender, _to, _value);
            return true;
    }

    function approve(address _spender, uint256 _value)
        public
        returns (bool success)
    {
        allowance[msg.sender][_spender] = _value;
        emit Approval(msg.sender, _spender, _value);
        return true;
    }

    function transferFrom(address _from, address _to, uint256 _value)
        public
        returns (bool success)
    {
        require(_value <= balanceOf[_from]);
        require(_value <= allowance[_from][msg.sender]);

        balanceOf[_from] -= _value;
        balanceOf[_to] += _value;
        allowance[_from][msg.sender] -= _value;
        emit Transfer(_from, _to, _value);
        return true;
    }
}
```

Before continuing with the rest of our crowdsale project, let's first look at some of the other main token standards that are available.

ERC-223 token standard

(For reference during this section, the standard can be found at the following link: `https://github.com/ethereum/EIPs/issues/223`)

This standard was created as a response to a potential issue with the original ERC-20 standard; namely, if a user calls `transfer()` with a contract account as the to address, then those tokens are lost forever. There is no way that the contract, who owns the receiving address, can itself ever call `transfer()`, thus rendering the tokens stuck.

ERC-223, which, at the time of writing, is still in an open draft and not finalized, attempts to remedy the problem of stuck tokens by only allowing transfers to accounts owned by contracts if those contracts have a way of handling the tokens transferred to their ownership.

The standard defines a new interface for the `transfer()` function, and states that any contract expecting to receive tokens must implement a `tokenFallback()` function, which is called as part of the transfer. If the function isn't defined, tokens cannot be transferred to the contract's ownership, making it impossible to accidentally send tokens to addresses owned by contracts if those contracts are not expecting them.

The general flow is presented in the following diagram:

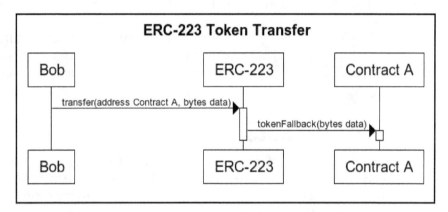

Note that the transfer now only requires a single call to be initiated by Bob, as opposed to the two calls – `approve()` and `transferFrom()` – for the equivalent ERC-20 flow. This means both gas costs and blockchain state costs are reduced.

Two other important token standards, which we won't discuss in detail, but which could both be considered successors to ERC-20 and ERC-223, are ERC-677 and ERC-777.

ERC-677 was designed to make the functionalities provided by ERC-223 backward-compatible with ERC-20, while ERC-777 is particularly complex, and uses a registry contract defined in a further new standard, ERC-820, to allow any address to register which type of interface it implements. The registry then allows an ERC-777 contract to check the implementation of the to address as part of any transfer.

ERC-721 non-fungible token standard

(For reference during this section, the standard can be found at the following link: `https://github.com/ethereum/eips/issues/721`)

The tokens we've discussed so far have all been based on the idea of value, where that value was initially defined at the time of crowdsale in terms of an existing currency: you buy a given number of tokens for a given amount of ETH.

It's possible, however, to allow tokens to represent other things, such as physical objects or a reputation. In contrast to an abstract unit of value, such as a dollar, bitcoin, or ether, such things aren't fungible. Fungibility is the characteristic of an asset that determines whether assets of the same type can be considered interchangeable during an exchange. One ether has the same value and utility of any other ether, and so they are considered completely interchangeable and fungible. One item, such as a car, a baseball card, or a CryptoKitty (`https://www.cryptokitties.co/`), is not directly interchangeable with another, so is considered non-fungible. ERC-721 was proposed to tokenize such non-fungible assets.

Token sale contracts

We have so far implemented our new token in the form of an ERC-20 contract. We could deploy this contract and it would function perfectly well. When the contract is deployed, its constructor is called, and the total token balance is initially assigned to the contract owner. What we want to do now is distribute the tokens, while at the same time raise money for our fictional project, and to do this we need to run an ICO, or token sale.

The simplest type of token sale allows participants to buy tokens over a fixed period of time, ending either at a predefined date, or once all of the tokens are sold. This is the simple implementation we'll undertake. There are, however, more complex forms of token sale, which we'll briefly summarize here.

Hard cap

This type of sale involves selling a fixed number of tokens at a fixed price, either until all the available tokens are sold, that is, the cap is reached, or until a predefined time or block number. This is the form of sale we'll implement.

Soft cap

An initial cap is set, but if this is reached, then the sale continues until a certain point in time. A soft cap can be mixed with a hard cap, allowing the sale to continue after a soft cap, and up until the hard cap is reached.

Uncapped

In this case, there is no cap on the number of tokens being sold, and the sale runs for a fixed time. The exchange ratio can either be constant, or changed as the sale progresses. A common form of this sale gives better rates to early contributors, with the rate decreasing as the sale proceeds. This mixed-ratio scheme is similar to how the original Ethereum ICO was run.

The schemes presented thus far have involved a simple token purchase at a given price. Auctions are a form of sale that are more interesting.

Dutch auction

A Dutch auction uses a mechanism that results in the discovery of what participants consider to be a fair price. The auction begins at a high asking price, which is then incrementally lowered until the bids received cover the total amount of tokens on offer. The price at which the auction closes, that is, when all tokens are accounted for, is the price at which all bidders will receive their tokens. Dutch auctions are popular because they offer this process of price discovery, and because they are transparent: all bidders have visibility into the total available supply, current prices, and changes in price over time. Each bid is visible, so supply and demand characteristics can be understood throughout the auction.

Reverse dutch auction

This is another form of capped sale, but in this case, the portion of tokens sold to participants is dependent on the length of the sale. If all tokens are sold on day one, then a proportion, P %, would be distributed among participants, and the rest retained by the project team. If the sale finishes on day two, then $P+X$ % would be distributed, and so on. The idea in this type of auction is to guarantee that if a participant buys at time T, then they are buying at a value that is at most $1 / T$. The reality often doesn't match the theory, as was shown with the Gnosis token sale, where the fear of missing out caused everyone to buy in at day one, and the sale therefore finished earlier than expected.

Considerations

With any type of token sale, certain aspects should be decided beforehand:

- The time or block number at which the sale will start.
- Whether there are any caps, and their type.
- How long the sale will last.
- The end conditions for the sale.
- The currency in which tokens can be bought.
- The proportion of the tokens that will be sold, and the proportion kept.
- The exchange rates, that is, how much the tokens will cost. If the rate isn't fixed, it should be understood how they will change.

These considerations, together with the type of sale you will use, will depend on the characteristics and requirements of your particular project. For the purposes of our project code, we will be using a simple, fixed-cap token sale.

Implementing our token sale contract

Our token sale contract will handle the mechanics of buying and selling our token in ether. To do this, our token sale contract will have to communicate with our ERC-20 contract in order to perform transfers from our token sale contract's balance to the balances of participants. For this communication, the token sale contract must know which functions are supported in our ERC-20 contract. This can be done in one of two ways:

- **Define an interface**: We can use Solidity's interface keyword to define the parts of the ERC-20 contract that the token sale contract needs to use. We would make this declaration in the same file, above the token-sale contract body.

- **Import the ERC-20 contract**: We can use an import statement to include the entire ERC-20 contract. For our implementation, this is the method we'll use.

First, create a new file in our project's `contracts/` directory, named
`PacktTokenSale.sol`. At the top of our new file, we want to declare the compiler version
and import the ERC-20 contract:

```
pragma solidity ^0.4.24;

import "./PacktToken.sol";

contract PacktTokenSale {

}
```

Constructor

The constructor of our token sale contract will take two arguments:

- The address of our ERC-20 token contract
- The token price

At the head of our contract, we will assign two public state variables to hold the values
passed into the constructor. Importantly, we use the type definition from our token contract
when assigning the passed-in address:

```
contract PacktTokenSale {
    PacktToken public tokenContract;
    uint256 public tokenPrice;
    address owner;

    constructor(PacktToken _tokenContract, uint256 _tokenPrice) public {
        owner = msg.sender;
        tokenContract = _tokenContract;
        tokenPrice = _tokenPrice;
    }
}
```

Token supply

One of the considerations mentioned in the *Token sale contracts* section was the total number of tokens to offer in the crowd sale. Often a portion of the total number of tokens is kept by the project, perhaps to be sold in the future as a way to supplement funding. In our implementation, we will be selling 50% of the total tokens we create when we deploy our ERC-20 token contract. Whenever we need to query the balance associated with our token sale contract, we will call our ERC-20 contract directly:

```
tokenContract.balanceOf(this);
```

This will give us the remaining balance associated with our token sale, but for convenience, we will keep track of the number of tokens sold with a separate public variable:

```
uint256 public tokensSold;
```

Buying tokens

The main functionality of our token sale contract is defined in buying and selling tokens, which will be handled by a single function, buyTokens():

```
function buyTokens(uint256 _numberOfTokens)
    public
    payable
{
    require(msg.value == _numberOfTokens * tokenPrice);
    require(tokenContract.balanceOf(this) >= _numberOfTokens);
    tokensSold += _numberOfTokens;
    emit Sell(msg.sender, _numberOfTokens);
    require(tokenContract.transfer(msg.sender, _numberOfTokens));
}
```

Let's look at what's happening in the preceding code:

- The function must be marked payable for it to accept the ether required to pay for the tokens.
    - It first requires that the ether sent with the function call, msg.value, is equal to the price of the number of tokens we want to buy.
- It then requires that the number of tokens left in the token sale contract's balance will cover the requested number of tokens. As mentioned previously, we do this by calling into our ERC-20 contract and checking the balance owned by the token sale contract.

- We emit an event marking the sale.
- We increment the counter for the number of tokens sold.
- Finally, we require that the transfer of the tokens is successful. To make the transfer, we call into the ERC-20 contract directly.

The `Sell` event emitted as part of the function takes the following form:

```
event Sell(address indexed _buyer, uint256 indexed _amount);
```

Ending the sale

The only remaining part of our contract is the functionality to end the sale. We previously stated that our sale will be a fixed-price, fixed-period sale. In this sale, the owner will be able to end the sale at any time. In the real world, this would not be ideal, and would be a red flag to any potential investors. The code is defined as follows:

```
function endSale() public {
    require(msg.sender == owner);
    require(tokenContract.transfer(owner,
                            tokenContract.balanceOf(this)));
    msg.sender.transfer(address(this).balance);
}
```

The `endSale()` function first transfers all remaining tokens from the address of our ERC-20 contract to the address of the contract owner. It then transfers the ether held by the sale contract to the same address.

An alternative would be to have a call to `selfdestruct()` at the end of this function. This both sends any held ether to the admin account, as well as removing the smart contract's code from storage, thereby freeing space in the blockchain, and generating a refund for the owner.

The complete token sale contract

Our basic implementation is now complete, and can be compiled by running the following from our project directory:

```
truffle compile
```

Here is the full code of our token sale contract as is. You will notice that an additional helper function, `safeMultiply()`, has been added – this will be explained in the next section:

```solidity
pragma solidity ^0.4.24;

import "./PacktToken.sol";

contract PacktTokenSale {
    PacktToken public tokenContract;
    uint256 public tokenPrice;
    uint256 public tokensSold;
    address owner;
    event Sell(address indexed _buyer, uint256 indexed _amount);

    constructor(PacktToken _tokenContract, uint256 _tokenPrice) public {
        owner = msg.sender;
        tokenContract = _tokenContract;
        tokenPrice = _tokenPrice;
    }

    function buyTokens(uint256 _numberOfTokens)
        public
        payable
    {
        require(msg.value == safeMultiply(_numberOfTokens, tokenPrice));
        require(tokenContract.balanceOf(this) >= _numberOfTokens);
        tokensSold += _numberOfTokens;
        emit Sell(msg.sender, _numberOfTokens);
        require(tokenContract.transfer(msg.sender, _numberOfTokens));
    }

    function endSale() public {
        require(msg.sender == owner);
        require(tokenContract.transfer(owner,
                                tokenContract.balanceOf(this)));
        msg.sender.transfer(address(this).balance);
    }

    function safeMultiply(uint256 x, uint256 y)
        internal
        pure
        returns (uint z)
    {
        require(y == 0 || (z = x * y) / y == x);
    }
}
```

Contract security

Our two contracts are now complete, and we'll shortly describe how to deploy them to a network. Once they are deployed to the blockchain, we won't be able to change them: they will be immutable. This immutability means that it's important to ensure the code is correct the first time, as any bugs found after deployment will be difficult to fix.

To this end, when developing smart contracts, it's important to follow best practices. Here are some important considerations to keep in mind when writing smart contracts:

- Prepare for failure and bugs.
- Deploy carefully.
- Keep contracts as simple as possible.
- Ensure your tools and components are up to date.
- Understand how the blockchain works.

Known attack vectors

Together with the general considerations we just mentioned, it's important to understand specific attacks that your smart contract could be vulnerable to. We will briefly discuss several of the most common attack vectors, and how to protect against them, but our discussion won't be exhaustive since the field of smart contract security is very broad.

Integer overflow/underflow

Our token sale contract makes use of a `safeMultiply()` function, though at the time, we didn't explain its use further. The function is specifically used to protect against our first attack vector: integer overflow.

Here is a version of our `buyTokens()` function that does not use the call to `safeMultiply()`:

```
function buyTokens(uint256 _numberOfTokens)
    public
    payable
{
    require(msg.value == _numberOfTokens * tokenPrice);
    require(tokenContract.balanceOf(this) >= _numberOfTokens);
    emit Sell(msg.sender, _numberOfTokens);
    require(tokenContract.transfer(msg.sender, _numberOfTokens));
}
```

The `msg.value`, `_numberOfTokens`, and `tokenPrice` variables are all of the `uint256` type. When their maximum value of 2^{256} is reached, they circle round back to zero. In the unsafe implementation, it would be possible in certain cases for a user to pass in a large enough value for `_numberOfTokens` such that the product on the right-hand side would overflow to the point where it could still equal `msg.value`. Our `safeMultiply()` implementation prevents this from happening.

Of course, in our implementation, the next call to `require()` would likely fail anyway with a large value for `_numberOfTokens`, but this should serve as an example of when such safety is required.

Reentrancy

A reentrancy bug was the cause of the infamous attack on the DAO, where 3,600,000 of the DAO's 11,500,000 ether were drained from the DAO contract, eventually resulting in the Ethereum network forking, and the Ethereum Classic chain being created.

Here is some code that is vulnerable to this type of attack. It's a generic withdrawal function that might be seen in any type of contract that deals with ether balances:

```
// This code is unsafe - do not use.
mapping (address => uint) private userBalances;

function withdrawBalance(uint256 amount) public {
    require(userBalances[msg.sender] >= amount);
    require(msg.sender.call.value(amountToWithdraw)());
    userBalances[msg.sender] = 0;
}
```

The issue is that we are using `call.value()` to transfer the user's balance to their address. However, it's possible that the address belongs to a contract, and not an externally owned account (that is, a wallet address). In such a case, when we use `call.value()`, we are making a call into the contract's code, which could have been engineered in such a way to call `withdrawBalance()` again. We have therefore created a loop in which we are able to withdraw multiple times.

To mitigate this type of risk, `transfer()` should be used instead of `call.value()` (or `send()`, which is another option), which would prevent external code from being executed. To further protect against reentrancy, the Checks-Effects-Interactions pattern should also be used.

Let's now rewrite the vulnerable `withdrawBalance()` function using what we've learned:

```
mapping (address => uint) private userBalances;

function withdrawBalance(uint256 amount) public {
    require(userBalances[msg.sender] >= amount);
    userBalances[msg.sender] -= amount;
    msg.sender.transfer(amount);
}
```

First, we conduct the necessary checks, and, in this case, the only check we need to run is that the user isn't trying to withdraw more than their balance holds. The next step is to apply the effects, which, in this case, means applying the change to the user's balance. The final step is to carry out any external calls, in this case, the transfer of the balance to the user's address.

In the vulnerable version of our function, the external interactions were carried out before the effects were applied, which led to the vulnerability and allowed a loop to exist.

OpenZeppelin

In a similar vein to the *Don't roll your own crypto* adage, it's often better to use pre-existing code when writing smart contracts, especially when writing code aimed at mitigating attack vectors. The `safeMultiply()` function that we wrote in our token sale contract could have contained bugs, rendering it dangerous rather than safe. To mitigate the risk of trying to write code such as this, we can use contracts and libraries that have been widely used and vetted by the community.

OpenZeppelin is an open source framework used to build secure smart contracts. The project provides open source, audited smart contracts and libraries that can be included and imported into other projects. One of their most widely-used libraries is `SafeMath.sol` (which can be found in OpenZeppelin's contracts GitHub repository), which includes safe implementations of the four basic mathematical operations:

```
pragma solidity ^0.4.24;

/**
```

```
 * @title SafeMath
 * @dev Math operations with safety checks that throw on error
 */
library SafeMath {

   /**
    * @dev Multiplies two numbers, throws on overflow.
    */
   function mul(uint256 _a, uint256 _b) internal pure returns (uint256 c)
{
        // Gas optimization: this is cheaper than asserting 'a' not being
zero, but the
        // benefit is lost if 'b' is also tested.
        // See:
https://github.com/OpenZeppelin/openzeppelin-solidity/pull/522
        if (_a == 0) {
            return 0;
        }

        c = _a * _b;
        assert(c / _a == _b);
        return c;
   }

   /**
    * @dev Integer division of two numbers, truncating the quotient.
    */
   function div(uint256 _a, uint256 _b) internal pure returns (uint256) {
        // assert(_b > 0); // Solidity automatically throws when dividing
by 0
        // uint256 c = _a / _b;
        // assert(_a == _b * c + _a % _b); // There is no case in which
this doesn't hold
        return _a / _b;
   }

   /**
    * @dev Subtracts two numbers, throws on overflow
    * (i.e. if subtrahend is greater than minuend).
    */
   function sub(uint256 _a, uint256 _b) internal pure returns (uint256) {
        assert(_b <= _a);
        return _a - _b;
   }

   /**
    * @dev Adds two numbers, throws on overflow.
    */
```

```
    function add(uint256 _a, uint256 _b) internal pure returns (uint256 c)
{

        c = _a + _b;
        assert(c >= _a);
        return c;
    }
}
```

We will alter our token sale contract to remove our own implementation of
`SafeMultiply()`, and instead include the `SafeMath.sol` library from OpenZeppelin. The
simplest way to do this for our project is to manually create a file called `SafeMath.sol` in
our `contracts/` directory. Copy the code from OpenZeppelin's repository, and import the
file into `PacktTokenSale.sol`:

```
pragma solidity ^0.4.24;

import "./PacktToken.sol";
import "./SafeMath.sol";

contract PacktTokenSale {
...
```

Our multiplication line then becomes the following:

```
require(msg.value == SafeMath.mul(_numberOfTokens, tokenPrice));
```

Testing the code

The next step in our implementation is to test the code. We could do this by manually
calling the functions in our contracts and checking for the expected outcome, but the better
way is to write tests using Truffle's test framework, thereby allowing us to automate the
testing process.

Note that we could have developed our contracts in a test-driven way, by first defining the
expected behavior of our contracts, writing an initially-failing test to test that behavior, and
then writing code to allow the test to pass. In our case, we haven't done this, but **Test-
Driven Development** (**TDD**) is a popular option for developers using the Truffle
framework.

Truffle allows tests to be written in both JavaScript and Solidity. For our implementation,
we'll use JavaScript, which, under Truffle, uses the Mocha testing framework and Chai
assertion library. If you are familiar with Mocha, then you will be familiar with the general
structure of the test code.

We'll create two test files in our project's `test/` directory, one for each of the token and token sale contracts. These will be `.js` files and will contain code that Mocha is able to understand. We will describe the basic layout of the test code, and write two sets of tests for each contract, but our tests won't be exhaustive. That is left as an exercise for the reader.

Before we write any test code, we need to be able to interact with our contracts in Truffle, and to do that we must first migrate them. We'll be using both Ganache and a public test network for our testing, as in previous chapters. Having previously used the Ropsten test network, in this chapter, we will introduce and use the Rinkeby test network. So, before diving into the testing, let's take a quick detour to look in more detail at the available test networks.

The public test networks

There are three main test networks supported by the two main Ethereum clients, Geth and Parity. All of them are available for public use, with all of them using their own sandboxed version of the ETH currency. The different networks are not able to communicate together, so each should be considered a completely different platform. It should also be noted that test ether has no real-world value. Though a monetary value for test ether could be created by normal market forces within each network, the fact that any of the networks could be wound down at any time means that this value would be misplaced.

Ropsten

Ropsten (`https://ropsten.etherscan.io/`) is the oldest of the available networks, though the current iteration of the network is a replacement for the original, which was taken down due to a DoS attack. It is a **Proof-of-Work (PoW)** network with mining being open to the public, and therefore provides the best reproduction of the main network. Unlike the other networks, Ropsten is supported by both Geth and Parity.

Rinkeby

Rinkeby (`https://rinkeby.etherscan.io/`), like Kovan, is a **Proof-of-Authority (PoA)** network, which means that new blocks are not publicly mined as in a PoW network, but are created by trusted nodes in the network at regular time intervals. This makes PoA networks immune to spam attacks, and generally more stable. Rinkeby was started by the Ethereum team, and, as such, is only supported by the Geth client.

Kovan

Kovan (`https://kovan.etherscan.io/`) is the second of the PoA networks, and was created by the Parity team. As such, it is only supported by the Parity client.

Migrating the code

In Truffle, migration files are JavaScript files that help you deploy your contracts to a network, be it Ethereum's mainnet, a public testnet, or a personal test environment such as Ganache. For the purposes of our testing, we will be using Ganache, but later we will deploy our contracts to the Rinkeby public test network.

To connect with Ganache, we first have to download and install it from `https://truffleframework.com/ganache`. Once installed, running Ganache will create a local, in-memory blockchain instance for the purposes of testing.

Once Ganache is installed, we have to configure Truffle to be able to use it, and to do that we must edit the `truffle.js` file in the root of our project (Windows users must edit the accompanying `truffle-config.js` file instead). The following code tells Truffle how to communicate with Ganache. Note that it's possible Ganache will be configured with a different port, `7545`, in which case the following port should be changed:

```
module.exports = {
  networks: {
    development: {
      host: "127.0.0.1",
      port: 8545,
      network_id: "*"
    }
  }
};
```

Before we can migrate our contracts, we must also add a further file to our project's `migrations/` directory. When we initialized Truffle, a standard file called `1_initial_migration.js` was generated, but this only provides a bootstrapping facility for the test framework.

We will create a new file, `2_deploy_contracts.js`, and add the following code:

```
var PacktToken = artifacts.require('./PacktToken.sol');
var PacktTokenSale = artifacts.require('./PacktTokenSale.sol');

module.exports = function (deployer) {
  deployer.deploy(PacktToken, 1000000).then(function () {
```

```
     return deployer.deploy(
       PacktTokenSale,
       PacktToken.address,
       1000000000000000);
   });
 };
```

This migration file takes the following actions:

- It deploys the `PacktToken` contract, and passes in 1000000 as the total number of tokens to the constructor.
- It then deploys the `PacktTokenSale` contract, and passes in the address of the token contract together with 1000000000000000 as the token price, in wei (this is equivalent to 0.001 ether per token).

We can now migrate our two contracts by running the following:

```
truffle migrate
```

Testing our token contract

As a first step, we need to create a new test file, and tell Truffle which contract we will be interacting with during the test. We can't use the contracts directly, because our JavaScript test framework has no way of understanding the Solidity code. Instead, we use a contract abstraction, which is created at compile time, and which can be included in our test file using Truffle's `artifacts.require()` syntax.

Create a new file in the `test/` directory called `PacktToken.test.js` and add the following:

```
var PacktToken = artifacts.require('./PacktToken');
```

If you are familiar with Mocha, then you may expect our test file to include a call to `describe()`. Truffle, however, uses `contract()`, which behaves in the same way, but includes initialization and clean-up handling. Note that we pass a callback as the second parameter, and to that callback we're passing a reference to accounts. This makes Ganache's accounts available for the tests:

```
contract('PacktToken', async (accounts) => {
});
```

In our tests, we will use the JavaScript ES2017 async/await notation, but it's possible to use JavaScript ES2015 promises just as easily. Let's define a simple test first, then break down what it involves:

```
it ('initialises the contract with the correct values', async () => {
    let instance = await PacktToken.deployed();

    let name = await instance.name();
    assert.equal(name, 'Packt ERC20 Token', 'has the correct name');
});
```

This will be the basic form of our test cases. The preceding code does the following:

- It defines a test case using Mocha's it() syntax.
- It asynchronously gets a reference to our token contract, which has been deployed as part of the running truffle test.
- Using the returned contract instance, it asynchronously calls into the contract to get the name of our token.
- It asserts that the returned name is what we are expecting.

We could extend this initial test to include a further call to check the symbol in our contract:

```
let symbol = await instance.symbol();
assert.equal(symbol, 'PET', 'has the correct symbol');
```

Our second test will check that, as part of the deployment, we passed the correct value for our token supply to the contract constructor:

```
it ('allocates the total supply on deployment', async () => {
    let instance = await PacktToken.deployed();

    let supply = await instance.totalSupply();
    assert.equal(supply, 1000000, 'sets the correct total supply');
});
```

We could write more tests specifically for the token contract, but instead we will implicitly test the code as part of testing the token sale contract.

Testing our token sale contract

The tests for out token sale contract will be slightly more involved as they will require references to both our contracts.

We will start by creating a new file, `PacktTokenSale.test.js`, in the `test/` directory of our project. At the head of the file we require abstractions of both contracts:

```
var PacktTokenSale = artifacts.require('./PacktTokenSale.sol');
var PacktToken = artifacts.require('./PacktToken');
```

We can then set up some variables for use during the tests:

```
contract('PacktTokenSale', async (accounts) => {
  let owner = accounts[0];
  let buyer = accounts[1];
  let tokensToSell = 500000;
  let tokenPrice = 1000000000000000;
  let numberOfTokens;
  ...
});
```

We are using Ganache's first address as the owner of the sale, and its second address as the participant in the sale. The `tokensToSell` value equates to 50% of the token supply defined in our token contract deployment. In a real token sale, the owner of the contracts would be responsible for allocating the desired amount of token to the token sale contract. In our token sale test, we are allocating 50%.

Again, we won't write an exhaustive set of tests here, but will cover enough to give an idea of how to write further tests. We'll aim to cover enough to check that both buying tokens and transferring them between addresses works correctly. Our first test will check that both contracts have been deployed, and that the token price has been set correctly by the constructor of the token sale contract:

```
it ('initialises the contract with the correct values', async () => {
  let tokenSaleInstance = await PacktTokenSale.deployed();

  let tokenSaleAddress = await tokenSaleInstance.address;
  assert.notEqual(tokenSaleAddress, 0x0, 'has an address');

  let tokenAddress = await tokenSaleInstance.tokenContract();
  assert.notEqual(tokenAddress, 0x0, 'has an address');

  let tokenPrice = await tokenSaleInstance.tokenPrice();
  assert.equal(tokenPrice,
              1000000000000000,
              'sets the correct token price');
});
```

Our next test is more involved and checks the buying functionality:

```
it ('allows users to buy tokens', async () => {
  let tokenSaleInstance = await PacktTokenSale.deployed();
  let tokenInstance = await PacktToken.deployed();

  // Transfer half of the tokens to the sale contract.
  let success = await tokenInstance.transfer(
    tokenSaleInstance.address, tokensToSell, { from: owner });

  numberOfTokens = 40;
  let receipt = await tokenSaleInstance.buyTokens(
    numberOfTokens,
    { from: buyer, value: numberOfTokens * tokenPrice });

  let buyerBalance = await tokenInstance.balanceOf(buyer);
  assert.equal(buyerBalance, numberOfTokens);

  let contractBalance = await tokenInstance.balanceOf(
    tokenSaleInstance.address);
  assert.equal(contractBalance, tokensToSell - numberOfTokens);
});
```

Here's a breakdown of what's happening:

- We first get a reference to both deployed contracts.
- As in a real token sale, before the sale starts, we allocate a proportion of the tokens to the sale contract, here 50%.
- The buyer account buys a set number of tokens from the token sale contract.
- We then check that the balances of the buyer and token sale contract have been updated correctly in the token contract.

In this test, we have checked that both the token sale contract's buying functionality and the token contract's transfer functionality work.

Deploying to a test network

Development and testing so far has used Ganache as a local blockchain instance. We now want to go a step further, and deploy our contracts to a public testnet so that other users can interact with them.

There are multiple options for deploying to a public test network, including:

- Using Remix and Metamask
- Using the Ethereum Wallet and Mist browser
- Using MyCrypto (`https://mycrypto.com`) or MyEtherWallet (`https://www.myetherwallet.com`)
- Using the Geth or Parity command line
- Using Truffle with Geth or Parity

Our development so far has been based on Truffle, so we will continue in that vein. The deployment will involve several steps:

- Running a Geth client and syncing it with the Rinkeby test network
- Creating and funding a new account
- Configuring Truffle to communicate with the new Geth instance
- Deploying the code

Running Geth on Rinkeby

Geth is the most popular Ethereum client, and can be used with any of the public test networks. We will be using the Rinkeby Proof-of-Authority test network for our deployment.

First, ensure you have Geth installed on your system. If Geth isn't already installed, official download instructions can be found at `https://geth.ethereum.org/downloads/`.

Once Geth is installed, it's important to initialize and run it with the correct parameters. The easiest way to do this is to follow the instructions at `https://www.rinkeby.io/#geth`, specifically those for running a full node.

After running the appropriate Geth `init` command found in the instructions, to sync the chain data, the following command should be run:

```
geth --networkid=4 --datadir=$HOME/.rinkeby --rpc --cache=1024 --
bootnodes=enode://a24ac7c5484ef4ed0c5eb2d36620ba4e4aa13b8c84684e1b4aab0cebe
a2ae45cb4d375b77eab56516d34bfbd3c1a833fc51296ff084b770b94fb9028c4d25ccf@52.
169.42.101:30303
```

This will start a new Geth process, which will begin syncing the Rinkeby blockchain data. It's advised to attach a second console to the running process to allow further commands to be run while syncing is ongoing. This can be achieved in a new terminal by running the following command:

```
geth attach ~/.rinkeby/geth.ipc
```

The syncing process may take several hours, but the progress can be checked periodically by running the following command in the attached console:

```
> eth.syncing
```

Once this returns false, syncing is complete, and we can proceed with creating a new account:

```
> personal.newAccount("<password>")
```

Running this command, with an appropriate password substituted in, will create a new account, and return the new account address. At any point, your accounts can be viewed by running the following:

```
> personal.listAccounts
```

Having created an account to work with, we now have to give it some testnet ether, and the best way to do this is from the Rinkeby faucet. Navigating to `https://www.rinkeby.io/#faucet` will display a series of instructions that should be followed, which include inputting your new address, and selecting the amount of testnet ether you would like. It's recommended to pick the highest available amount, 18.75. While you're waiting for your ether to arrive, we can continue on the configure Truffle.

Configuring Truffle to work with Geth

We earlier configured Truffle to work with Ganache by adding the relevant details to `truffle.js`. We now want to add the equivalent details for our local Geth instance, so that Truffle can communicate with the public testnet. Underneath the development entry used by Ganache, add the following:

```
rinkeby: {
    host: "localhost",
    port: 8545,
    network_id: "4", // Rinkeby
    from: "<your_account_address>",
    gas: 5000000,
},
```

There are several things to note:

- The network ID is 4, which is Rinkeby.
- The from account is the new account created and funded in the steps described in the *Running Geth on Rinkeby* section.
- The gas value is the most gas you want to spend on deploying the contracts (I have picked a value that will be high enough to cover the cost).

Before we deploy, we need to check that our account is unlocked and ready for use. To do this, you can run the following command with the password used at creation:

```
> personal.unlockAccount(personal.listAccounts[0],"<password>")
```

Having ensured the account is unlocked from our Geth console, we can then run the migration from our Terminal:

```
truffle migrate --network rinkeby
```

This should give the following output:

```
Running migration: 2_deploy_contracts.js
  Deploying PacktToken...
  ... 0xb62b416b2d33235ca9e59693db0ed7c5485457a3fef77b8ac8b807c094619c5d
  PacktToken: 0xe35949af5cd0c957c6ef54f92ef59dc311f40114
  Deploying PacktTokenSale...
  ... 0x338b60c9a6d916695d8a30835a273a4625f7e3a084c5514818a19288b34431c4
  PacktTokenSale: 0x601baf6e646cbe4fa91fdd6cc9619c6e5d538d22
Saving successful migration to network...
  ... 0x7ff158ab6d363441326a7402d3c137d322cd3a7283c732839579ab25f3cd8288

  Saving artifacts...
```

In the preceding output, the longer hashes are the transactions that deployed the contracts, while the shorter hashes are the addresses at which the contracts now reside. Your hashes will differ from those here. These hashes can all be checked on Rinkeby's block explorer, https://rinkeby.etherscan.io.

The Truffle console

Now that we've deployed our contracts, let's check that the deployment initialized them as expected. To do this we'll call our deployed contracts directly, and to do this we'll use truffle console, which we can run with the following command:

```
truffle console --network rinkeby
```

At the prompt, we can then get a reference to our deployed token contract:

```
truffle(rinkeby)> PacktToken.deployed().then(function(instance) {
tokenInstance = instance; })
undefined
```

And, from here, we can check our public state variables:

```
truffle(rinkeby)> tokenInstance.name()
'Packt ERC20 Token'

truffle(rinkeby)> tokenInstance.symbol()
'PET'

truffle(rinkeby)> tokenInstance.totalSupply().then(function(supply) {
tokenSupply = supply; })
undefined

truffle(rinkeby)> tokenSupply.toNumber()
1000000
```

In the constructor of our token contract, we also assigned the total supply of tokens to the token creator. We deployed the contracts via the Geth client, so the contract owner is the account we created in the Geth console, which we can also read in Truffle's console:

```
truffle(rinkeby)> web3.eth.accounts
```

This will output the account that deployed the contracts, which we can then confirm was assigned the total supply in the constructor:

```
truffle(rinkeby)>
tokenInstance.balanceOf("<your_account_address>").then(function(balance) {
ownerBalance = balance; })
undefined

truffle(rinkeby)> ownerBalance.toNumber()
1000000
```

Provisioning the token sale contract

When the token contract is deployed, it assigns the total balance to the contract owner, as we showed in the previous section. However, during the token sale, we only want to sell a portion of the total number of tokens, keeping the remainder under ownership of the project owner. To achieve this, we want to transfer a portion of the tokens to the address of the token sale contract.

When we wrote the sample test file for our token sale contract in testing our token sale contract, one of the first steps was to provision the contract with the number of tokens defined by `tokensToSell`. We defined this as 500,000, or 50% of the total supply. We will provision the same proportion of tokens to our publicly-deployed token sale contract.

First, get a reference to our deployed token sale contract:

```
truffle(rinkeby)> PacktTokenSale.deployed().then(function(saleInstance) {
tokenSaleInstance = saleInstance; })
undefined
```

We can then get the deployed address using `tokenSaleInstance.address`.

Before transferring the tokens, ensure that the account is unlocked as described in the *Configuring Truffle to Work with Geth* section. We can then transfer the tokens by submitting a transaction with the following command:

```
truffle(rinkeby)> tokenInstance.transfer(tokenSaleInstance.address, 500000,
{ from: web3.eth.accounts[0] })
```

This should take about 15 to 30 seconds to complete, after which a transaction receipt will be returned in the console. From here, we can check that the balances have been updated:

```
truffle(rinkeby)>
tokenInstance.balanceOf("<your_account_address>").then(function(balance) {
ownerBalance = balance; })
Undefined

truffle(rinkeby)> ownerBalance.toNumber()
500000

truffle(rinkeby)>
tokenInstance.balanceOf(tokenSaleInstance.address).then(function(balance) {
saleBalance = balance; })
Undefined

truffle(rinkeby)> saleBalance.toNumber()
500000
```

Our token sale contract is now provisioned and ready to sell its tokens!

Verifying our contract code on Etherscan

Having deployed our contracts to Rinkeby, we can now start telling the public about our token sale and wait for the investment to roll in. However, any conscientious investor would likely question the transparency of our deployments – how do they know our contracts can be trusted? As it stands, our contracts' bytecode can be viewed on EtherScan, but this isn't human-readable, and doesn't immediately help with convincing investors of our transparency.

One solution to this problem is to verify and publish our contract code on Etherscan, using the tool at `https://rinkeby.etherscan.io/verifyContract`. To do this, we require the following:

- The contract addresses, which can be found in the output of the deployment stage.
- The contract names, which we defined as `PacktToken` and `PacktTokenSale`.
- The compiler version used by Truffle to compile our contracts, which can be found by running the version of Truffle and checking the Solidity version.
- Whether optimization was turned on when we compiled our contracts. By default, this is always false.
- The contract source code, which can be copied directly from our project's Solidity files.
- The ABI of the constructor arguments. To find this, enter the address of a contract into EtherScan, click the **Code** tab on the contract's page, and the constructor arguments can be copied directly from the second box down.

 This procedure will work for our token contract, but the process for our token sale contract is slightly more complex because it imports both our token contract and the `SafeMath.sol` library. These three files must be combined for the verification to work, and to do this the recommendation is to follow the instructions at the head of EtherScan's verification page, namely to use one of the flattening tools mentioned in the web page itself.

Our contracts are now deployed to the Rinkeby public testnet, and the code is verified. Our next step is to create a frontend web page to allow members of the public to participate in the sale.

Creating a frontend website

Our contracts are deployed and ready, but currently, the only way to interact with them is through a console attached to a client, or using a third-party website that is able to read the contracts. This is all well and good for a developer, but for investors and members of the public, this is likely too much of a barrier to participation – we need a simpler way for them to interact.

In the next part of our tutorial, we will create a simple, single-page website that will allow users to quickly and easily buy tokens in our token sale. The page we will be making is shown here:

The page contains the following:

- Information about the name of the token and the current token price.
- The user's current token balance.
- The user's account address.
- An input field and button to enter the amount of tokens to buy.
- A progress bar indicating the progress of the ICO.

There are many ways we could create such a page, but this tutorial isn't aimed at teaching the intricacies of frontend design, so our page will use a very basic set of technologies. If you are a frontend developer with a favorite frontend framework, then by all means adapt the following implementation to something you are more familiar with.

Setting up the frontend development

The first step is to ensure our environment is ready to work with. Certain dependencies will need to be pulled in using NPM, so it's important that this is installed and up to date. If you don't already have it installed, do so using the relevant instructions from `https://www.npmjs.com/get-npm`.

Once NPM is installed, run the following from the root directory of the project:

```
npm init
```

This will step through the fields that need to be set in our project's `package.json` file. An example file is shown here:

```
{
  "name": "packtcoin",
  "version": "1.0.0",
  "description": "\"Packt Token Sale ICO\"",
  "main": "app.js",
  "directories": {
    "test": "test"
  },
  "scripts": {
    "test": "test",
  },
  "author": "<your_name>",
  "license": "ISC",
}
```

The main dependencies that we will require are as follows:

- `lite-server`: A lightweight web server. Note that this should only be used for development – if you want to properly deploy your frontend, a suitable alternative should be used.
- `browser-sync`: A dependency of lite-server that allows us to expose the files required by the frontend.

For the first of these, install the package using the following:

```
npm install --save lite-server
```

We can then add a new entry in the package.json file to enable us to run our web server. In the scripts section, add a dev entry:

```
"scripts": {
    "test": "test",
    "dev": "lite-server"
},
```

To configure the browser-sync dependency, we need to create a new file at the root of our project, bs-config.json. In this file, add the build/contracts/ directory, as well as the src/ directory, which we will create shortly:

```
{
  "server": {
    "baseDir": ["./src", "./build/contracts"]
  }
}
```

Frontend directory structure

The files for the frontend will be added to a new directory, src/, placed in the root of our overall project. By making use of CDNs, we can keep the number of files to a minimum. The files we will need to create are shown in the following directory structure:

```
...
|
|--- src/
|    |
|    +--- js/
|    | |
|    | +--- app.js
|    |
|    +--- index.html
...
```

The index.html file will contain the HTML for our single-page site, while the app.js file will contain the JavaScript required to handle user interactions. There is no separate css/ directory, since we will be using Bootstrap for styling.

Together with these files, we will also be using JavaScript code sourced from CDNs for the following:

- Bootstrap, to provide the styling for the user interface
- Web3, to allow our frontend to interact with the blockchain
- Truffle Contract, to provide a more intuitive interface for our frontend code to interact with the deployed contracts
- jQuery, which is required by Bootstrap

index.html

We will briefly describe the main parts of the code, and then present the overall file. Again, the aim here isn't to provide a tutorial on HTML or frontends in general, but to give an example of one way of creating an ICO web page.

Starting at the end of the file, we import a series of JavaSscript files:

```
<script
src="https://cdnjs.cloudflare.com/ajax/libs/jquery/3.3.1/jquery.js"></scrip
t>
<script
src="https://stackpath.bootstrapcdn.com/bootstrap/4.1.3/js/bootstrap.min.js
" integrity="sha384-
ChfqqxuZUCnJSK3+MXmPNIyE6ZbWh2IMqE241rYiqJxyMiZ6OW/JmZQ5stwEULTy"
crossorigin="anonymous"></script>
<script
src="https://cdn.jsdelivr.net/gh/ethereum/web3.js/dist/web3.min.js"></scrip
t>
<script
src="https://cdn.jsdelivr.net/npm/truffle-contract@3.0.6/dist/truffle-contr
act.min.js"></script>
<script src="js/app.js"></script>
```

The imports are described as follows:

- `jquery.js` is sourced from a remote CDN, and required by Bootstrap.
- `boostrap.min.js`, together with the associated CSS, is sourced from a CDN, and provides the styling for our frontend.
- `web3.min.js` is sourced from a CDN, and allows us to interact with the blockchain via a web3 provider.

- `truffle-contract.min.js` is sourced from a CDN, and provides a more convenient interface through which we can interact with our contract.
- `app.js` is sourced from our `js/` directory, and will handle the interactions of users with our web page.

Now that when we have the appropriate styling imported in the form of Bootstrap, we can begin to create the rest of the page.

We begin with a heading:

```
<div class="col-lg-12">
  <h1 class="text-center" style="margin-top: 100px">
    Packt Token ICO Sale
  </h1>
  <hr />
</div>
```

Note that any additional styling, outside of that provided by Bootstrap, will be defined inline, rather than creating a separate `.css` file.

The next section provides the user with information about the sale, such as the token price, together with information personal to them, such as their address and how many tokens they have purchased so far. Note that there is an assumption that they are using a browser with MetaMask installed. The enclosing `div` is defined as follows:

```
<div id="content" class="text-center" style="display: none;">
  <p>
    This is the <span id="tokenName"></span> sale.
    The token price is <span id="tokenPrice"></span> ETH.
  </p>
  <p>
    Your token balance is: <span id="tokenBalance"></span>
    <span id="tokenSymbol"></span>
  </p>
  <p>Your active account is: <span id="accountAddress"></span></p>
</div>
```

Here, the ID values will be used by `app.js` to render information read from the contracts.

To enable users to enter the number of tokens required, the page requires a form, which, in this case, makes heavy use of Bootstrap's styling. Note also that the `onSubmit` handler is defined as a function in `app.js`, which we'll describe later in the *app.js* section:

```
<form onSubmit="App.buyTokens(); return false;" role="form">
  <div class="form-group">
    <div class="input-group mb-3">
```

```
        <input id="numberOfTokens" type="number" class="form-control"  aria-
describedby="basic-addon2" value="1" min="1" pattern="[0-9]">
        <div class="input-group-append">
          <button class="btn btn-outline-primary" type="submit">
            Buy PET Tokens
          </button>
        </div>
      </div>
    </div>
</form>
```

Finally, to give users an understanding of our ICO's progress, we show a progress bar:

```
<div>
  <div class="progress">
    <div id="progress" class="progress-bar progress-bar-striped progress-
bar-animated" role="progressbar" aria-valuenow="75" aria-valuemin="0" aria-
valuemax="100"></div>
  </div>
  <p>
    <span id="tokensSold"></span> / <span id="tokensAvailable"></span>
  </p>
  <hr />
</div>
```

With all the main parts of the user interface defined, our `index.html` file will look like the following:

```
<!DOCTYPE html>
<html lang="en">
<head>
  <link
href="https://stackpath.bootstrapcdn.com/bootstrap/4.1.3/css/bootstrap.min.
css" rel="stylesheet" integrity="sha384-
MCw98/SFnGE8fJT3GXwEOngsV7Zt27NXFoaoApmYm81iuXoPkFOJwJ8ERdknLPMO"
crossorigin="anonymous">
  <title>Packt Token ICO Sale</title>
</head>
<body>
  <div class="container" style="width: 650px">
    <div class="col-lg-12">
      <h1 class="text-center" style="margin-top: 100px">
        Packt Token ICO Sale
      </h1>
      <hr />
    </div>
    <div id="contentLoader">
      <p class="text-center">Loading...</p>
```

```
        </div>
        <div id="content" class="text-center" style="display: none;">
          <p>
            This is the <span id="tokenName"></span> sale.
            The token price is <span id="tokenPrice"></span> ETH.
          </p>
          <p>
            Your token balance is: <span id="tokenBalance"></span> <span
id="tokenSymbol"></span>
          </p>
          <p>Your active account is: <span id="accountAddress"></span></p>
          <br />

          <form onSubmit="App.buyTokens(); return false;" role="form">
            <div class="form-group">
              <div class="input-group mb-3">
                <input
                  id="numberOfTokens"
                  type="number"
                  class="form-control"
                  aria-describedby="basic-addon2"
                  value="1"
                  min="1"
                  pattern="[0-9]">
                <div class="input-group-append">
                  <button class="btn btn-outline-primary" type="submit">
                    Buy PET Tokens
                  </button>
                </div>
              </div>
            </div>
          </form>

          <br>
          <div class="progress">
            <div
              id="progress"
              class="progress-bar progress-bar-striped progress-bar-animated"
              role="progressbar"
              aria-valuenow="75"
              aria-valuemin="0"
              aria-valuemax="100"></div>
          </div>
          <p><span id="tokensSold"></span> / <span
id="tokensAvailable"></span></p>
          <hr />
        </div>
      </div>
```

```
    <script
src="https://cdnjs.cloudflare.com/ajax/libs/jquery/3.3.1/jquery.js"></scrip
t>
    <script
src="https://stackpath.bootstrapcdn.com/bootstrap/4.1.3/js/bootstrap.min.js
" integrity="sha384-
ChfqqxuZUCnJSK3+MXmPNIyE6ZbWh2IMqE241rYiqJxyMiZ6OW/JmZQ5stwEULTy"
crossorigin="anonymous"></script>
    <script
src="https://cdn.jsdelivr.net/gh/ethereum/web3.js/dist/web3.min.js"></scrip
t>
    <script
src="https://cdn.jsdelivr.net/npm/truffle-contract@3.0.6/dist/truffle-contr
act.min.js"></script>
    <script src="js/app.js"></script>
</body>
</html>
```

With the HTML code complete, we can turn our attention to the JavaSscript. Most of the Javascript code is sourced directly from **content delivery networks** (**CDNs**), so the code doesn't have to be included in our project directly. There is one file, however, that we must create ourselves: `app.js`.

app.js

First, create a `js/` directory inside the `src/` directory, and then create an empty file named `app.js`.

At the top of the file, create the variables we'll need later:

```
App = {
  web3Provider: null,
  contracts: {},
  account: '0x0',
  loading: false,
  tokenPrice: 0,
  tokensSold: 0,
  tokensAvailable: 500000,
  ...
```

Next, define the main initialization function:

```
init: function() {
    return App.initWeb3();
},
```

This calls our web3 initialization function:

```
initWeb3: function() {
    if (typeof web3 !== 'undefined') {
        App.web3Provider = web3.currentProvider;
        web3 = new Web3(web3.currentProvider);
    } else {
        App.web3Provider = new
Web3.providers.HttpProvider('http://localhost:8545');
        web3 = new Web3(App.web3Provider);
    }
    return App.initContracts();
},
```

This is a standard pattern for setting the web3 provider. The `if` clause checks whether a provider has been injected into the current page, which will be true if the user is using MetaMask. If web3 is undefined, the `else` clause sets an alternative, which, in this case is a client running locally on port `8545`. This could be Ganache, or an Ethereum client, such as Geth, connected to a public or private network. We will assume that anyone wanting to participate in our ICO has an appropriate provider.

Next, we get references to both the deployed contracts, and output their addresses to the console for debugging purposes:

```
initContracts: function() {
    $.getJSON("PacktTokenSale.json", function(packtTokenSale) {
        App.contracts.PacktTokenSale = TruffleContract(packtTokenSale);
        App.contracts.PacktTokenSale.setProvider(App.web3Provider);
        App.contracts.PacktTokenSale.deployed().then(function(packtTokenSale)
{
            console.log("Dapp Token Sale Address:", packtTokenSale.address);
        });
    }).done(function() {
        $.getJSON("PacktToken.json", function(packtToken) {
            App.contracts.PacktToken = TruffleContract(packtToken);
            App.contracts.PacktToken.setProvider(App.web3Provider);
            App.contracts.PacktToken.deployed().then(function(packtToken) {
                console.log("Dapp Token Address:", packtToken.address);
            });

            App.listenForEvents();
```

```
        return App.render();
    });
  });
},
```

The next part has the job of listening for `Sell` events from the deployed contracts, and re-rendering the page when they are received:

```
listenForEvents: function() {
    App.contracts.PacktTokenSale.deployed().then(function(instance) {
        instance.Sell({}, {
            fromBlock: 0,
            toBlock: 'latest',
        }).watch(function(error, event) {
            console.log("event triggered", event);
            App.render();
        });
    });
},
```

The next part is more involved, and is responsible for reading the values from the deployed contracts and rendering them as the user interface. With reference to the ID values set in `index.html`, the code should be self-explanatory. Of interest is the message output while the data is being loaded, and how this is controlled using the loader variable:

```
render: function() {
    if (App.loading) {
        return;
    }
    App.loading = true;

    const loader  = $('#contentLoader');
    const content = $('#content');

    loader.show();
    content.hide();

    web3.eth.getCoinbase(function(err, account) {
        if (err === null) {
            App.account = account;
            $('#accountAddress').html(account);
        }
    });

    App.contracts.PacktTokenSale.deployed().then(function(instance) {
        packtTokenSaleInstance = instance;
        return packtTokenSaleInstance.tokenPrice();
    }).then(function(tokenPrice) {
```

```
        App.tokenPrice = tokenPrice;
        $('#tokenPrice').html(web3.fromWei(App.tokenPrice,
"ether").toNumber());
        return packtTokenSaleInstance.tokensSold();
      }).then(function(tokensSold) {
        App.tokensSold = tokensSold.toNumber();
        $('#tokensSold').html(App.tokensSold);
        $('#tokensAvailable').html(App.tokensAvailable);

        var progress = (Math.ceil(App.tokensSold) / App.tokensAvailable) *
100;
        $('#progress').css('width', progress + '%');

        App.contracts.PacktToken.deployed().then(function(instance) {
          packtTokenInstance = instance;
          return packtTokenInstance.balanceOf(App.account);
        }).then(function(balance) {
          $('#tokenBalance').html(balance.toNumber());
          return packtTokenInstance.name();
        }).then(function(name) {
          $('#tokenName').html(name);
          return packtTokenInstance.symbol();
        }).then(function(symbol) {
          $('#tokenSymbol').html(symbol);
          App.loading = false;
          loader.hide();
          content.show();
        });
      });
    },
```

The final part of the code is the function called by the HTML's onSubmit handler, buyTokens(). This calls the associated function in the token sale contract:

```
    buyTokens: function() {
      $('#content').hide();
      $('#contentLoader').show();
      const numberOfTokens = $('#numberOfTokens').val();
      App.contracts.PacktTokenSale.deployed().then(function(instance) {
        return instance.buyTokens(numberOfTokens, {
          from: App.account,
          value: numberOfTokens * App.tokenPrice,
        });
      }).then(function(result) {
        console.log(result);
        $('form').trigger('reset');
      });
    }
```

Combining the preceding with a call to `App.init()` at the bottom of the file gives the following overall code:

```
App = {
  web3Provider: null,
  contracts: {},
  account: '0x0',
  loading: false,
  tokenPrice: 0,
  tokensSold: 0,
  tokensAvailable: 500000,

  init: function() {
    return App.initWeb3();
  },

  initWeb3: function() {
    if (typeof web3 !== 'undefined') {
      App.web3Provider = web3.currentProvider;
      web3 = new Web3(web3.currentProvider);
    } else {
      App.web3Provider =
        new Web3.providers.HttpProvider('http://localhost:7545');
      web3 = new Web3(App.web3Provider);
    }
    return App.initContracts();
  },

  initContracts: function() {
    $.getJSON("PacktTokenSale.json", function(packtTokenSale) {
      App.contracts.PacktTokenSale = TruffleContract(packtTokenSale);
      App.contracts.PacktTokenSale.setProvider(App.web3Provider);
      App.contracts.PacktTokenSale.deployed().then(function(packtTokenSale)
{

        console.log("Dapp Token Sale Address:", packtTokenSale.address);
      });
    }).done(function() {
      $.getJSON("PacktToken.json", function(packtToken) {
        App.contracts.PacktToken = TruffleContract(packtToken);
        App.contracts.PacktToken.setProvider(App.web3Provider);
        App.contracts.PacktToken.deployed().then(function(packtToken) {
          console.log("Dapp Token Address:", packtToken.address);
        });

        App.listenForEvents();
        return App.render();
      });
    });
```

```
    },

  listenForEvents: function() {
    App.contracts.PacktTokenSale.deployed().then(function(instance) {
      instance.Sell({}, {
        fromBlock: 0,
        toBlock: 'latest',
      }).watch(function(error, event) {
        console.log("event triggered", event);
        App.render();
      });
    });
  },

  render: function() {
    if (App.loading) {
      return;
    }
    App.loading = true;

    const loader  = $('#contentLoader');
    const content = $('#content');

    loader.show();
    content.hide();

    web3.eth.getCoinbase(function(err, account) {
      if (err === null) {
        App.account = account;
        $('#accountAddress').html(account);
      }
    });

    App.contracts.PacktTokenSale.deployed().then(function(instance) {
      packtTokenSaleInstance = instance;
      return packtTokenSaleInstance.tokenPrice();
    }).then(function(tokenPrice) {
      App.tokenPrice = tokenPrice;
      $('#tokenPrice').html(web3.fromWei(App.tokenPrice,
"ether").toNumber());
      return packtTokenSaleInstance.tokensSold();
    }).then(function(tokensSold) {
      App.tokensSold = tokensSold.toNumber();
      $('#tokensSold').html(App.tokensSold);
      $('#tokensAvailable').html(App.tokensAvailable);

      var progress = (Math.ceil(App.tokensSold) / App.tokensAvailable) *
100;
```

```
    $('#progress').css('width', progress + '%');

    App.contracts.PacktToken.deployed().then(function(instance) {
      packtTokenInstance = instance;
      return packtTokenInstance.balanceOf(App.account);
    }).then(function(balance) {
      $('#tokenBalance').html(balance.toNumber());
      return packtTokenInstance.name();
    }).then(function(name) {
      $('#tokenName').html(name);
      return packtTokenInstance.symbol();
    }).then(function(symbol) {
      $('#tokenSymbol').html(symbol);
      App.loading = false;
      loader.hide();
      content.show();
    });
  });
},

buyTokens: function() {
  $('#content').hide();
  $('#contentLoader').show();
  const numberOfTokens = $('#numberOfTokens').val();
  App.contracts.PacktTokenSale.deployed().then(function(instance) {
    return instance.buyTokens(numberOfTokens, {
      from: App.account,
      value: numberOfTokens * App.tokenPrice,
    });
  }).then(function(result) {
    console.log(result);
    $('form').trigger('reset');
  });
}
};

App.init();
```

Running the frontend code

Our frontend code is now complete, and we have lite-server installed as a dependency. We can now test our frontend by running our web server locally. To do so, run `lite-server` using the following command:

```
npm run dev
```

This will open a new browser tab and show our frontend.

Interacting with the frontend

To test the frontend, we need the following:

- Metamask to be running in the browser, and pointing to the Rinkeby network
- The accounts associated with MetaMask to be sufficiently funded to invest in the ICO

Once these are set up, entering the number of tokens and clicking on the button will trigger the MetaMask confirmation window to open, allowing the user to confirm the sale.

While the frontend waits for the associated `Sell` event to be emitted, the page will display a loading message. After 15-30 seconds, the page should re-render and display the updated token balance.

And that's it! Our ICO frontend is now fully functional, albeit in the form of a locally-hosted web page. To take our project to its logical conclusion, the next step would be to push the frontend to a publicly-accessible server, rather than having it running only locally. This is left as a further exercise to the reader.

Summary

In this chapter, we discussed all the important practical aspects of running an ICO. We described what an ICO is, looked at some of the different token standards available, and some of the different forms of token sales. We then implemented an ICO, starting with the implementation of an ERC-20 token, leading to the implementation of a token sale contract. We created a minimal set of tests, and deployed the contracts on a local Ganache instance, before deploying to the Rinkeby test network. Finally, we created a basic frontend web page to allow us to interact with the Rinkeby contracts.

The next logical step is to make our ICO frontend available to the world. In the next chapter, we will describe two ways of doing this without needing to use a standard, centralized hosting solution.

Suggestions for further work

This chapter has only touched on the core aspects of implementing an ICO, meaning there is further scope to look at certain aspects in depth. The following are some suggestions for improvements and additions:

- **Tests**: Our contract tests covered only the bare minimum, and don't fully test all aspects of our contracts. An exercise for the reader is to extend the tests to provide complete code coverage.
- **Token sales**: Though we discussed the different types of sales available, we have only implemented the most basic ones.
- **Token standards**: Again, we discussed several standards (or proposed standards), but only implemented the most popular ones.
- **OpenZeppelin**: We mentioned OpenZeppelin when discussing contract safety, and in implementing our `SafeMath.sol` code. However, OpenZeppelin has lots more open source code on the topic of ICOs, including implementations of many different token standards and token sales. Their code samples also come complete with ready-made test files.
- **Frontend code**: Our web page is very basic and could be improved in various ways using different frontend frameworks.

Distributed Storage IPFS and Swarm

9

In our discussions of Ethereum so far, it should have become clear that using the Ethereum blockchain to store large amounts of data is neither cost-effective, nor what it was designed for. Storing information in the blockchain means storing it as state data, and doing so requires payment in the form of gas.

In this chapter, we will look at ways that data can be stored in a distributed manner by way of two different platforms: IPFS and Swarm. After introducing both platforms, we will describe how to install and make basic use of them, and demonstrate how both can be used to host the ICO DApp we created in `Chapter 8`, *Creating an ICO*. Finally, we will create a small project to help us become familiar with how IPFS can be used programmatically in a website frontend.

Background

The Ethereum Virtual Machine (EVM) operates on words that are 256 bits, or 32 bytes, in size. Each 256-bit word of data costs 20,000 gas units to store, equating to 640,000 gas units per kilobyte. At the time of writing, the gas price is around 4.5 Gwei (0.0000000045 ETH), making a kilobyte of data cost 0.00288 ETH.

Scaling this up gives a cost of 2,880 ETH per GB of data, with the current price of $220 per ETH giving each GB a price tag of $621,000. This is an extremely high cost as compared to conventional centralized cloud storage, where the costs per GB are usually in the region of cents.

If we can't store large amounts of data in the blockchain itself, then the logical alternative would be to store it in a centralized storage layer, while making it available to the data layer located on a blockchain. An example of this would be a DApp that uses the blockchain as its decentralized data layer backend, but with the storage layer and frontend hosted on a conventional, centralized server.

The following diagram shows how this is usually achieved:

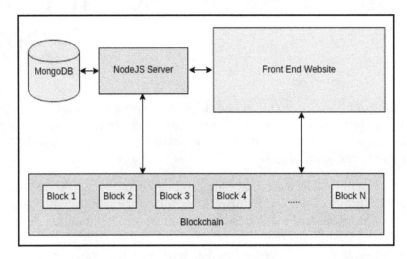

A decentralized blockchain backend with a centralized frontend and storage

For some, this is an acceptable compromise between a decentralized data layer and a centralized storage layer, the latter being a necessary evil to get around the costs of storing data in the blockchain itself. It is, however, possible to do better, and make the storage layer decentralized, as well, without needing to use a blockchain directly.

In early versions of the Web3 technology stack, decentralized storage was provided by Ethereum's **Swarm** platform, which was designed to store and distribute a DApp's frontend code, as well as general blockchain data:

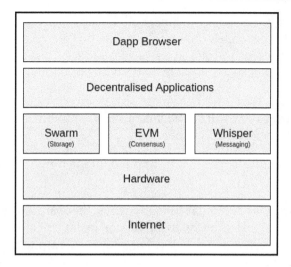

The Web3 technology stack

Another service, called **InterPlanetary File System** (**IPFS**), provides an alternative to Swarm. The two platforms are similar, and to some extent, they can be used interchangeably, as will be discussed in more detail in subsequent sections.

Swarm and IPFS

Before looking at how we can make use of each of the two alternatives for decentralized storage in detail, we'll first briefly look at their main similarities and differences.

The aim of each project is to provide both a general decentralized storage layer and a content delivery protocol. To do so, both technologies use peer-to-peer networks composed of client nodes, which are able to store and retrieve content. The files that are stored on each of the platforms are addressed by the hashes of their content.

A result of being able to store files is that both IPFS and Swarm are able to store and serve the HTML, CSS, and JavaScript of applications built on top of them, and can therefore take the place of traditional server backends.

For files that are too large to be stored whole, both projects offer a model whereby larger files can be served in chunks, much the same as in the BitTorrent protocol. One of the main issues with the BitTorrent protocol is that users are not incentivized to host, or seed, content, creating a one-sided system in which many downloaders feed from a few hosts.

To mitigate similar issues, IPFS and Swarm are able to incentivize users to run clients by way of monetary rewards. For Swarm, the incentives are built in, as Swarm must be run in conjunction with an Ethereum Geth client.

For IPFS, a separate incentive layer must be applied, in the form of Filecoin (see `http://filecoin.io`).

Although the two platforms are similar in many ways, there are also differences. Firstly—and perhaps most importantly, from the perspective of a developer—the IPFS project is more mature, and has a higher level of adoption, despite Swarm's more integral position in the Ethereum ecosystem.

Further differences mainly involve the technologies from which each platform is built. For example, Swarm uses a **content-addressed chunkstore**, rather than the **distributed hash table** (**DHT**) used by IPFS. A further example is that, due to its close association with the rest of the Ethereum stack, Swarm is able to make use of Ethereum's DevP2P protocol (`https://github.com/ethereum/wiki/wiki/%C3%90%CE%9EVp2p-Wire-Protocol`), whereas IPFS uses the more generic libp2p network layer (`https://github.com/libp2p`).

For the purposes of our discussion, these comparisons should be sufficient. A much more detailed comparison can be found online, at `https://github.com/ethersphere/go-ethereum/wiki/IPFS--SWARM`.

Installing IPFS

We will start by installing IPFS locally on our machine, which will give us the tools required to upload and view content on the IPFS network. Installation processes will vary depending on your machine's architecture—full instructions can be found at `https://ipfs.io/docs/install/`.

Once IPFS has been installed, we can initialize our node as follows:

```
ipfs init
```

Once this has completed correctly, the following output will displayed:

```
initializing ipfs node at /Users/jbenet/.go-ipfs
generating 2048-bit RSA keypair...done
```

```
peer identity: Qmcpo2iLBikrdf1d6QU6vXuNb6P7hwrbNPW9kLAH8eG67z
to get started, enter:

ipfs cat /ipfs/QmS4ustL54uo8FzR9455qaxZwuMiUhyvMcX9Ba8nUH4uVv/readme
```

Run the suggested `ipfs cat` command to read a welcome file:

```
Hello and Welcome to IPFS!
```

```
If you're seeing this, you have successfully installed
IPFS and are now interfacing with the ipfs merkledag!

-----------------------------------------------------
| Warning:                                          |
|   This is alpha software. Use at your own discretion! |
|   Much is missing or lacking polish. There are bugs.  |
|   Not yet secure. Read the security notes for more.   |
-----------------------------------------------------

Check out some of the other files in this directory:

  ./about
  ./help
  ./quick-start      <-- usage examples
  ./readme           <-- this file
  ./security-notes
```

We've now initialized our node, but we haven't yet connected to the network. To do so, we can run the following command:

```
ipfs daemon
```

To check that we are connected correctly, we can view the nodes in the network that we're directly connected to, as follows:

```
ipfs swarm peers
```

Having connected to the network, it will now be possible to access the documents stored and distributed by it. To test whether we can do this, we'll use a test file that already resides on the network.

In this case, it's an image of a cat, and, because it's an image file, we'll first need to direct the data to a new file for viewing:

```
ipfs cat /ipfs/QmW2WQi7j6c7UgJTarActp7tDNikE4B2qXtFCfLPdsgaTQ/cat.jpg
>cat.jpg
```

This is perhaps a confusing example: we're using the `ipfs cat` command to show an object stored in IPFS, where the object itself is a picture of a cat, named `cat.jpg`.

As well as accessing the file directly, the file can also be viewed by using any of the following options:

- A local browser-based userinterface (`http://localhost:5001/webui`):

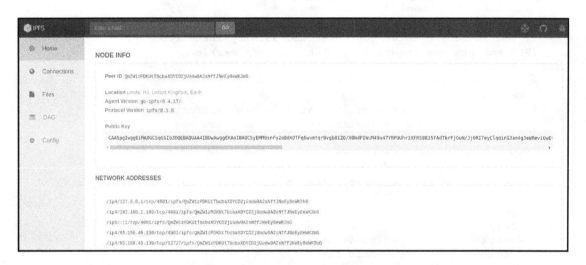

- The local IPFS gateway that is run by our client, on port `8080`:

```
curl
"http://127.0.0.1:8080/ipfs/QmW2WQi7j6c7UgJTarActp7tDNikE4B2qXtFCfLPdsgaTQ/
cat.jpg" > local_gateway_cat.jpg
```

- A remote public IPFS gateway URL:

```
curl
"https://ipfs.io/ipfs/QmW2WQi7j6c7UgJTarActp7tDNikE4B2qXtFCfLPdsgaTQ/cat.jp
g" > public_gateway_cat.jpg
```

Now that our local client is running correctly, and we are able to interact with the network, we can move on to adding files and directories.

The simplest way to add a single file is to use the following command, passing it the path to the file that you want to upload:

```
ipfs add <file>
```

Running this command returns a hash, which is used as the file's IPFS address. This address is based on the contents of the file, and can be used to access the file, as shown previously.

We'll return to adding files later, when we add the files associated with our ICO website to the network.

Installing Swarm

Installing Swarm is slightly more involved than IPFS, and it depends on a running Geth client. If you haven't already done so, ensure that Geth is installed by using the appropriate instructions for your OS (see `https://github.com/ethereum/go-ethereum/wiki/Installing-Geth`).

Once this is complete, install Swarm, also using the appropriate instructions for your OS, from `https://swarm-guide.readthedocs.io/en/latest/installation.html`.

Once it has been installed, we can check for a successful installation by using the following command:

```
$ swarm version
Swarm
Version: 0.3.2-stable
Git Commit: 316fc7ecfc10d06603f1358c1f4c1020ec36dd2a
Go Version: go1.10.1
OS: linux
```

Before we run our local Swarm client, if Geth doesn't already have an account configured, we should create one by using the following command:

```
geth account new
```

This account can then be used to connect to the Swarm network, as follows:

```
swarm --bzzaccount <your_account_address>
```

Once the client is running, we can upload a test file from another Terminal. Here, we use the picture of the cat that we downloaded from IPFS:

```
$ swarm up cat.jpg
5f94304f82dacf595ff51ea0270b8f8ecd593ff2230c587d129717ec9bcbf920
```

The returned hash is the hash of the Swarm manifest associated with the file. This is a JSON file containing the `cat.jpg` file as its only entry. When we uploaded the `cat.jpg` file, the manifest was uploaded with it, allowing for the main file to be returned with the correct MIME type.

To check that the file has uploaded, we can use one of several options. First, we can access it through our local Swarm client's HTTP API on port `8500`, using a web page that it serves at `http://localhost:8500`. From here, entering the hash returned by Swarm will display the picture of our cat.

The second option is to access the file through Swarm's public gateway, at `http://swarm-gateways.net/bzz:/<file_hash>/` (substituting your own hash at the end).

Hosting our frontend

In `Chapter 8`, *Creating an ICO*, we created all of the necessary components of an ICO. Our backend consisted of the ERC-20 token contract, together with the token sale contract, both of which were deployed to the Rinkeby network.

We also created a frontend in the form of a standard HTML, CSS, and JavaScript website, hosted on a local web server. Our frontend interacted with the blockchain backend by way of the Web3 JavaScript library and the MetaMask browser add-on.

Now, we want to remove our reliance on the centralized frontend, and replace it with a frontend served by either IPFS or Swarm.

Serving your frontend using IFPS

Let's start by deploying our frontend to IPFS. First, we need to decide which files are required by the frontend, and add them to a directory that we can add to IPFS. With reference to `Chapter 8`, *Creating an ICO*, the following files will be required:

- The frontend code that we created in the `src/` directory
- The contract abstractions, in the form of JSON files, in the `build/contract/` directory

From the root of our ICO project, add the contents of these directories to a new directory that we'll use for the deployment to IPFS:

```
$ mkdir dist
$ rsync -r src/ dist/
$ rsync -r build/contract/ dist/
```

Then, add the new directory to IPFS by using the add command that we met earlier, passing it the recursive -r flag, as follows:

```
$ ipfs add -r dist/
added QmXnB22ZzXCw2g5AA1EnNT1hTxexjrYwSzDjJgg8iYnubQ dist/Migrations.json
added Qmbd5sTquZu4hXEvU3pQSUUsspL1vxoEZqiEkaJo5FG7sx dist/PacktToken.json
added QmeBQWLkTZDw84RdQtTtAG9mzyq39zZ8FvmsfAKt9tsruC
dist/PacktTokenSale.json
added QmNi3yyX7gGTCb68C37JykG6hkCvqxMjXcizY1fb1JsXv9 dist/SafeMath.json
added Qmbz7fF7h4QaRFabyPUc7ty2MN5RGg9gJkodq2b8UydkYP dist/index.html
added QmfKUdy8NGaYxsw5Tn641XGJcbJ1jQyRsfvkDKej56kcXy dist/js/app.js
added Qmc3xyRTJ2wNt2Ep5BFvGnSRyQcjk5FhYXkVfvobG26XAm dist/js
added QmQytFqNoyk8H1ZEaHe9wkGcbcUgaRbReEzurPBYRnbjNB dist
```

With the files required for our site uploaded, we can access our fully decentralized ICO web page by taking the hash corresponding to the parent directory and viewing it via a public IPFS URL, as follows:

```
https://ipfs.io/ipfs/QmQytFqNoyk8H1ZEaHe9wkGcbcUgaRbReEzurPBYRnbjNB/.
```

This will bring up a fully decentralized version of our ICO website, which can be interacted with in the usual way, using the MetaMask browser add-on.

Note that the page may take longer to load than a centrally served frontend: this decrease in performance should perhaps be considered the price paid to make our site truly decentralized and censorship-resistant.

Using IPNS

Whenever we need to update any of our ICO frontend files, the associated IPFS file hashes will change, meaning that the IPFS path that we first generated for our project will no longer equate to the most recent version of the files. This will cause the public URL to change whenever file changes are made.

To solve this problem, we can use **IPNS** (short for **InterPlanetary Naming System**), which allows us to publish a link that won't change when the underlying files are changed.

Let's publish the first iteration of the site to IPNS, using the hash of the main directory:

```
ipfs name publish QmQytFqNoyk8H1ZEaHe9wkGcbcUgaRbReEzurPBYRnbjNB
```

After a while, this will return a hash similar to the following:

```
Published to QmZW1zPDKUtTbcbaXDYCD2jUodw9A2sNffJNeEy8eWK3bG:
/ipfs/QmQytFqNoyk8H1ZEaHe9wkGcbcUgaRbReEzurPBYRnbjNB
```

This shows a new hash, which is the peerID, along with the path that we are publishing to it. We can check that the peerID correctly resolves to our IPFS path, as follows:

```
$ ipfs name resolve QmZW1zPDKUtTbcbaXDYCD2jUodw9A2sNffJNeEy8eWK3bG
/ipfs/QmQytFqNoyk8H1ZEaHe9wkGcbcUgaRbReEzurPBYRnbjNB
```

The most recent version of our site will now be available at the following URL (note that we are now using ipns/ instead of ipfs/): https://ipfs.io/ipns/ QmZW1zPDKUtTbcbaXDYCD2jUodw9A2sNffJNeEy8eWK3bG/.

Whenever the files of the frontend are updated, they can be published to the same IPNS path:

```
$ ipfs add -r dist/
$ ipfs name publish <new_directory_hash>
```

We can now access the most up-to-date version of our site without needing to know the updated hash associated with our changed dist/ directory.

Our IPNS hash, however, is still not very user-friendly. Therefore, the next logical step would be to bind our IPNS file path to a static domain, something which can be done by purchasing a domain and making that domain publicly known. Doing this, would require us to alter the DNS TXT record associated with our domain, to point to our IPNS URL.

There is one problem with this: it increases our reliance on centralization. Using a centralized DNS server to resolver our site's address would defeat the object of using IPFS and IPNS to begin with. For now, this isn't something that we will do.

Our site is now fully decentralized, and we have published our files on IPNS. In the next section, we will explore the equivalent operations with Swarm.

Serving your frontend using Swarm

The method for adding our site to Swarm is almost identical to the previous method. With Swarm running, as outlined earlier, we will use our existing `dist/` directory, along with the `--recursive` flag.

In addition, we will pass a default path that specifies the file to render in the case of a request for a resource with an empty path, as follows:

```
$ swarm --defaultpath dist/index.html --recursive up dist/
  2a504aac8d02f7715bea19c6c19b5a2be8f7ab9442297b2b64bbb04736de9699
```

Having uploaded our files, the site can then be viewed through our local Swarm client using the generated hash, as follows: `http://localhost:8500/bzz:/` `2a504aac8d02f7715bea19c6c19b5a2be8f7ab9442297b2b64bbb04736de9699/`.

In the same way that we can use a public gateway to view our IPFS-hosted site, we can also use Swarm's public gateway: `http://swarm-gateways.net/bzz:/` `2a504aac8d02f7715bea19c6c19b5a2be8f7ab9442297b2b64bbb04736de9699/`.

Our frontend is now deployed to Swarm, but, as with the case for IPFS, our public-facing URL isn't very user-friendly. To solve this problem, we will use the **Ethereum Name Service** (**ENS**), which is a distributed and extensible naming system based on the Ethereum blockchain.

ENS

The aim of ENS is to provide a better and more secure user experience when dealing with Ethereum addresses or Swarm hashes. It allows the user to register and associate an address or hash with a more user-friendly string, such as `packttoken.eth`. This is similar to the way in which DNS maps a user-friendly URL to an IP address.

We will register a test domain on the Rinkeby testnet, which supports `.test` domains, but not the `.eth` domains supported by the mainnet and the Ropsten testnet. This is to our benefit—registering a `.test` domain is a much quicker process than registering the `.eth` equivalent, as it doesn't involve going through an auction process. It should be noted that the `.test` domain expires after 28 days.

ENS is composed of a series of smart contracts, which we will describe briefly, as follows:

- **ENS root contract**: This contract keeps track of the registrars that control the top-level .eth and .test domains, and of which resolver contract to use for which domain.
- **Registrar contracts**: These contracts are similar to their DNS namesakes, and are responsible for administering a particular domain. There is a separate registrar for the .eth domain on the mainnet, .test on Ropsten, and .test on Rinkeby.
- **Resolver contracts**: These contracts are responsible for the actual mapping between Ethereum addresses or Swarm content hashes and the user-friendly domain names.

The first step is to register our .test domain on Rinkeby. To begin, we need to download a JavaScript file that contains certain contract ABI definitions and helper functions that will simplify the overall registration process. The file can be found at https://github.com/ensdomains/ens/blob/master/ensutils-testnet.js.

The contents should be copied into a local file which we will access later.

We will be working on the Rinkeby testnet, but the file that we have downloaded contains the addresses associated with the Ropsten testnet ENS contracts, so we'll need to change it to point to the equivalent contracts on Rinkeby.

On line 220, change the line to point to the Rinkeby ENS root contract, as follows:

```
var ens = ensContract.at('0xe7410170f87102df0055eb195163a03b7f2bff4a');
```

The second change that we need to make is to the address associated with the Rinkeby public resolver contract. On line 1,314, change it to point to the following address:

```
var publicResolver =
resolverContract.at('0x5d20cf83cb385e06d2f2a892f9322cd4933eacdc');
```

Registering our domain requires a running Geth node connected to the Rinkeby network, which we used in Chapter 8, *Creating an ICO,* for deploying our ICO contracts. If it hasn't been left running, restart the Geth node using the following command, and allow it to sync to the latest block:

```
geth --networkid=4 --datadir=$HOME/.rinkeby --rpc --cache=1024 --
bootnodes=enode://a24ac7c5484ef4ed0c5eb2d36620ba4e4aa13b8c84684e1b4aab0cebe
a2ae45cb4d375b77eab56516d34bfbd3c1a833fc51296ff084b770b94fb9028c4d25ccf@52.
169.42.101:30303
```

From a second Terminal, we now need to attach to the running client and load the edited `.js` file with the abstractions of our Rinkeby ENS contracts:

```
$ geth attach ~/.rinkeby/geth.ipc
> loadScript("./ensutils-testnet.js")
true
```

We will now have access to the relevant functions inside both the registrar and resolver contracts deployed on Rinkeby. First, check that the name you want to use is available:

```
> testRegistrar.expiryTimes(web3.sha3("packt_ico"))
0
```

This will return a timestamp equal to the time at which the name expires. A zero timestamp means that the name is available.

We can then register the name with the registrar contract, first ensuring that we have a funded account that our Geth client can access:

```
> testRegistrar.register(web3.sha3("packt_ico"), eth.accounts[0], {from:
eth.accounts[0]})
"0xe0397a6e518ce37d939a629cba3470d8bdd432d980531f368449149d40f7ba92"
```

This will return a transaction hash that can be checked on EtherScan, for inclusion in the blockchain. Once included, we can query the registrar contract to check the expiry time and owner account:

```
> testRegistrar.expiryTimes(web3.sha3("packt_ico"))
1538514668

> ens.owner(namehash("packt_ico.test"))
"0x396ebfd1a0ec6e6cefe6035acf487900a10fcf56"
```

We now own an ENS domain name, but it doesn't yet point to anything useful. To do that, we need to use the public resolver contract whose address we also added to ensutils-testnet.js.

The next step is to create a transaction to the public resolver contract, in order to associate our Swarm file hash with our new domain name. Note that `0x` must be added to the front of our hash in order for the contract to parse it correctly:

```
> publicResolver.setContent(namehash("packt_ico.test"),
'0x2a504aac8d02f7715bea19c6c19b5a2be8f7ab9442297b2b64bbb04736de9699',
{from: eth.accounts[0]});
"0xaf51ba63dcedb0f5c44817f9fd6219544a1d6124552a369e297b6bb67f064dc7"
```

So far, we have registered our domain name with the public registrar contract and set a public resolver to map our domain name to the Swarm hash.

The next connection to make is to tell the ENS root contract the address of the resolver to use for our domain name:

```
> ens.setResolver(namehash("packt_ico.test"), publicResolver.address,
{from: eth.accounts[0]})
"0xe24b4c35f1dadb97b5e00d7e1a6bfdf4b053be2f2b78291aecb8117eaa8eeb11"
```

We can check whether this has been successful by querying the ENS root contract:

```
> ens.resolver(namehash("packt_ico.test"))
"0x5d20cf83cb385e06d2f2a892f9322cd4933eacdc"
```

The final piece of the puzzle is to tell our local Swarm client how to find and use the correct resolver contract. To do this, we need to start it by using the --ens-api option, which tells Swarm how to resolve ENS addresses. In this case, we pass an IPC path connecting to our Geth client, which is itself connected to the Rinkeby network where our ENS contract resides.

As a part of this command, we also pass the address of Rinkeby's ENS root contract:

```
swarm --bzzaccount <your_rinkeby_account> --ens-api
0xe7410170f87102df0055eb195163a03b7f2bff4a@/home/<your_home_directory>/.rin
keby/geth.ipc --datadir ~/.rinkeby
```

Our site can now be viewed at the following local URL: http://localhost:8500/bzz:/packt_ico.test/.

If we wanted to make our new domain publicly accessible, rather than just accessible on our local machine, we would need to register a .eth domain on the mainnet. At present we are accessing our website using our .test domain through our local Swarm client, which we've connected to our Rinkeby Geth client.

The public Swarm gateway, however, is connected to the Ethereum mainnet, so it can only access the mainnet ENS contracts, and not those on Rinkeby.

IPFS file uploader project

In the second part of this chapter, we will take a more detailed look at how we can use IPFS's HTTP API programmatically. To do so, we will create a simple HTML and JavaScript web page from which we can upload files to IPFS directly, without the need to first upload the files to a backend server.

To do this, we will use the JS-IPFS-API JavaScript library, which will allow a browser-based frontend to communicate directly with the local IPFS node that we created earlier in the chapter. Note that this API library should not be confused with JS-IPFS, which is a JavaScript implementation of the main IPFS protocol.

The aim here is not to explore the HTTP API completely, but to provide a basic example of how it can be used. To learn more about the methods made available by the API, the relevant documentation should be consulted, at `https://github.com/ipfs/js-ipfs-api`.

Project setup

First, we need to run IPFS by using the appropriate configuration, which will differ from the configuration that we used earlier in the chapter. If IPFS is still running from earlier, first, stop the process.

Next, we need to apply some configurations that will allow IPFS to perform cross-origin requests, or **Cross-Origin Resource Sharing** (**CORS**). This will allow our web page, which will be run by a local web server on its own local domain, to interact with the local IPFS gateway, itself hosted locally on a different domain:

```
$ ipfs config --json API.HTTPHeaders.Access-Control-Allow-Methods '["GET",
"POST", "PUT", "OPTIONS"]'
$ ipfs config --json API.HTTPHeaders.Access-Control-Allow-Origin '["*"]'
```

Having done this, we can start IPFS again by using the `ipfs daemon` command.

For the purposes of this project, we will run our web page on a local development web server. An exercise for the reader would be to follow the instructions earlier in this chapter to upload the site itself to IPFS, thereby giving us an IPFS-hosted IPFS file uploader!

First, let's create our project directory structure:

```
$ mkdir packtIpfsUploader
$ cd packtIpfsUploader
```

We can initialize npm and walk through the suggested values:

```
npm init
```

Then, we'll install the web server package:

```
npm install --save lite-server
```

And finally, we'll edit the `package.json` file to include a way to easily start the server:

```
...
"scripts": {
  "test": "echo \"Error: no test specified\" && exit 1",
  "dev": "lite-server"
},
...
```

The web page

Our web site will be a single page, created from two files: an `index.html` file and a `main.js` JavaScript file. It will have a single input for specifying the local file to upload, and a button to initiate the upload.

Once uploaded, a link to the file on IPFS will be shown on the page, as shown in the following screenshot:

User interface following a successful file upload

index.html

Our HTML will clearly be very simple. The styling will be provided by Bootstrap, with any additional minor styling being declared inline, rather than in a separate CSS file. Our HTML file will pull in the following dependencies from external CDN sources:

- **Bootstrap**: Both the CSS and JS components
- **jQuery**: Required by Bootstrap

- **IPFS API**: Required to interact with our local IPFS client
- **Buffer**: Required to convert our file data into buffer, so that it can be passed to IPFS

The file itself is perhaps not interesting enough to explore in detail, so it is shown in full as follows, without further explanation:

```html
<!DOCTYPE html>
<html lang="en">
<head>
  <meta charset="UTF-8">
  <meta name="viewport" content="width=device-width, initial-scale=1.0">
  <meta http-equiv="X-UA-Compatible" content="ie=edge">
  <link
href="https://stackpath.bootstrapcdn.com/bootstrap/4.1.3/css/bootstrap.min.
css" rel="stylesheet" integrity="sha384-
MCw98/SFnGE8fJT3GXwEOngsV7Zt27NXFoaoApmYm81iuXoPkFOJwJ8ERdknLPMO"
crossorigin="anonymous">
  <title>IPFS File Uploader</title>
</head>
<body>
  <div class="container" style="width: 650px">
    <div class="col-lg-12">
      <h1 class="text-center" style="margin-top: 100px">
        IPFS File Uploader
      </h1>
      <hr />
    </div>
    <div class="input-group">
      <div class="custom-file">
        <input type="file" class="custom-file-input" id="fileToUpload">
        <label class="custom-file-label" for="fileToUpload">
          Choose file...
        </label>
      </div>
      <div class="input-group-append">
        <button
          class="btn btn-outline-secondary"
          type="button"
          onclick="uploadFile()">
          Upload
        </button>
      </div>
    </div>
    <hr />
    <div id="filePath" style="display: none;">
      File uploaded to:
```

```
        <a id="ipfsUrl" href="">
          <span id="ipfsUrlString"></span>
        </a>
      </div>
    </div>

    <script
src="https://cdnjs.cloudflare.com/ajax/libs/jquery/3.3.1/jquery.js"></scrip
t>
    <script
src="https://stackpath.bootstrapcdn.com/bootstrap/4.1.3/js/bootstrap.min.js
" integrity="sha384-
ChfqqxuZUCnJSK3+MXmPNIyE6ZbWh2IMqE241rYiqJxyMiZ6OW/JmZQ5stwEULTy"
crossorigin="anonymous"></script>
    <script src="https://wzrd.in/standalone/buffer"></script>
    <script src="https://unpkg.com/ipfs-api@9.0.0/dist/index.js"
integrity="sha384-5bXRcW9kyxxnSMbOoHzraqa7Z0PQWIao+cgeg327zit1hz5LZCEbIMx/L
WKPReuB"
    crossorigin="anonymous"></script>
    <script src="main.js"></script>

</body>
</html>
```

main.js

Our JavaScript code is more interesting, and it is where the interaction with IPFS takes place. The main work happens in the function that we will pass to the HTML button as the onclick handler, `uploadFile()`. This function performs the following tasks:

- Reads the file into a raw binary data buffer using `FileReader`
- Initializes an `ipfs` object and binds it to our IPFS client by calling the `IpfsApi` constructor
- Adds the file to IPFS using the `ipfs.files.add()` method
- Uses the resulting hash to create a URL that can be output to the user

The following is the full file, showing the commented code. Along with the main upload function, the file contains a small amount of jQuery code, used in parsing the filename from the input and in showing the resulting IPFS URL:

```
// Get a reference to the file path from the HTML.
const filePath = $('#filePath');

// Change the string displayed in the input to reflect the selected file.
$('#fileToUpload').on('change', function() {
```

```
    let fileName = $(this).val().split('\\').pop();
    $(this).next('.custom-file-label').html(fileName);
    filePath.hide();
});

function uploadFile() {
  // Create a new FileReader instance to read the file.
  const reader = new FileReader();

  // Define a function to be called once reading the file is complete.
  reader.onloadend = () => {
    // Call the IpfsApi constructor as a method of the global window
object.
    const ipfs = window.IpfsApi('localhost', 5001);

    // Put the file data into a buffer that IPFS can work with.
    const buf = buffer.Buffer(reader.result);

    // Add the file buffer to IPFS, returning on error.
    ipfs.files.add(buf, (err, result) => {
      if (err) {
        console.error(err);
        return
      }

      // Form the IPFS URL to output to the user.
      const outputUrl = `https://ipfs.io/ipfs/${result[0].hash}`;
      const link = document.getElementById('ipfsUrl');
      link.href = outputUrl;
      document.getElementById("ipfsUrlString").innerHTML= outputUrl;

      // Show the URL to the user.
      filePath.show();
    });
  };

  // Get the file from the HTML input.
  const file = document.getElementById("fileToUpload");

  // Read the file into an ArrayBuffer, which represents the file as a
  // fixed-length raw binary data buffer.
  reader.readAsArrayBuffer(file.files[0]);
}
```

Once the files have been created inside of the project directory, we can run the project by starting the web server:

npm run dev

This will serve the page locally, at `http://localhost:3000`, or on the next available port (if port `3000` is taken).

From here, clicking on **Input** will open a file browser, from which a local file can be selected. Clicking on **Upload** will then add the file to IPFS via our IPFS node, and will display the URL at which the file can be viewed via the public IPFS gateway.

Our file uploader is now running on our local machine. To make our file uploader available to the public, we can either host it on a centralized hosting platform, or, as mentioned earlier, push the frontend files to IPFS itself.

Summary

In this chapter, we introduced the idea of complimenting a decentralized blockchain data layer with a decentralized storage layer, in the form of either IPFS or Swarm. We described the installation and basic uses of both technologies, before moving on to the more involved process of hosting our ICO website.

Finally, we introduced a very simple example of how the IPFS API can be used programmatically.

Supply Chain on Hyperledger

10

In a previous chapter, we shed light on blockchain adoption in business by building an inter-business network using Quorum. In this chapter, we will continue in the same direction by introducing an enterprise blockchain solution called **Hyperledger Fabric**. Hyperledger (or the Hyperledger project) is one of the biggest projects in the blockchain industry. It is a global collaboration, hosted by the Linux foundation, and includes leaders in different sectors aiming to build a robust business-driven blockchain framework.

In this and the next chapter, you will develop, from a practical standpoint, a strong grasp of core Hyperledger, understand what Fabric is and how it works, and learn key vocabulary and concepts commonly used when discussing Hyperledger.

This chapter presents a first introduction to Hyperledger by building a blockchain-based supply chain application. It will be an occasion to show how blockchain, and in particular Hyperledger, enables global business transactions with greater visibility and trust and less entanglement.

This chapter will help you to achieve the following practical goals:

- Setting up a private Hyperledger network
- Writing and deploying your first Chaincode (smart contract)
- Building a web interface to query your Chaincode

Food industry supply chain

The main reason for classical supply chain inefficiency is the lack of transparency and reliable reporting. Many companies suffer from the lack of visibility regarding the entire supply chain of their products, and hence lose an immediate competitive advantage over competitors in their industries.

In the traditional supply chain models, the information about an entity is not fully transparent to others, which leads to inaccurate reports and a lack of interoperability. Emails and printed documents provide certain information, but still can't contain fully detailed visibility and traceability information since the products across the entire supply chain are hard to trace. It is almost impossible for the consumer to know the true value of the product they purchased.

Since the blockchain is a transparent, immutable, and secure decentralized system, it is considered to be a game-changing solution for traditional supply chain industries. It can help to build an effective supply chain system by improving the following areas:

- Tracking the products in the entire chain
- Verifying and authenticating the products in the chain
- Sharing the entire chain information between supply chain actors
- Providing better auditability

The food industry's supply chain use case is a difficult landscape, where multiple actors need to coordinate with each other in order to deliver the goods to their final destination, that is, the customers. The following picture depicts the actors we will consider in our example of a food supply chain (multi-echelon) network.

Every stage of the chain introduces potential security vulnerabilities, integration issues, and other inefficiency issues. The main growing threat in current food supply chains remains counterfeit food and food fraud. Given these threats, in this example we will build a food-tracking system based on the Hyperledger blockchain, which will enable full visibility, tracking, and traceability. More importantly, it will assure the authenticity of food by recording a product's details in an immutable and viable way. By sharing a product's details over an immutable framework, we will enable the end consumer to self-verify a product's authenticity.

Now that we have an idea about the project we will build, let's take a quick overview of the Hyperledger project before we start coding.

Quick Hyperledger overview

As introduced in `Chapter 7`, *Blockchains in Business*, there are three main types of blockchain networks; public blockchains, consortium or federated blockchains, and private blockchains. Hyperledger is a blockchain framework which aims to help companies to build private or consortium permissioned blockchain networks, where multiple organizations can share the control and the permission to operate a node within the network.

Hyperledger is a set of open source tools and blockchain subprojects resulting from cross-industry collaboration. We will present two main components in this chapter – Hyperledger Fabric and Hyperledger Composer – while in the next chapter we will have the opportunity to discover other tools.

Hyperledger Fabric

Hyperledger Fabric is the cornerstone of the Hyperledger projects hosted by the Linux Foundation. It is a permission-based blockchain, or more accurately a **distributed ledger technology** (**DLT**), which was originally created by IBM and Digital Asset. It is designed as a modular framework with different components, such as the orderer and **Membership Services Provider** (**MSP**). It is also a flexible solution, offering a pluggable consensus model, although it is currently only providing permissioned, voting-based consensus, with the assumption being that any current Hyperledger networks will be operating in a partially trustworthy environment.

Given this, there is no need for anonymous miners to validate any transactions, there is no need either for an associated currency to act as an incentive. All participants are required to be authenticated in order to participate and transact on the blockchain. As with Ethereum, described earlier in the book, it supports smart contracts, which in Hyperledger are called Chaincode and these contracts describe and execute the application logic of the system. Unlike Ethereum, however, Hyperledger Fabric doesn't require expensive mining computation to commit transactions and thus can help us to build blockchains that can scale up with less latency.

Hyperledger Fabric is different from blockchains such as Ethereum or Bitcoin, not only in its type or because it is currency-agnostic, but also in terms of its internal machinery. In a typical Hyperledger network we have the following key elements:

- **Ledger**: This stores a chain of blocks, which keeps all immutable historical records of all state transitions.
- **Nodes**: These are the logical entities of the blockchain. There are three types of nodes :
  - **Client**: Clients are applications that act on behalf of a user to submit transactions to the network.
  - **Peer**: This is an entity that commits transactions and maintains the ledger state.
  - **Orderer**: This creates a shared communication channel between clients and peers, and it packages blockchain transactions into blocks and sends them to committing peers.

Together with these key elements, Hyperledger Fabric is based on the following key design features:

- **Chaincode**: Chaincode is a similar concept to a smart contract in other networks such as Ethereum. It is a program written in a higher level language, executing against the ledger's current state database.
- **Channels**: A channel is a private communication subnet for sharing confidential information between multiple network members. Each transaction is executed on the channel which is only visible to the authenticated and authorized parties.
- **Endorsers**: These validate transactions and invoke chaincode, sending back the endorsed transaction results to the calling applications.
- **MSP**: This provides identity validation and authentication processes by issuing and validating certificates. It identifies which certification authorities (CAs) are trusted to define the members of a trust domain, and determines the specific roles an actor might play (member, admin, and so on).

End-to-end transaction flow

To understand how Hyperledger Fabric is different and how it works under the hood, let's look at how a transaction gets validated. In a typical Hyperledger network, the following figure depicts the end-to-end system flow for processing a transaction:

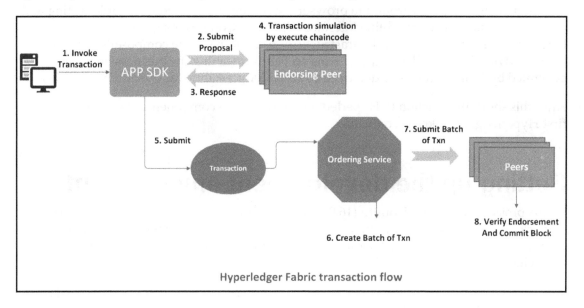

Hyperledger Fabric transaction flow

As a first step, the client initiates a transaction by sending a request to a Hyperledger Fabric-based application client, which submits the transaction proposal to endorsing peers. These peers simulate the transaction by executing the Chaincode (using a local copy of the state) specified by the transaction and sending back the results to the application. At this point, the application combines the transaction along with the endorsements and broadcasts it to the Ordering Service. The Ordering Service checks the endorsements and creates a block of transactions for each channel before broadcasting them to all peers in the channel. Peers will then verify the transactions and commit them.

In our use case, the Hyperledger Fabric blockchain can connect participants through a transparent, permanent, and shared record of food origin data, processing data, shipping details, and more. The Chaincode we defined will be invoked by authorized participants in the food supply chain. All executed transaction records will be permanently saved in the ledger, and all entities will be able to look up this information.

Hyperledger Composer

Alongside blockchain frameworks such as Fabric or Iroha, the Hyperledger project provides us with tools such as Composer, Hyperledger Explorer, and Cello. Composer provides a tool set to help build blockchain applications more easily. It consists of CTO (a modelling language), Playground (a browser-based development tool for rapid testing and deployment), and a command-line interface (CLI) tool. Composer supports the Hyperledger Fabric runtime and infrastructure, and internally the composer's APIs utilize the underlying Fabric API. Composer runs on Fabric, meaning the business networks generated by Composer can be deployed to Hyperledger Fabric for execution.

After this short introduction to Hyperledger Fabric's main components, it's time to run the first Hyperledger blockchain network.

Setting up the development environment

In this project, we will use Ubuntu (16.04, 64 bits) as the lab environment, and run the Hyperledger application in a virtual machine. For that, we recommend your system to have at least 4 GB of memory. To get started with Hyperledger Fabric, we need first to meet the following prerequisites.

Prerequisites

Before advancing any further we need to install the following third-party tools :

- Virtual box available at `https://www.virtualbox.org/wiki/Downloads` or native Linux (Ubuntu)
- Git (`https://git-scm.com/`)
- Go Language (`https://golang.org/dl/`)
- Docker engine available at `https://docs.docker.com/install/linux/docker-ce/ubuntu/` (version +17.03)
- Docker Compose available `https://docs.docker.com/compose/install/` (version +1.8)
- Curl (`https://curl.haxx.se/`)

- Node available at `https://nodejs.org/en/` (version 8.x < 9)
- NPM (version 5.x)
- Python 2.7.x and Pip

Once you install Go, you should set the environments variables properly :
```
export GOPATH=$HOME/go
export PATH=$PATH:$GOROOT/bin:$GOPATH/bin
```

You can refer to their official documentation for further installation instructions.

Installing Hyperledger Fabric

The next step is to build a local Hyperledger Fabric runtime to deploy your business networks to.

Make sure you have installed all the dependencies required for us to make the Fabric environment run. Then, create a folder with the name `food-supply-chain/`, which will host our Fabric project and network configurations files.

Enter the project's directory and install the platform-specific binaries:

```
curl -sSL
https://raw.githubusercontent.com/hyperledger/fabric/release-1.2/scripts/bo
otstrap.sh | bash
```

As a result, you'll preload all of the requisite Docker images for Hyperledger Fabric 1.2 in one shot.

You can change the release to install by using `bash -s 1..` or changing the release in the script URL `/release-1.*/`

Fabric's Chaincode

Now, let's begin the fun part of the chapter – writing smart contracts.

Chaincode is the smart contract that handles the business logic agreed to by members of the network. It is a piece of code that performs the logic operation in the blockchain network, and can be written in any conventional programming language and executed in a container. Currently, since Fabric 1.1, Golang and Javascript are the supported Chaincode languages. In this example, we will use Golang (Go) as the Chaincode language to implement our food supply chain example. Therefore, I recommend learning about the Go lanauge before starting. You can refer to the official documentation, or to Go playground (`https://play.golang.org/`), which is a web-based IDE where you can learn to code in Go online.

As creating the entire supply chain logic may not be within the scope of this chapter, we will implement some very simple logic for our food industry supply chain example.

Writing Chaincode

Before we start coding, you can choose to use an IDE for Go, or you may choose the old-fashioned route of Vim or Notepad. There are many popular IDEs which support Go development, for example Visual Studio Code (VSC) (`https://code.visualstudio.com/docs/languages/go`), JetBrains Goland, or Eclipse with the `goEclipse` plugin. Here, we recommend using VSC. You can refer to the official VSC documentation for setup and configuration instructions.

To start writing Chaincode, it's recommended that you download the project files from the code file section for this book on the Packt website. There is a starter project called `food-supply-chain_start`. You can import this project to your VSC and open the `foodcontract.go` file located under `food-supply-chain_start/chaincode/foodcontract`.

When writing the Chaincode, we first need to import the necessary Go dependencies – the `shim`, `peer`, and `protobuf` packages – as follows:

```
package main
import (
    "encoding/json"
    "fmt"
    "strconv"
    "time"
    "github.com/hyperledger/fabric/core/Chaincode/shim"
    pb "github.com/hyperledger/fabric/protos/peer"
)
```

All Chaincode implements the following interface (from the shim package at `https://godoc.org/github.com/hyperledger/fabric/core/chaincode/shim#Chaincode`), which declares these three core functions with the following signatures:

```
type Chaincode interface {
    Init(stub *ChaincodeStub, function string, args []string) ([]byte,
error)
    Invoke(stub *ChaincodeStub, function string, args []string) ([]byte,
error)
    Query(stub *ChaincodeStub, function string, args []string) ([]byte,
error)
}
```

Therefore, any Chaincode should define these main functions in its code. For our first Chaincode, `FoodContract`, along with the previous package, we will import the following structure:

```
type FoodContract struct{}
// We declare chaincode objects and variables
func (t *SimpleChaincode) Init(stub shim.ChaincodeStubInterface)
pb.Response {
    return shim.Success([]byte("Init called"))
}

func (t *SimpleChaincode) Invoke(stub shim.ChaincodeStubInterface)
pb.Response {
    return shim.Success([]byte("Invoke called"))
}

// We declare other functions
func main() {
    err := shim.Start(new(FoodContract))
    if err != nil {
        fmt.Printf("Error creating new Food Contract: %s", err)
    }
}
```

We now need to fill in this empty Chaincode. Let's start by implementing the `Init()` function.

The Init function

The `Init` function is called when the Chaincode is instantiated by the blockchain network for the first time to initialize its internal data. You can think of it as a constructor in other languages (though Go doesn't support constructors).

As we are building Chaincode to manage a food supply chain, we need to start by defining a struct called `Food` to represent a food asset. The following picture shows the UML representation of a given asset:

Food

OrderId : String
FoodId : String
ConsumerId: String
ManufactureId: String
WholesalerId: String
RetailerId: String
LogisticsId: String
Status: String
RawFoodProcessDate: String
ManufactureProcessDate: String
WholesaleProcessDate: String
ShippingProcessDate: String
RetailProcessDate: String
DeliveryDate: String
OrderPrice: Int

As you may guess, `OrderId` is the order-tracking ID for the entire supply chain. Besides, each entity in the chain will have its unique entity ID and timestamp when it starts processing the transaction. For example, the raw food producer entity has `FoodId` and `RawFoodProcessDate`, and retailers have `RetailerId` and `RetailProcessDate`. Each step will update the current status, the entity-related ID, and the process date in the food supply chain.

By querying `orderId`, we can easily track the current transaction information and status. In the final step, the blockchain will update `deliverDate` and mark the status as completed once the consumer has received the order.

Here is the equivalent food struct code in our chaincode:

```
type FoodContract struct {}
type food struct {
    OrderId                string
    FoodId                 string
    ConsumerId             string
    ManufactureId          string
    WholesalerId           string
    RetailerId             string
    LogisticsId            string
```

```
    status                   string
    RawFoodProcessDate       string
    ManufactureProcessDate   string
    WholesaleProcessDate     string
    ShippingProcessDate      string
    RetailProcessDate        string
    OrderPrice               int
    ShippingPrice            int
    DeliveryDate             string
}
```

We then define our `Init` function as follows:

```
func (t *FoodContract) Init(stub shim.ChaincodeStubInterface) pb.Response {
    return setupFoodSupplyChainOrder(stub)
}
```

As you may notice, the `Init` function takes a `ChaincodeStubInterface` stub as an argument and calls `setupFoodSupplyChainOrder` for initializing the object attributes. The best practice when writing Chaincode is to have the initialization process in a separate function:

```
func setupFoodSupplyChainOrder(stub shim.ChaincodeStubInterface)
pb.Response {
    _, args := stub.GetFunctionAndParameters()
    orderId := args[0]
    consumerId := args[1]
    orderPrice, _ := strconv.Atoi(args[2])
    shippingPrice, _ := strconv.Atoi(args[3])
    foodContract := food{
        OrderId:        orderId,
        ConsumerId:     consumerId,
        OrderPrice:     orderPrice,
        ShippingPrice:  shippingPrice,
        Status:         "order initiated"
    }
    foodBytes, _ := json.Marshal(foodContract)
    stub.PutState(foodContract.OrderId, foodBytes)
    return shim.Success(nil)
}
```

`ChaincodeStub` provides us with the `GetFunctionAndParameters()` to read the arguments passed to the Chaincode when `Init()` or `Invoke()` are called. These arguments can be used to pass the function (defined within the Chaincode) to execute, along with other arguments used to initialize local variables. These parameters are passed when we initialize our `foodContract` with predefined values from the client application. For instance, when the consumer places an order with the product price and shipment price, the `order ID` is generated to track the entire order process for the blockchain. The newly generated `foodContract` data is converted to a byte stream using the `json.Marshal` method. The contract data is then recorded in the Fabric ledger using the `ChaincodeStubInterface.putstate` method, with `orderId` as a key. Finally, the method returns the success status by returning `shim.success(nil)`.

The Invoke function

The `Invoke()` function, as its name implies, is executed when an application wants to invoke a specific function in the Chaincode. The calling application will pass the particular function name to be executed, with the needed arguments. In our code we will define the following `Invoke()` function:

```
func (t *FoodContract) Invoke(stub shim.ChaincodeStubInterface) pb.Response
{
    function, args := stub.GetFunctionAndParameters()
    if function == "createRawFood" {
        return t.createRawFood(stub, args)
    } else if function == "manufactureProcessing" {
        return t.manufactureProcessing(stub, args)
    } else if function == "wholesalerDistribute" {
        return t.wholesalerDistribute(stub, args)
    } else if function == "initiateShipment" {
        return t.initiateShipment(stub, args)
    } else if function == "deliverToRetail" {
        return t.deliverToRetail(stub, args)
    } else if function == "completeOrder" {
        return t.completeOrder(stub, args)
    } else if function == "query" {
        return t.query(stub, args)
    }
    return shim.Error("Invalid function name")
}
```

The `Invoke` function is called per transaction on the Chaincode,
with `ChaincodeStubInterface` being passed as an argument, and
the `GetFunctionAndParameters` returning the function name and arguments. Based on
the received function name, it invokes the appropriate Chaincode application method.

To keep it simple, and to avoid any irrelevant Golang coding details, we will present a
single example of an invoked Chaincode function—`createRawFood`. The other Chaincode
functions associated with subsequent steps in the chain will be similar to this method:

```go
func (f *FoodContract) createRawFood(stub shim.ChaincodeStubInterface, args
[]string) pb.Response {
    orderId := args[0]
    foodBytes, _ := stub.GetState(orderId)
    fd := food{}
    json.Unmarshal(foodBytes, &fd)
    if fd.Status == "order initiated" {
        fd.FoodId = "FISH_1"
        currentts := time.Now()
        fd.RawFoodProcessDate = currentts.Format("2006-01-02 15:04:05")
        fd.Status = "raw food created"
    } else {
        fmt.Printf("Order not initiated yet")
    }
    foodBytes, _ = json.Marshal(fd)
    stub.PutState(orderId, foodBytes)
    return shim.Success(nil)
}
```

As you will notice, the `createRawFood` method accepts a `ChaincodeStubInterface` stub
and command-line inputs as arguments. We set `orderId` to the value of the first command-
line argument. Then, we query food data from the Fabric and convert encoded data to a
readable JSON format by using `jsonUnmarshal`. We check using the returned data, if the
current status is "order initiated" before updating the food asset process using a system date
with the format `YYYY-mm-dd hh:mm:dd`. In Go, we
use `currentts.Format("2006-01-02 15:04:05")` to return the date timestamp in the
specified format. We also update the food status as raw food created. At the end, we
commit food to the blockchain data by calling the `stub.PutState` method, and we return
a successful response to the client using `shim.Success`.

As we discussed in the previous section, in the food industry supply chain example, we have six kinds of actor: the raw food producers, the manufacturing processors, wholesalers, logistics operators, retailers, and consumers. Consequently, for a complete Chaincode, we will define an associated function to each actor representing their roles and interactions with the blockchain as follows:

- `createRawFood`: function called to produce the food
- `manufatureProcessing`: function called to send the food to the manufacturing processor
- `wholesaleDistribute`: function called to transport the food product to the wholesaler for distribution
- `initiateShipment`: function called to initiate the shipment process from wholesalers
- `deliverToRetail`: function called to deliver the food product to the retailers from logistics
- `completeOrder`: function called to complete the order process after the consumers can pick up their products

The overall process is shown in the following sequence diagram:

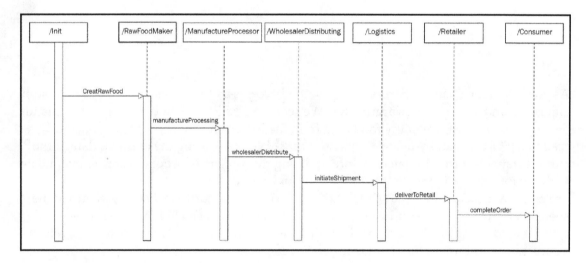

Once the customer receives the product, the order is completed and, per consequence, we update the status as completed by calling `completeOrder`, which is defined as follows:

```
func (f *FoodContract) completeOrder(stub shim.ChaincodeStubInterface, args
[]string) pb.Response {
    orderId := args[0]
```

```
    foodBytes, err := stub.GetState(orderId)
    fd := food{}
    err = json.Unmarshal(foodBytes, &fd)
    if err != nil {
        return shim.Error(err.Error())
    }
    if fd.Status == "Retailer started" {
        currentts := time.Now()
        fd.DeliveryDate = currentts.Format("2006-01-02 15:04:05")
        fd.Status = "Consumer received order"
    } else {
        fmt.Printf("Retailer not initiated yet")
    }
    foodBytes0, _ := json.Marshal(fd)
    err = stub.PutState(orderId, foodBytes0)
    if err != nil {
        return shim.Error(err.Error())
    }
    return shim.Success(nil)
}
```

Hyperledger data storage

At this level, let's introduce an important concept in Hyperledger—the world state.

As you will have noticed, at the end of the createRawFood function we called the putState(key, value) method to store or update any validated state values on the ledger.

Here, a question can be raised about data immutability: Does the putState function change the data in the blockchain? In Hyperledger Fabric we need to make a distinction between two parts of the ledger—the world state and the blockchain.

The world state is a database that stores (as a key value pair) the current values of all ledger states (all Chaincode states). It is populated when each peer validates and commits a transaction. Fabric supports two database infrastructure options for state databases including LevelDB, as used by Ethereum, and CouchDB. The former is the default state database, which supports key value storage, while the latter is a more advanced choice used to store complex data types to support business functions. However, Fabric provides a flexible pluggable design for state databases, meaning it can be configured to use other types of database.

The second part is the blockchain. It represents a transaction log that records all historical changes of the world state, and is a file-based ledger which stores an immutable sequence of blocks, and contains a set of ordered transaction data.

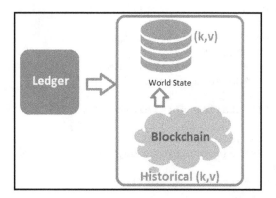

Given that, we understand now that `putState(key, value)` will update the ledger state data in the world state, and the transaction log will keep the entire state data as an immutable record visible only to permitted nodes in the blockchain.

The Query function

The final important function to define is the `Query` function. It is called when the application queries the Chaincode state. In our case `Query` definition is straightforward: we just need to pass a key—`orderId`—to get, in result, the corresponding food struct, as follows :

```
func (f *FoodContract) query(stub shim.ChaincodeStubInterface, args
[]string) pb.Response {
    var ENIITY string
    var err error
    if len(args) != 1 {
        return shim.Error("Incorrect number of arguments. Expected ENIITY
Name")
    }
    ENIITY = args[0]
    Avalbytes, err := stub.GetState(ENIITY)
    if err != nil {
        sonResp := "{\"Error\":\"Failed to get state for " + ENIITY + "\"}"
        return shim.Error(jsonResp)
    }
    if Avalbytes == nil {
        jsonResp := "{\"Error\":\"Nil order for " + ENIITY + "\"}"
```

```
          return shim.Error(jsonResp)
      }
      return shim.Success(Avalbytes)
  }
```

The important part in the code above is the call to the `GetState(ENIITY)` method, which reads the values from the world state corresponding to the given key.

Error handling

Interestingly, Hyperledger Fabric has its own error-handling package, `github.com/pkg/errors`, which allows you to handle errors in a much better way than the built-in error handling provided by Go. For example:

```
import (
    "fmt"
    "github.com/pkg/errors"
)

//wrapping error with stack
func wrapWithStack() error {
    err := displayError ()
    return errors.Wrap(err, "wrapping an application  error with stack
trace")
}
func displayError() error {
    return errors.New("example error message")
}
func main() {
    err := displayError()
    fmt.Printf("print error without stack trace: %s\n\n", err)
    fmt.Printf("print error with stack trace: %+v\n\n", err)
    err = wrapWithStack()
    fmt.Printf("%+v\n\n", err)
}
```

The aforementioned package provides several helpful functions. For instance, `error.wrap` is used to generate a call stack trace for a given error (the standard error handling does not come with stack traces), which is very helpful for debugging, while `error.New` generates a new error with the supplied message and records the stack trace at the point it was called. The `shim` package also provides an error-handling method, `shim.error()`, which returns an error message with a serialized response to the client.

As an example, we can define the `initiateShipment` function as the following, with the ability to warn the client if an error occurs using `shim.error` as follows:

```go
func (f *FoodContract) initiateShipment(stub shim.ChaincodeStubInterface,
args []string) pb.Response {
    orderId := args[0]
    foodBytes, err := stub.GetState(orderId)
    fd := food{}
    err = json.Unmarshal(foodBytes, &fd)
    if err != nil {
        return shim.Error(err.Error())
    }
    if fd.Status == "wholesaler distribute" {
        fd.LogisticsId = "LogisticsId_1"
        currentts := time.Now()
        fd.ShippingProcessDate = currentts.Format("2006-01-02 15:04:05")
        fd.Status = "initiated shipment"
    } else {
        fmt.Printf("Wholesaler not initiated yet")
    }
    foodBytes0, _ := json.Marshal(fd)
    err = stub.PutState(orderId, foodBytes0)
    if err != nil {
        return shim.Error(err.Error())
    }
    return shim.Success(nil)
}
```

At this level, we have successfully written the main parts of our first Chaincode using the Golang language. Next, we need to build a local Hyperledger network to deploy the Chaincode and start tracking the food along the supply chain.

Building a business network

Hyperledger Fabric has a built-in docker image to run peer nodes, and in order to set up a supply chain network we would typically use Docker Composer to launch various Fabric component containers. Before we run the Fabric network, we need to design the food supply chain network topology properly. In the chain, we have six types of entity: the raw food producer, a manufacturing processor, wholesalers, logistics operators, retailers, and consumers. For demonstration purposes we will define three different organizations to contain these entities, a single orderer, and a channel in our business network. The entities will interact with the blockchain application by invoking Chaincode in the Fabric network, updating the ledger world state, and writing transaction logs.

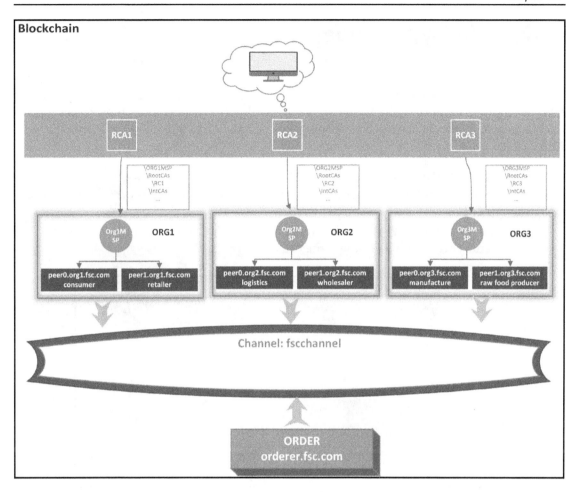

In this design, the organisation **ORG1** hosts two peer nodes (`peer0.org1.fsc.com` and `peer1.org1.fsc.com`) representing the consumer and retailer peers, and handles the interaction involved in the consumer ordering food through the retailer store. Elsewhere, **ORG2** hosts two peer nodes (`peer0.org2.fsc.com` and `peer1.org2.fsc.com`) representing the logistic and wholesaler peers, and handles the wholesaler's initial shipment request to the logistical entity. Meanwhile, **ORG3** hosts two peer nodes (`peer0.org3.fsc.com` and `peer1.org3.fsc.com`) representing the manufacturing processor and raw food producer peers, and handles the interaction of sending raw food to manufacturers for processing and packaging.

Privacy in Hyperledger

Hyperledger is a permissioned blockchain, meaning all participants and components in the network have identities which are assigned to a certificate such as x.509. The main element behind this schema, is the MSP which ensures the privacy of all members in the network. It has the ability to identify each participant's roles within the organization they represent, and set access privileges for the context of a network and channel. There are three types of MSPs:

- **Network MSP**: Defines members in the network
- **Channel MSP**: Defines who can participate in certain actions on a given channel according to channel policies
- **Peer/Orderer MSP**: Defined as the local MSP for a single peer or orderer, for identifying members of the same organization

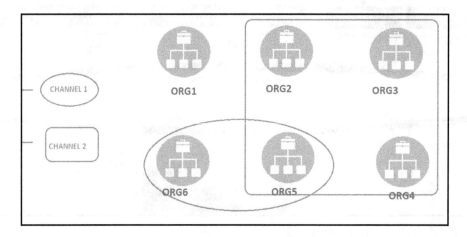

In the preceding example, there are two channels for two groups of members. **CHANNEL 1** is for **ORG5** and **ORG6**, and **CHANNEL 2** is for **ORG2**, **ORG3**, **ORG4**, and **ORG5**. Two different channel MSPs apply to these groups separately. **ORG5** and **ORG6** can see transactions in **CHANNEL 1**, while **ORG2**, **ORG3**, **ORG4**, and **ORG5** can see transactions in **CHANNEL 2**. **ORG5** participates in both channels, and can see both sets of transactions, but **ORG6** can't see transactions in **CHANNEL 1**. Similarly, **ORG2**, **ORG3**, and **ORG4** can't see transactions in **CHANNEL 1** .

Define services in a compose file

After presenting the business network's logical architecture, we will now adopt something similar for our food supply chain. We'll be using Docker Compose to launch the corresponding Fabric containers, and as a first step we will define the services run in the container using a `docker-compose.yml` file.

Before we start to define our config files, let's have a look at the project's structure. You should remember that you can get the project code from the Packt website. We have a root folder `food-supply-chain/` structured as follows:

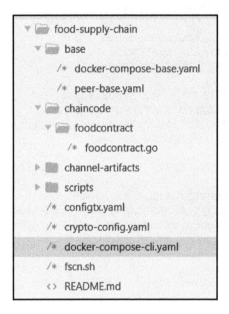

There is a `base/` folder which contains two base files — `peer-base.yaml` and `docker-compose-base.yaml` — which are needed to configure the Docker containers as fabric peers. The `chaincode/` folder contains a subfolder `foodcontract/` which hosts the Chaincode files.

As we will discover later, the `configtxgen` tool will generate the output in the `channel-artifacts/` folder, as configured in `configtx.yaml`. Finally, the `scripts/` folder contains `script.sh` and `utils.sh`, which sets up the Hyperledger network and defines a Chaincode execution scenario, while `fscn.sh` will be be the script which triggers the execution of the others.

That said, let's start configuring Docker. To make it easy for you, copy the file and `base/` directory, along with the `docker-compose-cli.yaml` file, to your working directory from the Packt source code or `fabric-samples/first-network` directory (`https://github.com/hyperledger/fabric-samples/tree/release-1.2/first-network`). Here is an example defining the parameters of the orderer service and a network peer:

```
# Blockchain by example
version: '2'
services:
  orderer.fsc.com:
    container_name: orderer.fsc.com
    image: hyperledger/fabric-orderer
    environment:
      - ORDERER_GENERAL_LOGLEVEL=debug
      - ORDERER_GENERAL_LISTENADDRESS=0.0.0.0
      - ORDERER_GENERAL_GENESISMETHOD=file
      -
ORDERER_GENERAL_GENESISFILE=/var/hyperledger/orderer/orderer.genesis.block
      - ORDERER_GENERAL_LOCALMSPID=OrdererMSP
      - ORDERER_GENERAL_LOCALMSPDIR=/var/hyperledger/orderer/msp
      - ORDERER_GENERAL_TLS_ENABLED=true
      -
ORDERER_GENERAL_TLS_PRIVATEKEY=/var/hyperledger/orderer/tls/server.key
      -
ORDERER_GENERAL_TLS_CERTIFICATE=/var/hyperledger/orderer/tls/server.crt
      - ORDERER_GENERAL_TLS_ROOTCAS=[/var/hyperledger/orderer/tls/ca.crt]
    working_dir: /opt/gopath/src/github.com/hyperledger/fabric
    command: orderer
    volumes:
    - ../channel-
artifacts/genesis.block:/var/hyperledger/orderer/orderer.genesis.block
    - ../crypto-
config/ordererOrganizations/fsc.com/orderers/orderer.fsc.com/msp:/var/hyper
ledger/orderer/msp
    - ../crypto-
config/ordererOrganizations/fsc.com/orderers/orderer.fsc.com/tls/:/var/hype
rledger/orderer/tls
    ports:
    - 7050:7050
  peer0.org1.fsc.com:
    container_name: peer0.org1.fsc.com
    extends:
    file: peer-base.yaml
    service: peer-base
    environment:
      - CORE_PEER_ID=peer0.org1.fsc.com
      - CORE_PEER_ADDRESS=peer0.org1.fsc.com:7051
```

```
        - CORE_PEER_GOSSIP_EXTERNALENDPOINT=peer0.org1.fsc.com:7051
        - CORE_PEER_LOCALMSPID=Org1MSP
    volumes:
        - /var/run/:/host/var/run/
        - ../crypto-
config/peerOrganizations/org1.fsc.com/peers/peer0.org1.fsc.com/msp:/etc/hyp
erledger/fabric/msp
        - ../crypto-
config/peerOrganizations/org1.fsc.com/peers/peer0.org1.fsc.com/tls:/etc/hyp
erledger/fabric/tls
    ports:
        - 7051:7051
        - 7053:7053

  peer1.org1.fsc.com:
    container_name: peer1.org1.fsc.com
    extends:
      file: peer-base.yaml
      service: peer-base
...
```

You can define the other peers, peer*.org*.fsc.com, in the same way as we did
for peer0.org1.fsc.com using their corresponding domain names. For a more complete
example, you can have a look at the example listed in the Hyperledger GitHub repository
(https://github.com/hyperledger/composer/blob/master/packages/composer-tests-
functional/hlfv1/docker-compose.yml). As you may notice, the docker-compose.yml
file extends a peer-base.yaml configuration, which can be used as the configuration file
for each node:

```
# Peer network configuration for food Supply Chain
version: '2'
services:
  peer-base:
    image: hyperledger/fabric-peer
    environment:
        - CORE_VM_ENDPOINT=unix:///host/var/run/docker.sock
        - CORE_VM_DOCKER_HOSTCONFIG_NETWORKMODE=${COMPOSE_PROJECT_NAME}_fscn
        - CORE_LOGGING_LEVEL=DEBUG
        - CORE_PEER_TLS_ENABLED=true
        - CORE_PEER_GOSSIP_USELEADERELECTION=true
        - CORE_PEER_GOSSIP_ORGLEADER=false
        - CORE_PEER_PROFILE_ENABLED=true
        - CORE_PEER_TLS_CERT_FILE=/etc/hyperledger/fabric/tls/server.crt
        - CORE_PEER_TLS_KEY_FILE=/etc/hyperledger/fabric/tls/server.key
        - CORE_PEER_TLS_ROOTCERT_FILE=/etc/hyperledger/fabric/tls/ca.crt
    working_dir: /opt/gopath/src/github.com/hyperledger/fabric/peer
    command: peer node start
```

The most important part of the previous file is the line starting with command, which specifies the command that is issued when the container starts.

Resources and profiles

The next step is to edit the configtx.yaml file, which represents an exhaustive list of all the internal resources defined by Fabric. It will be used later to create a channel and related artifacts. Here's the configuration we need for our network:

```yaml
# Blockchain by example.
Profiles:
    FSCOrgsOrdererGenesis:
        Orderer:
            <<: *OrdererDefaults
            Organizations:
                - *OrdererOrg
        Consortiums:
            FoodSupplyChainConsortium:
                Organizations:
                    - *Org1
                    - *Org2
                    - *Org3
    FSCOrgsChannel:
        Consortium: FoodSupplyChainConsortium
        Application:
            <<: *ApplicationDefaults
            Organizations:
                - *Org1
                - *Org2
                - *Org3
################################################################################
#####
#    Section: Organizations
#    - This section defines the different organizational identities which
will
#    be referenced later in the configuration.
################################################################################
#####
Organizations:
    - &OrdererOrg
        Name: OrdererOrg
        ID: OrdererMSP
        MSPDir: crypto-config/ordererOrganizations/fsc.com/msp
    - &Org1
        Name: Org1MSP
        ID: Org1MSP
```

```
            MSPDir: crypto-config/peerOrganizations/org1.fsc.com/msp
            AnchorPeers:
                - Host: peer0.org1.fsc.com
                  Port: 7051
        - &Org2
            Name: Org2MSP
            ID: Org2MSP
            MSPDir: crypto-config/peerOrganizations/org2.fsc.com/msp
            AnchorPeers:
                - Host: peer0.org2.fsc.com
                  Port: 7051
        - &Org3
            Name: Org3MSP
            ID: Org3MSP
            MSPDir: crypto-config/peerOrganizations/org3.fsc.com/msp
            AnchorPeers:
                - Host: peer0.org3.fsc.com
                  Port: 7051
Orderer: &OrdererDefaults
    OrdererType: solo
    Addresses:
        - orderer.fsc.com:7050
    BatchTimeout: 2s
    BatchSize:
        MaxMessageCount: 10
        AbsoluteMaxBytes: 20 MB
        PreferredMaxBytes: 512 KB
    Kafka:
        Brokers:
            - 127.0.0.1:9092
    Organizations:
Application: &ApplicationDefaults
    Organizations:
```

We define, among other things, the path which contains the MSP configuration for every organization.

You can refer to the sample `configtx.yaml` shipped with Fabric (`https://github.com/ hyperledger/fabric-test/blob/master/feature/configs/configtx.yaml`) for all possible configuration options.

Fabric channel and Genesis block

We can use the `configrxgen` tool to create important artifacts for the food supply chain network, namely: the Genesis block, channel, and anchor peer transactions. To achieve that goal, we run the following commands:

```
> configtxgen -profile FSCOrgsOrdererGenesis -outputBlock ./channel-
artifacts/genesis.block

> export CHANNEL_NAME="fscchannel"
> configtxgen -profile FSCOrgsChannel -outputCreateChannelTx ./channel-
artifacts/channel.tx -channelID $CHANNEL_NAME
```

The first command creates the orderer Genesis block, whereas the last command initiates a channel configuration transaction, `channel.tx`. At each step we supply to the `configtxgen` tool the profiles defined earlier in the `configtx.yaml` file.

After creating a channel with multiple organizations, we need to define `AnchorPeers` to initiate gossip communication between peers from different organizations. As stated in the official documentation at `https://hyperledger-fabric.readthedocs.io/en/release-1.2/glossary.html#anchor-peer`, an anchor node serves as the entry point for another organization's peer on the same channel to communicate with each of the peers in the anchor peer's organization.

Next, we need to use `configtxgen` to create a configuration update transaction to include those anchor peers for the different `Orgs`:

```
configtxgen -profile FSCOrgsChannel -outputAnchorPeersUpdate ./channel-
artifacts/Org1MSPanchors.tx -asOrg Org1MSP -channelID $CHANNEL_NAME
 configtxgen -profile FSCOrgsChannel -outputAnchorPeersUpdate ./channel-
artifacts/Org2MSPanchors.tx -asOrg Org2MSP -channelID $CHANNEL_NAME
   configtxgen -profile FSCOrgsChannel -outputAnchorPeersUpdate ./channel-
artifacts/Org3MSPanchors.tx -asOrg Org3MSP -channelID $CHANNEL_NAME
```

To update an anchor peer in the `FSCOrgsChannel` channel, run the following commands:

```
peer channel update -f ./channel-artifacts/Org${ORG}MSPanchors.tx -c
$CHANNEL_NAME -o orderer.fsc.com:7050 --tls $CORE_PEER_TLS_ENABLED --cafile
$ORDERER_CA >&log.txt
```

As a result, you should see output similar to the following screenshot:

```
Update Anchor ...
CORE_PEER_TLS_ROOTCERT_FILE=/opt/gopath/src/github.com/hyperledger/fabric/peer/crypto/peerOrganizations/org1.fsc.com/peers/peer0.org1.fsc.com/tls/ca.crt
CORE_PEER_TLS_KEY_FILE=/opt/gopath/src/github.com/hyperledger/fabric/peer/crypto/peerOrganizations/org1.fsc.com/peers/peer0.org1.fsc.com/tls/server.key
CORE_PEER_LOCALMSPID=Org1MSP
CORE_VM_ENDPOINT=unix:///host/var/run/docker.sock
CORE_PEER_TLS_CERT_FILE=/opt/gopath/src/github.com/hyperledger/fabric/peer/crypto/peerOrganizations/org1.fsc.com/peers/peer0.org1.fsc.com/tls/server.crt
CORE_PEER_TLS_ENABLED=true
CORE_PEER_MSPCONFIGPATH=/opt/gopath/src/github.com/hyperledger/fabric/peer/crypto/peerOrganizations/org1.fsc.com/users/Admin@org1.fsc.com/msp
CORE_PEER_ID=cli
CORE_LOGGING_LEVEL=DEBUG
CORE_PEER_ADDRESS=peer0.org1.fsc.com:7051
2018-09-29 23:37:29.688 UTC [msp] GetLocalMSP -> DEBU 001 Returning existing local MSP
2018-09-29 23:37:29.688 UTC [msp] GetDefaultSigningIdentity -> DEBU 002 Obtaining default signing identity
2018-09-29 23:37:29.691 UTC [channelCmd] InitCmdFactory -> INFO 003 Endorser and orderer connections initialized
2018-09-29 23:37:29.691 UTC [msp] GetLocalMSP -> DEBU 004 Returning existing local MSP
2018-09-29 23:37:29.691 UTC [msp] GetDefaultSigningIdentity -> DEBU 005 Obtaining default signing identity
2018-09-29 23:37:29.692 UTC [msp] GetLocalMSP -> DEBU 006 Returning existing local MSP
2018-09-29 23:37:29.692 UTC [msp] GetDefaultSigningIdentity -> DEBU 007 Obtaining default signing identity
2018-09-29 23:37:29.692 UTC [msp/identity] Sign -> DEBU 008 Sign: plaintext: 0A92060A074F72673J4D53501286062D...2A0641646D696E732A0641646D696E73
2018-09-29 23:37:29.692 UTC [msp/identity] Sign -> DEBU 009 Sign: digest: F9A28ED47E853F4A6D1701F11EFE0D0E3395C4B3B96CC660A029A54596A6E35
2018-09-29 23:37:29.692 UTC [msp] GetLocalMSP -> DEBU 00a Returning existing local MSP
2018-09-29 23:37:29.692 UTC [msp] GetDefaultSigningIdentity -> DEBU 00b Obtaining default signing identity
2018-09-29 23:37:29.692 UTC [msp] GetDefaultSigningIdentity -> DEBU 00d Obtaining default signing identity
2018-09-29 23:37:29.692 UTC [msp/identity] Sign -> DEBU 00e Sign: plaintext: CACA060A1608021A0608B599C0DD0522...4108FCF53F27D313D77ECD4FFB9D6DFE
2018-09-29 23:37:29.693 UTC [msp/identity] Sign -> DEBU 00f Sign: digest: 94451A0C82591021ED77DC1F4ADB7B0DF2E50FF705486DAC46E35C890DFACEF0
2018-09-29 23:37:29.707 UTC [channelCmd] update -> INFO 010 Successfully submitted channel update
2018-09-29 23:37:29.707 UTC [main] main -> INFO 011 Exiting.....
=========== Updated Anchor peer1.org1 on the channel "fsccchannel" ===================
```

Generate peers and orderer certificates

As stated earlier, nodes are allowed to access business networks using an MSP, which is typically a **Certificate Authority (CA)**.

In this section, we will generate, for all the components that we need to run in the network, the required X.509 certificates using the `cryptogen` tool, which uses the `crypto-config.yaml` file as its configuration input. Here is an example which defines the orderer and peer organizations:

```
OrdererOrgs:
    # ---------------------------------------------------------------------------
    ----
    # Orderer
    # ---------------------------------------------------------------------------
    ----
    - Name: Orderer
      Domain: fsc.com
      Specs:
        - Hostname: orderer
# ---------------------------------------------------------------------------
--
# "PeerOrgs" - Definition of organizations managing peer nodes
# ---------------------------------------------------------------------------
--
PeerOrgs:
    # ---------------------------------------------------------------------------
    ----
    # Org1
```

```
      # -------------------------------------------------------------------
----
      - Name: Org1
        Domain: org1.fsc.com
        Template:
          Count: 2
        Users:
          Count: 2
      # -------------------------------------------------------------------
----
      # Org2
      # -------------------------------------------------------------------
----
      - Name: Org2
        Domain: org2.fsc.com
        Template:
          Count: 2
        Users:
          Count: 2
      # -------------------------------------------------------------------
----
      # Org3
      # -------------------------------------------------------------------
----
      - Name: Org3
        Domain: org3.fsc.com
        Template:
          Count: 2
        Users:
          Count: 2
```

We have now defined three organizations for peers and single orderer organization. You can use the sample file provided by Hyperledger sample projects at https://github.com/hyperledger/fabric-samples. Afterward, we run the following command to generate the certificates for the peers and the orderer:

```
cryptogen generate --config=./crypto-config.yaml
```

As a result, you should see the following output in the console:

```
ubuntu@ip-172-31-15-76:~/apps/blockchain-by-example/food-supply-chain$ sudo bin/cryptogen generate --config=./crypto-config.yaml
org1.fsc.com
org2.fsc.com
org3.fsc.com
```

Start the Docker containers

We are now ready to run our network, but first we need to perform one last step—editing the `compose-cli.yaml`.

This file defines the `networks` and `services` including the `peer`, `order`, and `cli` containers, the last of which is where you issue commands that interact with the peers (creating channels, deploying Chaincode, and so on).

Below is an example of a `docker-compose-cli.yaml`:

```
version: '2'
networks: #Define blockchain network name
  fscn:
#service section define all peers service and related container services:
  #name of service will serve as an orderer in the fabric network
  orderer.fsc.com:
  extends:
  file: base/docker-compose-base.yaml
  service: orderer.fsc.com
  container_name: orderer.fsc.com
  networks:
  - fscn
  peer0.org1.fsc.com:
  container_name: peer0.org1.fsc.com
  extends:
  file: base/docker-compose-base.yaml
  service: peer0.org1.fsc.com
  networks:
  - fscn
  peer1.org1.fsc.com:
  container_name: peer1.org1.fsc.com
  extends:
  file: base/docker-compose-base.yaml
  service: peer1.org1.fsc.com
  networks:
  - fscn
  ....
#client section
  cli:
```

```
container_name: cli
image: hyperledger/fabric-tools
tty: true
```

Defining environment variable environment:

```
- GOPATH=/opt/gopath
- CORE_VM_ENDPOINT=unix:///host/var/run/docker.sock
- CORE_LOGGING_LEVEL=DEBUG
#- CORE_LOGGING_LEVEL=INFO
- CORE_PEER_ID=cli
- CORE_PEER_ADDRESS=peer0.org1.fsc.com:7051
- CORE_PEER_LOCALMSPID=Org1MSP
- CORE_PEER_TLS_ENABLED=true
-
CORE_PEER_TLS_CERT_FILE=/opt/gopath/src/github.com/hyperledger/fabric/peer/
crypto/peerOrganizations/org1.fsc.com/peers/peer0.org1.fsc.com/tls/server.c
rt
-
CORE_PEER_TLS_KEY_FILE=/opt/gopath/src/github.com/hyperledger/fabric/peer/c
rypto/peerOrganizations/org1.fsc.com/peers/peer0.org1.fsc.com/tls/server.ke
y
-
CORE_PEER_TLS_ROOTCERT_FILE=/opt/gopath/src/github.com/hyperledger/fabric/p
eer/crypto/peerOrganizations/org1.fsc.com/peers/peer0.org1.fsc.com/tls/ca.c
rt
-
CORE_PEER_MSPCONFIGPATH=/opt/gopath/src/github.com/hyperledger/fabric/peer/
crypto/peerOrganizations/org1.fsc.com/users/Admin@org1.fsc.com/msp
 working_dir: /opt/gopath/src/github.com/hyperledger/fabric/peer
 command: /bin/bash -c './scripts/script.sh ${CHANNEL_NAME} ${DELAY}; sleep
$TIMEOUT'
```

Mapping the directories that are being used in the environment configurations:

```
volumes:
- /var/run/:/host/var/run/
- ./Chaincode/:/opt/gopath/src/github.com/Chaincode
- ./crypto-
config:/opt/gopath/src/github.com/hyperledger/fabric/peer/crypto/
- ./scripts:/opt/gopath/src/github.com/hyperledger/fabric/peer/scripts/
- ./channel-
artifacts:/opt/gopath/src/github.com/hyperledger/fabric/peer/channel-
artifacts
depends_on:
- orderer.fsc.com
- peer0.org1.fsc.com
- peer1.org1.fsc.com
```

```
   - peer0.org2.fsc.com
   - peer1.org2.fsc.com
   - peer0.org3.fsc.com
   - peer1.org3.fsc.com
   networks:
```

We define the following environment variables:

```
CHANNEL_NAME=$CHANNEL_NAME
TIMEOUT=$CLI_TIMEOUT
DELAY=$CLI_DELAY
```

The first variable, `CHANNEL_NAME`, holds the name of the channel that was specified earlier as an input for the `configtxgen` tool. For the timeout, you can provide a value (specified in seconds), otherwise the CLI container, by default, will exit after 60 seconds.

Finally, we can launch our network by calling the `docker-compose` command with the `docker-compose-cli.yaml` file, as follows:

```
sudo docker-compose -f docker-compose-cli.yaml up
```

If we run the command, it will launch our network, shown as follows:

```
ubuntu@ip-172-31-15-76:~/apps/blockchain-by-example/food-supply-chain$ sudo docker-compose -f docker-compose-cli.yaml up
WARNING: The CHANNEL_NAME variable is not set. Defaulting to a blank string.
WARNING: The DELAY variable is not set. Defaulting to a blank string.
WARNING: The TIMEOUT variable is not set. Defaulting to a blank string.
WARNING: The COMPOSE_PROJECT_NAME variable is not set. Defaulting to a blank string.
Creating peer0.org3.fsc.com ... done
Creating peer0.org2.fsc.com ... done
Creating peer1.org2.fsc.com ... done
Creating peer1.org3.fsc.com ... done
Creating peer0.org1.fsc.com ... done
Creating orderer.fsc.com    ... done
Creating peer1.org1.fsc.com ... done
Creating cli                ... done
Attaching to peer0.org2.fsc.com, peer0.org1.fsc.com, peer1.org2.fsc.com, peer0.org3.fsc.com, orderer.fsc.com, peer1.org3.fsc.com, peer1.org1.fsc.com, cli
peer0.org2.fsc.com  | 2018-09-29 07:30:03.955 UTC [viperutil] getKeysRecursively -> DEBU 001 Found map[string]interface{} value for peer.BCCSP
peer0.org2.fsc.com  | 2018-09-29 07:30:03.956 UTC [viperutil] getKeysRecursively -> DEBU 002 Found map[string]interface{} value for peer.BCCSP.
PKCS11
peer0.org2.fsc.com  | 2018-09-29 07:30:03.956 UTC [viperutil] getKeysRecursively -> DEBU 003 Found map[string]interface{} value for peer.BCCSP.
```

> To check if everything is running successfully, you can use `docker ps` to list the executing containers (peers, orderer, and CLI).

Join the channel and install Chaincode

Once we have started the Fabric network, we need to execute a series of commands to interact with the blockchain. You may already notice that we have a command configuration in the CLI section of the `docker-compose-cli.yaml`:

```
/bin/bash -c './scripts/script.sh ${CHANNEL_NAME} ${DELAY}; sleep $TIMEOUT'
```

Since there are six peers and three organizations, when we call the above commands, we don't want to hardcode the peers and organizations inside any functions. To avoid ending with a cumbersome script, we can simply pass the peer and organization parameters to a script function and trigger the peer-related Fabric command. Here is an example of `scripts/script.sh` to join all peers to a channel and install Chaincode for the consumer and retailer peer nodes.

```
#check script.sh utils.sh
joinChannel () {
  for org in 1 2 3; do
    for peer in 0 1; do
      joinChannelWithRetry $peer $org
      echo "======= peer${peer}.org${org} joined on the channel
\"$CHANNEL_NAME\" ============ "
      sleep $DELAY
      echo
    done
  done
}

joinChannelWithRetry () {
  PEER=$1
  ORG=$2
  setGlobals $PEER $ORG
  peer channel join -b $CHANNEL_NAME.block >&log.txt
  ..
}

echo "Installing Chaincode on consumer peer: peer0.org1..."
installChaincode 0 1
echo "Installing Chaincode on retailer peer: peer1.org1..."
installChaincode 1 1

..

#function for install Chaincode, check utils.sh
installChaincode () {
  PEER=$1
  ORG=$2
  setGlobals $PEER $ORG
```

```
  peer Chaincode install -n fsccc -v 1.0 -l ${LANGUAGE} -p
github.com/Chaincode/foodcontract >&log.txt
  res=$?
  cat log.txt
  verifyResult $res "Chaincode installation on peer${PEER}.org${ORG} has
Failed"
  echo "================== Chaincode is installed on remote
peer${PEER}.org${ORG} ================= "
  echo
}
```

We can also define additional important environment variables such as the following (an example when interacting with Peer 0 of Organization 2):

```
CORE_PEER_MSPCONFIGPATH=/opt/gopath/src/github.com/hyperledger/fabric/peer/
crypto/peerOrganizations/org2.fsc.com/users/Admin@org2.fsc.com/msp
CORE_PEER_ADDRESS=peer0.org2.fsc.com:7051
CORE_PEER_LOCALMSPID="Org2MSP"
CORE_PEER_TLS_ROOTCERT_FILE=/opt/gopath/src/github.com/hyperledger/fabric/p
eer/crypto/peerOrganizations/org2.fsc.com/peers/peer0.org2.fsc.com/tls/ca.c
rt
```

However, to automate the process and to avoid handling environment variables from the CLI, I have defined a `utils.sh` script located under the `scripts/` folder which we will be using later in this chapter.

Chaincode compilation and deployment

After setting up the network and writing the Chaincode, it's time to deploy the Chaincode. For that, we start by building and compiling the Chaincode using the following command: `go build`.

Many developers directly compile and install Chaincode from the project `Chaincode` folder, which isn't the best practice. Typically, we define `GOPATH` at `/opt/gopath` in the `docker-compose-cli.yaml` file, under the `cli` section:

```
cli:
  container_name: cli
  image: hyperledger/fabric-tools
  tty: true
  environment:
  - GOPATH=/opt/gopath
  - CORE_VM_ENDPOINT=unix:///host/var/run/docker.sock
  - CORE_LOGGING_LEVEL=DEBUG
  ....
  working_dir: /opt/gopath/src/github.com/hyperledger/fabric/peer
  command: /bin/bash -c './scripts/script.sh ${CHANNEL_NAME} ${DELAY}; sleep
$TIMEOUT'
  volumes:
  - /var/run/:/host/var/run/
  - ./Chaincode/:/opt/gopath/src/github.com/Chaincode
  - ./crypto-
config:/opt/gopath/src/github.com/hyperledger/fabric/peer/crypto/
```

The configuration will map the project `Chaincode/` folder to `/opt/gopath/src/github.com/Chaincode`, and when we start to bring up the Fabric network through our Composer command, the Chaincode will be copied to the preceding-mapped address with the compiled Chaincode file. Afterwards, we start the Docker CLI using: `docker exec -it cli bash`.

From here, we deploy Chaincode on the default peer (Peer 0 of Organization 1) using:

```
peer Chaincode install -n fsccc -v 1.0  -p
github.com/Chaincode/foodcontract
```

Here the -n argument specifies the network name and -v the Chaincode version. When this command executes successfully you will see a response indicating a status of 200.

Interacting with Chaincode

Once the Chaincode is deployed and installed, we can then instantiate the Chaincode as follows:

```
peer Chaincode instantiate -o orderer.fsc.com:7050 -C $CHANNEL_NAME -n
fsccc  -v 1.0 -c '{"Args":["init","order_001","John_1","100","5"]}' -P
"OR('Org1MSP.member','Org2MSP.member','Org3MSP.member')"
```

Here we pass a JSON array of arguments to trigger the `Init` function defined earlier, using the `-c` option (lowercase). If you remember, when `Init` is executed it calls the `setupFoodSupplyChainOrder` function internally, which initiates the order details. Along with this, we assign the values `order_001`, `John_1`, `100`, and `5` to the variables `orderId`, `consumerId`, `orderPrice` and `shippingPrice` respectively. The `-P` flag represents the endorsement policy associated with this Chaincode.

Running the project

Throughout the previous sections we have gone over Chaincode deployment, network setup and many other Fabric features. In this section, we will use the Fabric tool to run an end-to-end application for our food supply chain application. I assume here that you have already downloaded the project code from the Packt website.

To run the network we provide a bash script—`fscn.sh`—that leverages the Docker images to bootstrap a Hyperledger Fabric network quickly. You can run it using: `sudo ./fscn.sh -m up`.

Once up, the script `script.sh` defined earlier will be executed. As a consequence, a series of events will be set in motion, including channel creation, the joining of all peers into the channel, the installation and instantiation of Chaincode in all peers, and the execution of different queries. These are all defined in `script.sh`, which is associated with `utils.sh`.

The following picture shows the execution results of the first part of the script, ending with the creation of the channel, `fscchannel`:

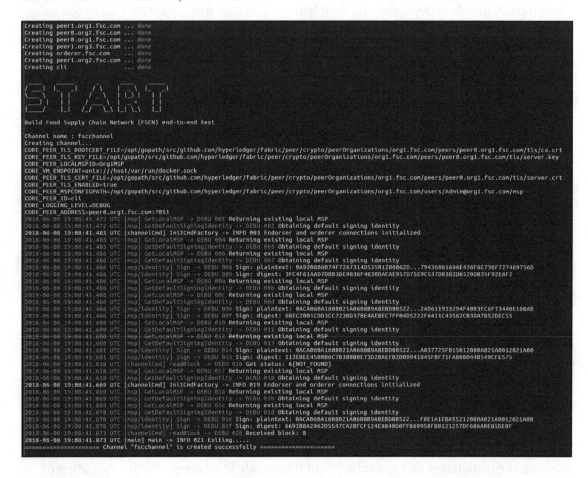

All the functions defined in the Chaincode will be called within `script.sh`. For the sake of brevity, we present here the output showing the result of the invocation of the `createRawFood` method:

```
2018-06-08 19:09:44.452 UTC [msp] GetLocalMSP -> DEBU 001 Returning existing local MSP
2018-06-08 19:09:44.452 UTC [msp] GetDefaultSigningIdentity -> DEBU 002 Obtaining default signing identity
2018-06-08 19:09:44.456 UTC [chaincodeCmd] checkChaincodeCmdParams -> INFO 003 Using default escc
2018-06-08 19:09:44.456 UTC [chaincodeCmd] checkChaincodeCmdParams -> INFO 004 Using default vscc
2018-06-08 19:09:44.456 UTC [chaincodeCmd] getChaincodeSpec -> DEBU 005 java chaincode disabled
2018-06-08 19:09:44.456 UTC [msp/identity] Sign -> DEBU 006 Sign: plaintext: 0A9D070A6908031A0C08F8A8EBD80510...77466F6F640A096F726465725F303031
2018-06-08 19:09:44.456 UTC [msp/identity] Sign -> DEBU 007 Sign: digest: BD8C413514D311420164AAE79FE0F1081B145AD99A3C2E08FA7309031BC04194
2018-06-08 19:10:01.659 UTC [msp/identity] Sign -> DEBU 008 Sign: plaintext: 0A9D070A6908031A0C08F8A8EBD80510...E884B0AC618961080981C0251F8CDE38
2018-06-08 19:10:01.659 UTC [msp/identity] Sign -> DEBU 009 Sign: digest: 3EECC396A1F95540B5D9E64FE02FBE604FB17350781952BE7370A9C8205B28B4
2018-06-08 19:10:01.663 UTC [chaincodeCmd] chaincodeInvokeOrQuery -> DEBU 00a ESCC invoke result: version:1 response:<status:200 message:"OK" > payload:"\n \262\361k\000\312\036\364\020
\251\022\1\310\325\312\002\217\037\027\315E\233\275\301\022\306!#\276\231+m+\022\303\003\n\255\003\027\223\003\n\005fsccc\022\211\003\n\017\n\torder_001\022\002\010\001\032\365\002\n\tor
der_001\032\347\002{\"OrderId\":\"order_001\",\"FoodId\":\"FISH_1\",\"ConsumerId\":\"John_1\",\"ManufactureId\":\"\",\"WholesalerId\":\"\",\"RetailerId\":\"\",\"LogisticsId\":\"\",\"Sta
tus\":\"raw food created\",\"RawFoodProcessDate\":\"2018-06-08 19:10:01\",\"ManufactureProcessDate\":\"\",\"WholesaleProcessDate\":\"\",\"ShippingProcessDate\":\"\",\"RetailProcessDate\
:\"\",\"OrderPrice\":100,\"ShippingPrice\":5,\"DeliveryDate\":\"\"}\022\025\n\004\sccc\022\r\n\013\n\005fsccc\022\002\010\001\032\003\010\310\001\"\014\022\005fsccc\032\031.0" endorsem
ent:<endorser:"\n\007Org3MSP\022\206\006-----BEGIN CERTIFICATE-----\nMIICDTCCAbSgAwIBAgIRAIyg7o0OJcvrzRoJepbRdnQwCgYIKoZIzj0EAwIwazEL\nMAkGA1UEBhMCVVMxEzARBgNVBAgTCknhbGlnb3Jua6zJua
NVBAcTDVNhb18G\ncmFuУ2l2Y28xF1ATBgNVBAoTDG9yЗ2MuZnN1LmNvbTEYMBYGA1UEAxMPY2Eub33n\nMySmcZMuY29tMB4XDTE4MDYwNTE4MDYwDES5MDEymVoXDTI4MDYwNTE8MDEymVoAwZELMAkG\nA1UEBhMCVVMxEzARBgNVBAgTCknhbGlmb3
JWExFjAUBgNVBAcTDVNhb18GcnFu\nY2lzY28xGzA28gNVBAMTEnB1ZXIxLm9yZzMuZnN1LmNvbTBZMBMGByqGSM49AgEG\nCCqGSM49AwEHA03ABKYzknAPgGJb+rFH0wBkaUk13vZu7IqrYvyv4WUHLUPHmarV\na6IZ70Z1Zr3dVuyxfS3n3ibU
njzx4Zp2nPP6Awa3TTBLMA4GA1UdDwEB/wQEAwIH\ngDAMBgNVHRMBAf8EAjAAMCSGA1UdIwQkMCKA1Brk2Kl7MnB1yZUVnltF228D\lpDc\nS+5AM0L+0QJzaCcuMAoGCCqGSM49BAMCA0cAMEQCIAt/uyezzonQYgECtzVPhk6R\nA11B2nRx+7w
6zcx6C1DtA1AdjzcNwmrwPRUM1ZOJd2x9wwAwZEhUBchfYe7wHGCD\nVA==\n-----END CERTIFICATE-----\n" signature:"00\002 .\354\202\3319\\345\220\282Ce\031\257+F\004 B5\355\244\224\to\377o\354\241\24
3\254\210\363\002 \017g\327\376\"W/\274\346\337j\2468Lt\021\350\204\260\254a\211a\013\t\261\300%\037\214\3368" >
2018-06-08 19:10:01.663 UTC [chaincodeCmd] chaincodeInvokeOrQuery -> INFO 00b Chaincode invoke successful. result: status:200
2018-06-08 19:10:01.663 UTC [main] main -> INFO 00c Exiting.....
Invoke:CreateRawFood transaction on PEER PEER5 on channel 'fscchannel' is successful.
```

This is the result of the execution of `chaincodeInvokeCreateRawFood` defined in the `utils.sh` script as follows:

```
#create rawfood by invoke chaincode
chaincodeInvokeCreateRawFood() {
    PEER=$1
    ORG=$2
    setGlobals $PEER $ORG
    if [ -z "$CORE_PEER_TLS_ENABLED" -o "$CORE_PEER_TLS_ENABLED" = "false"
]; then
        peer chaincode invoke -o orderer.fsc.com:7050 -C $CHANNEL_NAME -n
fsccc -c '{"Args":["createRawFood","order_001"]}' >&log.txt
    else
        peer chaincode invoke -o orderer.fsc.com:7050  --tls
$CORE_PEER_TLS_ENABLED --cafile $ORDERER_CA -C $CHANNEL_NAME -n fsccc -c
'{"Args":["createRawFood","order_001"]}' >&log.txt
    fi
    res=$?
    cat log.txt
    verifyResult $res "Invoke:CreateRawFood execution on PEER$PEER failed "
    echo "Invoke:CreateRawFood transaction on PEER $PEER on channel
'$CHANNEL_NAME' is successful. "
    echo
}
```

At the end, we can see the result of querying the Chaincode for the current food state data:

At this level, we are able to communicate with the deployed Chaincode through Linux scripts and commands. I know you might find it a bit tricky, therefore, in the following sections, we will use a more abstract approach using RESTful calls.

Interacting over REST API/JSON-RPC

So far, we have successfully run the end-to-end food supply chain via a script, simulating the entire business flow. In this section, we will explore using the Fabric RESTful API to demonstrate how a web page can interact with Fabric through a web application. We will demo how a CA can join the network and query the ledger data. We will use a previous food supply chain example to demonstrate how we can utilize the Fabric RESTful API to get information from the blockchain.

Setting up the development environment

Get the source code of this from the PacktPub GitHub repository if you haven't already done so. Once you download the source code, navigate to the directory `blockchain-by-example/fsc-restful`. The example we will run here is based on a Fabric sample project, located at `github: https://github.com/hyperledger/fabric-samples`.

To run the web application shipped with the book's code, we first need to bring up the Fabric network. We make sure that no other active container is running by using:

```
sudo ./script.sh -m down
```

Then, clear any unused networks:

```
docker network prune
```

Navigate to the `webapp/` folder and run:

```
npm install
```

You'll have to wait for npm to install a few packages. Once the operation is successfully finished, navigate back to the `fsc-restful` folder, and launch the Fabric network by running:

```
sudo ./script -m up
```

Install the Chaincode, and instantiate it with initial customer order data, before invoking `createRowfoodChaincode`:

```
peer Chaincode install -n fsccc -v 1.0 -p "$CC_SRC_PATH" -l "$LANGUAGE"
peer Chaincode instantiate -o orderer.example.com:7050 -C mychannel -n
fsccc -l "$LANGUAGE" -v 1.0 -c
'{"Args":["init","order_001","John_1","100","5"]}'
peer Chaincode invoke -o orderer.example.com:7050 -C mychannel -n fsccc -c
'{"Args":["createRawFood","order_001"]}'
```

Register users

As the Chaincode is instantiated and the needed dependencies are installed, launch the Node.js server using `node server.js`. Once the server is running, open the web browser by navigating to `http://yourserverip:3000`. You will see a web page similar to the one here:

You can start by assigning the admin to the Fabric client. For that, click the **Register Admin** button, which will register you in Fabric as the admin client user:

In this step, we send a request for an admin as the authorized user and register with the CA. The certificate-related folder, `hrc-key-store`, should be generated.

 You need to clean up this folder when you rebuild your Fabric network or you will get an error, since the CA was generated from a previous network.

Let's take a look at how `server.js` registers admin users in a Fabric blockchain.

The client application uses `fabric-ca-client`, `fabric-client`, and GRpc node libraries to interact with the Fabric network.

The `fabric-ca-client` manages Fabric's user certificate life cycles, including registering, enrolling through API, and interacting with the Fabric CA.

The `fabric-client` interacts with peers and orderers to install and instantiate Chaincodes, send transactions, and perform queries.

Here are a few steps to register admin users:

1. Set up `hfc-key-store` for `Fabric_Client`
2. Initialize Fabric client—new
   `Fabric_CA_Client('http://localhost:7054', tlsOptions ,
   'ca.example.com', crypto_suite)`
3. Get admin user—`context - fabric_client.getUserContext('admin',
   true)`

4. Create admin user—`fabric_client.createUser`

Here is some sample code, serving to register an admin:

```
app.get('/registerAdmin',function(req,res) {
    var fabric_client = new Fabric_Client();
    var fabric_ca_client = null;
    var admin_user = null;
    var member_user = null;
    var store_path = path.join(__dirname, 'hfc-key-store');
    Fabric_Client.newDefaultKeyValueStore({ path: store_path
}).then((state_store) => {
        // assign the store to the fabric client
        fabric_client.setStateStore(state_store);
        var crypto_suite = Fabric_Client.newCryptoSuite();
        var crypto_store = Fabric_Client.newCryptoKeyStore({path:
store_path});
        crypto_suite.setCryptoKeyStore(crypto_store);
        fabric_client.setCryptoSuite(crypto_suite);
        var    tlsOptions = {
            trustedRoots: [],
            verify: false
        };
fabric_ca_client = new Fabric_CA_Client('http://localhost:7054', tlsOptions
, 'ca.example.com',crypto_suite);
        return fabric_client.getUserContext('admin', true);
    }).then((user_from_store) => {
        if (user_from_store && user_from_store.isEnrolled()) {
            console.log('Successfully loaded admin from persistence');
            admin_user = user_from_store;
            return null;
        } else {
            // need to enroll it with CA server
            return fabric_ca_client.enroll({
              enrollmentID: 'admin',
              enrollmentSecret: 'adminpw'
```

```
            }).then((enrollment) => {
                console.log('Successfully enrolled admin user "admin"');
                return fabric_client.createUser({username: 'admin',mspid:
    'Org1MSP',
                    cryptoContent: { privateKeyPEM: enrollment.key.toBytes(),
    signedCertPEM: enrollment.certificate }});
            }).then((user) => {
                admin_user = user;
                return fabric_client.setUserContext(admin_user);
            }).catch((err) => {
            });
        }
    }).then(() => {
    ..
    }).catch((err) => {
    });
});
```

Once the admin is registered, we register a user as the Fabric client by clicking the **Register User** button. This step is similar to the precedent, and the user will be registered with the CA server and enrolled as a new user with an assigned identity, which can query and update the ledger. This authority is granted and authorized by the admin user through the Fabric network:

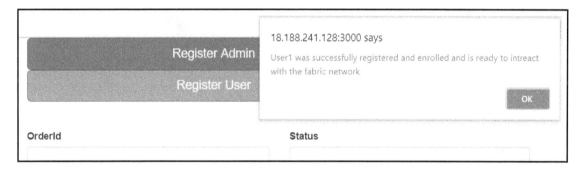

Querying the Chaincode from UI

Now, it is time to query the Chaincode status using the authorized user, who can read the data from the ledger, which is returned in JSON format.

By clicking **Query Chaincode**, the node server triggers the query Chaincode API to get the current ledger state information. We can see that `orderId`, `orderPrice`, `shippingPrice`, and `rawFoodProcessDate` are returned from the ledger and shown on the page:

Similarly to what we did before, the `queryChaincode` uses the `fabric_client` API to connect to a channel with peer and query data as follows:

```
app.get('/queryChaincode',function(req,res){
        // setup the fabric network
        var fabric_client = new Fabric_Client();
        var channel = fabric_client.newChannel('mychannel');
        var peer = fabric_client.newPeer('grpc://localhost:7051');
        channel.addPeer(peer);
        var member_user = null;
        var store_path = path.join(__dirname, 'hfc-key-store');
        var tx_id = null;
        Fabric_Client.newDefaultKeyValueStore({ path: store_path
        }).then((state_store) => {
                ...
            return fabric_client.getUserContext('user1', true);
        }).then((user_from_store) => {
            ....
            const request = {
                chaincodeId: 'fsccc',
                fcn: 'query',
                args: ['order_001']
            };
            // send the query proposal to the peer
            return channel.queryByChaincode(request);
```

Congratulations! We just used our application and queried it via Hyperledger Fabric. At this level, you should get a good sense for how web applications can be integrated with the Fabric blockchain.

Hyperledger Composer

You have witnessed how difficult it can be to build a Hyperledger network and to deploy and interact with the Chaincode. This situation will change with Composer.

As mentioned earlier, Hyperledger Composer is based on Hyperldeger Fabric. It is an open development tool set and a framework for making the development of blockchain applications much easier. Hyperledger Composer was built with JavaScript, making it very easy to define your business network, create assets, and run transactions.

Get Hyperledger Composer and Playground

In this project we will make use of the Hyperledger Composer development tools. Hyperledger Composer is an application development framework, which helps us in getting started quickly, and which simplifies the creation of Hyperledger Fabric (`https://hyperledger-fabric.readthedocs.io/en/latest/`) blockchain applications.

We start by installing the most important utility, `composer-cli`, which will help us to perform administrative, operational, and development tasks:

```
npm install -g composer-cli@0.19
```

Next, we'll also pick up `generator-hyperledger-composer` and `composer-rest-server`. We start by installing the first package, which is a Yeoman module that creates project templates for using with Hyperledger Composer:

```
npm install -g generator-hyperledger-composer
```

Then, we install the Hyperledger Composer REST server, which allows for RESTful interactions between our deployed business network and a web client:

```
npm install -g composer-rest-server
```

Afterwards, we install Yeoman, which is a tool for generating skeleton web applications. We install it in order to use the previously installed generator, `generator-hyperledger-composer` :

```
npm install -g yo
```

We need then to install Hyperledger Playground, which provides you with a user interface for viewing and demonstrating your business networks, as follows:

```
npm install -g composer-playground
```

Composer Playground

As Composer Playground has already been installed, we can start the corresponding container using:

```
sudo docker run --name composer-playground --publish 8080:8080 --detach
hyperledger/composer-playground
```

Once the container has started, open a browser and navigate to `localhost:8080`, where you should see the following welcome page:

You can shut down playground at any time, using:

```
sudo docker rm --force composer-playground
```

If everything is ready, let's start to play!

First, let's create a new business network by clicking on **Deploy a new business network.** Afterwards you'll need to provide some details about your new business network, for example a name—`fsn-business-network`. Then select `empty-business-network`, and click **Deploy**.

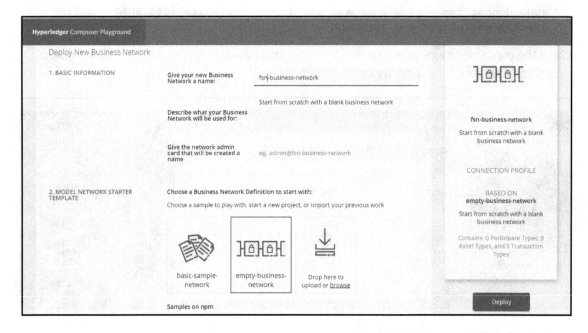

Once created, you have to connect to the `fsn-business-network` by clicking **Connect now**:

You'll get a few files, and among them will be a model file. Hyperledger Composer provides an object-oriented-like modeling language, which allows us to define the domain model for a business network definition in a `.cto` file. You can learn more about this modeling language and this file's structure from the official documentation at: `https://hyperledger.github.io/composer/v0.19/reference/cto_language`. For the sake of our example, let's adopt the following sample:

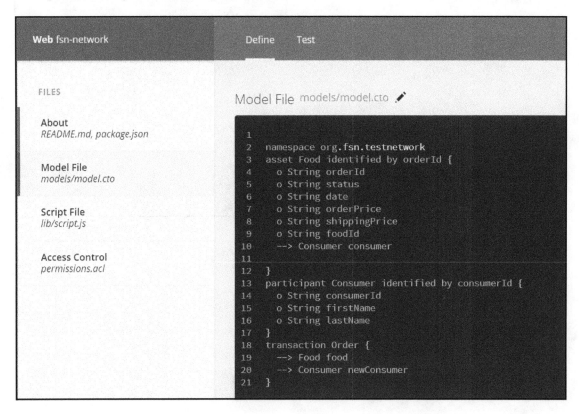

After that, we need to define your transaction processor script file by adding a JavaScript file with the following content:

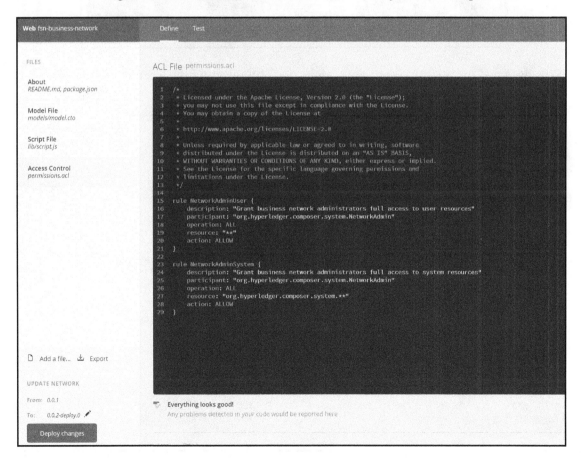

Then, we need to define the access control policy. We use the default network administrator to give full access to the business network and system-level operations:

Once you have finished, click **Deploy changes** in the bottom left to upgrade the business network, and click **Test** to get a test started.

We should add a participant to our business network. To do that, create a participant by selecting the left menu's **Consumer** tab, and clicking **Create new participant** in the upper right. Modify the value with your details, then click **Create new** to create the new participant.

In registry: **org.fsn.testnetwork.Consumer**

JSON Data Preview

```
1  {
2      "$class": "org.fsn.testnetwork.Consumer",
3      "consumerId": "Brian",
4      "firstName": "Brian",
5      "lastName": "Wu"
6  }
```

Now, we need to create an asset. This can be done by selecting the left menu **Food** tab under assets, and clicking **Create new asset** in the upper right. Enter or modify the value you need to test. Then click **Create new** to create the new asset.

You should see the newly created asset in the **Food** tab:

Web fsn-network   Define   Test   admin

PARTICIPANTS

Consumer   Asset registry for org.fsn.testnetwork.Food

                          ID   Data

ASSETS
                          001   {
Food   "$class": "org.fsn.testnetwork.Food",
                                                  "orderId": "001",
                                                  "status": "New",
                                                  "date": "2018-06-10 10:22:01",
                                                  "orderPrice": "100",
TRANSACTIONS   "shippingPrice": "5",
                                                  "foodId": "food001",
All Transactions   "consumer": "resource:org.fsn.testnetwork.Consumer#0531"
                                                }

                                                              Collapse

Submit Transaction

At this level, you can submit a transaction by entering the corresponding `orderId` and `consumerId` defined in previous steps:

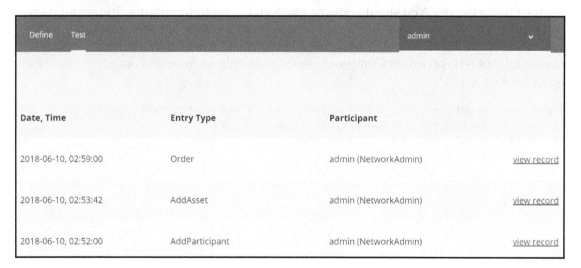

Once submitted, you can view the log of your transactions by clicking **All transactions** on the left. Click **View record** to inspect the transaction details. You can see the transaction ID and when this transaction was processed:

Date, Time	Entry Type	Participant	
2018-06-10, 02:59:00	Order	admin (NetworkAdmin)	view record
2018-06-10, 02:53:42	AddAsset	admin (NetworkAdmin)	view record
2018-06-10, 02:52:00	AddParticipant	admin (NetworkAdmin)	view record

By checking the food asset value, we can see that the consumer data is updated:

Now, you have an idea how Composer works and how easy it is to work with such a tool, instead of using the native Fabric infrastructure directly.

Summary

In this chapter, we have learned a lot about the Hyperledger project and, in particular, about Fabric. We have introduced, among other things, how to write and deploy a smart contract using Golang. You should now be comfortable enough to start writing your own smart contracts. We have also discovered how to build a web application that can interact with the Hyperledger Fabric API using the RPC protocol. At the end, we introduced an important tool—Hyperledger Composer—which can help us to build Fabric applications easily.

I hope you are not tired, since, in the next chapter, we will continue discovering Hyperledger by building another project—a letter of credit.

11
Letter of Credit (LC) Hyperledger

In the previous chapter, we learned the important basics and key concepts of Hyperledger Fabric by building a blockchain-based supply chain for the food industry. In this chapter, we will continue learning and exploring the essential components of the Hyperledger project by exploring an important financial concept—a **letter of credit** (**LC**). You will almost certainly come across an LC example while learning about blockchain's application to finance, as it provides a perfect example of how certain thorny issues can be resolved.

Throughout this chapter, we will deepen our knowledge of Hyperledger Fabric and introduce several advanced tools, while also learning how to develop and manage scalable, highly interoperable business solutions based on Hyperledger.

In this chapter, we will take a look at the following main topics:

- Hyperledger Composer
- Enrollment and identity management in a Hyperledger network
- Writing Chaincode for an LC
- Hyperledger on IBM's cloud

An LC is far too complex a process to be fully implemented and covered in a single chapter, hence, we will restrict our attention to how to implement the main concepts.

LC concepts and design

An LC, also known as a draft, a documentary credit, or bankers' commercial credit, is a letter from a bank guaranteeing that a buyer's payment to a seller will be received with a specified sum in a specified currency, provided the seller meets precisely defined terms within a fixed time frame. In the event that the buyer is unable to make the payment, the bank will cover the full or remaining amount of the purchase.

LCs are one of the most common payment methods available in international trade, as in such contexts, banking channels are used for payment between parties involved who may not trust each other. An LC issued by an issuing bank is often sent to a confirming bank that will undertake to pay the exporter according to the terms of the LC. The following diagram shows a simplified example of an LC process, although a real transaction could be much more complex:

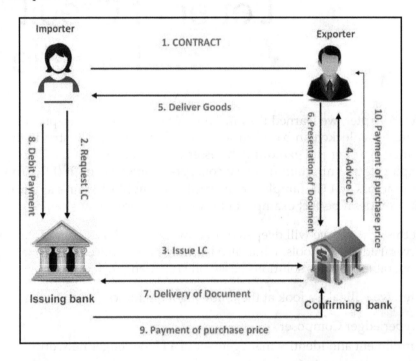

The LC process is inefficient and typically time-consuming, as it depends on complex financial and administrative operations involving multiple actors. Blockchain technology can help to simplify the process by sharing financial data and documentation through a secure network that requires no third-party verification. It is reported that the global finance company BBVA was able to reduce the time required to send, verify, and authorize an international trade transaction, which normally takes from around 7 to 10 days, to just 2.5 hours by using the blockchain.

We will walk through an example of an LC by using Hyperledger Fabric technologies, and demonstrate how these technologies can improve the efficiency of the overall LC process.

Development environment

If you found Golang a difficult option to deal with when creating your Chaincode, then here is your relief. Instead of using Golang, we will discover how Hyperledger Composer can abstract Chaincode development using JavaScript and other easy-to-learn modeling languages.

Before getting started, make sure you have installed all the necessary prerequisites (except Golang) by following the instructions in the relevant section of `Chapter 10`, *Supply Chain on Hyperledger*.

Setting up the IDE

In the LC example, we will use Hyperledger Composer to work on our business network code and smart contract logic. For this, you can choose your preferred IDE, but for our example we will use Visual Studio Code. From `https://code.visualstudio.com`, download and install Visual Studio Code.

Open Visual Studio Code and navigate to **View | Extensions**, and search for and install the Hyperledger Composer extension. It will help you to write a composer's model files and report errors for you easily, as demonstrated in the following screenshot:

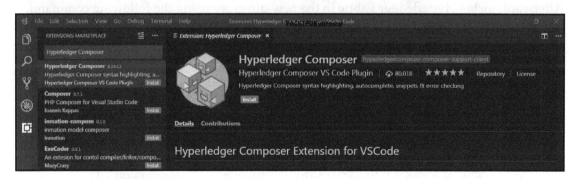

If you don't want to use an IDE, you can continue using your favorite text editor.

Getting Hyperledger Fabric running

In the previous chapter, we introduced how to build a Fabric network, and how to install and use the composer and playground utilities. In this chapter, we will discover a new way to start a Hyperledger Fabric V1.2 (or earlier) network for development purposes using a set of helper scripts (https://github.com/hyperledger/composer-tools/tree/master/packages/fabric-dev-servers).

Let's start by creating a directory called `fabric-dev-servers/` under the home (~) location:

```
mkdir ~/fabric-dev-servers && cd ~/fabric-dev-servers
```

Next, we install Yeoman, which is a tool for generating skeleton web applications. We install it so that we may use the generator `generator-hyperledger-composer` later:

```
npm install -g yo
```

Next, we install `generator-hyperledger-composer` mentioned in the previous step, which is a Yeoman module serving to create project templates for use with Hyperledger Composer:

```
npm install -g generator-hyperledger-composer
```

Afterward, install Hyperledger Fabric in the new directory using the following command. Make sure that both Bash and Docker are installed on the target system before running the script:

```
curl -O
https://raw.githubusercontent.com/hyperledger/composer-tools/master/package
s/fabric-dev-servers/fabric-dev-servers.tar.gz
tar -xvf fabric-dev-servers.tar.gz
```

You'll get a dev server package containing scripts to set up three different levels of Fabric—versions 1.0, 1.1, and 1.2. You can select a version by setting the environment variable `HL_FABRIC_VERSION` to `hlfv1*` (for example, `hlfv11` for version 1.1).

 In the official documentation, it's stated that if you are using Hyperledger Composer v0.16.x, then you will want to use Hyperledger Fabric V1.0. If you are using Hyperledger Composer v0.17, v0.18, or v0.19, then you will want to use Hyperledger Fabric V1.1. If you are using Hyperledger Composer v0.20 or later, then you will want to use Hyperledger Fabric V1.2.

Run `./teardownAllDocker.sh` and `./teardownFabric` to make sure any previous Docker or Fabric runtimes are cleaned up:

```
sudo ./teardownAllDocker.sh ./teardownFabric.sh
```

You'll be asked in the prompt to choose between three options. You can choose the option kill and remove to clean all of the containers.

Afterwards, run `./downloadFabric.sh` to download a local Hyperledger Fabric runtime:

```
sudo ./downloadFabric.sh
```

This script will download a set of runtime Docker images for the Hyperledger project representing the core Fabric components, which will comprise our Hyperledger Fabric network—Fabric CA, Fabric Peer, Fabric Chaincode environment, Couchdb, and Fabric Orderer.

All set? Now, let's start building our composer LC application.

Creating a composer Fabric application

As we introduced briefly in the previous chapter, Hyperledger Composer is built on top of the Hyperledger Fabric blockchain. It provides a set of tools to help developers rapidly develop use cases and deploy a blockchain solution quickly. Hyperledger Composer is built with JavaScript, leveraging modern tools including Node.js and NPM. It involves a business-centric, driven development process and helps developers to digitize and model business networks.

Hyperledger Composer is a toolbox of helpful tools that includes the following:

- A modeling language called CTO
- Composer Playground, which is a web interface for the rapid building and testing of a business network
- **Command-line interface** (**CLI**) tools for integrating modeled business networks (created using Hyperledger Composer) in a running instance of the Hyperledger Fabric network

We introduced the Composer Playground in the previous chapter. In this chapter, we will discover the CTO and CLI tools.

Creating our first business network using Hyperledger Composer

Hyperledger Composer helps you to model your current business network quickly, which involves identifying the parties doing business, and their roles. Multiple participants will access the business network, and each maintainer of the network will host several peer nodes, which will replicate the ledger data between them.

If you have run through the example in the previous chapter, navigate to the `blockchain-by-example/` folder, and create a folder called `letterofcredit/`. If you don't have a `blockchain-by-example/` folder, just create the `letterofcredit/` folder at a location you prefer.

Use `yo hyperledger-composer:businessnetwork` to generate a business network project template with Yeoman's help. You'll need to answer a few questions about your new application:

```
Welcome to the business network generator
? Business network name: lc-network
? Description: LC Business network
? Author name:  your name
? Author email: your Email
? License: Apache-2.0
? Namespace: org.example.lc
? Do you want to generate an empty template network? Yes: generate an empty template network
   create package.json
   create README.md
   create models/org.example.lc.cto
   create permissions.acl
   create .eslintrc.yml
```

If you choose to generate an empty template, you'll get a set of files, as shown in the following screenshot:

```
├── models
│   └── org.example.lc.cto
├── package.json
├── permissions.acl
└── README.md
```

Let's look at each part of the Composer network definition.

Models definition

Composer helps you to model business networks representing your assets and the transactions related to them using model files. Such files have a `.cto` file suffix and they are written using a special object-oriented modeling language (called CTO). Generally, a modeling file is composed of the following elements:

- A single namespace
- A set of resource definitions, including assets, participants, transactions, and events
- Optional imported resources and declarations from other namespaces

To give you an idea of how modeling works, let's start with a simple example, introducing the basic concepts before building the LC business network.

Open the `org.example.lc.cto` file generated by Yoeman and paste in the following code snippets:

```
namespace org.example.lc

asset SampleAsset identified by assetId {
  o String assetId
  o String value
    --> SampleParticipant owner
}
transaction TransactionExample {
    --> SampleAsset asset
  o String newValue
  }

event AssetEvent{
    -->SampleAsset asset
}

participant SampleParticipant identified by participantId {
o String participantId
  }
```

In this simple model, we define four different types of objects, representing an `asset`, `transaction`, `participant`, and an `event`.

An asset, for example `SampleAsset`, is defined using the `asset` keyword and `identified by` syntax. An asset contains fields, where each field, as for other objects, is expressed in the format `o Fieldtype fieldname`.

Here, we also model a transaction called `TransactionExample` that contains a relationship to an existing instance of `SampleAsset` (asset), which will be changed, and a string value (`newValue`) used to update the asset's property (`value`). A relationship is a typed pointer to an instance represented in the model by an arrow, `-->`, pointing to the object.

Using the same syntax as for `asset` and `transaction`, we define a participant type using the `participant` keyword.

JavaScript transaction logic

After we have modeled the example's participants, assets, and transactions, it's time to encode the business logic in the form of transaction processor functions. These functions are typically considered as a Chaincode or smart contract function.

For that purpose, create a new directory called `lib/`, under which we will define the JavaScript files written in ECMAScript ES5. This script (or scripts) will contain transaction processor functions that will be called when a transaction is submitted.

In your `lib/` directory, create a `logic.js` file (optionally from Visual Studio Code), and then paste in the following transaction processor function:

```
/**
 * Create the sample asset
 * @param {org.example.lc.cto.TransactionExample} tx- the
TransactionExample transaction
 * @transaction
 */
async function  TransactionExample (tx) {

    // Get the factory.
    var factory = getFactory();
    // Create a new vehicle.
    var asset= factory.newResource('org.example.lc', 'SampleAsset',
'ASSET_1');
    // Create a new relationship to the owner.
    asset.owner=
factory.newRelationship(namespace,'SampleParticipant',tx.owner.getIdentifie
r());
    // Get the asset registry for the asset.
    let assetRegistry = getAssetRegistry('org.example.lc.SampleAsset');
    // Update the asset in the asset registry.
    await assetRegistry.add(tx.asset);

    // Emit an event for the new created asset.
    let event = getFactory().newEvent('org.example.lc',  'SampleEvent');
```

```
        event.asset = tx.asset;
        emit(event);


    }
```

In the preceding example, the first line comment contains a human-readable description of what `TransactionExample` does. The second line must include the `@param` annotation to indicate which resource name of the transaction defined in the model file will be triggered by this transaction processor function. After the resource name, we define the parameter name (`tx` in this case), which must be supplied to the JavaScript function as an argument. The last line must contain the `@transaction` annotation to indicate that this function is defined as a transaction processor function.

The transaction processor function defines the `TransactionExample` type as the associated transaction and passes the parameter, `tx`.

The `getFactory` and `newResource` functions are used to create a new instance of the asset `SampleAsset`. The properties of the newly created instance can be set as standard JavaScript object properties, for instance, `asset.value=xyz`.

We instantiate a new relationship using `newRelationship` with the given namespace, type, and identifier to point at an existing instance of the specified namespace and identifier.

Finally, once we have updated its attribute, we store the new instance in the appropriate asset registry using the `Add` function (from `AssetRegistry` API), and then an event is emitted.

Access control definition

It's possible, optionally, to define an **access control list** (**ACL**) to set the permissions of the business network. The rules in the ACL can determine which user (roles) are permitted to create, read, update, or delete the business network domain model elements. There are two types of ACL rules: simple and conditional.

Simple ACL rules are used to control the resources that participants can access, for example:

```
rule ExampleSimpleRule {
    description: "Example Description of Simple Rule"
    participant: "org.example.SampleParticipant"
    operation: ALL
    resource: "org.example.SampleAsset"
```

```
        action: ALLOW
    }
```

The preceding simple rule, shows that the participant `SampleParticipant` can perform all operations on the resources of the `org.example.SampleAsset` asset.

Conditional rules can specify the rules to apply depending on variable conditions. If the transaction is defined in ACL rules, when a participant submits a transaction, the ACL rule applies and only allows the participant to access the resources defined by the conditions:

```
rule ExampleConditionalRuleWithTransaction {
    description: "Description of the Condition Rule With Transaction"
    participant(u): "org.example.SampleParticipant"
    operation: READ, CREATE, UPDATE
    resource(m): "org.example.SampleAsset"
    transaction(tx): "org.example.TransactionExample"
    condition: (m.owner.getIdentifier() == u.getIdentifier())
    action: ALLOW
}
```

The preceding example shows that a participant user can perform all operations on the resource of the `org.example.SampleAsset` asset if the participant is the owner of the asset and he submitted a transaction called `org.example.TransactionExample` to perform the operation.

In our case, for the sake of simplicity, we opened the permissions for all participants, but, in a real-world project, you should define a detailed ACL rule to limit participant access to the resources and transactions:

```
/**
 * Access control rules for lc-network
 */
rule Default {
    description: "Allow all participants access to all resources"
    participant: "ANY"
    operation: ALL
    resource: "org.example.lc.*"
    action: ALLOW
}

rule SystemACL {
  description: "System ACL to permit all access"
  participant: "ANY"
  operation: ALL
  resource: "org.hyperledger.composer.system.**"
  action: ALLOW
}
```

We just developed a minimalistic Hyperledger Composer business network model, Chaincode, and permissions ACL.

As you now have an idea about how we can model a business network, let's extend this model to implement our letter of credit use case. We first need to keep the same ACL file and you can also optionally clean up the other files (`logic.js` and `model.cto`)

LC business network

Until now, we have covered the basic, necessary Hyperledger Composer business network components, namely, the model, script, and permission ACL. Now, it's time to start developing our LC use case. We will be basing this on a sample generated previously by Yeoman and the modeling elements presented earlier.

Initial LC model

As presented earlier in the *LC concepts and design* section, we have four actors in our LC use case, namely, a buyer, a seller, an issuing bank, and a confirming bank. Let's define these participants in our CTO model as follows:

```
namespace org.example.lc
enum ParticipantType {
  o BUYER
  o SELLER
  o ISSUING_BANK
  o CONFIRMING_BANK
}

// PARTICIPANTS
//BANK
participant Bank identified by bankID {
  o String bankID
  o String name
  o ParticipantType type
}
//USER
participant User identified by userId {
  o String userId
  o String name
  o String lastName optional
  o String companyName
```

```
        o ParticipantType type
        --> Bank bank
    }
```

We first define four types of participants—a buyer, seller, issuing bank, and confirming bank—in an enumeration, which is declared using the keyword `enum ParticipantType`. Then, we define a bank participant with the attribute `ParticipantType` to differentiate between the issuing and confirming banks.

A participant `User`, is defined with the property `userId` as the identity field, the associated company name, and the bank he will deal with. For example, the buyer will deal with the issuing bank and the seller will deal with the confirming bank.

Now, let's define the letter of credit asset:

```
// ENUMS
enum LCStatus {
    o CONTRACT
    o REQUEST_LC
    o ISSUE_LC
    o ADVICE_LC
    o DELIVER_PRODUCT
    o PRESENT_DOCUMENT
    o DELIVERY_DOCUMENT
    o BUYER_DEBIT_PAYMENT
    o BANKS_PAYMENT_TRANSFER
    o SELL_RECEIVED_PAYMENT
    o CLOSED
}
// ASSETS
asset LetterOfCredit identified by letterId {
    o String letterId
    --> User buyer
    --> User seller
    --> Bank issuingBank
    --> Bank confirmingBank
    o Rule[] rules
    o ProductDetails productDetails
    o String [] evidence
    o LCStatus status
    o String closeReason optional
}
concept ProductDetails {
    o String productType
    o Integer quantity
    o Double pricePerUnit
}
```

```
concept Rule {
  o String ruleId
  o String ruleText
}
```

As we saw in the *LC concepts and design* section, the entire LC process has 10 steps. Therefore, we have defined the possible status in the `LCStatus` enumeration. We have also added a final `CLOSED` status to signal the end of the LC process.

We define the `ProductDetails` concept, which contains information on the kind of product and total price that the buyer is paying to the seller. In Composer's modeling language, concepts are abstract classes contained by an asset, participant, or transaction.

We model the LC as an asset with an ID, `letterId`, which can be used by all participants in the network to trace this LC. The LC is related (relationship) to the four participants, and defines certain rules (`Rule[] rules`) that only permitted, authorized parties can perform. The `evidence` array provides proof of certain steps needed to display the required documents. The variable `LCStatus` will keep track of the current blockchain LC status (as defined in the `LCStatus` enum).

We have defined the assets and participants, so now it is time to define the requisite transactions following the LC process steps.

Participant onboarding

Before the LC process starts, we need to onboard all participants in the network. For demonstration purposes, in this example, we will suppose we have a buyer with the name David Wilson, a seller, Jason Jones, the issuing bank (First Consumer Bank), and the confirming bank (Bank of Eastern Export).

We declare a transaction in the model file. We then define the corresponding transaction processor function in `lib/logic.js` as follows:

```
/**
 * Create the participants needed for the demo
 * @param {org.example.lc.CreateDemoParticipants} createDemoParticipants -
 * the CreateDemoParticipants transaction
 * @transaction
 */
async function createDemoParticipants() { // eslint-disable-line no-
unused-vars
    const factory = getFactory();
    const namespace = 'org.example.lc';
```

```
        // create the banks
        const bankRegistry = await getParticipantRegistry(namespace +
'.Bank');
        const issuingbank = factory.newResource(namespace, 'Bank', 'BI');
        issuingbank.name = 'First Consumer Bank';
        issuingbank.type = 'ISSUING_BANK';
        await bankRegistry.add(issuingbank);
        const confirmingbank = factory.newResource(namespace, 'Bank', 'BE');
        confirmingbank.name = 'Bank of Eastern Export';
        confirmingbank.type = 'CONFIRMING_BANK';
        await bankRegistry.add(confirmingbank);

        // create users
        const userRegistry = await getParticipantRegistry(namespace +
'.User');
        const buyer = factory.newResource(namespace, 'User', 'david');
        buyer.name = 'David';
        buyer.lastName= 'Wilson';
        buyer.bank = factory.newRelationship(namespace, 'Bank', 'BI');
        buyer.companyName = 'Toy Mart Inc';
        buyer.type = 'BUYER';
        await userRegistry.add(buyer);
        const seller = factory.newResource(namespace, 'User', 'jason');
        seller.name = 'Jason';
        seller.lastName= 'Jones';
        seller.bank = factory.newRelationship(namespace, 'Bank', 'EB');
        seller.companyName = 'Valley Toys Manufacturing';
        seller.type = 'SELLER';
        await userRegistry.add(seller);
    }
```

Here, we define an asynchronous function instantiating the objects (participants) representing the actors involved in the LC and add them to the participant registry.

As discussed earlier, there are 10 steps in the LC process flow. Therefore, we will add the related model objects and define the transaction logic for each step.

Initial agreement

As defined in our LC design, the first step in the agreement between buyer and seller is where the buyer agrees to purchase the goods from the seller. Therefore, we define an `InitialApplication` transaction in our model for all attending participants, including the buyer, seller, and banks. In this step, we define a transaction, which creates a letter of credit with an ID, `letterId`, and then define the related participants along an event firing a notification regarding the LC creation:

```
transaction InitialApplication {
  o String letterId
  --> User buyer
  --> User seller
  --> Bank issuingBank
  --> Bank confirmingBank
  o Rule[] rules
  o ProductDetails productDetails
}
event InitialApplicationEvent {
  --> LetterOfCredit lc
}
```

The following function represents the process behind the `InitialApplication` transaction as follows:

```
#related the transaction processor function
/**
 * Create the LC asset
 * @param {org.example.lc.InitialApplication} initalAppliation - the
InitialApplication transaction
 * @transaction
 */
async function initialApplication(application) { // eslint-disable-line no-
unused-vars
    const factory = getFactory();
    const namespace = 'org.example.lc';

    const letter = factory.newResource(namespace, 'LetterOfCredit',
application.letterId);
    letter.buyer = factory.newRelationship(namespace, 'User',
application.buyer.getIdentifier());
    letter.seller =
        factory.newRelationship(namespace,
'User',application.seller.getIdentifier());
    letter.issuingBank =
        factory.newRelationship(namespace, 'Bank',
application.buyer.bank.getIdentifier());
```

```
    letter.confirmingBank =
factory.newRelationship(namespace,'Bank',application.seller.bank.getIdentif
ier());
    letter.rules = application.rules;
    letter.productDetails = application.productDetails;
    letter.evidence = [];
    letter.status = 'CONTRACT';
    letter.step=0;
    //save the application
    const assetRegistry = await
getAssetRegistry(letter.getFullyQualifiedType());
    await assetRegistry.add(letter);
    // emit event
    const applicationEvent = factory.newEvent(namespace,
'InitialApplicationEvent');
    applicationEvent.lc = letter;
    emit(applicationEvent);
}
```

When this function is called, it instantiates a new resource representing our new LC, and then defines the relationship between the LC and the participants using the `newRelationship` method. Afterward, it sets the letter status to `CONTRACT`, and LC `step` to 0 (`letter.step=0`).

We use the `getAssetRegistry` method to find the current LC (modeled as an asset in the CTO) in the blockchain using the `getfullyQualifiedType` method, which returns the fully qualified type name of the indicated instance. Then, we use the `add` function to add the LC asset to the blockchain.

At the end, we create an event object for the new asset using `newEvent` with the event namespace, type (`InitialApplicationEvent`), and then publish the event using the `emit` function.

LC request

After the initial agreement, the buyer requests an LC from the issuing bank by signing the bank's LC form. We define the `BuyerRequestLC` transaction and the related event in the model CTO file as follows:

```
transaction BuyerRequestLC {
  --> LetterOfCredit lc
  --> User buyer
}
```

```
event BuyerRequestLCEvent {
  --> LetterOfCredit lc
  --> User buyer
}
```

In the transaction processor function, we check if the letter's status is not closed or under creation before updating its status to REQUEST_LC, and the step to 1, as follows:

```
/**
 * Buyer submit LC requst to issuing bank
 * @param {org.example.lc.BuyerRequestLC} buyerLCRequest - the Buyer
request LC transaction
 * @transaction
 */
async function buyerLCRequest(request) { // eslint-disable-line no-unused-
vars
    const factory = getFactory();
    const namespace = 'org.example.lc';

    let letter = request.lc;

    if (letter.status === 'CLOSED') {
        throw new Error ('This letter of credit has already been closed');
    } else if (letter.step !== 0) {
        throw new Error ('This letter of credit should be in step 0 -
CONTRACT');
    }
    letter.status = 'REQUEST_LC';
    letter.step = 1;

    const assetRegistry = await
getAssetRegistry(letter.getFullyQualifiedType());
    await assetRegistry.update(letter);

    // emit event
    const buyerRequestLCEvent = factory.newEvent(namespace,
'BuyerRequestLCEvent');
    buyerRequestLCEvent.lc = letter;
    emit(buyerRequestLCEvent);
}
```

As you will have noticed, Composer provides us with the ability to handle exceptions in transaction processor functions using throw new Error with a detailed message. Once thrown, the transaction will fail and roll back any changes already made.

The rest of the code is pretty similar to what we have done for the previous function, except here we use the `update` function to update the LC asset in the blockchain.

LC approval

After the buyer submits an LC request, the issuing bank approves the LC form, and sends it to the confirming bank. In our model file, we define the related `IssuingBankApproveLC` transaction and the related event as follows:

```
transaction IssuingBankApproveLC {
   --> LetterOfCredit lc
}

event IssuingBankApproveLCEvent {
   --> LetterOfCredit lc
}
```

The transaction logic here is similar to the previous step, where we use `getAssetRegistry` to find the existing LC asset and we update the LC status, before emitting the `IssuingBankApproveLCEvent`. The letter status is set to `ISSUE_LC`, and the LC `step` to 2:

```
/**
  * issuing bank approval buyer LC
  * @param {org.example.lc.IssuingBankApproveLC} issuingBankApproveLC -
  * Issuing Bank approval LC transaction
  * @transaction
  */
 async function issuingBankApproveLC(request) { // eslint-disable-line no-
unused-vars
     const factory = getFactory();
     const namespace = 'org.example.lc';

     let letter = request.lc;

     if (letter.status === 'CLOSED') {
         throw new Error ('This letter of credit has already been closed');
     } else if (letter.step!== 1) {
         throw new Error ('This letter of credit should be in step 1 -
REQUEST_LC');
     }
     letter.status = 'ISSUE_LC';
     letter.step=2;

     const assetRegistry = await
```

```
getAssetRegistry(request.lc.getFullyQualifiedType());
    await assetRegistry.update(letter);

    // emit event
    const issuingBankApproveLCEvent = factory.newEvent(namespace,
'IssuingBankApproveLCEvent');
    issuingBankApproveLCEvent.lc = letter;
    emit(issuingBankApproveLCEvent);
}
```

LC advising

Once the issuing bank approves the LC form, the confirming bank receives LC advice and sends it to the seller. We define the ConfirmingBankAdviceLC transaction and an event for the LC update as follows:

```
transaction ConfirmingBankAdviceLC {
  --> LetterOfCredit lc
}

event ConfirmingBankAdviceLCEvent {
  --> LetterOfCredit lc
}
```

The letter status is set to ADVISE_LC, and the step property is updated to 3. We define the related transaction, along with an event firing a notification about the LC advised by the confirming bank:

```
/**
  * confirming bank approval LC
  * @param {org.example.lc.ConfirmingBankAdviceLC} confirmingBankAdviceLC -
  * confirming bank advice LC transaction
  * @transaction
  */
async function confirmingBankAdviceLC(request) { // eslint-disable-line no-
unused-vars
    const factory = getFactory();
    const namespace = 'org.example.lc';

    let letter = request.lc;

    if (letter.status === 'CLOSED') {
        throw new Error ('This letter of credit has already been closed');
    } else if (letter.step!== 2) {
        throw new Error ('This letter of credit should be in step 2 -
ISSUE_LC');
```

```
    }
    letter.status = 'ADVICE_LC';
    letter.step=3;

    const assetRegistry = await
getAssetRegistry(request.lc.getFullyQualifiedType());
    await assetRegistry.update(letter);

    // emit event
    const confirmingBankAdviceLCEvent =
        factory.newEvent(namespace, 'ConfirmingBankAdviceLCEvent');
    confirmingBankAdviceLCEvent.lc = letter;
    emit(confirmingBankAdviceLCEvent);
}
```

Goods shipping

After the seller receives LC advice from the confirming bank, the seller ships the goods. In this step, we define the `SellerDeliverGoods` transaction and related event for the LC update:

```
transaction SellerDeliverGoods {
  --> LetterOfCredit lc
  o String evidence
}

event SellerDeliverGoodsEvent {
  --> LetterOfCredit lc
}
```

The letter status is set to `DELIVER_PRODUCT`, and the `step` to 4:

```
/**
 * seller deliver product
 * @param {org.example.lc.SellerDeliverGoods} sellerDeliverGoods - seller
deliver product
 * @transaction
 */
async function sellerDeliverGoods(request) { // eslint-disable-line no-
unused-vars
    const factory = getFactory();
    const namespace = 'org.example.lc';

    let letter = request.lc;

    if (letter.status === 'CLOSED') {
```

```
        throw new Error ('This letter of credit has already been closed');
    } else if (letter.step!== 3) {
        throw new Error ('This letter of credit should be in step 3 -
ADVICE_LC');
    }
    letter.status = 'DELIVER_PRODUCT';
    letter.step=4;
    letter.evidence.push(request.evidence);
    const assetRegistry = await
getAssetRegistry(request.lc.getFullyQualifiedType());
    await assetRegistry.update(letter);

    // emit event
    const sellerDeliverGoodsEvent = factory.newEvent(namespace,
'SellerDeliverGoodsEvent');
    sellerDeliverGoodsEvent.lc = letter;
    emit(sellerDeliverGoodsEvent);
}
```

Present document

After the seller has shipped the goods, he presents a written document to the confirming bank. Therefore, we define the `SellerPresentDocument` transaction and related event for the LC update:

```
transaction SellerPresentDocument {
  --> LetterOfCredit lc
  o String evidence
}
event SellerPresentDocumentEvent {
  --> LetterOfCredit lc
}
```

The letter status is set to PRESENT DOCUMENT, and the `step` to 5:

```
/**
  * seller Presentation the Document
  * @param {org.example.lc.SellerPresentDocument} sellerPresentDocument -
seller present document
  * @transaction
  */
async function sellerPresentDocument(request) { // eslint-disable-line no-
unused-vars
    const factory = getFactory();
    const namespace = 'org.example.lc';

    let letter = request.lc;
```

```
    if (letter.status === 'CLOSED') {
        throw new Error ('This letter of credit has already been closed');
    } else if (letter.step!== 4) {
        throw new Error ('This letter of credit should be in step 4 -
ADVICE_LC');
    }
    letter.status = 'PRESENT_DOCUMENT';
    letter.step=5;
    letter.evidence.push(request.evidence);
    const assetRegistry = await
getAssetRegistry(request.lc.getFullyQualifiedType());
    await assetRegistry.update(letter);

    // emit event
    const sellerPresentDocumentEvent = factory.newEvent(namespace,
'SellerPresentDocumentEvent');
    sellerPresentDocumentEvent.lc = letter;
    emit(sellerPresentDocumentEvent);
}
```

The LC asset has an evidence array data field, which contains all the document proofs for the entire process. When a seller presents a written document to the confirming bank, the document will be added to the LC evidence using the JavaScript push function: `letter.evidence.push(request.evidence)`. As you know, the `push()` method adds new items to the end of an array.

Document delivery

At this step, the confirming bank delivers the document to the issuing bank. We define the `ConfirmingBankDeliverDocument` transaction and related event and update the LC status with the document evidence:

```
transaction ConfirmingBankDeliverDocument {
  --> LetterOfCredit lc
  o String evidence
}
event ConfirmingBankDeliverDocumentEvent {
  --> LetterOfCredit lc
}
```

The letter status is set to DELIVERY_DOCUMENT, and the step is 6:

```
/**
 * seller deliver product
 * @param {org.example.lc.ConfirmingBankDeliverDocument}
confirmingBankDeliverDocument -
 (seller deliver product
 * @transaction
 */
async function confirmingBankDeliverDocument(request) { // eslint-disable-
line no-unused-vars
    const factory = getFactory();
    const namespace = 'org.example.lc';

    let letter = request.lc;

    if (letter.status === 'CLOSED') {
        throw new Error ('This letter of credit has already been closed');
    } else if (letter.step!== 5) {
        throw new Error ('This letter of credit should be in step 5 -
PRESENT_DOCUMENT');
    }
    letter.status = 'DELIVERY_DOCUMENT';
    letter.step=6;
    letter.evidence.push(request.evidence);
    const assetRegistry = await
getAssetRegistry(request.lc.getFullyQualifiedType());
    await assetRegistry.update(letter);

    // emit event
    const confirmingBankDeliverDocumentEvent =
        factory.newEvent(namespace,'ConfirmingBankDeliverDocumentEvent');
    confirmingBankDeliverDocumentEvent.lc = letter;
    emit(confirmingBankDeliverDocumentEvent);
}
```

Debit payment

The buyer makes a payment for the goods. In this step, we define the
BuyerDepositPayment transaction and related event and update the LC status:

```
transaction BuyerDepositPayment {
  --> LetterOfCredit lc
}

event BuyerDepositPaymentEvent {
```

```
    --> LetterOfCredit lc
}
```

The letter status is set to BUYER_DEBIT_PAYMENT, and the step to 7:

```
/**
 * buyer Deposit Payment
 * @param {org.example.lc.BuyerDepositPayment} buyerDepositPayment - buyer
Deposit Payment
 * @transaction
 */
async function buyerDepositPayment(request) { // eslint-disable-line no-
unused-vars
    const factory = getFactory();
    const namespace = 'org.example.lc';

    let letter = request.lc;

    if (letter.status === 'CLOSED') {
        throw new Error ('This letter of credit has already been closed');
    } else if (letter.step!== 6) {
        throw new Error ('This letter of credit should be in step 6 -
DELIVERY_DOCUMENT');
    }
    letter.status = 'BUYER_DEBIT_PAYMENT';
    letter.step=7;

    const assetRegistry = await
getAssetRegistry(request.lc.getFullyQualifiedType());
    await assetRegistry.update(letter);

    // emit event
    const buyerDepositPaymentEvent = factory.newEvent(namespace,
'BuyerDepositPaymentEvent');
    buyerDepositPaymentEvent.lc = letter;
    emit(buyerDepositPaymentEvent);
}
```

Payment transfer

When the buyer receives the goods, the issuing bank transfers payment to the confirming bank. In this step, we define the BanksTransferPayment transaction and related event and update the LC status:

```
transaction BanksTransferPayment {
    --> LetterOfCredit lc
```

```
}

event BanksTransferPaymentEvent {
  --> LetterOfCredit lc
}
```

The letter status is set to BANKS_PAYMENT_TRANSFER, and the step to 8:

```
/**
 * banks Transfer Payment
 * @param {org.example.lc.BanksTransferPayment} banksTransferPayment -
banks Transfer Payment
 * @transaction
 */
async function banksTransferPayment(request) { // eslint-disable-line no-
unused-vars
    const factory = getFactory();
    const namespace = 'org.example.lc';

    let letter = request.lc;

    if (letter.status === 'CLOSED') {
        throw new Error ('This letter of credit has already been closed');
    } else if (letter.step!== 7) {
        throw new Error ('This letter of credit should be in step 6 -
BUYER_DEBIT_PAYMENT');
    }
    letter.status = 'BANKS_PAYMENT_TRANSFER';
    letter.step=8;

    const assetRegistry = await
getAssetRegistry(request.lc.getFullyQualifiedType());
    await assetRegistry.update(letter);

    // emit event
    const banksTransferPaymentEvent = factory.newEvent(namespace,
'BanksTransferPaymentEvent');
    banksTransferPaymentEvent.lc = letter;
    emit(banksTransferPaymentEvent);
}
```

Pay the seller

After receiving the payment from the issuing bank, the confirming bank makes the payment to the seller. In this step, we define the `sellerReceivedPayment` transaction and related event and update the LC status:

```
transaction SellerReceivedPayment {
  --> LetterOfCredit lc
}

event SellerReceivedPaymentEvent {
  --> LetterOfCredit lc
}
```

The letter status is set to `SELL_RECEIVED_PAYMENT`, and the `step` to 9:

```
/**
 * seller Received Payment
 * @param {org.example.lc.SellerReceivedPayment} sellerReceivedPayment -
seller Received Payment
 * @transaction
 */
async function sellerReceivedPayment(request) { // eslint-disable-line no-
unused-vars
    const factory = getFactory();
    const namespace = 'org.example.lc';

    let letter = request.lc;

    if (letter.status === 'CLOSED') {
        throw new Error ('This letter of credit has already been closed');
    } else if (letter.step!== 8) {
        throw new Error ('This letter of credit should be in step 6 -
BANKS_PAYMENT_TRANSFER');
    }
    letter.status = 'SELL_RECEIVED_PAYMENT';
    letter.step=9;

    const assetRegistry = await
getAssetRegistry(request.lc.getFullyQualifiedType());
    await assetRegistry.update(letter);

    // emit event
    const sellerReceivedPaymentEvent =
factory.newEvent(namespace,'SellerReceivedPaymentEvent');
```

```
    sellerReceivedPaymentEvent.lc = letter;
    emit(sellerReceivedPaymentEvent);
}
```

LC closure

This will be the final step in the LC process, where the buyer receives the goods and the seller receives the payment. Therefore, we define a closing transaction referencing the targeted LC and the reason behind the closure:

```
transaction Close {
  --> LetterOfCredit lc
  o String closeReason
}

event CloseEvent {
  --> LetterOfCredit lc
  o String closeReason
}
```

The letter status is set to CLOSED, and the step to 10:

```
/**
 * Close the LOC
 * @param {org.example.lc.Close} close - the Close transaction
 * @transaction
 */
async function close(closeRequest) { // eslint-disable-line no-unused-vars
    const factory = getFactory();
    const namespace = 'org.example.lc';

    let letter = closeRequest.lc;

    if (letter.status === 'SELL_RECEIVED_PAYMENT') {
        letter.status = 'CLOSED';
        letter.closeReason = closeRequest.closeReason;

        // update the status of the lc
        const assetRegistry = await
getAssetRegistry(closeRequest.lc.getFullyQualifiedType());
        await assetRegistry.update(letter);

        // emit event
        const closeEvent = factory.newEvent(namespace, 'CloseEvent');
        closeEvent.lc = closeRequest.lc;
        closeEvent.closeReason = closeRequest.closeReason;
```

```
        emit(closeEvent);
    } else if (letter.status === 'CLOSED') {
        throw new Error('This letter of credit has already been closed');
    } else {
        throw new Error('Cannot close this letter of credit');
    }
}
```

This was the final part of our Chaincode. Now, let's deploy it in the Fabric network and check whether it works as expected.

Deploying the LC

First off, we need to start Hyperledger Fabric. For that, change the directory to `fabric-dev-servers/` and start the `./startFabric.sh` script as follows:

```
cd ~/fabric-dev-servers
sudo ./startFabric.sh
```

Next, create a peer admin card by executing the script `./createPeerAdminCard.sh`. As a result, you'll get an output similar to the following:

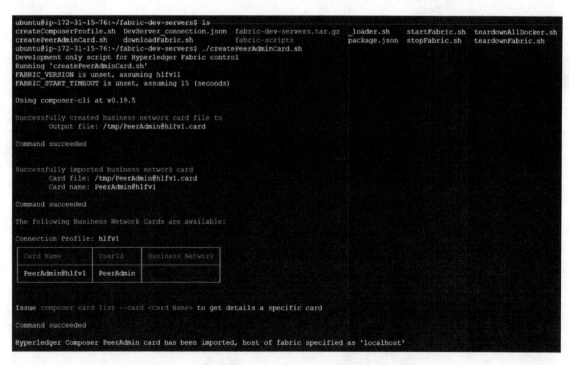

If everything goes as expected, we can move on to building the business network archive.

Deploying business network

The first step is to create a business network archive from a directory on disk, by using the **Composer command Line interface** (**Composer CLI**) as follows:

```
composer archive create -t dir -n .
```

As a result, a business network archive file called `lc-network@0.0.1.bna` will be created in the `lc-network/` folder. Next, we need to install the business network `lc-network@0.0.1.bna` archive file:

```
composer network install --card PeerAdmin@hlfv1 --archiveFile lc-network@0.0.1.bna
```

As you may have noticed, we need to specify a `PeerAdmin` business network card (using the `--card` option), which was created earlier when we ran `./createPeerAdminCard.sh`. You can run `composer card list` to verify that you have the `PeerAdmin` card.

To start the business network, we run the following command:

```
composer network start --networkName lc-network --networkVersion 0.0.1 --networkAdmin admin --networkAdminEnrollSecret adminpw --card PeerAdmin@hlfv1 --file networkadmin.card
```

As a result, a `networkadmin.card` file will be generated to authenticate the specified admin (`--networkAdmin admin`) later in the REST server.

Then, import the network administrator identity as a usable business card:

```
composer card import --file networkadmin.card
```

You can check that the business network has been deployed successfully using the following command:

```
composer network ping --card admin@lc-network
```

Generating a REST server

REST calls are a convenient way to communicate with the Fabric network. As we did in the previous chapter, we will generate a RESTful interface to access the business network by using the `composer-rest-server` tool. For that, navigate to the project folder and type the following command:

```
composer-rest-server
```

You'll be asked a few questions, for which you can provide the same answers as in the following screenshot:

```
ubuntu@ip-172-31-15-76:~/apps/blockchain-by-example/letterofcredit/lc-network$ composer-rest-server
? Enter the name of the business network card to use: admin@lc-network
? Specify if you want namespaces in the generated REST API: never use namespaces
? Specify if you want to use an API key to secure the REST API: No
? Specify if you want to enable authentication for the REST API using Passport: No
? Specify if you want to enable event publication over WebSockets: Yes
? Specify if you want to enable TLS security for the REST API: No

To restart the REST server using the same options, issue the following command:
   composer-rest-server -c admin@lc-network -n never -w true

Discovering types from business network definition ...
Discovered types from business network definition
Generating schemas for all types in business network definition ...
Generated schemas for all types in business network definition
Adding schemas for all types to Loopback ...
Added schemas for all types to Loopback
Web server listening at: http://localhost:3000
Browse your REST API at http://localhost:3000/explorer
```

 For a production environment, you should enable the TLS API key security setting.

As a next step, we will use the REST interface to test the LC business network we have developed. If you open a browser and navigate to `http://youIpAddress:3000`, you will see something similar to the following page:

You can expand each list of items (transactions, assets) on the page to invoke the associated transaction we defined in the network model. Let's simulate an LC process and test each step using the REST interface.

Testing LC project

In this section, we will test the LC transactions in a sequential step-by-step manner. The steps are ordered following the order in which the transactions were implemented in the previous section. Therefore, we start with the `CreateDemoParticipants` transaction to onboard the parties involved.

Participant onboarding

In this test case, we onboard all participants in the network with the details we used previously in the demo: buyer (David Wilson), seller (Jason Jones), issuing bank (First Consumer Bank), and confirming bank (Bank of Eastern Export). For that, click on `CreateDemoParticipants` to submit a transaction, then expand the `POST` method, and then click the **Try it out!** button to invoke the transaction. If it succeeds, you'll see an `HTTP 200` response code, as shown here:

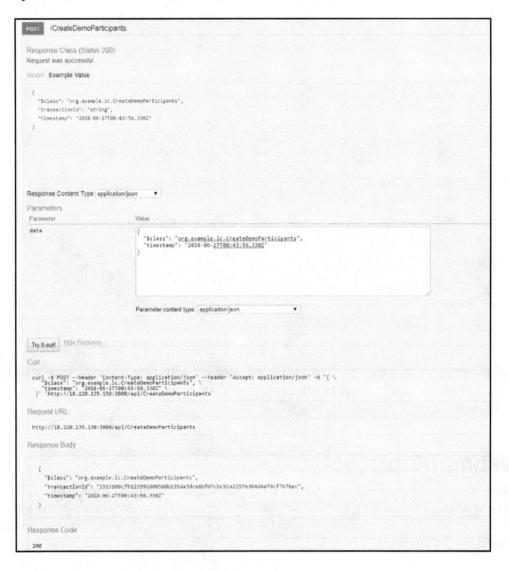

If we get the/USER, we can see that both users are created in the blockchain.

```
Curl

 curl -X GET --header 'Accept: application/json' 'http://18.220.135.130:3000/api/User'

Request URL

 http://18.220.135.130:3000/api/User

Response Body

 [
   {
     "$class": "org.example.lc.User",
     "userId": "david",
     "name": "David",
     "lastName": "Wilson",
     "companyName": "Toy Mart Inc",
     "type": "BUYER",
     "bank": "resource:org.example.lc.Bank#BI"
   },
   {
     "$class": "org.example.lc.User",
     "userId": "jason",
     "name": "Jason",
     "lastName": "Jones",
     "companyName": "Valley Toys Manufacturing",
     "type": "SELLER",
     "bank": "resource:org.example.lc.Bank#EB"
   }
 ]
```

If we GET the /BANK, we can see both banks are created in the blockchain.

```
Curl

  curl -X GET --header 'Accept: application/json' 'http://18.220.135.130:3000/api/Bank'

Request URL

  http://18.220.135.130:3000/api/Bank

Response Body

  [
    {
      "$class": "org.example.lc.Bank",
      "bankID": "BE",
      "name": "Bank of Eastern Export",
      "type": "CONFIRMING_BANK"
    },
    {
      "$class": "org.example.lc.Bank",
      "bankID": "BI",
      "name": "First Consumer Bank",
      "type": "ISSUING_BANK"
    }
  ]

Response Code

  200
```

Initial agreement

In this step, the buyer and seller agree that the buyer will purchase the goods, and afterward the InitialApplication transaction is submitted. The buyer and seller have uploaded the agreement rule associated with this newly created letter of credit.

Run the `POST` method for `InitialApplication`:

```
{
  "$class": "org.example.lc.InitialApplication",
  "letterId": "LC-CA-501P10",
  "buyer": "resource:org.example.lc.User#david",
  "seller": "resource:org.example.lc.User#jason",
  "issuingBank": "resource:org.example.lc.Bank#BI",
  "confirmingBank": "resource:org.example.lc.Bank#EB",
  "rules": [ {
      "ruleId": "LC-CA-501P10-AGREEMENT-1",
      "ruleText": "The Scooter will be received in working order"
    },
    {
      "ruleId": "LC-CA-501P10-AGREEMENT-2",
      "ruleText": "The Scooter will be received within 35 days"
    }],
  "productDetails": {
    "$class": "org.example.lc.ProductDetails",
    "productType": "Scooter",
    "quantity": 50000,
    "pricePerUnit": 30
  }
}
```

You can then verify the LC's content, and you should see a successful response with the status 200.

LC request

When the buyer requests an LC from the issuing bank by signing the bank's LC form, the letter's status is set to `REQUEST_LC`.

To check that, click on the `BuyerRequestLC` POST method and provide the following data:

```
{
 "$class": "org.example.lc.BuyerRequestLC",
  "lc": "resource:org.example.lc.LetterOfCredit#LC-CA-501P10"
}
```

Here, we pass two JSON variables, `$class` and `lc`. The former is the transaction function's name we defined in the model file—`BuyerRequestLC` appended to the file namespace `org.example.lc`—whereas the latter specifies the targeted resource with the following structure:

```
"resource:{model name space}.{asset}#{assetId}".
```

As you may remember, in the previous step, we set the LC `assetid` as `LC-CA-501P10`.

As a result, the Composer tool will find LC in the blockchain and update the LC status to `REQUEST_LC`. If it succeeds, you'll see an HTTP `200` response code.

LC approval

At this level, the issuing bank approves the LC form, and sends it to the confirming bank. Therefore, the letter's status is set to `ISSUE_LC`, and provides the following data:

```
{
    "$class": "org.example.lc.IssuingBankApproveLC",
    "lc": "resource:org.example.lc.LetterOfCredit#LC-CA-501P10"
}
```

Click `IssuingBankApproveLC`—POST method. The passing value is similar to the previous step. We pass `resource:org.example.lc.LetterOfCredit#LC-CA-501P10` to specify the LC.

As a result, you should see that the letter's status is set to `ISSUE_LC`.

LC advising

Afterward, the confirming bank sends LC advice to the seller, and the letter status is set to `ADVISE_LC`.

Click `ConfirmingBankAdviceLC`—POST method, with the following arguments:

```
{
    "$class": "org.example.lc.ConfirmingBankAdviceLC",
    "lc": "resource:org.example.lc.LetterOfCredit#LC-CA-501P10"
}
```

To verify the LC's content, you should see that the letter status is set to `ADVISE_LC`.

Goods shipping

At this stage, the seller ships the goods and the status is set to DELIVER_PRODUCT. Click SellerDeliverGoods—POST method and provide the following data:

```
{
   "$class": "org.example.lc.SellerDeliverGoods",
   "lc": "resource:org.example.lc.LetterOfCredit#LC-CA-501P10",
   "evidence": "77603075985295a937b28cf0128f4e7f"
}
```

To verify the LC's content, you should see that the letter status is set to DELIVER_PRODUCT.

Present document

The seller presents a written document to the confirming bank and the status is set to PRESENT_DOCUMENT.

Click SellerPresentDocument—POST method:

```
{
   "$class": "org.example.lc.SellerPresentDocument",
   "lc": "resource:org.example.lc.LetterOfCredit#LC-CA-501P10",
   "evidence": "acd2280df872c844ccfdf60ec7360819"
}
```

To verify the LC's content, you should see that the letter status is set to PRESENT_DOCUMENT.

Deliver document

The confirming bank delivers the document to the issuing bank and the status is set to DELIVERY_DOCUMENT.

Click ConfirmingBankDeliverDocument—POST method, and provide the following data:

```
{
   "$class": "org.example.lc.ConfirmingBankDeliverDocument",
   "lc": "resource:org.example.lc.LetterOfCredit#LC-CA-501P10",
   "evidence": "a61524a8d2b5986c90dd3b84e8406290"
}
```

To verify the LC's content, you should see the letter status is set to DELIVERY_DOCUMENT.

Debit payment

The buyer makes the payment for the goods and the letter status is set to
BUYER_DEBIT_PAYMENT.

Click BuyerDepositPayment—POST method, and provide the following data:

```
{
    "$class": "org.example.lc.BuyerDepositPayment",
    "lc": "resource:org.example.lc.LetterOfCredit#LC-CA-501P10"
}
```

To verify the LC's content, you should see that the letter status is set to
BUYER_DEBIT_PAYMENT.

Payment transfer

The issuing bank transfers payment to the confirming bank and the letter status is set to
BANKS_PAYMENT_TRANSFER.

Click BanksTransferPayment—POST method, and provide the following data:

```
{
    "$class": "org.example.lc.BanksTransferPayment",
    "lc": "resource:org.example.lc.LetterOfCredit#LC-CA-501P10"
}
```

To verify the LC's content, you should see that the letter status is set to
BANKS_PAYMENT_TRANSFER.

Pay the seller

The confirming bank pays the payment to the seller and the letter status is set to
SELL_RECEIVED_PAYMENT.

Click SellerReceivedPayment—POST method, and provide the following data:

```
{
    "$class": "org.example.lc.SellerReceivedPayment",
    "lc": "resource:org.example.lc.LetterOfCredit#LC-CA-501P10"
}
```

To verify the LC's content, you should see that the letter status is set to
`SELL_RECEIVED_PAYMENT`.

LC closure

This is the final step in the LC process, where we send a closing transaction to update the
letter's status to `CLOSED`.

Click `Close—POST` method, and provide the following data:

```
{
    "$class": "org.example.lc.Close",
    "lc": "resource:org.example.lc.LetterOfCredit#LC-CA-501P10",
    "closeReason": "LC completed"
}
```

If you were able to follow the instructions and successfully get to this step, congratulations!
You are now able to build an application and generate a business domain REST API based
on the deployed business network model!

Hyperledger Fabric on IBM Cloud

IBM Cloud (`https://www.ibm.com/cloud/`), previously known as IBM Bluemix, provides
an enterprise blockchain platform as a flexible **blockchain-as-a-service (BaaS)**, which is
based on the open source Hyperledger Fabric. The customer can easily create, deploy, and
manage a secure enterprise blockchain on IBM Cloud without caring about the underlying
infrastructure.

IBM Cloud is an expensive service for a developer who wants to learn. Therefore, instead of
deploying a custom example, such as the previous LC, which requires a premium plan, we
present here one of the samples—Marbles—provided by IBM from its free starter plan.

The application will create a marble (a glass ball used as a children's toy) and store it in the
blockchain by invoking Chaincode. We will create a UI that creates or updates the marble's
attributes and stores them in the ledger. The Hyperledger Fabric Client SDK will call the
network Chaincode through the RPC protocol.

To run this sample in the IBM Cloud, we need to create an IBM Cloud account and select the blockchain service:

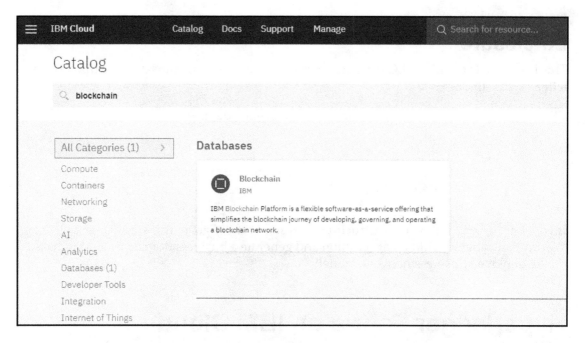

Select the **Starter Membership Plan**, which is free:

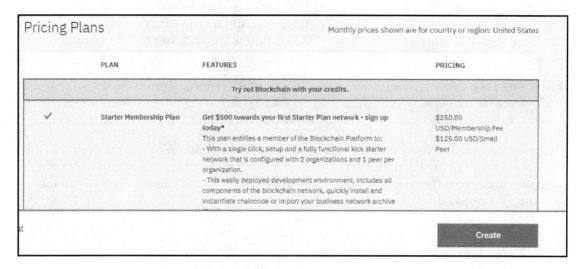

Once created, you'll need to launch the network and set up the toolchain for Marbles. For that, browse to the IBM Blockchain GitHub link at `https://github.com/IBM-Blockchain/marbles/blob/master/.bluemix/README.md`, and click **Get Marbles**. You should see a page similar to the following one, where you should click **Create** to create the Marbles sample toolchain:

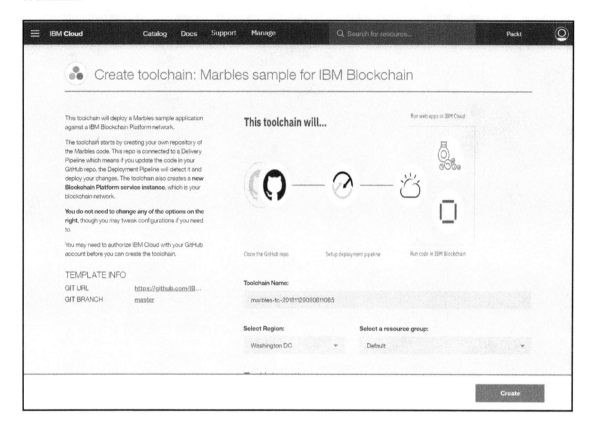

During setup, it will ask you for your GitHub login. Enter all the required login information, and click **Authorize IBM-Cloud**.

Once GitHub's code is set up in IBM Cloud, click **Create** to continue to the next step—**Delivery Pipeline**:

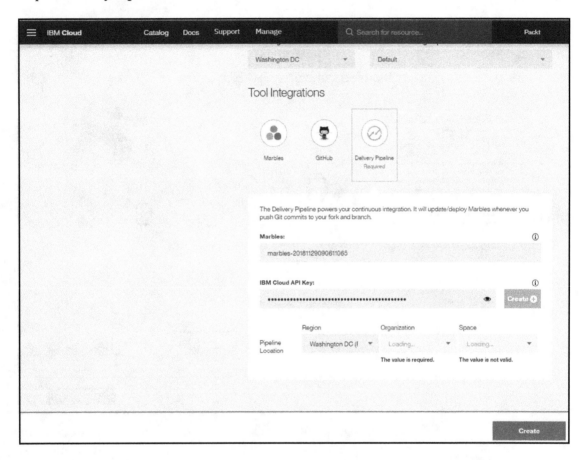

Click on **Delivery Pipeline** and it will start deploying the Marbles application to the blockchain:

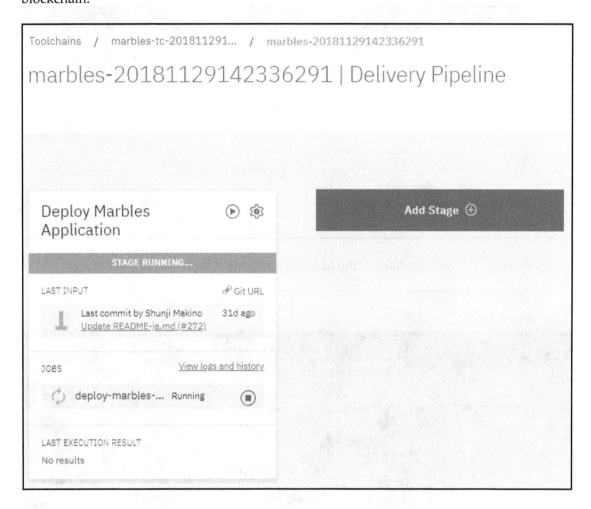

Once completed, click on the Marbles Node.js application:

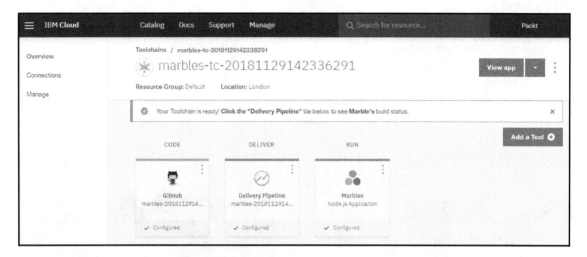

You should see the web interface of the Marbles application launched in the browser:

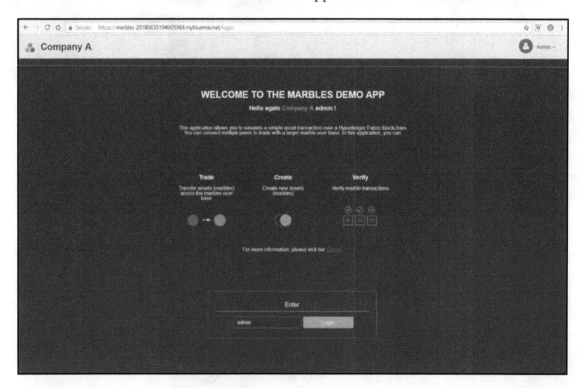

Login as admin, and a welcome demo page will pop up. You can select **Express** or **Guided** setup. Let's click the **Express** button:

The Marbles application is now loaded:

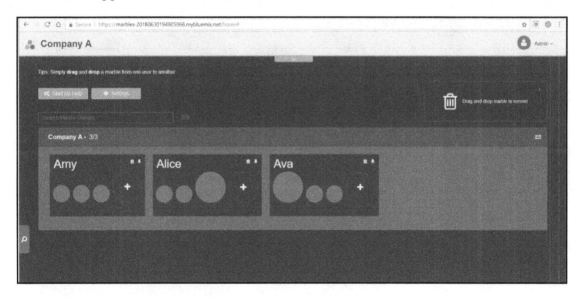

Try to add one Marble by clicking the **Ava add (+)** button. Add the marble, and then click **Create**:

You should see that a new green Marble is added to Ava:

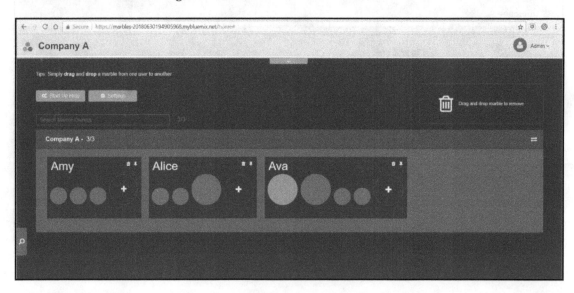

Congratulations! You have just run a sample Hyperledger Fabric blockchain application on the IBM Cloud platform!

IBM Cloud is a powerful platform with built-in services that can easily be integrated into your blockchain project. For instance, we can utilize Watson, which is IBM's AI solution, to analyze and customize application data to share among authorized network participants.

Summary

In this chapter, we have learned about the Hyperledger Composer through the letter of credit example. We have defined and built a business network model and then packaged it as a `.bna` file and deployed it to a Fabric network. We also set up a Composer REST server to communicate with the business network over HTTP. At the end, we have introduced IBM BaaS by running a marble application example in the IBM blockchain.

From now on, you should be able to build more complex blockchain projects using Hyperledger Fabric and Composer. If you have read the previous chapters, you'll now have an idea about the difference between business-driven blockhains, such as Hyperledger, and cryptocurrency-driven blockchains, such as Bitcoin or Ethereum. Finally, if you are not happy with Hyperledger and you are searching for an alternative, you should explore the Corda project (`https://www.corda.net/`).

Other Books You May Enjoy

If you enjoyed this book, you may be interested in these other books by Packt:

Blockchain for Enterprise
Narayan Prusty

ISBN: 9781788479745

- Learn how to set up Raft/IBFT Quorum networks
- Implement Quorum's privacy and security features
- Write, compile, and deploy smart contracts
- Learn to interact with Quorum using the web3.js JavaScript library
- Learn how to execute atomic swaps between different networks
- Build a secured Blockchain-as-a-Service for efficient business processes
- Achieve data privacy in blockchains using proxy re-encryption

Hands-On Blockchain with Hyperledger
Nitin Gaur

ISBN: 9781788994521

- Discover why blockchain is a game changer in the technology landscape
- Set up blockchain networks using basic Hyperledger Fabric deployment
- Understand the considerations for creating decentralized applications
- Learn to integrate business networks with existing systems
- Write Smart Contracts quickly with Hyperledger Composer
- Design transaction model and chaincode with Golang
- Deploy Composer REST Gateway to access the Composer transactions
- Maintain, monitor, and govern your blockchain solutions

Leave a review - let other readers know what you think

Please share your thoughts on this book with others by leaving a review on the site that you bought it from. If you purchased the book from Amazon, please leave us an honest review on this book's Amazon page. This is vital so that other potential readers can see and use your unbiased opinion to make purchasing decisions, we can understand what our customers think about our products, and our authors can see your feedback on the title that they have worked with Packt to create. It will only take a few minutes of your time, but is valuable to other potential customers, our authors, and Packt. Thank you!

Index

www.ingramcontent.com/pod-product-compliance
Lightning Source LLC
Chambersburg PA
CBHW060639060326
40690CB00020B/4452